PHILOSOPHY OF MIND IN ANTIQUITY

Spanning 1200 years of intellectual history – from the 6th century BCE emergence of philosophical enquiry in the Greek city-state of Miletus, to the 6th century CE closure of the Academy in Athens in 529 – *Philosophy of Mind in Antiquity* provides an outstanding survey of philosophy of mind of the period. It covers a crucial era for the history of philosophy of mind, examining the enduring and controversial arguments of Plato and Aristotle, in addition to the contribution of the Stoics and other key figures.

Following an introduction by John Sisko, fifteen specially commissioned chapters by an international team of contributors discuss key topics, thinkers, and debates, including:

- the Presocratics,
- Plato,
- cognition,
- Aristotle,
- intellect,
- natural science,
- time,
- mind, perception, and body,
- the Stoics,
- Galen, and
- Plotinus.

Essential reading for students and researchers in philosophy of mind, ancient philosophy, and the history of philosophy, *Philosophy of Mind in Antiquity* is also a valuable resource for those in related disciplines such as Classics.

John E. Sisko is Professor of Philosophy and Dean of the College of Arts and Sciences at Queens University of Charlotte, USA. He has published in ancient philosophy of mind and physics, including papers in *Ancient Philosophy, Apeiron, Archiv fur Geschichte der Philosophie, Classical Quarterly, Mind, Oxford Studies in Ancient Philosophy*, and *Phronesis*.

The History of the Philosophy of Mind
General Editors: Rebecca Copenhaver and Christopher Shields

The History of the Philosophy of Mind is a major six-volume reference collection, covering the key topics, thinkers and debates within philosophy of mind, from Antiquity to the present day. Each volume is edited by a leading scholar in the field and comprises chapters written by an international team of specially commissioned contributors.

Including a general introduction by Rebecca Copenhaver and Christopher Shields, and fully cross-referenced within and across the six volumes, *The History of the Philosophy of Mind* is an essential resource for students and researchers in philosophy of mind, and will also be of interest to those in many related disciplines, including Classics, Religion, Literature, History of Psychology, and Cognitive Science.

VOL.1 PHILOSOPHY OF MIND IN ANTIQUITY
edited by John E. Sisko

VOL.2 PHILOSOPHY OF MIND IN THE EARLY AND HIGH MIDDLE AGES
edited by Margaret Cameron

VOL.3 PHILOSOPHY OF MIND IN THE LATE MIDDLE AGES AND RENAISSANCE
edited by Stephan Schmid

VOL.4 PHILOSOPHY OF MIND IN THE EARLY MODERN AND MODERN AGES
edited by Rebecca Copenhaver

VOL.5 PHILOSOPHY OF MIND IN THE NINETEENTH CENTURY
edited by Sandra Lapointe

VOL.6 PHILOSOPHY OF MIND IN THE TWENTIETH AND TWENTY-FIRST CENTURIES
edited by Amy Kind

PHILOSOPHY OF MIND IN ANTIQUITY

The History of the Philosophy of Mind, Volume 1

Edited by John E. Sisko

Routledge
Taylor & Francis Group
LONDON AND NEW YORK

First published 2019
by Routledge
2 Park Square, Milton Park, Abingdon, Oxon OX14 4RN

and by Routledge
605 Third Avenue, New York, NY 10017

First issued in paperback 2020

Routledge is an imprint of the Taylor & Francis Group, an informa business

© 2019 selection and editorial matter, John E. Sisko; individual chapters, the contributors

The right of John E. Sisko to be identified as the authors of the editorial material, and of the authors for their individual chapters, has been asserted in accordance with sections 77 and 78 of the Copyright, Designs and Patents Act 1988.

All rights reserved. No part of this book may be reprinted or reproduced or utilised in any form or by any electronic, mechanical, or other means, now known or hereafter invented, including photocopying and recording, or in any information storage or retrieval system, without permission in writing from the publishers.

Trademark notice: Product or corporate names may be trademarks or registered trademarks, and are used only for identification and explanation without intent to infringe.

British Library Cataloguing-in-Publication Data
A catalogue record for this book is available from the British Library

Library of Congress Cataloging-in-Publication Data
Names: Sisko, John E., editor.
Title: Philosophy of mind in antiquity / edited by John E. Sisko.
Description: New York : Routledge, 2018. | Series: The history of the philosophy of mind ; Volume 1 | Includes bibliographical references and index.
Identifiers: LCCN 2017060250| ISBN 9781138243927 (hardback : alk. paper) | ISBN 9780429508219 (e-book)
Subjects: LCSH: Philosophy of mind—History.
Classification: LCC BD418.3 .P484 2018 | DDC 128/.209—dc23
LC record available at https://lccn.loc.gov/2017060250

ISBN 13: 978-0-367-73413-8 (Vol I, pbk)
ISBN 13: 978-1-138-24392-7 (Vol I, hbk)

ISBN: 978-1-138-24393-4 (Vol II, hbk)
ISBN: 978-1-138-24394-1 (Vol III, hbk)
ISBN: 978-1-138-24395-8 (Vol IV, hbk)
ISBN: 978-1-138-24396-5 (Vol V, hbk)
ISBN: 978-1-138-24397-2 (Vol VI, hbk)
ISBN: 978-1-138-92535-9 (6-volume set, hbk)

Typeset in Times New Roman
by Apex CoVantage, LLC

CONTENTS

Notes on contributors   vii
General introduction   x
REBECCA COPENHAVER AND CHRISTOPHER SHIELDS

Introduction to volume 1   1
JOHN E. SISKO

1 **Presocratic interest in the soul's persistence after death**   23
JOHN PALMER

2 **Presocratic accounts of perception and cognition**   44
PATRICIA CURD

3 **Soul, perception and thought in the Hippocratic corpus**   64
HYNEK BARTOŠ

4 **Plato's guide to living with your body**   84
RUSSELL E. JONES AND PATRICIA MARECHAL

5 **Plato and tripartition of soul**   101
RACHEL SINGPURWALLA

6 **Cosmic and human cognition in the *Timaeus***   120
GÁBOR BETEGH

7 **The power of Aristotle's hylomorphic approach**   141
KELSEY WARD AND RONALD POLANSKY

CONTENTS

8 Aristotle on the intellect and limits of natural science 160
   CHRISTOPHER FREY

9 Aristotle on the perception and cognition of time 175
   JOHN BOWIN

10 Aristotle on mind, perception, and body 194
   JOHN E. SISKO

11 Rational impressions and the stoic philosophy of mind 214
   VANESSA DE HARVEN

12 Mind in an atomistic world: Epicurus and
   the Epicurean tradition 236
   FRANCESCA MASI AND FRANCESCO VERDE

13 Galen's philosophy of mind 258
   R.J. HANKINSON

14 Plotinus' theory of affection 279
   ANA LAURA EDELHOFF

15 Intellect in Alexander of Aphrodisias and John Philoponus:
   divine, human or both? 299
   FRANS A.J. DE HAAS

Index 317

CONTRIBUTORS

Hynek Bartoš is Associate Professor at Charles University, Faculty of Humanities. He has published in ancient Greek philosophy and medicine, including papers in *Ancient Philosophy*, *Apeiron*, *Classical Quarterly*, and *Rhizai*, as well as a book: *Philosophy and Dietetics in the Hippocratic On Regimen* (Brill 2015). He co-edits a series of the first Czech translations with commentaries of the Hippocratic treatises.

Gábor Betegh is Laurence Professor of Ancient Philosophy at the University of Cambridge and Fellow of Christ's College. His work focuses on ancient metaphysics, philosophy of nature, and cosmology, as well as the relationship between philosophy and religion. He is the author of *The Derveni Papyrus. Cosmology, Theology and Interpretation*, Cambridge, MA: Cambridge University Press, 2004 (paperback 2007), and the co-editor with Julia Annas of *Cicero's De Finibus: Philosophical Approaches*, Cambridge, MA: Cambridge University Press, 2015.

John Bowin is an Associate Professor of Philosophy at the University of California, Santa Cruz. He is the author of a number of articles on Aristotle.

Patricia Curd is Professor of Philosophy at Purdue University. She is the author of *The Legacy of Parmenides: Eleatic Monism and Later Presocratic Thought* (Princeton University Press, 1998; reprinted with an additional introduction by Parmenides Publishing in 2004); of *Anaxagoras of Clazomenae: Fragments; Text and Translation with Notes and Essays for the Phoenix Presocratics Series of the University of Toronto Press* (2007); and is co-editor (with Daniel W. Graham) of *The Oxford Handbook of Presocratic Philosophy* (Oxford University Press, 2008) and has published work on early Greek philosophers including Xenophanes, Heraclitus, Parmenides, Empedocles, Democritus, Anaxagoras, and Gorgias.

Ana Laura Edelhoff studied philosophy, Greek, and Latin at the Freie Universität Berlin and the University of Oxford. She is specialising in ancient philosophy and contemporary ethics. Currently she is finishing her Ph.D. in philosophy at the Humboldt University Berlin. From October 2016 until September 2017 she was a teaching fellow in philosophy at the University of Tübingen. Since October 2017 she is a teaching fellow in philosophy at the University of Hamburg.

Christopher Frey is Assistant Professor at the University of South Carolina. He is the author of several articles on ancient Greek metaphysics and natural philosophy as well as on topics in contemporary philosophy of perception and mind. He is writing a book on Aristotle's conception of the soul as a principle of life.

R.J. Hankinson is Professor of Philosophy and Classics at the University of Texas at Austin. He has published numerous articles on many aspects of ancient philosophy and science; his books include *The Sceptics* (1995), *Cause and Explanation in the Ancient Greek World* (1998), and *Galen on Antecedent Causes* (1998); he has also edited *The Cambridge Companion to Galen* (2008).

Frans A.J. de Haas is Professor of Ancient and Medieval Philosophy at the Institute for Philosophy at Leiden University (The Netherlands). Since his dissertation on John Philoponus' notion of prime matter (1995), he has published widely on Aristotle, Neoplatonism, and the late ancient commentary tradition. His current research is focused on the psychology of Alexander of Aphrodisias and its significance for Alexander's new design of Peripatetic philosophy.

Vanessa de Harven is Assistant Professor of Philosophy at the University of Massachusetts, Amherst. She specializes in Ancient Philosophy of the Greek and Roman eras, with a central research focus on Stoic metaphysics, including the ontological status of Stoic incorporeals and in particular the physicalist nature of the Stoics' novel semantic entities called *lekta*, roughly the meanings of our words. In addition to her interests in contemporary metaphysics, epistemology, philosophy of mind, and theory of meaning, she also has research interests in Plato's metaphysics and epistemology, Socratic intellectualism, and Presocratic philosophy.

Russell E. Jones is Associate Professor of Philosophy at Harvard University. He has published articles on various aspects of the thought of Plato and Aristotle, especially on Platonic ethics and epistemology.

Patricia Marechal is Assistant Professor of Philosophy at Northwestern University. Her research focuses on ancient Greek metaphysics, philosophy of action, and moral psychology. She also works on the history of medicine in Late Antiquity.

Francesca Masi is Tenure-Track Researcher (in History of Ancient Philosophy) at University Ca' Foscari of Venice. Her research is dedicated to ontology, physics, psychology, and ethics in ancient thought. In addition to several articles mainly devoted to Epicurus' and Aristotle's philosophy, she's the author of two books: *Epicuro e la filosofia della mente* (2006) and *Qualsiasi cosa capiti. Natura e causa dell'ente accidentale. Aristotele, Metafisica Epsilon 2–3* (2015). She has also co-edited with Maddalena Bonelli a volume on *Aristotle's*

Categories (2011) and with Stefano Maso two volumes on *Fate, Chance and Fortune in Ancient Thought* (2013) and on *Eidola* in Epicurus' *Peri Physeos Book II* (2015).

John Palmer is Professor of Philosophy at the University of Florida. He is the author of *Plato's Reception of Parmenides* (Oxford, 1999) and *Parmenides and Presocratic Philosophy* (Oxford, 2009), as well as articles on the Presocratics, Plato, Aristotle, and Ancient Skepticism.

Ronald Polansky is Professor of Philosophy and Department Chair at Duquesne University. He edits *Ancient Philosophy* and has published a commentary on Aristotle's *De Anima*.

Rachel Singpurwalla is Associate Professor of Philosophy at the University of Maryland. She has published numerous articles on Plato's moral psychology, ethics, and politics.

John E. Sisko is Professor of Philosophy and Dean of the College of Arts and Sciences at Queens University of Charlotte. He has published in ancient philosophy of mind and physics, including papers in *Ancient Philosophy*, *Apeiron*, *Archiv fur Geschichte der Philosophie*, *Classical Quarterly*, *Mind*, *Oxford Studies in Ancient Philosophy*, and *Phronesis*.

Francesco Verde is currently adjunct professor of History of Ancient Philosophy at Sapienza, University of Rome and Humboldt Experienced Researcher at JMU Würzburg. His research interests focus of Ancient Atomism, Ancient Physics from Aristotle to Epicurus, and Herculaneum Papyrology. In addition to articles devoted to Ancient Skepticism and Epicureanism, he has published an Italian translation with commentary of Epicurus' *Letter to Herotodus* (2010), *Elachista: La dottrina dei minimi nell'Epicureismo* (2013), and an introduction to Epicurus' philosophy (2013). He has also co-edited, with Stéphane Marchand, a volume on Epicureanism and Skepticism.

Kelsey Ward is Assistant Professor of Philosophy at Hobart and William Smith Colleges.

GENERAL INTRODUCTION

Rebecca Copenhaver and Christopher Shields

How far back does the history of philosophy of mind extend? In one sense, the entire history of the discipline extends no further than living memory. Construed as a recognized sub-discipline of philosophy, philosophy of mind seems to have entered the academy in a regular way only in the latter half of the twentieth century. At any rate, as an institutional matter, courses listed under the name 'Philosophy of Mind' or 'The Mind-Body Problem' were rare before then and seem not to have become fixtures of the curriculum in Anglo-American universities until the 1960s.[1] More broadly, construed as the systematic self-conscious reflection on the question of how mental states and processes should be conceived in relation to physical states and processes, one might put the date to the late nineteenth or early twentieth century.

One might infer on this basis that a six-volume work on *The History of Philosophy of Mind* extending back to antiquity is bound to be anachronistic: we cannot, after all, assume that our questions were the questions of, say, Democritus, working in Thrace in the fifth century BC, or of Avicenna (Ibn-Sînâ), active in Persia in the twelfth century, or of John Blund, the Oxford- and Paris-trained Chancellor of the see of York from 1234–1248, or, for that matter, of the great German philosopher and mathematician Leibniz (1646–1716). One might on the contrary think it *prima facie* unlikely that thinkers as diverse as these in their disparate times and places would share very many preoccupations either with each other or with us.

Any such immediate inference would be unduly hasty and also potentially misleading. It would be misleading not least because it relies on an unrealistically unified conception of what *we* find engaging in this area: philosophy of mind comprises today a wide range of interests, orientations, and methodologies, some almost purely *a priori* and others almost exclusively empirical. It is potentially misleading in another way as well, heading in the opposite direction. If we presume that the only thinkers who have something useful to say to us are those engaging the questions of mind we find salient, using idioms we find congenial, then we will likely overlook some surprising continuities as well as instructive discontinuities across these figures and periods.

Some issues pertinent to mental activity may prove perennial. Of equal importance, however, are the differences and discontinuities we find when we investigate questions of mind assayed in earlier periods of thought. In some cases, it is true, we find it difficult to determine without careful investigation whether difference in idiom suffices for difference in interest or orientation. For instance, it was once commonplace to frame questions about mental activity as questions about the soul, where today questions posed about the nature of the soul and its relation to the body are apt to sound to many to be outmoded or at best quaintly archaic. Yet when we read what, for instance, medieval philosophers investigated under that rubric, we are as likely as not to find them reflecting on such core contemporary concerns as the nature of perception, the character of consciousness, the relation of mental faculties to the body, and the problem of intentionality – and to be doing so in a manner immediately continuous with some of our own preoccupations.

That said, even where upon examination we find little or no continuity between present-day and earlier concerns, this very difference can be illuminating. Why, for instance, is the will discussed so little in antiquity? Hannah Arendt suggests an answer: the will was not discussed in antiquity because it was not discovered before St. Augustine managed to do so in the third century.[2] Is she right? Or is the will in fact discussed obliquely in antiquity, enmeshed in a vocabulary at least initially alien to our own? On the supposition that Arendt is right, and the will is not even a topic of inquiry before Augustine, why should this be so? Should this make us less confident that we have a faculty rightly called 'the will'? Perhaps Augustine not so much discovered the will as *invented* it, to give it pride of place in his conception of human nature. A millennium later Thomas Aquinas contended that the will is but one power or faculty of the soul, as an intellectual appetite for the good (*ST* I 82, resp.). Is he right? Is the will as examined by Augustine and Aquinas the same will of which we ask, when we do, whether our will is free or determined?

A study of the history of philosophy of mind turns up, in sum, some surprising continuities, some instructive partial overlaps, and some illuminating discontinuities across the ages. When we reflect on the history of the discipline, we bring into sharper relief some of the questions we find most pressing, and we inevitably come to ask new and different questions, even as we retire questions which we earlier took to be of moment. Let us reflect first then on some surprising continuities. Three illustrations will suffice, but they could easily be multiplied.

First, consider some questions about minds and machines: whether machines can be conscious or otherwise minded, whether human intelligence is felicitously explicated in terms of computer software, hardware, or functional processes more generally. Surely such questions belong to our era uniquely? Yet we find upon reading some early modern philosophy that this is not so. In Leibniz, for instance, we find this striking passage, known as 'Leibniz's mill':

> Imagine there were a machine whose structure produced thought, feeling, and perception; we can conceive of its being enlarged while maintaining the same relative proportions, so that we could walk into it as we can walk into a mill. Suppose we do walk into it; all we would find there

> are cogs and levers and so on pushing one another, and never anything to account for a perception. So perception must be sought in simple substances, not in composite things like machines. And that is all that can be found in a simple substance – perceptions and changes in perceptions; and those changes are all that the internal actions of simple substances can consist in.
>
> (*Monadology* §17)

Leibniz offers an argument against mechanistic conceptions of mental activity in this passage, one with a recognizably contemporary counterpart. His view may be defensible or it may be indefensible; but it is certainly relevant to questions currently being debated.

Similarly, nearly every course in philosophy of mind these days begins with some formulation of the 'mind-body problem', usually presented as a descendant of the sort of argument Descartes advanced most famously in his *Meditations*, and defended most famously in his correspondence with Elisabeth of Bohemia. Centuries before Descartes, however, we encounter the Islamic polymath Avicenna (Ibn-Sînâ) wondering in detail about the question of whether the soul has or lacks quantitative extension, deploying a striking thought experiment in three separate passages, one of which runs:

> One of us must suppose that he was just created at a stroke, fully developed and perfectly formed but with his vision shrouded from perceiving all external objects – created floating in the air or in space, not buffeted by any perceptible current of the air that supports him, his limbs separated and kept out of contact with one another, so that they do not feel each other. Then let the subject consider whether he would affirm the existence of his self. There is no doubt that he would affirm his own existence, although not affirming the reality of any of his limbs or inner organs, his bowels, or heart or brain or any external thing. Indeed he would affirm the existence of this self of his while not affirming that it had any length, breadth or depth. And if it were possible for him in such a state to imagine a hand or any other organ, he would not imagine it to be a part of himself or a condition of his existence.
>
> (Avicenna, '*The Book of Healing*')

Avicenna's 'Floating Man' or 'Flying Man', reflects his Neoplatonist orientation and prefigures in obvious ways Descartes' more celebrated arguments of *Meditations* II. Scholars dispute just how close this parallel is,[3] but it seems plain that these arguments and parables bear a strong family resemblance to one another, and then each in turn to a yet earlier argument by Augustine,[4] more prosaically put, but engaging many of the same themes.

The point is not to determine who won the race to this particular argument, nor to insist that these authors arrive at precisely the same finish line. Rather, when we study each expression in its own context, we find illuminating samenesses and differences, which in turn assist us in framing our own questions about the character of the quantitative and qualitative features of mind, about the tenability of solipsism, and about the nature of the human self. One would like to know, for instance, whether such a narrow focus on the internal states of human consciousness provides a productive method for the science of mind. Or have our philosophical forebears, as some today think, created impediments by conceiving of the very project in a way that neglects the embodied characteristics of cognition? From another angle, one may wonder whether these approaches, seen throughout the history of the discipline, lead inexorably to Sartre's conclusion that 'consciousness is a wind blowing from nowhere towards objects'?[5] One way to find out is to study each of these approaches in the context of its own deployment.

For a final example, we return to the birthplace of Western philosophy to reflect upon a striking argument of Democritus in the philosophy of perception. After joining Leucippus in arguing that the physical world comprises countless small atoms swirling in the void, Democritus observes that *only* atoms and the void are, so to speak, really real. All else exists by convention: 'by convention sweet and by convention bitter, by convention hot, by convention cold, by convention colour; but in reality atoms and void' (DK 68B9). This remark evidently denies the reality of sensible qualities, such as sweetness and bitterness, and even colour. What might Democritus be thinking? By judging this remark alongside his remaining fragments, we see that he is appealing to the variability of perception to argue that if one perceiver tastes a glass of wine and finds it sweet, while another perceiver tastes the same glass and finds it bitter, then we must conclude – on the assumption that perceptual qualities are real – that either one or the other perceiver is wrong. After all, they cannot both be right, and there seems little point in treating them as both wrong. The correct conclusion, Democritus urges, is that sensible qualities, in contrast to atoms and the void, are not real. The wine is neither sweet nor bitter; sweetness and bitterness are wholly subjective states of perceivers.

Readers of seventeenth- and eighteenth-century British philosophy will recognize this argument in Locke and Berkeley. Locke presents the argument to support his distinction between primary and secondary qualities: primary qualities being those features of objects that are (putatively) *in* objects, independently of perception, such as number, shape, size, and motion; secondary qualities being those features of objects subject to the variability of perception recognized by Democritus. Locke struggles with the reality of secondary qualities, sometimes treating them as ideas in our minds and other times as dispositions of the primary qualities of objects that exist independently of us. Democritus, by contrast, aligning the real with the objective, simply banishes them to the realm of convention. And Berkeley appeals to the same phenomenon on which Locke founds his famous distinction – the variability of perception – to argue that the distinction is unsustainable and thus embraces the anti-Democritean option: the real is the ideal.

We may ask which if any of these philosophers deserves to be followed. As an anecdotal matter, when beginning philosophy students grasp the point of arguments from the variability of perception, they become flummoxed, because before having their attention focussed on the phenomenon of variability, most tend to think of sensible qualities as intrinsic monadic properties of the external objects of perception. This issue in the philosophy of perception, straddling as it does different periods and idioms, remains a live one, proving as vivid for us as it was for Democritus and Locke.

When we find similar philosophical arguments and tropes recurring in radically different periods and contexts throughout the history of philosophy, that is usually at least a strong *prima facie* indication that we are in an area demanding careful scrutiny. Unsurprisingly, arguments concerning the nature of perception and perceptible qualities offer one telling illustration. Still, we should resist the temptation to find continuities where none exist, especially where none exist beyond the verbal or superficial. We should moreover resist, perhaps more strongly still, the tendency to minimize or overlook differences where they appear. One of the intellectual joys of studying the history of philosophy resides precisely in uncovering and appreciating the deep discontinuities between disparate times and contexts.

On this score, examples abound, but one suffices to illustrate our point. The title of a widely read article written in the 1960s posed a provocative question: 'Why Isn't the Mind-Body Problem Ancient?'.[6] This question, of course, has a presupposition, namely that the mind-body problem is in fact *not* ancient. It also seems to betray a second presupposition, namely that there is *a* mind-body problem: a single problem that that engages philosophers of the modern era but that escaped the ancients. This presupposition raises the question: what *is* the single, unified, mind-body problem that the ancients failed to recognize? In fact, when we turn to the range of questions posed in this domain, we find a family of recognizably distinct concerns: the hard problem, the explanatory gap, mental causation, and so on. Not all these questions have a common orientation, even if they arise from a common anxiety that the mind and the body are at once so dissimilar that inquiring into their relationship may already be an error, and yet so similar in their occupation and operation as to obliterate any meaningful difference.

We might call this anxiety *categorial*. That is, it has seemed to various philosophers in various eras that there is some basic categorial distinction to be observed in the domain of the mental, to the effect that mental states belong to one category and physical states to another. That by itself might be true without, however, there being any attendant problem. After all, we might agree that there is a categorial distinction between, say, biological properties and mathematical properties, and even that these families of properties are never co-instantiable. After all, no number can undergo descent with modification, and no animal can be a cosine. That is hardly a problem: no one expects numbers to be biological subjects, and no one would ever mistake an organism for a mathematical function. The problem in the domain of the mental and physical seems to arise only when we assume that some objects – namely ourselves – exhibit both mentality and physicality, and do so in a way that is systematic and unified. Bringing these thoughts together we arrive at a mind-body problem: if mental and physical properties are categorially exclusive while we ourselves are mental and physical at once, we must be what we cannot be, namely subjects of properties that cannot coincide.

In this sense, Cartesian dualism might be regarded as a solution to the mind-body problem, at least *this* mind-body problem, one which simply concedes its conclusion by affirming that minds and bodies are irredeemably different sorts of substances displaying different sorts of properties. Needless to say, this 'solution' invites a series of still more intractable problems concerning the interaction of these postulated disparate substances, about the location of the mental, and so forth. Even so, when the Cartesian expedient is rejected on these or other grounds, the old problem re-emerges, in one guise yielding an equally desperate seeming sort of solution, namely the total elimination of the mental as ultimately not amenable to a purely physicalistic characterization.[7] Eliminativism, no less than Cartesianism, solves the mind-body problem by effectively by concession.

One should accordingly look afresh at the problem as formulated. In fact, when one asks *what* these purportedly mutually excluding properties may be, several candidates come to the fore. Some think properties such as *being conscious* are mental and cannot possibly be physical, perhaps because conscious states are ineliminably subjective, whereas all physical properties are objective, or because mental properties are essentially qualitative, whereas physical properties are only quantitative. Descartes' own reasons, though disputed, seem to have been largely epistemic: possibly one can doubt the existence of one's body, whereas it is impossible, because self-defeating, to doubt the existence of one's own mind or mental states (*Meditation* II). If these property-differences obtain in these domains and are in fact such as to be mutually exclusive, then we do now have the makings of a mind-body problem.

Returning, then, to the question pertinent to our study of the ancient period, we may ask: do the ancients draw these sorts of categorial distinctions? If so, why do they fail to appreciate the problems we find so familiar and obvious? Or do they in fact fail to draw these categorial distinctions in the first place? If they do not, then one would like to know why not. One can imagine a number of different options here: one could fault the ancients for failing to pick up on such starkly categorial differences; one could credit them for astutely avoiding the conceptual muddles of Cartesianism. Some argue, for instance, that Aristotelian hylomorphism embraces a framework of explanation within which Cartesian questions simply cannot arise, thereby obviating an array of otherwise intractable problems.[8] Although we do not attempt to litigate these issues here, one can appreciate how an investigation into ancient approaches to philosophy of mind yields palpable benefits for some modern questions, even if and perhaps precisely because such questions were not ancient.

Needless to say, we never know in advance of our investigations whether the benefits of such study are forthcoming. To make such discoveries as can be made in this area, then, we need ask a set of questions similar to those we asked regarding the mind-body problem, *mutatis mutandis*, for other philosophical problems in the mental domain, broadly construed, as they arise in other periods of philosophy beyond ancient philosophy as well.

If we proceed in this way, we find that the study of the history of philosophy of mind offers the contemporary philosopher perspectives on the discipline which, however far below the surface, may yet guide our own inquiries into the mental and physical, and into the character of mental and physical states and processes. This is, of course, but one reason to engage the studies these six volumes contain. Other researchers with a more purely historical orientation will find a wealth of material in these pages as well, ranging across all periods of western philosophy, from antiquity to that part of the discipline that resides in living memory. Our historical and philosophical interests here may, of course, be fully complementary: the history of philosophy of mind takes one down some odd by-ways off some familiar boulevards, into some dead-ends and cul-de-sacs, but also along some well-travelled highways that are well worth traversing over and again.

Notes

1 A perusal of the course offerings of leading universities in the US tends to confirm this. To take but one example, which may be multiplied, a search of the archives of the University of Notre Dame lists one course in 'Philosophy of Mind' offered as an advanced elective in 1918 and 1928, 1929, but then no further course until 1967, when 'The Mind-Body Problem,' began to be offered yearly off and on for two decades. In the 1970s, various electives such as 'Mind and Machines' were offered intermittently, and a regular offering in 'Philosophy of Mind' began only in 1982. This offering continues down to the present. While we have not done a comprehensive study, these results cohere with archive searches of several other North American universities.
2 Arendt sees prefigurations in St. Paul and others, but regards Augustine as 'the first philosopher of the will and the only philosopher the Romans ever had' (1978, vol. ii, 84).
3 For an overview of these issues, see Marmura (1986).
4 On the relation between Descartes and Augustine, see the instructive treatment in Matthews (1992).
5 Sartre (1943: 32–33).
6 Matson (1966). Citing Matson's question, King (2007) went on to pose a continuing question of his own: 'Why Isn't the Mind-Body Problem Medieval?'. In so doing, King meant to oppose Matson, who had claimed that the one should not assume that medieval philosophers, although writing in a recognizably Aristotelian idiom, similarly failed to engage any mind-body problem. After all, he noted, in addition to their Aristotelianism, they accepted a full range of theistic commitments alien to Aristotle.
7 Eliminativism about the mental has a long a chequered history, extending at least as far back as Broad (1925) (who rejects it), but has its most forceful and accessible formulation in Churchland (1988)
8 Charles (2008) has advanced this sort of argument on behalf of hylomorphism.

Bibliography

Arendt, Hannah. 1978. *The Life of the Mind*, vols. i and ii. New York: Harcourt Brace Jovanovich.
Broad, C. D. 1925. *The Mind and Its Place in Nature*. London: Routledge & Kegan.

Charles, David. 2008. "Aristotle's Psychological Theory". *Proceedings of the Boston Area Colloquium in Ancient Philosophy* **24**: 1–29.

Churchland, P. M. 1988. *Matter and Consciousness*. Cambridge, MA: MIT Press.

King, Peter. 2007. "Why Isn't the Mind-Body Problem Medieval?" In *Forming the Mind: Essays on the Internal Senses and the Mind/Body Problem From Avicenna to the Medical Enlightenment*, 187–205. Berlin: Springer.

Marmura, Michael. 1986. "Avicenna's Flying Man in Context". *The Monist* **69**(3): 383–395.

Matson, Wallace. 1966. "Why Isn't the Mind-Body Problem Ancient?" In *Mind, Matter, and Method: Essays in Philosophy and Science in Honor of Herbert Feigl*, 92–102. St. Paul: University of Minnesota Press.

Matthews, Gareth. 1992. *Thought's Ego in Augustine and Descartes*. Ithaca: Cornell University Press.

Sartre, Jean-Paul. 1943. "Une Idée fondamentale de la phénomenologie de Husserl: L'intentionalité". In *Situations I*. Paris: Gallimard.

INTRODUCTION TO VOLUME 1[1]

John E. Sisko

The chapters in this volume offer explorations into major figures and movements in ancient philosophy of mind.[2] The time period assayed herein spans about 1,200 years, from the 6th century BCE, with the emergence of philosophical enquiry in the Greek city-state of Miletus, to the 6th century CE, with the decline of pagan philosophy in the wake of Emperor Justinian's closure of the Academy in Athens in 529 CE. Some of the theories discussed in this volume are poorly aligned with what we moderns now take to be core issues in philosophy of mind. Some of the theories are over-broad and over-general in relation to more modern approaches to the mind, while remaining silent on crucial topics, such as intentionality, consciousness, and the nature of volition. Further, where such theories address legitimate topics, like the ontology of mind, they offer only surface-level assessments. For example, Anaximenes (*floruit c.*550 BCE) contends: "our soul, . . . which is air, controls us" (DK13B2).[3] Yet, there is no evidence that Anaximenes considers the issue of how air might go about controlling the body.[4] Other theories discussed in this volume appear over-narrow: they limit discussion to only a subset of problems, while neglecting topics that are now taken to be central to philosophy of mind. For example, in Plato's *Phaedo*, Socrates contends that, while reason belongs to the soul, emotion belongs to the body and not to the soul (94b7–e5). This suggests that Plato (*c.*428–*c.*347 BCE), during at least one period in his development, might accept the thesis that the study of emotion belongs to some domain of enquiry other than philosophy of mind.[5]

Still, other theories discussed in this volume are neither over-broad nor over-narrow. Aristotle (384–322 BCE), for example, engages in sophisticated and nuanced discussions on a host of important topics, including emotion, perception, intellection, consciousness, self-awareness, intentionality, judgment, volition, and the relation between mental states and bodily states. Further, Aristotle's theory of intellection is nicely calibrated with our modern interests: within his account, some scholars espy anti-reductive materialism, others discern the supervenience of the mental upon the physical, and still others see functionalism (see Shields). Another thinker who is discussed in this volume, Galen (*c.*130–*c.*210 CE), gains the respect of modern readers for his empiricism and his ingenuity with experimentation. Galen's most famous experiment – that of cutting the recurrent laryngeal nerves of a pig and, thereby, eliminating its vocalizations – provides strong evidence that the brain controls behavior (UP.VII.14–15; see Gross). Yet, even those theorists discussed in this volume who appear at times to be *modern-seeming* also advance views that will strike the modern reader as outlandish, uninformed, bizarre, and markedly *non-modern*. Aristotle, after all, thinks that the brain is a cooling system for the body (PA.II.10.656a14–36), Galen claims that appetites and desires originate in the liver (PHP.V.577; see Hankinson), and Plato suggests that, after death, the souls of pleasure-seeking humans go on to wander around graveyards as phantoms or ghosts (*Phaedo* 81c8–d4). So, we would be doing ourselves a great disservice were we to study ancient approaches to philosophy of mind with the aim of coming to understand the field at its contemporary and cutting edge. For that purpose, given modern advances in neuroscience and empirical psychology, much of what is discussed in this volume must be considered jejune. So, we might reasonable ask why we should concern ourselves with the early history of philosophy of mind.

One answer to the question is that the study of ancient philosophy of mind provides us with important instrumental benefits. By coming to grasp major themes in ancient thought, we move towards a more comprehensive understanding of our place in cultural and intellectual history. First, elements of ancient thought are part of the threadwork of modern culture and, while many of the views discussed in this volume do not harmonize with contemporary science, some of the views harmonize quite well with notions that are held to be true by many individuals within our society. For example, Plato has many (non-philosophically minded) contemporary allies when it comes to belief in ghosts. Still, this lingering and unenlightened belief seems rather trifling when compared to some of the more damaging holdovers from ancient times. So, the study of early philosophy of mind helps us place certain ingrained (and often broadly held) cultural beliefs at arm's length. Further, it affords us the opportunities to uncover our own unwitting presuppositions. This promotes intellectual autonomy: it positions the reader to embrace or reject such views, with cognizance of each view's genesis, development, and legacy (as well as cognizance of arguments advanced by the early critics of each view). Second, the ancient world is the crucible in which questions that are central to contemporary philosophy of mind are first forged. Thus, once we are able to understand why ancient thinkers discard or discount certain issues, while they accept, embrace, and champion others, we gain a second type of critical distance. Knowledge of ancient theories of mind positions us to consider whether the questions that are asked by contemporary philosophers are in fact the questions that they, or we, should be asking. By gaining this critical distance, we are empowered to assess whether contemporary philosophy of mind might be due for a bit of disruption: we gain an eye with which to gauge whether the field (or some part of it), as it stands today, may be in want of a new paradigm. Third, we cannot fully appreciate or properly contextualize later developments in the philosophy of mind if we lack knowledge of relevant ancient theories. It is no accident that both Plato and Aristotle are mentioned and discussed in each volume within this six-part series: in many ways, these two philosophical titans still shape and define the field. In addition, we cannot gain a robust understanding of Descartes, without also turning to Augustine (354–430 AD); we cannot master Brentano, without also studying Aristotle; and we cannot comprehend key changes that take place during the Renaissance, without also exploring Lucretius (*obit. c.*50 BCE) (see Greenblatt). Later philosophers of mind (including contemporary ones, whether they are aware of it or not), stand on the shoulders of giants. So, the study of ancient philosophy of mind has important instrumental value.

Another reply to the question of why we should study theories advanced by early thinkers is that ancient philosophy of mind has intrinsic worth; plus, there is significant value in studying history for history's sake (see Frede and Reis, p. 4). We cannot help but be awestruck by the brilliant flashes of insight that characterize this period. As an example, when Aristotle advances the theory of hylomorphism (see DA.II.1–3), his synthesis, through which both the thesis that mind is material substance and the antithesis that mind is immaterial substance are rejected and superseded, is a manifestly stunning advance. In this fresh and unheralded move, Aristotle gives birth to a new and impressive worldview. Simply put: when we study ancient philosophy of mind, we witness powerful intellectual wonders and adventurous theoretical delights.

In what follows, I provide an overview of the choppy and undulating seascape of ancient philosophy of mind. I resist the temptation to wade into debate over contentious issues. Still, within this synopsis, I do not shy away from introducing my own views, especially where I have a stake as a participant in some lively, ongoing debates. Further, my account falls short of providing an adequate survey of even just those theories that are advanced by the more prominent thinkers of the period: in respect to both breadth and depth, my outline is far from complete. I sketch a few common themes and shared questions concerning the nature of soul, soul's relation to the body, and models for the possible mortality or immortality of soul. I also chart out some of the explanatory schemes that are integral to ancient philosophy of mind. Herein I offer a general framework which may help the reader to contextualize the issues and topics that are explored in the probing, rich, and illuminating chapters that comprise the main body of this volume.

1. Soul: range, nature, and relation to body

Many early thinkers who touch on topics associated with mind have no conception of philosophy of mind as such. Their views on mind are part of the fabric of their explorations into psychology. Yet, to call these thinkers psychologists would be misleading, for the conception of psychology that they share is much broader than the modern conception (see Everson, pp. 2–5). These thinkers are engaged in, what we might call, general life science. They consider soul (*psuche*) to be the principle of life and they affirm that living things have soul (they are *empsuche*, ensouled), while dead or inanimate things lack soul (these are *apsuche*, or soulless). So, early thinkers excogitate on the nature of soul and on the characteristic abilities of living things. Given that reproduction, growth, and nutrification are common to all living things, many early thinkers suppose that, in addition to humans and in addition to animals, even plants have soul. Among the Presocratics, Empedocles (*floruit* c.460 BCE) most assuredly holds this view (see DK31B117) and, arguably, Pythagoras (*floruit* c.540 BCE) does as well (see DK44B89; cf. Huffman, p. 38, n. 50).[6] Further, some Presocratics not only think that plants have souls, but also assign powers to plants that we would attribute to only humans or to only animals and humans. The author of *On Plants* (Pseudo-Aristotle) indicates, "Anaxagoras and Empedocles say that [plants] are moved by desire and they affirm that they also perceive and feel pain and pleasure. . . . Anaxagoras, Democritus, and Empedocles held that plants possess mind and knowledge" (DK59A117). The passage suggests that certain early philosophers believe that the cause of desire, perception, and thought is the same as the cause of nutrification, reproduction, and growth: the cause is simply and plainly soul. Without considering the possibility of functional taxonomies of living things or of types (or aspects) of soul, these philosophers infer that anything with soul must think, perceive, desire, and digest. Some early thinkers go a step further by supposing that the set of living things is actually broader than the set of all plants, animals, and humans. Thales (*floruit* c.600 BCE), for example, who takes the power to cause motion to be definitive of life, expands the set of living things to include magnets. As Aristotle testifies, "it appears from what is recounted of him that Thales too understood the soul to be a source of motion, since he said the loadstone has a soul because it moves iron" (DA.I.2.405a19–21=DK11A22). (If Aristotle's report is accurate, Thales apparently conflates self-motion – both locomotion and growth – with the power to cause motion in external objects.) Perhaps going yet another step beyond the pale, Anaximenes, it is argued, thinks that all matter is alive: he appears to embrace hylozoism (see Guthrie 1965, p. 341).[7] Hylozoism, in effect, destroys the very distinction between the living and the non-living. So, the evidence shows that philosophy of mind, in its earliest stirrings, is part of an expansive and wildly imaginative, yet empirically uninformed and taxonomically misguided, shared theoretical campaign, focusing on general life science.

As early philosophers start to weigh the relative merits of competing theories of mind, they also begin developing perspicuous taxonomies both of living things and of types (or aspects) of soul. The Pythagorean philosopher Philolaus (*floruit* c.430 BCE), as an example, states,

> the head [is the seat] of thought, heart of life [soul] and sensation, navel of rooting and first growth, and genitals of sowing seed and begetting. The brain <contains> the source of man, the heart that of animal, the navel that of plant, the genitals the source of all of them. For all things sprout and grow from seed.
>
> (DK44B10)

So, for Philolaus, the powers of thought, desire, and reproduction are situated in different parts of the body. Further, Philolaus maintains that these powers are not equally distributed among living organisms: he holds that reproduction is shared by all living things, while desire is common to only animals (and humans), and thought is unique to humans. Aristotle and Augustine hold the same view, when it comes to perishable beings (see Aristotle DA.II.2.413a26–b1 and Augustine *De Quantitate Animae* 33.70). Aristotle, while rejecting the notion that the faculty of reason is located in the brain, further schematizes and develops Philolaus' taxonomy by considering not only faculties, but also sub-faculties and even faculty-specific sub-components (see Perler 2015). For example, he contends that all animals share the perceptual modalities of taste and touch, whereas only those animals capable of locomotion possess the distal senses: the modalities of sight, hearing, and smell (see DA.II.2.413b2–8 & III.11.433b31–434a2). So, on Aristotle's account, taste and touch are taxonomically separate from the other perceptual modalities.[8] Further, Aristotle questions whether all animal species possess imagination (see DA.III.11.433b31–434a5), asserts that some species lack memory (see *Meta*.I.1), and is curious about whether certain non-human species might convey pertinent information to their own kind through vocalization or speech (see HA.IV.9).

Philolaus is not the only thinker to affirm that different psychological powers manifest themselves, or have their sources in, spatially distinct parts of the body. Still, against Philolaus, certain early philosophers do not believe that the threefold division of plants, animals, and humans constitutes a taxonomy of living things: certain thinkers see the divide between animals and plants as marking a separation between the *empsuche* and the *apsuche*. For example, the Stoics affirm that plants lack soul (see Aëtius 5.26.3 and Sorabji, pp. 98–99). Nevertheless, Philolaus' taxonomy of living things, as codified and developed by Aristotle, comes to be accepted by many ancient philosophers. Subsequent to Philolaus, few serious thinkers advance the bold (and resolutely uninformed) thesis that anything with soul must think, perceive, desire, and digest. In addition, few suggest that magnets live (*contra* Thales) or that all matter is alive (*contra* Anaximenes). Further, with an emerging focus on the study of specific psychological faculties, sub-faculties, and faculty sub-components, philosophers of the era begin to ask the kinds of questions that we tend to associate with projects that are now pursued by contemporary philosophers of mind. These early thinkers ask: how might we explain intentionality? How are we to account for the apparent unity of cognitive awareness? What specific bodily structures underwrite memory? And how are non-latent universal concepts developed within us, when our immediate experience of the world concerns only particulars or even only sense data?

As part of the enterprise of explaining why psychological powers manifest themselves in spatially distinct parts of the body (and as part of the related enterprise, pursued by some, of explaining why certain powers, like reason, are not realized in the body), early thinkers focus their energies on two core questions:

what is the nature of soul? And how is soul related to the body? The theories of soul and of soul's relation to body that emerge in this period differ greatly. Still, early approaches to soul fall into two categories: the theories are either 'monistic' or 'dualistic.'[9] Some thinkers propose that body and soul are closely intermingled or interdependent: they advance theories that are monistic. On the monistic approach, soul is causally or ontologically dependent on, or co-dependent with, the body and, thus, the soul cannot be identified when it is considered in isolation from the body. There are two chief variants of monism in early Western philosophy. The first is 'harmony theory.' Simmias advances this variant in Plato's *Phaedo*. He states, "the body is stretched and held together by the hot and the cold, the dry and the moist and other such things, and our soul is a mixture and harmony of those things when they are mixed with each other rightly and in due measure" (*Phaedo* 86b7–c2). On one interpretation of harmony theory, soul is a secondary effect or byproduct (an epiphenomenon) of the properly structured and attuned body. Soul is not a substance in its own right. Plus, the characteristics that we tend to attribute to soul are actually caused by the body: soul, on this approach, is causally inefficacious. In addition, under harmony theory, the destruction of the body entails the destruction (or cessation) of soul. So, soul cannot be identified in separation from the body: under the harmony theory, soul is one with the living body.

The second variant of monism is 'hylomorphism.' Aristotle develops this theory of soul and its relation to the body. He states, "soul is substance as form of a natural body which has life potentially" and "soul is the first actuality of a natural body furnished with organs" (DA.II.1.412a19–20 & 412b4). According to Aristotle, soul is not a substance in its own right. Rather, soul is the organization-for-the-sake-of-functioning of the body. Plus, he contends that a body, which loses its dynamic organizational form, is a body only in name alone (a body homonymously): it is not a living body at all, but is instead a corpse (see DA.II.1.412b17–413a2). So, according to Aristotle, body and soul are definitional correlates: body is matter enformed by soul and soul is the form of a living body. Thus, under hylomorphism, the destruction of the body entails the destruction (or cessation) of soul and soul cannot be identified in separation from the body. Aristotle affirms as much when he states, "there is no need to enquire whether soul and body are one, any more than whether the wax and the imprint are one; or, in general, whether the matter of a thing is the same with that of which it is the matter" (DA.II.1.412b6–8). Under the hylomorphism, soul is one with the living body.

Other theories of soul and its relation to body are dualistic. Dualistic theories cut against the notion that body and soul are closely intermingled or interdependent. Under dualism, body and soul have only a loose connection and, thus, soul can be identified in isolation from the body. Two variants of soul-body dualism are explored in early philosophy of mind: 'material/material dualism' and 'immaterial/material' dualism. Under material/material dualism, soul is an aggregate of fundamental material stuffs or it is, perhaps, an emergent material kind that is produced through the chemical interaction of more rudimentary stuffs. Theories of material/material dualism vary greatly in respect to sophistication and complexity, but all share the underlying tenet that soul and body are, at some level of analysis, different material substances.[10] Democritus, for example, holds that soul is an aggregate of minute spherical and, consequently, fiery atoms, which, through their own motion, cause the motion of living bodies. Aristotle reports, "Democritus . . . identifies the soul with the hot, as primary shapes of his spherical particles" and "he says because the minute spheres are in constant motion . . . they animate and move the whole body" (*De Resp*.IV.472a3–5=DK68A106 and DA.I.3.406b15–22=DK68A104). In addition, the Pythagoreans think that soul is some sort of basic, yet dynamic, stuff: most likely air. Aristotle writes, "some of them <the Pythagoreans> have declared that soul is identical with the motes in the air, and others with what makes these motes move" (DA.I.2.404a17–19=DK58B40). Philolaus, specifically, among the Pythagoreans, contends that soul is air/breath (see DK44A27). Further, according to Heraclitus (*floruit c*.500 BCE), soul is fire. He states, "a dry soul [a dry gleam of light] wisest and best" (DK22B118). For Empedocles, together with the authors of the Hippocratic treatises *On Regimen* and *On Disease*, soul (or at least mind) is blood, or oxygenated blood in the region about the heart, or, more specifically, the oxygen/air that is in such blood (see DK31B105, *De Victu* IV.90, and *Morb*. I.30). On Empedocles' account, blood is an emergent kind: it is a chemical compound or, perhaps, a homoeomerous substance that is produced when four fundamental kinds of matter – air, fire, water, and earth – are blended in roughly equal proportions (see DK31B98). For Lucretius, soul is a mixture of air, wind, heat, and some mysterious unnamed fourth type of matter; plus, Lucretius often compares soul to smoke or vapor (see DRN.III.231–234 & 425–445). For the Stoics, soul is structured from one of the three kinds of *pneuma* that together comprise the basic material ingredients of the universe. This *pneuma* is mixed throughout the living body, but it has a special governing locus in the region about the heart (see *El.Eth*.col.4.38–53, Galen PHP.111.1.10–15, and Long, pp. 562–572). Also some Stoics compare the soul to air (see Calcidius 200: Long and Sedley, p. 315). So, as a brief overview shows, many early thinkers believe that body and soul are different aggregates, amalgams, or blends of matter. These thinkers are material/material dualists and they agree that soul can be identified in isolation from the body.

Immaterial/material dualism is the second variant of classical dualism. The view is advanced by some of the more prominent and influential thinkers of the period, including Plato, Plotinus (204/5–270 CE), and Augustine. In Plato's *Phaedo*, Socrates affirms that, while the body is a visible compound and, thus, is destined to suffer division and destruction, the soul, is an invisible and unitary substance and, thus, is indestructible (see *Phaedo* 78b–79e & 102a–107a).[11] Plotinus, who is influenced by Plato, advances fresh arguments for the thesis that soul is a non-bodily unity. Plotinus' arguments are based on reflections on key characteristics of our cognitive lives. He insists, for example, that the unity of perceptual awareness – the unity found in cognizance of a single object as being, say, both white and sweet – is possible only if the soul is an indivisible and non-material unity (see *Enneads* IV.3 and Emilsson). Augustine, who is influenced by Plotinus, affirms that the human soul is not a body, even though it is somehow present to the body. He too reflects on special characteristics of cognition. Augustine argues that our ability to become aware, in one instant, of different parts of our own bodies, say, of both the left hand and the right foot, is possible only because the soul is non-bodily in nature (see *Ep*.166.2–4 and Teske, pp. 118–119). Looking out beyond the common gambit that is occupied by the developmentally linked trio of Plato, Plotinus, and Augustine, some scholars view Aristotle as an immaterial/material dualist when it comes to the rational soul. On one interpretation, Aristotle carves out a special case exception from his general theory of hylomorphism for intellect: he contends that mind is a non-bodily faculty (see Sisko 1999).[12] So, a number of prominent and influential early thinkers affirm (or, more cautiously, in the case of Aristotle, are said to affirm) that soul is, in some manner, non-bodily substance.[13] Soul, on this model, can be identified in isolation from the body.

2. Mortalism and immortalism

Monists and dualists alike explore the question of whether soul persists consequent to the death of the body. For the Greeks, interest in post-mortem existence has pre-philosophical roots. Consider the opening lines of the *Iliad*:

> Rage – Goddess, sing the rage of Peleus' son Achilles,
> murderous, doomed, that cost the Achaeans countless losses,
> hurling down to the House of Death so many sturdy souls,
> great fighters' souls, but made their bodies carrion,
> feasts for the dogs and birds.
>
> (I.1–5, Fagles trans)

According to Homer, when a warrior dies, his soul leaves the body and travels to the afterworld. Further, the soul, which is associated with breath and warm vapor, persists in Hades as an image or phantom of the deceased (see *Iliad* XI.465–540 and Lorenz, section 1). Also, within Orphism, an early Greek religion, it is believed that our souls may be reincarnated: they may take up fresh residences in human bodies or even in animal bodies (see Guthrie 1950, pp. 318–326). The Orphics, thus, believe in *metempsychosis*: transmigration of soul among the bodies of different species. In addition, the Orphics believe that, for cases in which the deceased had been properly initiated into ritualized religious practices and his soul had completed a sufficient number of cycles of reincarnation, the soul might escape specific travails in the underworld or even escape from the cycle of reincarnation altogether (see Guthrie *ibid*.). So, some early Greeks have pre-philosophical, unexamined, and uncritical beliefs about the persistence of the soul after death. These pre-philosophical souls are blind to the thorny issues that surround the metaphysics of persistence and they fail to be mindful of the variety of conceptually possible modes of persistence which a soul might enjoy.

Early philosophical theories that address the question of persistence of soul fall into two categories: these are 'mortalism' and 'immortalism.' Thinkers who embrace mortalism reject the notion that the soul persists in any way after the death of the living thing. Those who posit immortalism reject mortalism. (In the next section, I examine three types of immortalism. But in this section, I treat immortalism somewhat generically, even though the theories upon which I here focus will later be identified as falling under 'weak immortalism.') Lets first consider mortalism. Mortalism is entailed by monism: as we have already seen, under harmony theory and under hylomorphism, the destruction of the body results in the destruction (or cessation) of soul. So, any thinker who accepts either harmony theory or hylomorphism (and who also does not muddy the waters by introducing qualifications or special case exceptions) must, if he or she is sufficiently reflective, endorse mortalism.

The monists are not alone in promoting mortalism: many material/material dualists also advance the thesis. Democritus, for example, thinks that functional structures of soul atoms are maintained within the body through the process of respiration and, when respiration ceases, death occurs. We are told that, for Democritus, "death is the passing out of such 'shapes' from the body owing to the pressure of the surrounding air" (Aristotle *De Resp*.IV.472a14–16=DK68A106). So, Democritus believes that, with sufficient outflow of soul atoms, the internal material structure – a knotted tangle of atoms – which had constituted the soul, is destroyed: the soul ceases to be. Lucretius, who champions a revamped form of atomism which he inherits from Epicurus (341–270 BCE), sets out a series of innovative arguments in support of mortalism. As an example, he argues that pharmaceuticals could not impact the health of the mind, were mind not a material composite (see DRN.III.508–515). The destruction of this composite is, for Lucretius, the annihilation of soul.[14] In addition, some Stoics think that death brings the destruction of soul (see Plutarch 53C: Long and Sedley, p. 314). Nevertheless, not all Stoics hold this view. Further, certain other material/material dualists, independent of the Atomists and the Stoics, reject mortalism. We will turn to representative theories in a moment. But, here I propose what I take to be an entailment from material/material dualism: if a defender of material/material dualism meets three conditions, then he/she must endorse mortalism. The conditions are: the thinker (1) posits a non-magical theory of physics, (2) denies the possibility that supernatural forces or entities might preserve material souls in contravention of the laws of physics, and (3) is sufficiently reflective about his/her own beliefs, placing a high value on logical consistency. If the entailment is correct, then any material/material dualist who posits immortalism fails to meet at least one of the three conditions.

Some Stoics affirm that, while the non-rational soul perishes together with the body, the rational soul, possessed by humans, persists: the souls of those who have led foolish lives linger for a short while after death, while the souls of the wise and virtuous persist for a long time (see Eusebius 53W: Long and Sedley, p. 318). Still, even the latter souls ultimately come to be annihilated within a periodic, grand, and wholly destructive cosmic conflagration. So, Stoics, within this group, affirm that the rational soul outlasts the body: they believe the soul may persist post-mortem for a significant period of time. Among the material/material dualists who are neither Stoics nor Atomists, Empedocles stands out as a proponent of quasi-Orphic metempsychosis. He suggests that he himself has already lived many lives: some as a human, some as an animal, and some as a plant. Empedocles writes, "for ere now I have been a boy, a girl, a bush, a fowl, and a fish travelling in the sea" (DK31B117). Further, Empedocles offers a description of a blood sacrifice that strongly indicates a belief in metempsychosis. He states, "the father lifting up his own son in a changed form slaughters him with a prayer in his great folly, and they are lost as they sacrifice the supplicant. But he, not heedful of their rebukes, having made slaughter has prepared in his halls a ghastly banquet" (DK31B137). According to Empedocles, the sacrifice of an animal could be, in effect, filicide (as in our passage) or fratricide, sororicide, matricide, patricide, or any of a host of taboo murders. Further, owing to his belief in metempsychosis, Empedocles practices vegetarianism: it would seem that, for Empedocles, eating meat amounts to cannibalism. Pythagoras also believes in metempsychosis (plus, he too is a vegetarian). We learn from Xenophanes (*floruit* c.540 BCE) that, on an occasion when Pythagoras passed by a puppy being beaten, he said, "stop, don't beat him, since it is the soul of a man, a friend of mine, which I recognized when I heard it cry" (DK21B7). Within this scenario, it appears that Pythagoras recognizes the soul of a once departed, and now returned, friend. Along with Empedocles and Pythagoras, it is likely that Philolaus believes in metempsychosis (see DK44A27 and Huffman). Heraclitus is, perhaps, not a champion of metempsychosis. Nevertheless, he thinks that the soul outlasts the body. We are told, "Heraclitus said, admirably, that souls use the sense of smell in Hades" (DK22B98). Post-mortem sensation presupposes post-mortem existence. Thus, Heraclitus is an immortalist. Further, Heraclitus states, "for men who die there await things they do not expect or anticipate" and "they rise up . . . and become watchful guardians of the living and the dead" (DK22B75 & 78). Heraclitus thinks that the souls of some of the dead go on to wander about as phantoms or ghosts: shadowy, yet informed and sage, overseers. So, Heraclitus accepts that souls can persist for an appreciable period of time after the destruction of the body. Further, it is possible that, for Heraclitus (like certain Stoics), persistence of soul is limited by periodic cosmic conflagration (see Guthrie 1962, pp. 455–459).

Philosophers who believe in reincarnation or metempsychosis are committed to the view that souls persist for some non-insignificant measure of time after the death of the body. The theory of metempsychosis would lose its luster were we to propose that each of us (i.e., each of our souls) lasts for only, say, two cycles: one as a human, whose unfortunate life happens to be brief and painful, and another, say, as a grub. Minimally, I would think, these theorists suppose that the soul persists through at least a fistful of life cycles. In the case of Pythagoras, we are told that he "beheld each of all existing things for ten or even twenty generations of men" (DK31B129). So, it would seem that, for Pythagoras, the soul persists for about five hundred or one thousand years. Empedocles suggests a lengthier time frame: he describes himself as "one of those deities (*daimones*) who has gained long life, thrice ten thousand seasons he is exiled from the blessed gods, through time growing to be all kinds of creatures going from one grievous path of life to another" (DK31B115).[15] Since the Greeks divide the year into three seasons, it appears that Empedocles thinks souls/*daimones* persist for about 10,000 years. Interestingly, one might reasonably surmise that, for Empedocles, the demise of soul occurs at a specific moment (or period) in his cosmological cycle: the dominion of Love. At this stage in the cycle, the entire universe forms into a static, unitary, and homogenous mass (see Sisko 2014, pp. 60–61). So, neither Empedoclean souls nor their oft-associated bodies could exist at this stage in the cycle. The evidence thus shows that, while the defenders of metempsychosis reject mortalism, they, together with Heraclitus and certain Stoics, do not posit the eternal persistence of soul.

The project of coupling material/material dualism with immortalism presents a rather conspicuous difficulty. These theories appear to be incongruous: without magic or the divine, matter simply does not behave in ways that would be required, were composite material souls to be preserved.[16] Amalgams and blends, together with biological or chemical compounds, are entropic. Over time, they break down and their more rudimentary bits separate or emerge. Further, while some mixtures are relatively durable (take metal alloys as examples), others, like gaseous blends, loose tangles of atoms, and liquid solutions or suspensions are quite markedly entropic. Here Democritus and Lucretius understand the basics. As they see it, soul atoms scatter helter-skelter, they disentangle and pour out in all directions, when, say, in battle, a limb is lopped off and a warrior, as a consequence, dies. But, Democritus and Lucretius are mortalists: not immortalists. We must infer that their immortalist colleagues in the material/material dualist camp, unless they also introduce deeper mysteries, fail to see the light. Fire, fiery blends, air, airy blends, and biological liquids (like blood) are outstanding candidates for dispersal, dissipation, decrepitancy, and mortification. So, it is not unreasonable to propose that Pythagorean souls, Philolausian souls, Heraclitean souls, Empedoclean souls, and certain Stoic souls, contrary to their namesakes' wishes, should be mortal. These souls should perish together with the body. Regarding air/breath souls and fire/fiery souls, the point is well made by Cebes in Plato's *Phaedo*. Cebes states, "certain men think that after the soul has left the body it no longer exists anywhere, but that it is destroyed and dissolved ... and that, upon leaving the body, the soul is dispersed like breath or smoke, has flown away and gone and is no longer anything anywhere" (*Phaedo* 70a1–7). Cebes marks out a reasonable conjecture, based, in part, on the presumption that theories of material/material dualism should be subsumed within overarching philosophical schemes that are neither metaphysically rococo nor ontologically extravagant. So, on one interpretation, it appears that the material/material dualists may embrace immortalism only if they are willing to introduce the rococo or the extravagant: the magical or the divine.

On one view, the non-atomist material/material dualists come to look more like Democritus and Lucretius than they might otherwise appear. On this approach, these thinkers contend that, while the soul is mortal, the rudimentary bits out of which the composite soul is formed come to scatter at the approach of death and these bits go on to persist for long periods of time. These airy or fiery bits are, in some manner, indestructible, even though the composite soul perishes. The interpretation can be supported through argument. However, its defenders face an uphill battle. To support this mortalist reading, they must explain away the suggestion that Empedocles remembers having already lived as a boy, a girl, a bush, and a fish (see DK31B117); they must explain away the testimony, which indicates that Pythagoras recognizes the soul of a once departed, and now returned, friend (see DK21B7); and they must counter the suggestion that, for Heraclitus, souls can persist as ghosts that retain some of the character of their former selves (see DK22B87). I leave this thread for others to explore.

Returning to the main line of investigation, it is important to be reminded that many theories advanced by early philosophers of mind are wildly imaginative and empirically unmoored. So, it should be of no surprise that certain of these theories are also metaphysically rococo. Consider the musings of Empedocles: we have already learned that he considers himself to be a deity (*daimon*) (see DK31B115). More importantly, magic is at play throughout Empedocles' physics and cosmology. Empedocles describes his four fundamental types of matter – earth, air, fire, and water – as gods: Hera, Aidoneus, Zeus, and Nestis (see DK31B6). Further, he postulates that change in the cosmos is governed by the powers of Love and Strife (see, for example, DK31B17). Empedocles' physics contains elements that the modern reader must view as supra-physical: his physics is magical. The same can be said for theories advanced by other non-atomist material/material dualists. Heraclitus, for example, not only thinks that soul is fire, he thinks that fire is both *logos* and Zeus (see DK22B2 & B32), and he affirms that fire/*logos*/Zeus, which he otherwise calls "thunderbolt" (see DK22B24), steers and directs change throughout the cosmos.[17] So, it is likely that the early material/material dualists who embrace immortalism do so, in part, because they lack an understanding of hardnosed physics. For these theorists, the magical plays a legitimate role within the material world: their theories are situated within a nexus that the modern reader must view as fanciful and unreal.[18]

Still, let us, for the sake of argument, cede immortalism to Empedocles, Pythagoras and to any other material/material dualist who is similarly inclined: let us accept that our souls persist for five hundred years or even ten thousand years. Generalizing, let us agree that our souls carry on for N years. On this model, we are long-lived. But, there is a worry: the merely long-lived are not truly immortal. Under this scheme, any one of us might now be living through year N-1 (or N-x, where x is a frightfully low number) (see Lucretius DRN.III.1092–1101). Thus, any one of us (body and soul) might not have long to live. Since you (the reader) and I might be in such a predicament, our next deaths could be our last: our immortalist souls could soon face their own mortality. So, immortalism, of the type we have studied thus far, merely delays or postpones the demise of soul: it fails to provide unqualified rescue from annihilation. This point is well made by our learned friend Cebes. Examining the kind of immortalism that is offered up by Empedocles and others, Cebes likens the soul and the various bodies that it has inhabited throughout its term of existence (on this approach to immortalism) to a weaver and the various cloaks that he has worn throughout his life; and Cebes notes that just as the weaver, having outlasted many of his former cloaks, goes on to die in his last cloak, so too the soul, having outlasted many of its former bodies, dies together with its last body (see *Phaedo* 87b3–d1). Cebes understands that, while Pythagorean souls, Philolausian souls, Heraclitean souls, Empedoclean souls, and certain Stoic souls may be relatively durable, all such souls, in the end, are mortal.[19] This tainted immortalism (sullied by mortality) is, for some thinkers, just not good enough. Happily, for those who desire more, tainted immortalism, or 'weak immortalism,' is just one of three types of immortalism that are explored by ancient philosophers of mind. In addition to weak immortalism, early thinkers examine both 'conferred immortalism' and 'strong immortalism.'[20] The latter approaches are unblemished: they do not carry the taint of mortality. Under conferred or strong immortalism the soul persists eternally. In the next section, I define our three types of immortalism and examine early theories of strong immortalism and conferred immortalism.

3. Three types of immortalism

In the ancient period, philosophers of mind who contend that the soul persists after the destruction of the body present accounts that can be divided into three general categories:

Weak Immortalism = As a matter of fact, the soul is long-lived: it persists for a significant period of time after the death of the body, yet the soul is ultimately annihilated (see Pakaluk, p. 95, esp. n. 8).
Strong Immortalism = Necessarily, the soul, owing to its very nature, persists after the destruction of the body: the annihilation of soul is a metaphysical impossibility and, thus, the soul persists eternally (see Pakaluk *ibid.*, and Sedley, pp. 146–153).
Conferred Immortalism = Even though its destruction is metaphysically possible, the soul will in fact never be destroyed, because a divine being, which itself possesses strong immortality, acts to preserve the soul (see Sedley, pp. 153–156).[21]

Empedocles, Pythagoras, and other like-minded theorists advance weak immortalism. As we have seen, these philosophers presume that the soul is long-lived, but ultimately mortal. Weak immortalism, then, is strong enough to underwrite theories of reincarnation and metempsychosis, but it is too weak to support eternal persistence of soul. Other theorists champion strong immortalism or conferred immortalism, with the aim of showing that the soul persists indefinitely.

Philosophers who posit immaterial/material dualism tend to embrace strong immortalism.[22] The earliest, and most influential, argument for strong immortalism is the Final Argument in Plato's *Phaedo*. On one construal, the argument has four basic steps:[23]

(1) Socrates affirms that whenever the soul enters the body, it brings life with it: soul always brings life when it approaches the body (*Phaedo* 105c9–d5).
(2) He infers that, since death is the opposite of life, the soul (always bringing life with it) cannot admit death: the soul is deathless (*ibid.* 105d6–e9).[24]
(3) Socrates infers that soul is deathless in a specific manner: it is deathless just as "the god and the Form of life itself <are deathless>" (106d5–6): the soul is indestructible (*ibid.* 105e11–106d9).
(4) He concludes that, as death approaches, the soul (being indestructible) must withdraw safely to Hades rather than suffer annihilation (*ibid.* 106e1–107a1).

For Socrates and many of his interlocutors, step (1) flows from their shared acceptance of substance dualism, and, specifically, immaterial/material dualism. As dualists they believe that whenever a soul enters a body, it brings life to that body. Further, they hold that soul (which is the principle of life) is empowered to bring life to the body, because soul itself is alive. Other thinkers, like Empedocles and Pythagoras, who accept substance dualism, but, specifically, material/material dualism, could happily accept step (1): they agree that soul brings life to the body, because the soul itself is alive. Turning to step (2), let us accept that if something 'always brings life,' or 'whenever arriving in a new body always brings life,' then it is in some manner 'deathless.' Accordingly, Empedoclean and Pythagorean souls are 'deathless': they possess weak immortality and undergo metempsychosis, cheating death many times. So, thinkers like Empedocles and Pythagoras could also accept step (2). Thus, in light of historical context, there is little that is controversial in the first half of the Final Argument.

Many scholars consider the inference from step (2) to step (3) to be controversial. The Peripatetic philosopher Strato of Lampsacus (*c*.335–*c*.269 BCE) is the first to identify the chief difficulty with the inference (Damascius, *in Phd.* I 442; cf. Sedley, p. 150). Strato's criticism is as follows: step (2) of the argument requires that souls cannot be dead as long as they exist: there are no dead souls (see Sedley *ibid.*, and Frede, p. 31). But an annihilated soul is not a dead soul; rather such a soul simply is not. An annihilated soul ceases to be: it no longer exists either as alive or as dead. Thus, as we have already discovered, step (2) is compatible with weak immortalism. But, in step (3), Socrates affirms that the specific kind of 'deathlessness,' which is to be attributed to soul, is that of eternal indestructibility: the deathlessness of "the god and the Form of life itself" (106d5–6). So, in step

(3), Socrates postulates unqualified rescue from annihilation. However, since the annihilation of soul is logically compatible with step (2), step (3) is not entailed by step (2). Strato contends that there is an inferential gap in Socrates' argument. He is correct in his analysis. Still, though, Socrates does not present the argument as a bare entailment. His reasoning is informed by another argument that comes earlier in the *Phaedo*: the Affinity Argument (78b–80b).

The Affinity Argument is an argument by analogy. In the argument, Socrates reminds his interlocutors that material compounds are subject to dissolution and destruction and, accordingly, he affirms that the body, being a material compound, is mortal. He also notes that the soul is not akin to the body, insofar as the body is visible, while the soul is invisible. Socrates then goes on to identify certain other invisible substances.[25] These include the Forms, "the Equal itself, the Beautiful itself, and each thing in itself, the real" (*Phaedo* 78d3–4), together with "the divine" (*ibid.* 80a3) and "the good and wise god" (*ibid.* 80d7). The Forms are immaterial unities that are invisible, changeless, and immortal. The divine, which rules, directs, and steers (the cosmos) is indestructible, deathless, and eternal. Socrates goes on to note that the soul is akin to the Forms insofar as it is invisible; and it is akin to the divine insofar as it rules, directs, and steers (the body). Thus, he concludes that, since the Forms and the divine are indestructible, "soul is altogether indissoluble, or nearly so" (80b10). With the caveat 'or nearly so,' Socrates reveals that the Affinity Argument only shows, under its most favorable interpretation, that there is a likelihood that the soul possesses strong immortality. Socrates' caution is well justified: for any argument by analogy, even if all premises are true, it remains possible that the conclusion is false.

We are now in a position to see that, within the Final Argument, Socrates, by referring to the deathlessness enjoyed by "the god and the Form of life itself" (106d5–6), harkens back to the Affinity Argument. The interlocutors' attention is meant to be drawn back to the purported deathlessness of "the Equal itself, the Beautiful itself, and each thing in itself, the real" (*Phaedo* 78d3–4), "the divine" (*ibid.* 80a3), and "the good and wise god" (*ibid.* 80d7), as canvased in the Affinity Argument. So, within the Final Argument, the outcome of the Affinity Argument is offered as a buttressing consideration to help strengthen the inference from step (2) to step (3). Nevertheless, the extra consideration does not provide the Final Argument with sufficient strength to underwrite strong immortalism. As we have shown, the Affinity Argument does not provide us with certainty. Thus, the Final Argument does not show that soul must exist eternally.[26]

We have seen that, in the *Phaedo*, Socrates advances the idea that immaterial souls are indissoluble and indestructible. The notion can be questioned. Without an otherwise definitive metaphysics of immaterial substance, it remains possible that immaterial souls are immaterial compounds and these compounds might be subject to destruction. In this context, a creative thinker might explore the possibility that a god, possessing strong immortality, might ward off the destruction of our composite immaterial souls.[27] It appears that ancient philosophers do not explore this topic (yet, perhaps, Aristotle *Meta*.VII.17 bears on it). However, some early thinkers do explore a parallel issue. Some ancient philosophers, who consider our souls to be material compounds, also suggest that a god, possessing strong immortality, eternally wards off the dissolution and destruction of our souls. These thinkers champion conferred immortalism. Here we return to material/material dualism.

The earliest defense of conferred immortalism is found in Plato's *Timaeus*. Timaeus claims that our rational souls are formed by a divine craftsperson (*demiurge*) out of impure samples of Being, the Same, and the Other (*Timaeus* 40d–44d). Our souls are created as analogues of the world soul, which the *demiurge* also creates, but out of pure samples (*ibid*. 35a–39e). On this model, the rational soul rotates within the skull in a way that parallels the rotation of the heavens about the Earth.[28] Timaeus, echoing Empedocles and Pythagoras, posits metempsychosis (*ibid*. 90e6–92c3). He also allows that the souls of the truly just might escape from the cycle of reincarnation. Timaeus states, "he who has lived well throughout his appropriate time would make his way back to the dwelling of his lawful star and would have a life that was happy and habitual to him" (*ibid*. 42b3–5, trans. Kalkavage). Unlike earlier champions of metempsychosis, Timaeus contends that the soul has conferred immortality. He does not think that the soul is immortal in its own right. Rather, he thinks that immortality is conferred to the soul by the *demiurge*, which by its own essential nature is wholly deathless. Timaeus states,

> Now, to be sure, all that is bound together can be dissolved, and yet only one who is bad would be willing to dissolve that which is beautifully joined together and in good condition. For these reasons, and since indeed you have been born, you are not immortal nor entirely indissoluble, yet in no way shall you suffer this very dissolution, nor shall you happen to meet with the doom of death, since through my will you have been allotted a bond greater still and more lordly than those bonds with which you, when born, were bound together.
>
> (41b1–c6)

On this account, physical bonds hold the composite rational soul together, and these bonds can be broken. However, Timaeus insists that the *demiurge* provides a greater bond: an eternal commitment to ward off destruction of our souls. Thus, for Timaeus, our souls are, by nature, perishable: in themselves they are mortal (or, perhaps, they possess weak immortality). Yet, owing to the divine, our souls gain conferred immortality and are, thereby, eternally deathless.[29]

Timaeus and other advocates of conferred immortality presume that there exists a powerful god, possessing strong immortality.[30] Further, they insist that the god is resolutely good and, in virtue of its goodness (and power), the god provides us with unqualified rescue from annihilation by gifting us a derived form of immortality. Certain modern readers will view the thesis of conferred immortality as standing on tremulous and unsteady ground: the thesis, some suggest, rests upon a basis that is ontologically extravagant. Nevertheless, the topic of conferred immortality resurfaces in both medieval and early modern philosophy of mind.

4. Conclusion

In this chapter, I have suggested that early philosophers of mind are, at first, unclear about which objects in the world have soul (or are soul): candidates include humans, animals, and plants, but also magnets, selected rudimentary material elements (like air), and, for that matter, even all material stuffs. Second, I have shown that philosophers in this period explore three general positions on the relation between soul and body: monism, material/material dualism, and immaterial/material dualism. Third, I have shown that these thinkers examine four positions on the mortality or immortality of soul: mortalism, weak immortalism, strong immortalism, and conferred immortalism.

* * *

In Table I.1, I arrange the major theorists (together with some minor thinkers and envisioned ones) who are discussed in this chapter, indexing them by their underlying positions both on the soul-body relation and on the issue of the mortality or immortality of soul. I invite you (the reader), as you peruse this volume and the other volumes in the six-part series, to consider whether the chart is sufficiently complex. Have other conceptual possibilities been overlooked? Do some categories remain unexplored because they are metaphysically impossible? Plus, are there interesting sub-categories that should be fleshed out and examined? These kinds of questions and issues are part and parcel of the evolving project of philosophy of mind.

Table I.1 Soul-body relations & mortalism/immortalism in early philosophy of mind

	Mortalism	*Weak Immortalism*	*Strong Immortalism*	*Conferred Immortalism*
Monism	Simmias (Plato's *Phaedo*) & Aristotle			
Material/ Material Dualism	The Atomists (Democritus, Epicurus, & Lucretius) & Some Stoics	The Proponents of Magical Physics: Empedocles, Pythagoras, Heraclitus, Philolaus, & Some Stoics	Envisioned Proponents of Hyper-Robust Magical Physics (see endnote 19)	Timaeus (Plato's *Timaeus*)
Immaterial/ Material Dualism			Socrates (Plato'S *Phaedo*)	Arnobius of Sicci (see endnote 29)

Notes

1 I would like to thank Christopher Shields for very helpful comments on an earlier draft of this chapter.
2 Here 'ancient' is meant to cover a range of historical periods. In other contexts, some of these philosophical periods (including Hellenistic, Roman, and Late Antique) would typically not be referred to as ancient.
3 Translations of the Presocratic philosophers are based on those in Graham 2010.
4 What is probable is that Anaximenes, like some of the Pythagoreans, surmises that air is self-moving, given that the air around us appears to be in constant motion. Regarding the Pythagoreans, Aristotle writes, "some of them have declared that the soul is identical with the motes in the air, and others with what makes the motes move" (DA.I.2.404a16–20=DK58B40). Anaximenes does not explain how air-caused motion might be directed and controlled as opposed to being random and chaotic.
5 Plato's theory of soul in the *Phaedo* is, as Lorenz (section 3.1) indicates, "far from fully articulated." On the one hand, Socrates claims that only reason is to be attributed to soul. On the other hand, two of his arguments concerning the ontological status of soul (the 'Cyclical Argument,' 69e–72d; and the 'Final Argument,' 102b–107a) rely on the supposition that all livings things – plants, animals, and humans – have soul. Through these arguments, Plato aims to show that the soul is immortal. So, we must agree with Bostock (p. 189) when he claims that if the arguments succeed, Plato proves "that all living things have immortal souls, . . . <including> . . . (e.g.) aphids, jellyfish, and (presumably) cabbages."
6 I use 'Presocratic' to refer to the Greek philosophers and physicians who flourished prior to Plato's death (*c*.347 BCE). Certain Presocratics, such as Democritus (*nat. c*.460 BCE), are contemporaries of Socrates and, so, following a strictly chronologically approach, they are not Presocratic.
7 Thales also might be a hylozoist (see DK31A22 and McKirahan, p. 30).
8 Some contend that this distinction plays a key role in shaping Aristotle's theory of temperance (*sophrosyne*) (cf. Sisko 2003).
9 The distinction between body/soul monism and body/soul dualism in ancient philosophy of mind is advanced by Inwood, pp. 71–72, and affirmed by Frede & Reis, p. 2.
10 Anaximenes and Diogenes of Apollonia (*floruit c*.430 BCE) are marginal outliers: they are not material/material dualists. Instead, they are material phase-state dualists. Each affirms that soul is air (see DK13B2 and DK64B4, respectively). Yet, these thinkers are material monists: they contend that there is only one type of matter in the universe and they agree that this lone material kind is air. (Graham (2006, pp. 67–84) argues that Anaximenes is not a material monist. However, see Sisko 2007.) So, for this pair of thinkers, both body and soul are air: neither Anaximenes nor Diogenes proposes that body and soul are composed of different material substances. The distinction they offer, which is of immediate relevance, is that air can be condensed or rarified and so, as examples, what we call fire is rarified air (air in one phase-state) and what we call earth is condensed air (air in another phase-state) (see DK13B1 and DK64A5). So, for Anaximenes and Diogenes, soul is air in one phase-state, while bone, flesh, sinew, and the like are air in other phase-states. Thus, they are material phase-state dualists.
11 Plato's treatment of soul in other dialogues, like *Republic*, *Phaedrus*, and *Timaeus*, is not consistent with the theory that is advanced in the *Phaedo*. Consider *Timaeus*. In the dialogue, we learn that reason is located in the skull, it is spatially extended, and it rotates (see *Timaeus* 69c1–70a2). Further, we learn that reason's turnings can be warped by alien motions, which travel up from the torso, through the neck, and into the skull (see *Timaeus* 43d10–e3). The soul (or reason), as described in the *Timaeus*, possesses spatio-physical characteristics: it is not an immaterial substance.

12 Debate over Aristotle's view on the ontology of mind is nothing new. For example, John Philoponus (485–559 CE) contends that, according to Aristotle, the human rational soul is immaterial substance (see *In DA* 10, 10–11, 29).
13 Anaxagoras (*floruit c*.460 BCE) is a tricky case. He states, "mind is mixed with no object... it is the finest of all objects and the purest... mind rules all things that possess life, both the larger and the smaller... <and> mind is all alike, both the larger and the smaller" (DK59B12). Anaxagoras clearly thinks that mind animates all living things. What is at issue is whether he thinks that mind is a very fine homogeneous substance (like, say, Philolausian air) or that, struggling to find appropriate language to describe the incorporeal, he thinks that mind is an immaterial substance. For a defense of the former view, see Palmer, pp. 187–188 & 252–255. I favor the latter view. While I cannot argue it here, I think that were Anaxagoras to posit that mind is a type of matter, this would generate inconsistencies within his, otherwise cogent and mathematically ordered, physics. So, it may be that charity requires us to view Anaxagoras as an immaterial/material dualist.
14 Lucretius famously affirms, "death is nothing to us" (DRN.III.831). He contends that, since those who have died are not (i.e., they have ceased to be), they most certainly do not feel pain or experience suffering in some sort of afterlife. Plus, thinking that pain and suffering are all that we should ever fear, Lucretius concludes that we – the living – should not fear death: 'it is nothing to us.' On this model, we may be justified in not fearing the null state of being dead. However, it remains to be shown whether we should be justified in not fearing either the prospect of dying or the process of dying.
15 For a compact, but useful, overview of perspectives on Empedocles' self-proclaimed status as a deity, see Warren, pp. 146–152.
16 For a fine examination of Presocratic attitudes towards magic and the divine, see Gregory.
17 Together with Heraclitus, other Presocratics believe that a rational divinity, or divine power, organizes and directs change in the world (see, as examples, Xenophanes DK21B29 & 33, Parmenides (*floruit c*.480 BCE) DK28B12.3, and Anaxagoras DK59B12).
18 Robinson, focusing on Heraclitus and considering the impact of Homer, Hesiod, and the Orphics, states, "like so many other Greek philosophers, he <Heraclitus> may have found it impossible fully to break with his cultural inheritance, whatever the force of his own philosophical insights and convictions" (Robinson, p. 105). I agree with Robinson: in the writings of many early philosophers, the notion that the soul persists after death is presented as if it were a received truth and there is little or no evidence of a philosophical defense of the notion.
19 These thinkers, as I have indicated, espouse a magical physics within which souls outlast bodies, yet still are ultimately destroyed. A conceptually possible variant, which is not explored in ancient philosophy, is (let us call it) 'hyper-robust magical physics.' On this model, the magic is ever present and strong enough to guarantee the eternal deathlessness of soul.
20 Pakaluk introduces and masterfully explores the topics of weak immortalism and strong immortalism. Sedley studies conferred immortalism and another approach that he calls intrinsic immortalism. As I understand the categories, Sedley's intrinsic immortalism is equivalent to Pakaluk's strong immortalism. So, I employ only the later moniker in the body of this chapter.

Sedley also theorizes about 'earned immortalism.' Under earned immortalism, certain special or high-achieving humans, like, say, Heracles and the Dioskouroi (= St. Elmo's Fire) are said to undergo *apotheosis*: they are transformed from mortal beings into deathless gods (see Sedley, pp. 145–146 & 156–161). Reference to *apotheosis* is not uncommon in early Greek myth. Sedley contends that Plato flirts with the notion of earned immortality in the *Symposium*. In the dialogue, while considering the man who fully communes with Beauty itself, Diotima states, "it belongs to him to become loved by the gods, and to him it belongs, if to any human being, to become immortal" (trans. Sedley, p. 160). The passage suggests that Plato is willing to explore the possibility that those who complete the ascent to the Beautiful might, as a consequence, be transformed into deathless gods.

21 Here is another way to approach the same set of distinctions: some think that the soul is by nature immortal (Strong Immortalism), others think that it is perishable. Among those in the later group, some think that the soul in fact perishes (Weak Immortalism), while others suppose that some naturally immortal god prevents the demise of the disembodied soul (Conferred Immortalism).

22 This is not a logical requirement: one can develop a consistent scheme under which immaterial souls are destructible. Still, the impetus for experimenting with the idea that soul is immaterial is not irrational: without the wisdom of prior analysis, one might easily suppose that if material souls are destructible, then non-material souls are non-destructible.

23 Frede, p. 29, divides the argument into three steps. I separate what is, for Frede, step (III) into two steps: steps (3) and (4).

24 Death, of course, is not the opposite of life. If opposites are contradictories, then the opposite of life is non-life. The category of the non-living includes both the dead (i.e., those who have perished, having once been alive) and the wholly inanimate (material stuffs, say, like chalk and iron: items that have not perished, owing to the fact that they haven't ever been alive). Still, the central point in step (2) is that the only way to stop living is to die. Here, Socrates has it right.

25 Here Socrates' earlier defense of dualism is crucial (see *Phaedo* 63a3–69e5 and Pakaluk, pp. 98–108); for, as we have seen, monistic theories of soul (and notably Simmias' harmony theory, which is introduced, in the *Phaedo*, just five pages after the conclusion of the Affinity Argument) allow that the soul is both invisible and not a substance.

26 Augustine echoes Socrates' 'Final Argument' in *De immor. anim.* 4–5 & 9: see O'Daly, p. 407.

27 Further, even if immaterial souls are monads, one might suppose that some god has the power to destroy such souls. Still, if the god has the power, perhaps it would never act on that power.

28 Timaeus' notion that the human mind (or soul) is a collection of spatially extended circuits, which are analogous to the heavens in respect to both structure and motion, is prefigured in the Hippocratic Treatise *De Victu* (see Sisko 2006). The author of *De Victu*, however, does not propose that the soul has conferred immortality. Soul, in *De Victu*, appears to be mortal.

29 Arnobius of Sicca (*mort.* 330 AD) offers a peculiar variation on conferred immortalism. He claims that the immaterial soul is in a 'neutral state'; it is neither mortal nor immortal (*Adversus nationes* II.31 & 35). Further he contends that, in the final judgment, god will both confer immortality to the blessed and destroy the damned (*ibid.* II.36 & 61–62). On his account, neither outcome is a function of the metaphysical constitution of the soul itself. So, Arnobius posits both conferred immortality and conferred mortality.

Earned immortalism (see endnote 19) is a variation on conferred immortalism. Under conferred immortalism, all souls are granted eternal deathlessness by the divine. Under earned immortalism, only some souls (a select few) are granted eternal deathlessness. Each theory, as I see, requires the pre-existence of a god that possesses strong immortality. Not even Heracles, in a world without gods, could himself become a god.

30 Augustine champions conferred immortality at *Ep.*166.3: see O'Daly, p. 407.

Bibliography

Bostock, D. (1986) *Plato's Phaedo*. Cambridge, MA: Cambridge University Press.

Emilsson, E. (1991) Plotinus and soul-body dualism. In Everson, S. (ed.) *Companions to Ancient Thought 2: Psychology*. Cambridge, MA: Cambridge University Press, pp. 148–165.

Everson, S. (1991) *Companions to Ancient Thought 2: Psychology*. Cambridge, MA: Cambridge University Press.

Frede, D. (1978) The final proof of the immortality of the soul in Plato's Phaedo 102a–107a. *Phronesis* 23 (1): 27–41.

Frede, D., and Reis, B. (eds.) (2009) *Body and Soul in Ancient Philosophy*. Berlin: Walter de Gruyter.

Graham, D. (2006) *Explaining the Cosmos: The Ionian Tradition of Scientific Philosophy*. Princeton: Princeton University Press.

———. (2010) *The Texts of Early Greek Philosophy: The Complete Fragments and Selected Testimonies of the Major Presocratics*. Part I. Cambridge: Cambridge University Press.

Greenblatt, S. (2011) *The Swerve: How the World Became Modern*. New York: W.W. Norton and Company.

Gregory, A. (2013) *The Presocratics and the Supernatural: Magic, Philosophy, and Science in Early Greece*. London: Bloomsbury Publishing Plc.

Gross, C. (1998) Galen and the squealing pig. *The Neuroscientist* 4 (3): 216–221.

Guthrie, W. K. C. (1950) *The Greeks and Their Gods*. Boston: Beacon Press.

———. (1962) *A History of Greek Philosophy*. Vol. I. Cambridge, MA: Cambridge University Press.

———. (1965) *A History of Greek Philosophy*. Vol. II. Cambridge, MA: Cambridge University Press.

Hankinson, R. J. (1991) Galen's anatomy of soul. *Phronesis* 36 (3): 197–233.

Huffman, C. (2009) The Pythagorean conception of soul from Pythagoras to Philolaus. In Frede, D., and Reis, B. (eds.) *Body and Soul in Ancient Philosophy*. Berlin: Walter de Gruyter, pp. 29–43.

Inwood, B. (2009) Empedocles and metempsychosis: The critique of Diogenes of Oenoanda. In Frede, D., and Reis, B. (eds.) *Body and Soul in Ancient Philosophy*. Berlin: Walter de Gruyter, pp. 71–86.

Kalkavage, P. (2001) *Plato's Timaeus*. Newburyport: Focus Publishing.

Long, A. A. (1999) Stoic psychology. In Algra, K. et al. (eds.) *The Cambridge History of Hellenistic Philosophy*. Cambridge, MA: Cambridge University Press, pp. 560–584.

Lorenz, H. (2009) Ancient theories of soul. *Stanford Encyclopedia of Philosophy*. http://plato.stanford.edu/entries/ancient-soul/

Mckirahan, R. (2010) *Philosophy Before Socrates*. 2nd edn. Indianapolis: Hackett Publishing Company.

O'Daly, G. (1997) Augustine. In Furley, D. (ed.) *Routledge History of Philosophy, Volume II: From Aristotle to Augustine*. London: Routledge.

Pakaluk, M. (2003) Degrees of separation in the 'Phaedo'. *Phronesis* 48 (2): 89–115.

Perler, D. (ed.) (2015) *The Faculties: A History*. Oxford: Oxford University Press.

Robinson, T. M. (1987) *Heraclitus Fragments: A Text and Translation with Commentary*. Toronto: University of Toronto Press.

Sedley, D. (2009) Three kinds of platonic immortality. In Frede, D., and Reis, B. (eds.) *Body and Soul in Ancient Philosophy*. Berlin: Walter de Gruyter, pp. 145–161.

Shields, C. (1993/1968) Some recent approaches to Aristotle's De Anima. In Hamlyn, D. W. (ed.) *Aristotle's De Anima Books II and III*. Oxford: Oxford University Press, pp. 157–181.

Sisko, J. (1999) On separating the intellect from the body: Aristotle's De Anima III.4, 429a10-b5. *Archiv fur Geschichte der Philosophie* 81: 249–267.

———. (2003) Taste, touch, and temperance in Nicomachean Ethics III.10. *Classical Quarterly* 53 (1): 135–140.

———. (2006) Cognitive circuitry in Plato's 'Timaeus' and the Psuedo-Hippocratic 'Peri Diaites'. *Hermathena* 180: 5–17.

———. (2007) Review of Graham, D. *Explaining the Cosmos: The Ionian Tradition of Scientific Philosophy: Bryn Mawr Classical Review*. http://ccat.sas.upenn.edu/bmcr/2007/2007-07-64.html

———. (2014) Anaxagoras and Empedocles in the shadow of Elea. In Warren, J., and Sheffield, F. (eds.) *The Routledge Companion to Ancient Philosophy*. London: Routledge.

Sorabji, R. (1993) *Animal Minds and Human Morals*. Ithaca, NJ: Cornell University Press.

Teske, R. (2001) Augustine's theory of soul. In Stump, E., and Kretzmann, N. (eds.) *The Cambridge Companion to Augustine*. Cambridge, MA: Cambridge University Press.

Warren, J. (2007) *Presocratics: Natural Philosophers Before Socrates*. Berkeley and Los Angeles: University of California Press.

1

PRESOCRATIC INTEREST IN THE SOUL'S PERSISTENCE AFTER DEATH

John Palmer

As the characters of Plato's *Phaedo* discuss whether the soul survives the death of the individual and, if so, whether it possesses any of the intelligent capacity it had when embodied, they come to focus increasingly on what the soul must be to survive in this way. Socrates specifies that only something incomposite and unchanging could be indestructible, whereas anything composite and mutable is subject to destruction (*Phd.* 78c). Socrates goes on to argue that the soul should be regarded as indestructible or nearly so because its affinity to the incomposite, unchanging, and thus indestructible Forms indicates that it is likely to resemble them in respect of being indestructible as well (*Phd.* 78c–80b). While the argument from analogy is hardly conclusive, it marks a crucial moment in ancient Greek speculation regarding the possibility of the soul's persistence after death because it raises the crucial question of what the soul would have to be like to survive the death of the individual and, indeed, to be immortal by being indestructible. Plato recognizes that a serious treatment of the question of the soul's immortality must be grounded in consideration of the ontology of soul. Only if one understands what the soul is, he thinks, will one be in any proper position to determine whether it should be thought to be destroyed at the death of the individual. As we consider the interest of Greek philosophers prior to Plato in the soul's persistence after death, we need to consider the extent to which these early thinkers considered the ontology of soul.

It should be apparent from the conditions Plato specifies for an entity being indestructible that the soul, to be so, would have to be an immaterial entity. Since every material entity is spatially extended and as such divisible into parts, it would seem to be Plato's view that only if the soul is immaterial could it be indestructible. Plato in fact relaxes the *Phaedo*'s stringent requirement that an entity can be indestructible only if incomposite. In *Republic* X, he has Socrates say amidst discussion of the soul's nature and immortality: "It is not easy for something composed of many things to be eternal unless it has been provided with the finest possible composition" (*R.* X 611b). Here he is apparently suggesting that the rational part of the soul may be composite yet eternal (cf. *Ti.* 35a ff., 41a–b), though without suggesting that it is in any way a physical entity. None of the early Greek natural philosophers, however, ever posited the existence of immaterial entities, so that all those who reflected on the soul's nature or espoused its immortality conceived of the soul as a material entity. Such is certainly the case with Heraclitus of Ephesus, whose reflections on the soul and its fate will provide a touchstone for the rest of our discussion.

Heraclitus, most likely writing in the early 5th century BC, understood the changes all things undergo as governed in regular ways by a divine principle he variously speaks of as the order (λόγος), as fire, and as Zeus. What Heraclitus means by *logos* is notoriously difficult to capture, for it is at once both the underlying and non-apparent order of things and the active principle or source of this order. The element of fire occupies a special role in Heraclitus's system as the vehicle of *logos*. It is in some sense the most basic of the world's stuffs, for he describes it as transformed into other stuffs: "fire's turnings – first sea, and of sea the one half earth, the other half lightning storm . . . <earth> is dispersed as sea, and it is measured into the same order (λόγος) that there was before it became earth" (22B31 DK, cf. B76). These "turnings" or transformations he elsewhere describes as the "kindling" and "quenching" via which the world's fiery substance is transformed in generating the world as we know it. "This cosmos, the same for all," he says, "no god or human made, but it was always and is and will be, *ever-living fire*, kindled in measures and quenched in measures" (22B30 DK, cf. B67). In general, "all things are an exchange for fire and fire for all things, just as goods for gold and gold for goods" (22B90 DK). Fire is most suited to serve as the basic stuff in Heraclitus's cosmology because of its inherent dynamism. Because of its association with the *logos* and Zeus, moreover, one should think of it as not only a dynamic but an active principle, directing the changes it undergoes in regular and measured ways. Heraclitus perhaps most clearly ascribes an active capacity to fire when he says it will come suddenly upon all things to judge and convict them (22B66 DK, cf. B64). Heraclitus associates soul with fire by assigning it in the following fragment to the place occupied by fire in B31 (quoted previously): "for souls death is becoming water, and for water death is becoming earth – but from earth comes water, and from water soul" (22B36 DK). He associates soul with the order (λόγος) when he says, "soul's limits you could not go discover, though you travel along every path – such deep λόγος has it" (22B45 DK).

What, if anything, does Heraclitus's conception of the soul as essentially fiery and as having a limitlessly deep order (λόγος) imply regarding its ability to survive the death of the individual? A hint is perhaps implicit in the evident parallelism in the transformation schemata of B31 and B36. One thing that is particularly striking about B31 is that sea turns half into earth and half into lightning storm. Ephesus was in Heraclitus's day a major coastal city. When one hears the words of this fragment, it is hard not to think of the sea altering the coastline and of storm clouds rising from it and rolling inland. Heraclitus elsewhere speaks of the soul of an inebriated man as moist (22B117 DK) and says that "a dry soul is wisest and best" (22B118 DK). If the soul is something fiery, it makes sense that it should be incapacitated or even corrupted by becoming moistened and that it would be destroyed absolutely if it should suffer transformation into water. When he says that the dry soul is wisest and best, he evidently envisages the possibility of its being literally purified by becoming more fiery, more what it essentially is, and thus better. When Heraclitus describes the dry soul as "wisest" in B118, one cannot help recalling his assertions elsewhere that "the one and only wise thing is and is not willing to be called by the name of Zeus." Zeus, of course, is associated with the thunderbolt, and thunderbolt, Heraclitus says, "steers all things" (22B64 DK). The circle of associations is completed by his assertion that the one wise thing is "to understand the true judgment which steers all things through all" (22B41 DK). If an individual's soul when purified is wisest and best, then apparently it becomes more like the fiery principle governing the world, not only by governing the individual's own actions much more effectively than when moist or inebriated, but also by understanding at least something of what the divine principle understands as it governs the actions of the world. The substantial resemblance Heraclitus posits between the individual soul at the microcosmic level and the macrocosmic principle order (λόγος)/fire/Zeus makes it only natural that there should be such a possibility of the individual soul becoming more like this principle. That it should do so would appear to be for Heraclitus an ethical imperative.

Does Heraclitus also suppose that the soul that becomes wisest and best by being purified, dry, and fiery will in at least some cases survive the death of the individual? He does say, of course, in B36 that it is death for souls to become water and that soul comes to be from water. But other fragments suggest that some souls can achieve release from this cycle of destruction and regeneration: "souls dying in battle are more pure that those in disease" (22B136 DK), "better deaths achieve better fates" (22B25 DK), and, "†for it being there† they rise up and become wakeful guardians of the living and the dead" (22B63 DK, the first words of which are corrupt). Together these three fragments suggest that those whose souls are most fiery and so most pure are not destroyed but rewarded by becoming guardian spirits. If Heraclitus did envisage the possibility of such post-mortem survival for the purest souls, however, it can only have been temporary. For nothing in his system, not even the fiery substance of the order (λόγος)/Zeus, is exempt from the regular and continuous transformations he describes. Nonetheless, in Heraclitus's reflections on soul one encounters the two main strains of thought about the soul among the Presocratic philosophers. First is the idea that the possibility of the soul achieving a better or worse fate after the death of the individual is the ground for certain ethical imperatives. This idea is central to the tradition of thought about the soul that derives from Pythagoras and includes Empedocles and Philolaus. Second is the idea that the individual soul is made of the same stuff and engages in something like the same intelligent and directive activity as the divine principle that functions as the "soul" of the cosmos. This idea is central to the tradition of thought about the soul that originates with the early Ionian natural philosopher Anaximenes and continues in the neo-Ionian systems of Anaxagoras and Diogenes of Apollonia.

The notion that something of the individual survives death figures prominently in the early poetic and religious traditions of ancient Greece. Among the early Greek philosophers, this notion becomes central to the thought of Pythagoras of Samos and his followers. Our access to the doctrines of Pythagoras (c. 570–c. 490 BC) is made difficult by his having provided his students with exclusively oral instruction and by the practice that began with Plato's pupils and continued throughout later antiquity of attributing many of Plato's own doctrines to Pythagoras as their putative source. Heraclides Ponticus, for instance, a member of the early Platonic Academy, composed a number of dialogues that gave a decidedly Pythagorean cast to the sort of views regarding the fate of the soul found in Plato's eschatological myths. In this and other ways Plato's own pupils laid the groundwork for a view of Plato's philosophy as Pythagorean in its essentials that persisted in one way or another throughout most of antiquity. Aristotle's reports concerning Pythagoras counter this Platonizing tendency, but they tend to represent him more as the founder of a way of life than as a philosopher. Nevertheless, the earliest evidence associates Pythagoras with the doctrine that the soul or self survives the death of the body to be reborn in a series of reincarnations. The earliest attribution to Pythagoras of this doctrine of metempsychosis is by one of his contemporaries, the philosopher-poet Xenophanes of Colophon (c. 570–c. 475 BC): "And once while passing by a pup suffering rough abuse | They say he took pity on it and spoke this word: | 'Stop, do not beat him, because it is a dear man's | Soul, which I recognized upon hearing its utterance'" (21B7 DK). Certain verses on Pherecydes by Ion of Chios suggest that Pythagoras also taught that excellence in this life leads to a better afterlife (Ion 36B4 DK *ap.* D.L. I 120). Likewise, Herodotus reports the story that one of Pythagoras's slaves, the Thracian Zalmoxis, returned to his native land where he hosted its most prominent persons and taught that none of them would die but would go to a place where they would survive forever and have all good things (Hdt. IV 95; Herodotus himself thinks Zalmoxis was not Pythaogras's slave but in fact lived long before him).

Although the doctrine of metempsychosis is reliably regarded as one of the key teachings of Pythagoras, early evidence, such as that of Herodotus, indicates that the doctrine was not original with him but adapted from the Orphic mysteries and perhaps even from Egyptian cults. Thus when Plato in the *Meno* has Socrates introduce the idea that the human soul is not destroyed at the death of the individual but successively reborn so that one must live as piously as possible (*Men.* 81a–b), he does not attribute this view to Pythagoras or the Pythagoreans, either explicitly or implicitly, but instead to "wise men and women who treat of matters divine," who are further described as "those priests and priestesses concerned with providing some account of their practices" (*Men.* 81a–b). Plato also attributes the view to Pindar, quoting him at some length (*Men.* 81b–c, cf. Pi. *Ol.* II, esp. vv. 56–77), and to "numerous other divine figures among the poets" (*Men.* 81b). That Plato both here in the *Meno* and later at *Laws* IX 870d–e associates metempsychosis with the mystery cults and their initiatory rituals suggests that he was well aware that this particular doctrine, as central as it was to Pythagoras's teaching, did not originate with him. The doctrine was nevertheless firmly associated with him in the earliest tradition. Sometimes it is said that Pythagoras was the first to speak specifically of the "soul" (ψυχή) as successively reincarnated. Even if this is the case, it is far from clear what he understood the soul to be. It may well be that he did not consider what the soul would have to be in order to migrate repeatedly from life in one body to life in another, especially if he adapted his doctrine of metempsychosis from elements in the religious traditions with which he was familiar. He may have been more concerned with this doctrine as a basis for urging upon the members of his circle conduct designed to purify the soul. He appears to have taught that souls are judged after death, with the wicked punished and the good rewarded. When trying to discern Pythagoras's own views regarding the soul, one can scarcely add to what Porphyry in his *Life of Pythagoras*, most likely drawing on the work of the Peripatetic Dicaearchus, reports had become generally known: Pythagoras said that the soul is immortal, that it passes into other kinds of creatures, and that one should regard all things that have a soul as related (Dicaearch. fr. 33 Wehrli *ap*. Porph. *VP* 19).

These three views were espoused and developed by Empedocles of Acragas (c. 495–35 BC). A great admirer of Pythagoras, Empedocles accepted the doctrine of metempsychosis as the foundation for an ethical way of life focused on abstention from bloodshed and self-purification. He announces that he has already been a boy and a girl, a bush, a bird, and a fish in the sea (31B117 DK). He also envisages better reincarnations for those who have lived better lives, as here: "And at last seers and poets and healers | and leaders among earth-dwelling men they become, | whence they sprout anew as gods, greatest in honours" (31B146 DK). He describes a golden age when Aphrodite was queen and was worshipped with pure rituals rather than with impious bloodshed: "the altar was not drenched with the bulls' undiluted blood, | but this was the greatest defilement among men, | tearing out their life (θυμός) and eating their brave flesh" (31B128.8–10 DK). Elsewhere Empedocles bemoans the defilement he himself incurred by slaughtering and eating his fellow creatures in his previous reincarnations: "Alas that the merciless day did not first destroy me, | before I devised horrible deeds with my claws for meat" (*P. Strasb. gr.* 1665–1666, group d, 5–6). He encourages his addressees to cease their bloodshed and to recognize how they are eating each other (31B136 DK). He paints a vivid and horrific picture of how a father makes sacrificial slaughter of his own reincarnated son and consumes him "in an evil meal": "Likewise a son seizes his father and children their mother, | and tearing out their life (θυμός), they devour their loved ones' flesh" (31B137 DK). Thus the Pythagorean doctrine of metempsychosis has ethical implications for Empedocles in the prohibition against killing living creatures that he describes as a universal law: "But what is lawful for all extends continuously | through the wide-ruling aether and the boundless sunlight" (31B125 DK *ap*. Arist. *Rh*. I 13 1373b13–17, where it is made clear that "what is lawful for all" is this prohibition).

Empedocles also found in the doctrine of metempsychosis something of a touchstone for his own distinctive natural philosophy. Empedocles held that nothing ever perishes absolutely, that everything is instead continuously reborn in new forms, and that everything that comes to be has some sort of pre-existence. "No man wise in his thoughts," he says,

> would divine such things as these,
> that, so long as they live what indeed they call "life,"
> for so long then they are, and for them are there good and bad things,
> but prior to being formed and once dissolved as mortals, then they are
>   nothing.
>
> (31B15 DK)

In the same vein, though with more general scope, he says:

> And another thing I shall tell you: there is birth (φύσις) of none of all
> mortal things, nor any end in baneful death,
> but only mixture and interchange of what is mixed
> are there, though humans call these things "birth" (φύσις).
>
> (31B8 DK)

On his view, the so-called birth of each living thing, be it human, animal, or plant, in fact involves the coming together and intermingling of pre-existing entities that he identifies as the elemental constituents of all things. Empedocles calls fire, water, earth, and air the "four roots of all things" (31B6 DK) and describes them as united in various ways by Love and separated by Strife (31B17.6–8 DK). "And in rancour they are endowed with various forms and all separate," he says,

> while in Love they come together and are desired by each other.
> From these all things that were, that are, and that will be hereafter
> have sprung – trees, and men and women,
> and beasts, and birds, and water-fed fish,
> and even long-living gods supreme in their honours.
>
> (31B21.7–12 DK)

Empedocles appears to have identified the souls that undergo successive reincarnations with the "spirits" (δαίμονες) whose exile from the blessed he describes in the following verses:

> There is an oracle of Necessity, the gods' ancient decree,
> eternal, sealed and secured by great oaths:
> whoever in sinning pollutes his dear limbs with bloodshed
> as a spirit (δαίμων) – who have gained their portion of long-lasting life –
> for thrice ten thousand years he wanders apart from the blessed,
> being born during this time in manifold forms of mortals,
> interchanging one miserable path of life for another.

> For the aether's power chases him into the sea,
> sea spits him onto earth's surface, earth into the beams
> of the blazing sun, which hurls him into aether's whirls;
> one takes him from another, though all revile him.
> One of these I, too, now am, an exile from the gods and a wanderer,
> trusting in raving strife.
>
> (31B115 DK, with text as in Mansfeld-Primavesi 2011)

The place of these spirits within his physical theory is difficult to determine. If all things other than the forces Loves and Strife are either pure portions of the elements fire, water, earth, and air/aether or else compounds of these elements, then it would appear that the spirits sentenced to wander for 30,000 years through successive reincarnations must somehow be so as well. Here it will be useful to focus on the implications of Empedocles's psychology regarding the nature of the transmigrating spirit.

A number of fragments and doxographical reports indicate that Empedocles associated thought with the mixture of elements in the blood around the heart and life itself with the fiery element in the blood. The doxographer Aëtius attributes to Empedocles the views that the mind is in the compound of blood (Aët. IV 5.8) and that the soul and the intellect are the same (Aët. IV 5.12). Theophrastus in his treatise *On the senses* quotes Empedocles as having said that from the elements "all things have been fitted and formed, | and by these they think and are pleased and pained" (31B107 DK) before commenting that, on his view, we think with the blood because in it the elements are more evenly mixed than in any other part of the body (Thphr. *Sens.* 10). Elsewhere Empedocles says quite plainly that "blood about the heart is for humans thought (νόημα)" (31B105 DK). Theophrastus suggests that Empedocles accounted for variations in the content and quality of our thoughts by referencing variations in the mixture of elements in the blood (Thphr. *Sens.* 11, cf. 31B108 DK, Arist. *Metaph.* 1009b17–20). Two other reports in Aëtius indicate that Empedocles conceived of death as the separation of the fiery element from the blood: "Empedocles says sleep occurs due to a corresponding cooling of the heat (τοῦ θερμοῦ) in the blood, and death due to a total cooling" (Aët. V 24.2); and

> Empedocles says death occurs due to separation of the fiery element (τοῦ πυρώδους) from the things whose combination constituted a human being, so that on this account death is common to body and soul. Sleep, too, occurs due to separation of the fiery element.
>
> (Aët. V 25.4)

This evidence would seem to suggest that Empedocles associated life with the fiery element, which combines with the other elements in a measured manner to create the blood that he associates particularly with thought.

Other evidence, however, suggests that Empedocles associated life with air, so it may be that he understood the transmigrating spirit to be a compound of fire and air.

Amidst his survey of ancient Greek conceptions of the soul, the Christian bishop Theodoret of Cyrus reports that Empedocles called the soul a mixture formed from fiery and airy substance (Thdrt. *Gr.aff.cur.* V 18.9–10).[1] Aëtius reports Empedocles as having said that the first breath occurs when the moisture in newborns retreats and the air outside enters the empty space in the opened lungs, after which the airy element is expelled by the infant's internal heat, whereupon breathing proceeds regularly with successive inhalation and exhalation (Aët. IV 22.1). Evidently, the airy element is not entirely expelled when the infant exhales, but is mixed into the blood during inhalation, a view Aëtius also ascribes to Empedocles. This view regarding infants' first breath is strikingly similar to that of the 5th-century Pythagorean Philolaus. In a section of the medical papyrus known as the *Anonymus Londiniensis* that records a description, by Aristotle's pupil Meno, of Philolaus's views regarding the constitution of the body and the causes of disease, Philolaus is said to have held that embryos in the womb are constituted from the hot with no share of cold. "Immediately after birth," the report in the papyrus continues,

> the animal breathes in the external air (τὸ ἐκτὸς πνεῦμα) which is cold. Then it sends it out again like a debt. Indeed, it is for this reason that there is a desire for external air, so that our bodies, which were too hot before, by the drawing in of breath from outside are cooled thereby.
> (*Anon. Lond.* XVIII 21–8 = Philol. 44A27 DK, trans. Huffman)

This text has been brought to bear on the vexed question of whether Philolaus considered the soul to be an attunement (ἁρμονία), a view ascribed to both Philolaus and Pythagoras by the late Roman author Macrobius (*in Somn. Scip.* I 14.19 = 44A23 DK).

In Plato's *Phaedo*, Socrates's interlocutor Simmias, who is represented as having associated with Philolaus, raises the worry that the soul may not be immortal, as Socrates has been arguing, if it is a blending and attunement. For this evidently could not exist apart from the things it is a blending or attunement *of*:

> as the body is stretched and held together by the hot and the cold, the dry and the moist, and other such things, our soul is a blending (κρᾶσις) and attunement (ἁρμονία) of those things when they are mixed with each other rightly and in due measure.
> (*Phd.* 86b–c)

David Sedley has proposed that the report of Philolaus's views in the *Anonymus Londiniensis* enables one to reconstruct for Philolaus a theory of soul basically identical to the one Plato puts in the mouth of Simmias:

> a plausible reconstruction of Philolaus's doctrine of soul would be as follows. Our bodies are in their own constitution purely hot, and the admixture of cold which ensouled life requires must be constantly renewed by

breathing. Hot is an "unlimited," while the cold which is imposed upon it from birth is a "limiter." It is only in the harmonious combination brought about by breathing that hot and cold make up a living being, and soul *is* that harmonious combination.

(Sedley 1995, 24–5)

Sedley calls attention to the fact that the verb used in the papyrus for the cooling process that occurs upon the intake of air is *katapsuchousthai*, which Philolaus would likely have associated with *psuchē* or "soul," such that "it is only with the imposition of cooling breath on the 'hot' body that a creature acquires a soul." By identifying the soul with the harmonious combination of hot and cold, Sedley is guided not only by the view expressed by Simmias but also by Philolaus's own metaphysical views, according to which all things are either limiters, unlimiteds, or harmonious combinations thereof. "Nature in the cosmos," Philolaus himself announced in the opening of his book, "was harmoniously fitted together from both unlimiteds and limiters, both the cosmos as a whole and all things in it" (44B1 DK).

There is one glaring problem with the proposal that Philolaus identified soul with the harmonious combination of the hot as an unlimited and the cold as a limited. If this is what the soul is, then, as Simmias rightly points out, it could not survive the death of the individual to be reborn in another body, as Pythagoras taught. Although not impossible, it would certainly be surprising for Philolaus as a Pythagorean to espouse a theory of the soul that runs directly counter to one of the most fundamental teachings of Pythagoras himself. It is therefore worth considering as an alternative the possibility that Philolaus associated the transmigrating soul, not with the harmonious combination of the hot that constitutes the embryo and the cold that enters when it breathes in the external air, but with the external air itself. Although Aristotle is familiar with the view that the soul is an attunement (ἁρμονία), he does not associate this view with the Pythagoreans in his survey of views of the soul in *De Anima* I. He treats it instead as a generally popular idea:

> There is yet another opinion about soul which has commended itself to many as no less probable than any of those we have hitherto mentioned.... Its supporters say that the soul is a kind of attunement (ἁρμονία); for an attunement is a blend (κρᾶσις) or composition (σύνθεσις) of contraries, and the body is compounded out of contraries.
>
> (Arist. *de An.* I 4.407b27–32)

The views of the Pythagoreans regarding the soul Aristotle has referenced earlier, in chapter 2, where he sees them as exemplifying the broader tendency to identify soul as the originator of movement:

> what the Pythagoreans say seems to imply the same thing, for some said the motes in the air are soul, while others said it is what moves them.

> They mention these because they are seen moving continuously, even in perfectly calm conditions.
>
> (*de An.* I 2.404a16–20)

Aristotle's report appears to reflect an early view – that the motes in the air are soul – and a later attempt to rationalize it: what moves the motes in the air would most naturally be understood to be air itself. That the Pythagoreans associated soul with air is likewise reflected in the view recorded in the Pythagorean notebooks known to Alexander Polyhistor that the air is full of souls, which send portents and dreams to humans (D.L. VIII 32).

Something like this view has been suggested by Carl Huffman, in response to Sedley's proposal that Philolaus identified the soul with the harmonious compound of hot and cold. Huffman proposes that Pythagoras and the early Pythagoreans, including Philolaus, employed the term ψυχή or "soul" to refer to "the transmigrating soul, which is also the soul that is the center of personality during life" and that it "was conceived of primarily as the seat of emotions, which was closely connected to the faculty of sensation [and] distinct from the intellect" (Huffman 2009, 23). He develops this proposal by beginning with Philolaus's identification of the various psychological faculties:

> The head [is the seat] of intellect (νόος), the heart of soul (ψυχή) and sensation, the navel of rooting and first growth, the genitals of the sowing of seed and generation. The brain [contains] the source of a man, the heart that of an animal, the navel that of a plant, and the genitals that of all together. For all things grow and flourish from seed.
>
> (44B13 DK, after Huffman)[2]

Perhaps the most striking features of this text are its hierarchical division of psychological faculties and its association of the soul (ψυχή) with sensation in particular as something distinct from the intellect that is understood as peculiar to human beings. It is also striking how each faculty is associated with an organ or physiological feature, especially since this association raises the question of whether and how the faculty might possibly exist apart from its physiological seat. Huffman argues for understanding soul (ψυχή) here as something distinct from the sensation (αἴσθησις) with which it is paired and, more particularly, as the faculty associated with feelings of pleasure and pain and the emotions.[3] Huffman's interpretation is motivated in part by the idea that Philolaus, if he indeed accepted the Pythagorean doctrine of transmigration, would have wanted to identify the soul with a psychological capacity shared by humans and animals precisely because of the pressure on him as a Pythagorean to understand the soul as something capable of migrating from human to animal and back again. If he meant to identify the soul as something common to humans and animals, then the intellect (νόος) that is distinctive of humans would not be capable of migrating into animal form. Huffman is not especially clear, however, about just what it is that leaves the body at one creature's death to enter the body of another creature at its birth, in part because he is at pains to accommodate Sedley's suggestion that Philolaus understood the soul as a harmony. "When this balance of physical parts perishes," he says,

> the body does lose its soul, it is no longer ensouled, but this need not mean that the principle of the soul, the *archē*, which Philolaus locates in the heart, perishes. . . . We might suppose the initial breath of the newborn is a mechanical process in which the hot draws in the surrounding cool breath. With that initial breath, however, it also draws in the control-center *psychē*, the transmigrating soul, which resides in the heart and which will control the balance between hot and cold that makes the body ensouled.
>
> (Huffman 2009, 32)

What exactly the "principle of the soul" that does not perish when the body loses its soul or "the control-center *psyche*" that enters with the first breath is supposed to be is less than clear on Huffman's account. He nonetheless rightly notes that the evidence of the *Anonymus Londiniensis* indicates that Philolaus would not have thought the embryo has a soul. He also draws a comparison with the following report in the chapter of Aëtius devoted to the question of whether the embryo is a living creature:

> Empedocles says the embryo is not a living creature, but that it exists without breath in the womb. The living creature's first breath occurs during delivery when the moisture in the newborn infant is voided and the external airy element enters the voided area and comes into the opened up lungs.
>
> (Aët. V 15.3)

On Empedocles's view, then, the embryo is not a living creature until the air from outside first enters its lungs and it starts to breathe. It would be too simple, though, to say that the airy element that enters with its first breath is the creature's soul. In the first place, as we have seen, Empedocles is also said to have spoken of death as a separation of the fiery element from the elements as compounded in a person's makeup and particularly in the blood. Also, on Empedocles's view, the psychological faculty of thought is identified especially with the blood around the heart, and it is his view that in blood all four elements are near evenly mixed. Implicit in this evidence would seem to be the view that humans are not capable of any sort of thought until the element of air enters the blood after birth. While the intake of air is a responsible for their being alive, it is merely a necessary condition of their capacity for thought. It appears, therefore, that there is a distinction to be made between the transmigrating soul and the embodied soul. When the embryo at birth takes its first breath and thereby becomes a living creature, what enters interacts with what is already present within the creature's body, with the result that the physiological basis of its psychological capacities is completed and the capacities themselves first emerge. If thought (νόημα) for humans is, as Empedocles says, blood around the heart (αἷμα περικάρδιον), if blood is a mixture of all four elements, and if the element air only enters the creature's body with the first breath after birth, then the fluid in its veins and around its heart properly speaking only becomes blood and the vehicle of thought at this moment. It is as if Empedocles wanted to say that unoxygenated blood is not truly blood (though he apparently does not think of air entering the embryo's blood through its mother). It is important to appreciate that the external air that is breathed in does not persist unaltered and independent in the blood but is altered in its interaction with the material already present in generating new stuff. One should be very cautious, therefore, about attributing to the transmigrating soul the same psychological capacities that the living creature has. It would be highly implausible to do so, of course, since so many of these capacities evidently depend upon the bodily organs for their functioning.

At this point it will be instructive to consider briefly some of the background to Empedocles's conception in the Homeric poems. Michael Clarke has made a strong case against attributing to Homer the ideas that individual persons are composites of a body, on the one hand, and a spirit, soul, or mind on the other. Clarke takes his cue from the often observed fact that in Homer the word ψυχή, which we so readily translate as "soul," features only in contexts where life is lost or threatened to be lost and never in contexts suggesting that it is also the inner seat or principle of life, the self, and ordinary psychological function (Clarke 1999, 55–60). He goes on to show, via an exhaustive and attentive review of the Homeric psychological vocabulary, that

> Homer's understanding of thought and emotion revolves around a close-knit group of phenomena: the ebb and flow of breath [θυμός], the flow of fluids into and out of the breast, and the soft liquidity of the organs around and below the lungs [φρήν/φρένες] . . . the Homeric 'mind' is the same thing as the life of the physical substances in the breast [ἐν στήθεσσι ≈ ἐν θυμῷ or ἐνὶ φρέσι].[4]

Homer's psychological terminology does not indicate exclusively mental faculties, states, or activities but almost always something with a specific physiological identity as well: φρήν or φρένες are the lungs; ἦτορ, κραδίη, and κῆρ are different words for the heart; the πραπίδες is an organ situated above the liver. "[T]he ongoing process of thought," Clarke says,

> is conceived of as if it were precisely identified with the palpable inhalation of breath and the half-imagined mingling of breath with blood and bodily fluids in the soft, warm, flowing substances that make up what is behind the chest wall.[5]

One sees this, for example, in uses of the verb φρονεῖν, "to think" or "to ponder," which is etymologically related to φρένες or "lungs." In certain instances the phrase μέγα φρονέων evidently means "drawing deep breaths" or "gulping in air" rather than "thinking deep thoughts," for example in a simile describing Odysseus and Diomedes defending the Greek ships against the rampaging Hector: "as when a pair of boars gulping in air (μέγα φρονέοντε) rush at hunting dogs" (Hom. *Il*. XI 325).[6] This Homeric background makes it somewhat easier to understand Empedocles's identification of thought with the pericardial blood and, more generally, the important role he gives to the intake of the external air. Likewise, as variations in the balanced composition of the blood account in Empedocles for variations in the character of an individual's thought, so in Homer do variations in the impacting of the breath within the lungs and the region of the chest.

As *thumos* in Homer is the vital breath of thought, feeling, and life generally, so the moment of death is regularly described in terms of its loss, most often as a literally expiring hero breathes out his last breath (Clarke 1999, 130–133). Since its loss is the loss of physical strength and vitality, it is tempting to render *thumos* in such contexts as "life." This is in fact how the term has been rendered in the translations of Empedocles 31B128.10 and 31B137.2, where he describes the horrific crimes of tearing out the *thumos* of one's fellow living creatures and consuming their flesh in ritual sacrifice. "Spirit" would perhaps be the best rendering of *thumos*, since in this term the connection of breath and vitality is preserved. If we keep this connection in mind, then "spirit" will be appropriate for rendering *psuchē* as well. In Homer the *psuchē* that is lost at the moment of death is essentially indistinguishable from the *thumos* that is the dying person's last exhalation – except that *psuchē* can only be breath or spirit *lost* while *thumos* is breath or spirit either inhaled or exhaled (Clarke 1999, 133–143). Homer uses the term *psuchē* as well for the spirit that survives in Hades after the individual is dead, where it is an *eidōlon* or spectral image of that individual. How the two uses of *psuchē* are related is suggested by the verses with which Homer describes the deaths of first Patroclus and then later Hector: "Then as he spoke the end of death enveloped him; | and his ψυχή flying from his limbs was gone to Hades, | bemoaning its fate, leaving its manliness and youth" (Hom. *Il*. XVI 855–857 = XXII 361–363). It would be wrong to say that the *psuchē* in Homer is the soul of the individual that survives his or her death, for it never figures in the living individual as anything like the soul that will come to feature in Plato, and any number of philosophers and theologians after him, as something distinct from the body that is the principle of life and consciousness and that is as such the true self as opposed to the body. Whereas the Platonic soul is capable of surviving the death of the individual, the Homeric *psuchē* is not, for the very simple reason that it was not part of the individual when alive. It only begins to exist as something apart from the individual when he or she dies. It bears emphasizing that for Homer the dead body and not the *psuchē* that has flown off to Hades *is* the dead person. For Homer, strictly speaking, there is no survival of the person after death. And yet something of the dead individual is preserved in the spirit (ψυχή) and spectral image (εἴδωλον) that dwells in Hades. Each is, after all, the spirit or image *of* a particular individual who has died and is physically recognizable as such. When in the *Iliad* the *psuchē* of the dead Patroclus visits Achilles in a dream to ask for burial, it is said to be "most like to himself" (Hom. *Il*. XXIII 66, cf. 107). But it disappears like smoke, squealing and babbling, when Achilles tries to embrace it, whereupon he remarks that in the halls of Hades there is something, "a spirit and image, though inside it no wits (φρένες) at all" (*Il*. XXIII 99–104).

Exactly how and to what degree the ghostly spirits described in the Homeric poems retain something of the living individual's identity is a thorny and possibly irresolvable issue that need not concern us here. Enough has been said for us to understand why it would have been natural enough for an early Greek thinker such as Empedocles and others in the Pythagorean tradition to have associated the transmigrating soul with air or fire while conceiving of the embodied soul as something more complex and integrated into the individual creature's physiology. Given the Homeric background, it would hardly be surprising if Empedocles and Philolaus associated the transmigrating soul with the air the infant creature first breathes in at birth and that the individual last breathes out at death. In Homer, of course, there is no possibility that the *psuchē* might return to a person who has died, much less enter the body of another, newly born person or animal. The closest the Homeric shades come to re-embodiment is when Odysseus visits the underworld in the *Odyssey*. There the *psuchai* or spirits crowd round the pit where he has sacrificed sheep, all eager for the blood (Hom. *Od*. XI 23–50). When the spirit of his mother, Anticleia, does not recognize him, he learns from the spirit of Teiresias that only those who are allowed to drink the sacrificial blood, as he has, will speak to Odysseus (*Od*. XI 84–96, 138–149). Even though this rule is not strictly obeyed, it is reminiscent of Homer's physiologically integrated conception of life and thought. It may seem that Empedocles's transmigrating spirit must be something more substantial than a Homeric *psuchē* or *eidōlon*, that in it the identity of the individual must somehow persist more strongly. Empedocles claims, after all, that "*I* have already before been boy and girl, bush, bird, and mute fish in the sea" (31B117 DK). However, this assertion can be understood as a simple inference from the more fundamental teaching regarding the oracle of Necessity and the exile of the spirits that during their 30,000 years of wandering apart from the blessed they are born "in manifold forms of mortals" on the earth and in the air and sea. If Empedocles insists that it is he who has already been born in various forms, then a "self" or a bearer of personal identity would need to persist as both the embodied and the transmigrating soul. However, it is exceedingly difficult to imagine how he could explain this persistence given that his conception of thought as due to variations in the even mixture of elements in the pericardial blood is roughly on a par with Homer's physiological conception of psychological states and activities.

What is needed, it would seem, is a conception of the airy or fiery stuff that enters the body at birth as capable of thought and some sort of agency independent of and prior to its embodiment. We have already seen this in Heraclitus's conception of the individual soul as made of the same fiery stuff as the *logos*/fire/ Zeus governing the cosmos. Although there is little to suggest that Empedocles or Philolaus would have thought that the transmigrating soul was a portion of, or made of the same stuff as, a fiery or airy divine principle governing the cosmos, such a conception nevertheless figured prominently in the thought of a number of thinkers in addition to Heraclitus who belonged to the Ionian tradition of Presocratic philosophy.

Aëtius reports that Anaximenes of Miletus (mid- to late 6th century BC)

> declared air (ἀήρ) to be the principle of the things that are – for from this all things come to be and into it are again resolved. As our soul, he says, being air, holds us together, so does wind (πνεῦμα) and air embrace the world.
>
> (Aët. I 3.4)

Anaximenes identified ἀήρ – usually translated as "air" but something more like aether that is denser than fire and lighter than elemental air – as the originative stuff that is transformed into all other things via the processes of condensation and rarefaction. When rarefied Anaximenes's air becomes fire and when condensed it first becomes wind, which becomes cloud, which becomes water, which becomes earth, which becomes stone, with all other things then being produced from these basic stuffs. The processes of rarefaction and condensation are obviously reversible, so that elemental transformations are naturally understood as ongoing or even cyclical. Anaximenes's physical theory likely influenced that of Heraclitus, who must have been familiar with it. It is particularly striking how, like Heraclitean fire, Anaximenean air seems not to have been an inert material stuff but an active and even divine principle "embracing" and apparently governing all things as it transforms into them. Although our evidence for Anaximenes is more meager and indirect than for Heraclitus, Aëtius elsewhere reports, as does Cicero, that Anaximenes regarded air as a god (Aët. I 7.13, Cic. *ND* I 26). With Aëtius's report that Anaximenes said that wind and air embrace (περιέχει) the world, one may compare Aristotle's report that Anaximander's principle, the unlimited (τὸ ἄπειρον), which is also said to be divine, embraces (περιέχειν) all things and governs all things (Arist. *Ph.* III 4.203b10–15, cf. Hippol. *Haer.* I 6.1). Elsewhere Aristotle praises the traditions passed down from the ancients in the form of myth that "the divine embraces (περιέχει) the whole of nature" (Arist. *Metaph.* XII 1074a38–b3). What is important for our purposes is how Aëtius I 3.4 also indicates that Anaximenes identified the soul of the individual with air. Although Anaximenes conceived of the soul of the individual as a portion of the same air that is the directive principle of the world itself, there is no evidence that he thought the individual soul persisted as such after death. Presumably, the air itself that was an individual's soul would continue to exist after the individual's death and retain whatever capacities air itself has, but there is nothing to suggest that this simple material persistence would amount to the persistence of the individual. If the air in the body is affected by its embodiment so as to become a soul, then this air when it is finally separated from the body at death would presumably cease to be affected as it was when embodied and thus no longer properly be a soul. Although the lack of evidence makes it impossible to determine whether Anaximenes himself held such a view, it proves to be the *communis opinio* of the later Ionian philosophers.

The later Ionian philosopher Anaxagoras of Clazomenae (mid-5th century BC) similarly held that the individual intellect is a portion of the same intelligent and unlimited principle that governs both itself and all other things. He did not, however, identify this with any of the traditional elements but identified it directly as *nous* or "intellect." "Do we think with our blood, or air, or fire?" asks Plato's Socrates at *Phaedo* 96b. The question reflects what he regards as the reductive explanations of the natural scientists of his day. He goes on, of course, to report how excited he was when he heard someone reading from the book of Anaxagoras, who declared that *nous* or "intellect" directs and is the cause of everything (*Phd.* 97c). Although Socrates is excited by the prospect of teleological explanation broached by this hypothesis, it can also be seen as an improvement over reductive accounts of thought and the intellect, insofar as it makes intellect itself something fundamental rather than an attribute of something fundamental. Anaxagorean *nous* is still a material stuff, but it is intellect-stuff – a *res cogitans* – rather than some stuff such as blood, air, or fire to which it might have seemed reasonable to attribute (life and) thought because of its active and warm nature. As such, whether within or without a body, *nous* is capable of thought and agency. Anaxagoras's brilliantly imaginative physical theory posits that there is no lower limit on the size of portions of matter and likewise no upper limit. Every portion of matter, moreover, contains portions of every kind of stuff, and no stuff can be totally on its own once it has been mixed with other stuffs. The phenomenal characteristics of a thing are a function of the preponderance within it of stuffs with the relevant characters. *Nous* or intellect is one of Anaxagoras's basic stuffs, yet while it is everywhere the other stuffs are, it is not mixed with them and so remains independent and capable of affecting and directing all the other stuffs.[7] Anaxagoras is clear that if *nous* should ever be mixed with anything else, it would be mixed with everything else and would lose its distinctly pure character and consequently its power:

> The others have a portion of everything, but *nous* is unlimited and self-governing and is mixed with no thing, but it is alone itself on its own. For it were not on its own but was mixed with anything else, it would have a share of all things, if it were mixed with any. For in everything there is a portion of everything, just as I have said in what precedes; and the things commingled with it would restrict it, so that it could have power over no thing like it does now by being alone on its own. For it is the lightest of all things and the purest, it has all knowledge about everything, and it has the greatest power – and whatever has life, both the greater and the smaller, *nous* has power over them all.
>
> (excerpt from 59B12 DK)

The end of this text makes it clear enough that *nous* in individual creatures is supposed to be their governing principle even as the god-like *nous* that exerts its power in the creation and operation of the world functions as its governing principle.

The extant fragments of Anaxagoras's book have much more to say about *nous* in this cosmic role. Much of what Aristotle reports regarding Anaxagoras's view of the soul evidently depends on B12 (see, for example, the texts from Aristotle, *On the soul*, at 59A100 DK). One thing Aristotle's testimony adds is that the *nous* internal to a creature that functions as its soul is different in different creatures. Aristotle reports Anaxagoras as saying that *nous* belongs to all living things, both great and small, and that the *nous* that is spoken of in the sense of wisdom (φρόνησις) does not belong to all living things, nor even to all human beings (Arist. *de An.* I 2.404b3–6). If Aristotle is still reporting Anaxagoras with this last point, and not introducing an objection of his own, then it would seem that Anaxagoras made it part of his theory that the differences in the embodiment of *nous* in different types of creatures produces souls that are peculiar to each type. If Anaxagoras distinguished between simple *nous* and the variously embodied *nous* that is soul, this may account for some of Aristotle's difficulty in assessing whether he identified *nous* and soul. Aëtius groups Anaxagoras with Anaximenes, Archelaus, and Diogenes of Apollonia as having held that the soul is like air (Aët. IV 3.2). While the principle of thought (and life) in Anaxagoras is not simply air, as in the systems of these other thinkers, but *nous*, the description of it as the lightest and purest of all things suggests that it retains some of the characteristics of air. His insistence on saying that fish breathe, by taking in water through their gills and thereby generating air in their mouths that they then inhale (Arist. *de Resp.* 2. 470b33–471a2), and, more surprisingly, that even plants have respiration ([Arist.] *de Plant*. I 1.816b26), indicate that he continued to view the intake of air as essential to life even though he associated soul specifically with *nous*.

The traditional association of the soul with fire or warm breath persists in the atomist system of Democritus of Abdera (late 5th century BC). According to the early atomists Leucippus and Democritus, all things are ultimately composed of atoms and void. Their atoms are solid and indivisible entities, infinitely numerous, imperceptibly small, and of a limitless variety of shapes and sizes. They move unceasingly within the void, and from them all other things are composed. Despite the radical originality of the atomist physical theory, Democritus's views regarding the nature of the mind or soul connect with the previous tradition of Presocratic speculation on the subject in numerous ways even as it recasts its conventional features to make them consistent with the new theory. According to Aristotle, Democritus said that soul is a sort of fire and is hot, on the grounds that it must be a source of movement in other things, and that spherical atoms were fire and soul (Arist. *de An.* I 2.403b28–404a3). Democritus is even said to have compared these spherical soul and fire atoms, in a manner reminiscent of the view Aristotle attributes to some of the Pythagoreans, to the motes in the air visible in shafts of light (404a3–4). The reasons, Aristotle says, Democritus identified soul with spherical atoms is that atoms of this shape are most prone to permeate everything and are the most mobile of all shapes, apparently because they are least likely to get entangled with atoms of other shapes, and so they are best suited to be a source of motion for other things (404a5–9, cf. 405a8–13). Aristotle goes on to say that the atomists

> regard respiration as the characteristic mark of life; as the environment compresses the bodies of animals, and tends to extrude those atoms which impart movement to them, because they themselves are never at rest, there must be a reinforcement of these by similar atoms coming in from without in the act of respiration; for they prevent the extrusion of those which are already within by counteracting the compressing and consolidating force of the environment; and animals continue to live only so long as they are able to maintain this resistance.
> (404a9–16, rev. Oxford trans.; cf. Arist. *de Resp.* 4.471b30ff.)

Nothing in Democritus's atomistic theory of soul should be taken as suggesting that the soul is capable of surviving the death of the individual, neither as the soul of that individual nor even as soul. Only when they exist in the body of a living creature and are functioning as its motive principle are spherical atoms, properly speaking, soul.

Anaximenes's identification of the soul of the individual with air (ἀήρ) recurs in the system of Diogenes of Apollonia (late 5th century BC), who revived his view that air is the primary element and that all other things come to be as it undergoes alteration and differentiation via condensation and rarefaction (64B2 DK, cf. 64A5 DK). Diogenes's air was no inert stuff but an active and intelligent principle that is, as such, itself the cause of the changes it undergoes. It resembles not only Anaximenean air but even more so Heraclitean fire. Distinct from the elemental air that along with earth, water, and fire comes to be from it, elemental air seems to be the warm air associated with life and intelligence. "Humans and other living creatures that breathe," he wrote, "live by means of air. Indeed this is for them both soul (ψυχή) and intellect (νόησις), as will be clearly indicated in this work, and should this be disjoined they die and the intellect fails" (64B4 DK). The association of soul with the breath of life that leaves the body at death persists from Homer. Although Diogenes must suppose that the air that is an individual's soul will continue to exist after the individual's demise, given that elemental air is eternal and indestructible, he hardly supposes that the individual soul continues to exist as such. He takes pains to emphasize that, while soul is the same in all living creatures, it has a distinctive disposition not only in different species but also in different individuals of the same species:

> And the soul of all living creatures is the same, air hotter than that outside in which we are yet much colder than that near the sun. However

in no two living creatures is this heat alike (since it is not even so from one human being to the next), though the difference is not great but such that they are similar. Still none of the differentiated entities can become absolutely alike another without being the same. Since, then, the differentiation takes many types, living creatures are of many types as well as numerous, and they are like one another neither in form nor in way of life nor in intellect due to the sheer quantity of the differentiations.

(excerpt from 64B5)

In order for the soul of an individual to continue to exist as such, retaining its individual identity, after death, it would have to retain the peculiar differentiations that made it unique as the soul of a particular individual. But there is no evidence of Diogenes having supposed that the air that finally leaves the body at death retains its peculiar differentiation, any more than it possessed it before entering the body when the individual breathed.

The early Greek natural philosophers prior to Plato all conceived of the soul as a material entity associated in one way or another with active elemental principles of fire or air. Many associated it more specifically with breath and respiration, thus hearkening back to Homer. Although Empedocles and Philolaus inherited from Pythagoras the religious teaching that the soul repeatedly survives the death of one individual to be reborn in another, their biological and embryological theories drove them to distinguish the embodied soul from the transmigrating soul, making it problematic for the transmigrating soul to be the bearer of any persistent identity. Thinkers in the Ionian tradition, beginning with Anaximenes, conceived of the individual soul as a portion of the intelligent and active principle governing the cosmos as a whole. Although they would have supposed that the portion of air or intellect that is the soul in the individual continues to exist after the individual's death, they appear to have broadly shared with Empedocles and Philolaus the view that embodiment is crucial to the external principle's existence as a soul. In one way or another, then, the early Greek natural philosophers, like Homer, view whatever survives the death of the individual as an attenuated image of the soul that is the embodied principle of life.

Notes

1 Thanks to Dr. Simon Trépanier for bringing this reference to my attention and for sharing with me his work on fire and soul in Empedocles.
2 See Huffman 1993, 307–323, for discussion of the fragment's authenticity accompanied by extensive commentary.
3 Huffman 2009, 24–28, revising the view expressed in Huffman 1993, 307 and 318–319, that *psuchē* here is simply life.
4 Clarke 1999, 106, summarizing the results of the detailed discussion at 73–106. Cf. Jahn 1987, 255–258.
5 Clarke 1999, 75, drawing upon the insights of Onians 1951, 13–83 and *passim*, while correcting for the misguided anthropological theory of his era.

6 Clarke 1999, 83–84, drawing on Lockhart 1966. Clarke goes on to provide exhaustive evidence for the intimate connection between the vocabularies of breathing and thought in Homer.

7 For divergent views of *nous*'s directive role, see Laks 1993, Lesher 1995, and Curd 2007, 192–205.

Bibliography

Bétegh, G. (2006) Eschatology and cosmology: Models and problems. In Sassi, M. M. (ed.) *The Construction of Philosophical Discourse in the Age of the Presocratics*. Pisa: Edizioni della Normale, pp. 29–50.

———. (2013) On the physical aspect of Heraclitus' psychology (with new appendices). In Sider, D., and Obbink, D. (eds.) *Doctrine and Doxography: Studies on Heraclitus and Pythagoras*. Berlin: De Gruyter, pp. 225–261.

Bordoy, F. C. (2013) On the origin of the Orphic-Pythagorean notion of the immortality of the soul. In Cornelli, G., McKirahan, R., and Macris, C. (eds.) *On Pythagoreanism*. Berlin: De Gruyter, pp. 153–176.

Burkert, W. (1972) *Lore and Science in Ancient Pythagoreanism*. Cambridge, MA: Harvard University Press.

Clarke, M. (1999) *Flesh and Spirit in the Songs of Homer: A Study of Words and Myths*. Oxford: Clarendon Press.

Couloubaritsis, L. (1980) Considérations sur la notion de *noûs* chez Démocrite. *Archiv für Geschichte der Philosophie* 62 (2): 129–145.

Curd, P. (2007) *Anaxagoras of Clazomenae: Fragments and Testimonia*. Toronto: University of Toronto Press.

———. (2010) Thought and body in Heraclitus and Anaxagoras. *Proceedings of the Boston Area Colloquium in Ancient Philosophy* 25: 1–20.

DK = Diels, H., and Kranz, W. (1951–1952) *Die Fragmente der Vorsokratiker*. 6th edn. Berlin: Weidmann.

Frede, D., and Reis, B. (eds.) (2009) *Body and Soul in Ancient Philosophy*. Berlin: De Gruyter.

Huffman, C. (1993) *Philolaus of Croton: Pythagorean and Presocratic*. Cambridge, MA: Cambridge University Press.

———. (2009) The Pythagorean conception of the soul from Pythagoras to Philolaus. In Frede and Reis (2009), pp. 29–43.

Inwood, B. (2001) *The Poem of Empedocles*. Toronto: University of Toronto Press.

Jahn, T. (1987) *Zum Wortfeld 'Seele-Geist' in der Sprache Homers*. Munich: Beck.

Kirk, G. S., Raven, J. E., and Schofield, M. (1983) *The Presocratic Philosophers*. 2nd edn. Cambridge, MA: Cambridge University Press.

Laks, A. (1983) *Diogène d'Apollonie: la dernière cosmologie présocratique*. Lille: Presses Universitaires de Lille.

———. (1993) Mind's crisis: On Anaxagoras' Nous. *Southern Journal of Philosophy* 31 (Supplement): 19–38.

———. (1999) Soul, sensation, and thought. In Long, A. A. (ed.) *The Cambridge Companion to Early Greek Philosophy*. Cambridge, MA: Cambridge University Press, pp. 250–270.

Lesher, J. H. (1995) Mind's knowledge and power of control in Anaxagoras DK B12. *Phronesis* 40 (2): 125–142.

Lockhart, P. N. (1966) φρονεῖν in Homer. *Classical Philology* 61 (2): 99–102.

Long, A. A. (2015) *Greek Models of Mind and Self*. Cambridge, MA: Harvard University Press.
Mansfeld, J., and Primavesi, O. (2011) *Die Vorsokratiker*. Stuttgart: Philipp Reclam.
Nussbaum, M. C. (1972) Ψυχή in Heraclitus. *Phronesis* 17 (1): 1–16 and 17 (2): 153–170.
Onians, R. B. (1951) *The Origins of European Thought About the Body, the Mind, the Soul, the World, Time, and Fate*. Cambridge, MA: Cambridge University Press.
Primavesi, O. (2008) Empedocles: Physical and mythical divinity. In Curd, P., and Graham, D. W. (eds.) *The Oxford Handbook of Presocratic Philosophy*. Oxford: Oxford University Press, pp. 250–283.
Reichenauer, G. (2009) Demokrits Seelenmodell und die Prinzipien der atomistischen Physik. In Frede and Reis (2009), pp. 111–142.
Schäfer, C. (2009) Das Pythagorasfragment des Xenophanes und die Frage nach der Kritik der Metempsychosenlehre. In Frede and Reis (2009), pp. 45–69.
Schofield, M. (1991) Heraclitus' theory of soul and its antecedents. In Everson, S. (ed.) *Companions to Ancient Thought 2: Psychology*. Cambridge, MA: Cambridge University Press, pp. 13–34.
Sedley, D. (1995) The dramatis personae of Plato's *Phaedo*. In Smiley, T. (ed.) *Philosophical Dialogues: Plato, Hume, Wittgenstein: Proceedings of the British Academy* 85: 3–26.
Taylor, C. C. W. (2007) Democritus and Lucretius on death and dying. In Brancacci, A., and Morel, P.-M. (eds.) *Democritus: Science, the Arts, and the Care of the Soul*. Leiden: Brill, pp. 77–86.
Warren, J. (2002) Democritus, the Epicureans, death, and dying. *Classical Quarterly* 52 (1): 93–206.

2

PRESOCRATIC ACCOUNTS OF PERCEPTION AND COGNITION

Patricia Curd

Did early Greek philosophers have *theories* about perception and cognition? That depends on what counts as a theory. Nevertheless, some of the thinkers classified as Presocratics had views about the mechanism of sensation and about the nature of thinking.[1] The topics they discussed were connected with their interest in the possibility of human knowledge. Having raised the prospect that human beings can acquire the sort of epistemic security previously reserved for the divine, they were faced with related questions about sensation and cognition. Here, I consider Parmenides, Anaxagoras, and Democritus. As always when working with Presocratics, we must keep in mind the fragmentary nature of the evidence we have, as well as be aware of the role of the testimony of later philosophers and doxographers in shaping our interpretations. Lack of a settled vocabulary for perceptual and cognitive terms also makes for difficulty; it cannot be assumed that a single word or expression will maintain a fixed meaning across the views of the figures considered here.

1. Parmenides and some problems of interpretation

Parmenides suggests that there are two possible routes to knowledge of how things are: one relying fundamentally on the use of sensory perception; the other grounded in cognition or understanding (the human capacity for thinking and reasoning). He clearly rejects sense perception as an adequate path to knowledge.[2] Rather, Parmenides (or more precisely, the goddess who speaks in his poem) admonishes humans to rely on their capacity for understanding (i.e., to judge by reasoning) and to accept as true only those claims that are properly grounded in what-is:

> For not ever will this be forced through: that things that are not are;
> but you, block your understanding (νόημα) from this route of inquiry,
> nor allow habit to force you along this much-experienced pathway,
> to wield an aimless eye and an echoing ear
> and tongue, but judge by reasoning the much-contested testing spoken by me.
> (DK28 B7)

Here the contrast is between the controlled and careful use of thinking and understanding and the hit-or-miss process of sensory experience. Parmenides distinguishes between those human beings who are able to recognize the role that thinking and reasoning play in reaching a correct view of the world, and those whom he calls "mortals," who seem to rely only on sense experience and who take the senses as reliable reporters not only of how things appear at the moment, but of how things as a matter of fact are in reality. The goddess treats the mortal attitude as one that human beings can overcome, because they have the basic capacities for both sensing and understanding, and they can learn to use these correctly. The young man (κοῦρος) to whom the goddess speaks in the poem is taught by exhortation (the outline of the lesson in B1.28–32; the opening remarks of B2) and by example (the long set of proofs and argument in fragment B8) how to avoid the condition of the "undiscriminating hordes," attempting to follow an impossible route of inquiry:

> the one on which mortals, knowing nothing
> wander, two-headed; for helplessness in their
> breasts directs their wandering mind (νόος); they are borne along
> blind and deaf alike, amazed, undiscriminating hordes,
> by whom to be and not to be are held to be the same
> and not the same, and the path of all is backward turning.
> (DK28 B6.4–9)

The "know-nothing mortals" that Parmenides criticizes are not, I think, meant to be literally blind and deaf any more than they are literally two-headed. Rather, being amazed, undiscerning and failing to discriminate, they are swamped by their sensory experiences and although they may have visual and auditory experience, they are unable to see and hear correctly, in the sense of making proper judgments about their own experience, realizing that what is perceived may not be genuinely real. Part of the difficulty in grasping Parmenides' point is that he uses the same word, *noos*, to refer to the thinking or judging aspects of what we would call mental activity.[3] One can use one's *noos* well or badly (just as we can say that someone is thinking clearly or that someone else's thought is confused). In contrast, Heraclitus, while saying that "thinking is common to all" (B113) reserves *noos* for a success term, to indicate an achieved state of understanding (which he also terms "intelligence.")[4] For Parmenides, mortals have "wandering" *noos* because they fail to fix their thought on its proper object; they are instead distracted by ever-changing sensations.

Parmenides argues that when thought or reasoning disagrees with perception, the conclusions of reasoning must be trusted. Thus, Parmenides thinks that he has arguments (in B8) to show that anything that genuinely is (is real) cannot be subject to coming-to-be or passing-away and must have a stable and unique nature. Yet nothing that we experience is (apparently) like this. Parmenides here combines claims about knowledge, perception, thought, and the nature of what-is.

This is characteristic of Presocratic philosophy, where sharp categories have not yet been drawn between questions of metaphysics, epistemology, and the nature of mind. For Parmenides (as for, for instance, Xenophanes and Heraclitus) the ability to inquire, to ask questions, is the distinguishing mark of the human condition. In B3, we find the assertion that "the same thing is for thinking (νοεῖν) and for being (εἶναι)"; one's mind (νόος) – the capacity to think and understand – naturally seeks what is true, but it can be hindered by reliance on sense perception. Yet why should we not rely on our sensings? Human beings are, after all, creatures that perceive. What is so bad about perception that Parmenides apparently rejects confidence in our sensory evidence?

Within the early Greek tradition, theorists marked the distinction between the divine and the human by distinguishing not only between the immortal and the mortal, but between the knowing and the ignorant. Because mortal humans are "creatures of a day," they are limited to what they experience in a short life, and because their powers are so feeble, they are unaware of what happens outside of their particular concerns.[5] Empedocles, criticizing ordinary human attitudes to knowing, expresses this view of mortal limitations lucidly:

> For narrow fingers flow through the limbs,
> and many wretched things burst in, and blunt [mortals'] thoughts.
> Observing but a small portion of life in their living,
> quick-dying, like smoke, lifted up and wafted away to their doom. Each one persuaded only by that which he has chanced to meet,
> they are driven in all directions; each boasts of having seen the whole.
> (DK31 B2)

The narrow fingers through the limbs are the channels of sensation; the mortals are distracted by, and fail to think about or attend to, the experiences they happen to have in their short lives. Moreover, mortals take their own experiences as authoritative: for them, what seems is what is. The early Presocratics challenge this distinction between mortal and immortal: given the proper use of the intellect or mind, a mortal can have the same degree of certainty as the earlier poets attributed to the divine.[6] Heraclitus had claimed that sensory experience is necessary for knowledge.[7] In contrast, Parmenides argues that genuine knowledge or certainty has its own object (what-is) that is independent of sensory experience and is only to be grasped by intellect or mind (νόος). As the goddess says in the introduction to the poem (B1.28–32),

> it is right that you learn all things:
> both the unshaking heart of well-persuasive truth
> and the opinions of mortals, in which there is no true trust;
> yet nevertheless you will learn these too, how it were right that the things
>   that seem should be acceptable, being indeed the whole of things.[8]

The enigmatic last lines are a reference to the state of mortals who take what they experience (the things that are actually the objects of belief or opinion – *doxa*) to be the only things there are and hence "the whole of things"). The origin of that state is indicated in fragment 16, which gives a sense-based analysis of mind (νόος):

> For just as is the mixture of the much-wandering limbs on each occasion,
> so is *noos* present to humans; for the same thing
> is the very thing that cognizes – in all humans and in each: the nature of the
> limbs; for the full is thought.[9]

B16 is usually taken to belong to the Opinion (*Doxa*) part of Parmenides' poem, in which he describes the "beliefs of mortals" (referred to in the lines of B1 quoted previously).[10] I take the passage to describe the default state of cognition for human beings (note that Parmenides uses the descriptive word 'human being' here, rather than the more pejorative 'mortal'): all humans depend on sense experience. The "mixture of the much-wandering limbs" refers to the state of the body as affected by the external world (the continual impressions of sense-experience); these impressions determine the conditions in which all human thought originates.[11] Nevertheless, Parmenides also suggests through the imagery of the poem and through the views about mind and what-is that the goddess imparts that the default state of utter reliance on sense experience can give way to better thinking, in grasping what is stable and permanent, available only to a human thinker who has freed her thinking from dependence on the immediate present content of sense experience. Intellection seems to be a kind of direct insight, governed by the laws of necessity, which alone determine what can be true.[12] A human being stands between the mortal and immortal states: while being a sensing and perceiving creature, such a one also has the potential to think and understand, to grasp the truth directly with the mind.[13]

Unfortunately, Parmenides says almost nothing about the mechanisms involved here. Aristotle and Theophrastus, who both discuss sensation and thought in their predecessors, apparently were not entirely clear about Parmenides' views, and their difficulties with and interpretations of Presocratic views (including but not restricted to Parmenides) influenced later accounts. Theophrastus says,

> On the whole, Parmenides said nothing at all definite, only that, there being two elements, cognition (γνῶσις) is in accordance with the one that predominates. For if the hot or the cold is in excess, thought becomes different – that which is due to the hot being better and purer. Not but that what this too, requires an appropriate proportion. . . . For he speaks of perceiving and thinking as the same thing and this is why memory and forgetting result from the same things [the hot and the cold] on account of their blending. But he did not get so far as to determine whether or not there will be thinking and what the condition will be if they are equal in

the mixture. But that he makes sensation [occur] also by the contrary by itself is evident where he declares that a corpse does not perceive light, or heat, or sound on account of the absence of fire, but does perceive cold, silence, and the contraries. And in general everything that is has some sort of cognition (γνῶσις).

(28A46 = *De Sens.* 3–4)
(McKirahan's translation slightly revised)

Theophrastus clearly attributes an important role to fire (or the hot) to Parmenides' account of what makes a thing alive and able to sense. Unfortunately, we have no text from Parmenides himself that could help with this, except the claim that mortals named two forms as basic (and went astray in doing so): "ethereal fire of flame, being gentle, very light, everywhere the same as itself but not the same as the other; and then that one, in itself opposite, unknowing night, dense and heavy body" (B8.56–59). Later writers, following in many cases Aristotle's interpretation, saw Parmenides as having matter-based views of sensation and cognition with light and night as elements whose mixtures and proportions determine sensation and thought.[14]

Aristotle often claims that pre-Platonic thinkers failed to distinguish properly between perception and thought.[15] For instance, at *Metaphysics* IV.5 (1009b12ff.), Aristotle claims that Empedocles and Democritus say that sensation and thought are the same and occur by alteration, then adds, "And Parmenides declares the same thing," quoting B16. All of this is complicated by Aristotle's own views about perception and knowledge, and his insistence that sensation is neither sufficient nor necessary for the operation of intellect (νοῦς) in its best form. For Aristotle, thinking and sensation have different structures, and what he sees as the failure of earlier thinkers (including all of those discussed in this chapter) to discriminate between them in the right way. As if this were not complex enough, Aristotle's insistence that most pre-Platonic theories treated matter as their basic principle (*Met.* I.3) makes it easy for him (and those following him) to charge the Presocratics with erroneously making perception and thought "the same." Were Aristotle correct about this, Parmenides could not legitimately contrast the evidence of the senses and the dictates of genuine thought, and would instead have to treat thinking as a kind of perception (as one could interpret B16 as claiming).[16]

Now, it may be true that, as a matter of fact, Parmenides' own account of the way things are will not leave room for a legitimate contrast between thinking and sensing, or it may not allow that sensing can be in any way relevant to thinking. These claims depend on how we interpret the two main sections of Parmenides' poem and the extent to which we are willing to allow the doctrines of the *Doxa* to have any legitimacy. Indeed, the traditional interpretation of Parmenides has been that he rejected the senses altogether, distinguished cognition and sensation so sharply that thinking alone is epistemically legitimate, and that only Mind is real.[17] I have argued that the cosmological principles of the *Doxa* cannot themselves pass Parmenides' tests for what-is, and hence that scientific claims grounded in sense experience cannot count as genuine Parmenidean knowledge; but this need not reduce the sensible world and claims about it to illusion or to nonsense. In Book V of the *Republic* Plato makes metaphysical and epistemological distinctions that allow claims based on perception to have some degree of epistemic security as objects of belief. Parmenides does not make such claims, but it could be that he deemed the claims made in the *Doxa* to be acceptable but deceptive if taken to be genuinely true.[18] Only properly controlled thought (i.e., thinking that follows the rules exhibited in the arguments of B8) counts as genuine cognition.

2. Anaxagoras

Anaxagoras declares that the original state of the universe was a motionless universal mixture of all things; because of the completeness of the mixture, and because air and aether prevailed in it, "nothing was evident" (DK59 B1).[19] At some point, the mass began to be moved, and that movement caused separation out of the ingredients in such a way that an orderly cosmos began to form. Anaxagoras' cosmic mover is Mind (*nous: Νοῦς*):

> *Nous* controlled the whole revolution, so that it started to revolve in the beginning. First it began to revolve in a small region, but it is revolving yet more and will revolve still more. . . . And whatever sorts of things were going to be, and whatever sorts were and now are not, and as many as are now and whatever sorts will be, all these *nous* set in order.
> (DK59 B12 in part)

According to Diogenes Laertius (a not altogether reliable authority), Anaxagoras was given the nickname 'Mr. Mind,' because he claimed that Mind has control over matter (DK59 A1). Aristotle celebrates Anaxagoras for introducing a principle or cause that is separate from and controls matter:

> When someone said that *nous* is present, in nature just as it is in living animals, as the cause of the cosmos and of all its order, he appeared as a sober man among the random chatterers who preceded him. We know that Anaxagoras certainly held these views . . . those thinking this way posited at the same time a cause and principle in the things that are both of beauty and also of that from which motion is present in them.
> (*Met.* 984b15–19; 20–22)

We should remember that Aristotle's discussion assumes his own account of the four causes: material, formal, final, and efficient. Having claimed that most of his predecessors relied only on material causes, Aristotle now attributes to Anaxagoras the notion of an efficient (moving cause) and a final cause (of order and hence beauty). Clearly, Anaxagoras was seen by later philosophers as making a radical proposal: in the *Phaedo* (97b8ff.) Plato's Socrates proclaims the novelty of Anaxagoras' *nous* (although Socrates complains that Anaxagoras fails to make *nous* a cause of the goodness of the world). There are four fragments (B11, B12, B13, B14) that treat of *nous*: luckily B12, containing the fullest discussion, is (for a Presocratic text) quite long.[20] The material that we have from Anaxagoras allows us to make a few claims with some degree of confidence about his view of mind/intellect.

Aristotle is, I think, correct when says that Anaxagoras sees mind as analogously present in living things and in the cosmos. All Anaxagorean ingredients (the things in the original mixture) remain mixed together; as Anaxagoras says in B6, "nor is it possible that anything be separated out, nor come to be by itself, but just as in the beginning, now too, all things are together." The one exception, because it does not count as an ingredient and is not subject to mixture, is mind: "In everything there is a portion of everything, except *nous*, but *nous* is in some things, too." Those "some things" turn out to be living things with soul: "*nous* has control over all things that have soul, both the larger and the smaller" (B12). If we think of cosmic *nous*, that mind that controls the rotations, as "big *nous*," we can then suppose that the "larger and the smaller" here refers to anything that is alive, so that plants, animals, and humans all have *nous* to some degree or other. We can call this *nous* in ensouled living things "small *nous*." Fragment B4a asserts that "humans and the other animals were compounded, as many as have soul"; in A116 Plutarch says that Anaxagoras (along with the Platonists and Democritus) supposes that "a plant is an earth-bound animal." According to the author of the pseudo-Aristotelian *On Plants* (A117), Anaxagoras thought that plants have respiration, are moved by desire, and sense, and feel emotions: "they are animals and feel joy and sadness, taking the fall of their leaves as evidence . . . [in addition] Anaxagoras and Democritus and Empedocles say plants have perception and intelligence." Yet, unlike certain other Presocratics, as well as Plato and Aristotle, Anaxagoras does not claim that the heavenly bodies are divine, and so alive and ensouled. This is part of the reason that Anaxagoras acquired the reputation of being an atheist.[21]

Before going further with a discussion of mind, it worth pausing to consider these claims about the *nous*-capacities of plants and animals. Although he says little about it in any of the extant fragments, Anaxagoras apparently attributes all these characteristics to non-human plants and animals because they have soul. Thus, he views sensation, respiration and growth, emotional states, and intellect as aspects or functions of soul. It is unlikely that Anaxagoras thought that soul (as opposed to cosmic *nous*) is immortal, but the (admittedly meager) evidence suggests that soul is a cause of structure and activity (both motion and thought) in a living thing, including plants which have both motion (i.e., growth) and sensation (i.e., responding to wet or sunny conditions). Theophrastus reports that for Anaxagoras all sensation takes place through opposites (A92); in being affected in the appropriate way by something dissimilar, a living thing comes to have a sensory experience. For, as Theophrastus says, "the similar is unaffected by the similar." So, if I put my dry hand in water that is heated to approximately 37 degrees C it will not feel warm or cold, but it will feel wet. Sight is produced by reflection of light in the pupil (the dark part) of the eye, and Anaxagoras distinguishes between those animals that see well during the day from those that see better at night by referring to how light or dark their eyes are in relation to the amount of light during the day or night (A92). The size of the sense organ determines the sharpness of perception:

> Those animals that have large, clear, bright eyes see large and distant things; it is just the opposite for those with small eyes. It the same for hearing. Large animals hear large and distant perceptibles, while the smaller ones elude them, and small animals hear small and near perceptibles. It is also the same for smell: thin air has more odor, since air takes on an odor when heated and rarified. When a large animal inhales, it breathes in both the rare and the dense, but a small animal draws in the rare by itself; therefore the large animals perceive more. For scent is stronger when it is near rather than far away because it is denser; when dispersed, it is weaker.
>
> (A92)

I have quoted this passage at length because it gives some idea of how detailed some of Anaxagoras' accounts must have been and suggests something about the possible mechanism of sensation (although Theophrastus complains that "he is not clear on the more tactile senses . . . and Anaxagoras spoke superficially about colors"). Aëtius (*Plac.* 4.9.6 = Stobaeus *Ecl.* I.50.6) reports that for Anaxagoras (as for Parmenides, Empedocles, Democritus, Epicurus, and Heracleides) "each of the various sensations occur because of the symmetry of pores, with each of the appropriate objects of sensation fitting into each perceptual pathway."[22] This is the only report of sensation through the means of pores in Anaxagoras, and might well be inaccurate, but the mechanism is consistent with the perception-by-unlikes report in Theophrastus. Symmetry would allow the object of sensation to enter, while contrast with the character of the lining of the pores would explain perceptual awareness of the content. The mechanism of sensation by unlikes also accounts for one of the oddities of Anaxagoras' view that Aristotle, Theophrastus, Aspasius, and Aëtius report (and that is implied by the passage from Pseudo-Aristotle quoted previously): according to these reports, Anaxagoras claims that all perception is accompanied by some degree of pain, distress, or discomfort (A92, A94). Presumably this is because perception occurs through contraries: any noticeable contrast between the state of the perceiver and the object of sensation entering the body is noted as a difference; when difference is marked enough, pain results. Theophrastus notes that staring at the sun or hearing very loud noises can be painful.[23]

Anaxagoras notes that sensation can be deceptive: Sextus Empiricus quotes fragment 21, "Owing to their [the senses'] feebleness we are not able to determine the truth," and says that Anaxagoras offered the gradual change of colors (in mixing paints) as evidence. Sextus remarks, "sight will not be able to determine the gradual changes, although in nature they are real." We should conclude from this that Anaxagoras would say that we determine what is real by the use of our own (small) *nous* as intellect. One activity of cosmic (big) *nous* in B12 is that of discrimination. As Anaxagoras notes in B12,

> *Nous* has all discernment about everything, and has the greatest strength. . . . And *Nous* knew all things, the things that are being mixed together, the things that are being separated off, and the things that are being dissociated.
>
> (B12)

B13 stresses the continuing activity of *nous* as the rotation expands and infiltrates the surrounding unlimited cosmic mass. Anaxagoras makes it clear that cosmic *nous* could not act as it does without having understanding: although it causes the motions of the cosmos, it is not a blind efficient cause, but an ordering principle. In the same way that we control our own motions and order our emotions and desires, so Mind orders the cosmos. We can see the physical separation (and mixture) caused by the rotation that *nous* initiates, and in learning to use our own smaller *nous*, we each make discriminations and move beyond what is seen to what is the case.[24] Cosmic Mind alone has the power of direct insight into the fundamental natures of the ingredients and the mixtures. Although Anaxagoras notes that the senses are feeble in that there are limits to their powers of discrimination, for humans as minded entities, the senses are necessary: as B21a says, "appearances are a sight of the unseen." Like Democritus (who supposedly praised him for this remark), Anaxagoras builds his account of ordinary cognition on sense experience: reason may be the standard of truth (as Sextus says) but without the evidence of the senses we non-cosmic-minded things would be unable to think.

How should we conceive of Anaxagoras' cosmic Mind? Aëtius (A48) asserts that it is the mind of god that orders the ingredients, and that "Anaxagoras says that god is mind, the maker of the cosmos." Notwithstanding that report, although Anaxagoras' language in B12 is solemn enough to be appropriate for discussing the gods, he never says that *nous* is divine (and he certainly does not recognize the traditional Greek pantheon of gods). What he does say is this:

> The other things have a share of everything, but *Nous* is unlimited and self-ruling and has been mixed with no thing, but is alone itself by itself. For if it were not by itself, but had been mixed with anything else, then it would partake of all things, if it had been mixed with anything . . . and the things mixed together with it would thwart it, so that it would control none of the things in the way that it in fact does, being alone by itself. For it is the finest of all things, and the purest, and indeed it maintains all discernment about everything and has the greatest strength. . . . *Nous*, which always is, most assuredly is even now where all the other things

also are, in the surrounding multitude, and in the things that were joined together and in the things that have been separated off.

(B12; B14)

Anaxagoras' claims about the separateness, purity, and controlling powers of *nous*, along with his assertions that it somehow is where all the other things are also, make it clear that *nous* is not an ordinary ingredient in the world.[25] It is a power that moves and knows, and, I have argued, is not to be thought of as a mattered thing.[26] It pervades the cosmos as structuring and ordering it, just as it is present in living things as a structuring and ordering power. The idea of a rational and intelligible cosmos in this sense is strange to modern readers, but Anaxagoras' specific insistence on this is what makes him (at least in this respect) praiseworthy for Aristotle and Plato (yet, each was disappointed that Anaxagoras failed to anticipate his own version of teleology). Nevertheless, it is worth asking just how revolutionary Anaxagoras' view is. Earlier Greek philosophers had already indicated that there is a rational ordering principle at work in the cosmos and that this principle is similar to human intellect. Xenophanes' god is a divine mind, and Heraclitus' *logos* is a symbol of the rational self-ordering aspect of the cosmos.[27] We have seen Parmenides' insistence on the connection between thinking and what-is, and it is likely that Parmenides too thought of what-is as both intelligent and intelligible. Anaxagoras makes these claims explicit and, in contrasting the ingredients with *nous*, he does so in a way that seemed to Aristotle to move beyond the simple-minded matter-based theories of his predecessors.[28] I have already noted that I think that Aristotle's analysis is wrong, but that is not the point; given Aristotle's authority in the history of philosophy, Anaxagoras retains the title of Mr. Mind.

3. Democritus

Although I have argued that most of the Presocratics distinguish between sensation and cognition, Leucippus and Democritus indeed fall under Aristotle's too-sweeping generalization that most early philosophers thought that sensation and knowledge were somehow the same (see De Anima III.3).[29] As we have seen, in *Met.* IV.5 Aristotle also makes that claim mentioning both Empedocles and Democritus (as well as Parmenides later in the passage):

> In general, because these thinkers take knowledge to be perception, and that this is an alteration, they say that what appears to perception/sensation is necessarily true. It is because of this that both Empedocles and Democritus, and one may say, the others are liable to hold these sorts of views.
>
> (*Met.* 1009b12–17)

There is no doubt that Democritus claims that both sensation and cognition are states of body; for anything that is sensed or thought is the effect of atoms which are body. The problem is to determine the details of the view. The fundamental entities of the theory are atoms and void (or, the full and the empty). We have no direct quotations from Democritus himself about them, but the testimonia allow us to reconstruct the atomic view (although scholars both ancient and modern disagree about some of the details).[30] Atoms, named from the Greek *atomos* (ἄτομος uncuttable), are solid, infinitely varied in shape, and of many sizes (probably too small to be perceived by us).[31] The atoms move in or through the void (which is as real as the atoms); the motion produces interaction with other atoms.[32] This motion is eternal: as atoms move they either collide with or repel one another, producing more motions; and atoms can also become "entangled" because of variations in their shapes.[33] The entangled clusters themselves ultimately form the things that we perceive: things having certain characteristics determined by the size, shape, and arrangement of the atoms that constitute them. Anything we sense is the result of the interaction of these objects (various combinations of atoms of different sizes and shapes and of void) with those atoms and void that constitute the sense organs of living things. The characters that we attribute to perceptible objects are a function of (1) the objects perceived, (2) the state of the perceiver, and (3) the nature of the medium (air, itself a combination of atoms and void) through which perception occurs. Thus, we never perceive any external object directly; rather what we sense (or are aware of in sensing) are the states of our own perceptual mechanisms as affected by atoms entering them.[34] This claim has important consequences for Democritus' view of cognition.

Theophrastus is the most important source for information about Democritus' account of sensation and its objects, and his discussion (*De Sens.* sections 49–83) is quite detailed, especially in comparison with what he tells us about other Presocratics. Democritus shares with Empedocles the basic view that vision and other types of sensation depend on effluences from the perceived body; in Empedocles' system the effluences are composed of the four roots earth, water, air, and fire. According to Empedocles, these effluences impinge on the perceiver, and where the appropriate effluences meet the appropriate sense organs and enter the body through pores, sensing occurs.[35] Democritus' account is far more complex than Empedocles'. Democritus indeed begins with effluences: these are streams of atoms (often referred to as "thin films"; Democritus apparently called them ἔιδωλα) coming from the object. According to Theophrastus:

> He makes sight occur by means of the image (*emphasis*); his account of this is original, for he says that the image is not immediately produced in the eyeball, but that the air between the sight and the thing seen is compacted by the seer and the thing seen and an impression is made on it, as everything is always giving off effluences [the εἴδωλα]. This mass of air, which is solid and of a different color, is then imaged in the eyes, which are moist; a dense body does not take the image, but a moist one lets it pass through. That is why moist eyes are better at seeing than hard ones,

provided that the outer coating is as fine as possible, and the inside as porous as possible ... and the veins in the regions of the eyes are straight and free of moisture, so that they match the shape of the impressions; for everything most readily recognizes things of the same kind as itself.
(Theophrastus *De Sens*. 50; translated Taylor)

So Democritus claims that the image (ἔμφασις) in (or on the surface of) the eye is not the direct effect of the effluences from the object but is rather produced by those streams of εἴδωλα acting on the air that is between the object and the eye. The air is compacted by the streams of εἴδωλα in such a way that the appearance is transferred to the compacted air, and it is the streams of air hitting the eye that cause the appearance or image to form on the surface of the eyeball. The veins then transfer the images to what we might call a central processing center (the testimonia disagree strongly here; some say it is the brain, others that it is the collection for soul-atoms spread throughout the body).[36] The compaction of the air by the εἴδωλα may be a way for Democritus to explain how we can see (i.e., have images in our eyes) of large objects. If the films of atoms came directly from the cedar tree in the garden, remaining the same size as they travel, they would not fit into or onto the eye. What we are aware of in seeing, then, is not the cedar tree in the garden, but the effect of the air (which may contribute to the image formed in it by its own state of moistness or dryness) on the eyeball (the state of which also affects the image formed).[37] So, two persons standing next to one another may be looking at the same tree, but give different reports about the contents of their tree-perceptions. Both will be correct insofar as they are reporting the appearance; neither has direct visual access to what we might call 'the way the cedar tree really is.' Hearing works analogously: "air entering a void creates motion, except that it (the air) comes in all over the body, but especially and most of all through the ears, because there it travels through the most void and has the least delay." Again, it is the air that has been affected by the sounding that is transferred in hearing; both it and the state of the body that receives the sensory effluences make a difference to what is ultimately perceived. This is the same for all sensation (including touch, taste, and smell), and so the same sight, sound, or taste may seem different to different people.[38]

Although Democritus can give atomic explanations for why lead is heavy but soft, while iron is lighter but harder (this is due to the size of the atoms, and the way the atoms and void are arranged in each), and of their colors, the hardness and softness and colors are not real qualities in the lead and iron, but effects of interactions between the atoms and void constituting the object and those comprising the perceiver. It need not be that larger atoms are heavier (the vexed question of whether or not Democritean atoms have weight is not the issue here);[39] rather it is the amount and arrangement of void in iron and lead, as determined by the size, number, and arrangement of the atoms, that is relevant. In lead there is less void, but the atoms are more evenly aligned (*De Sens*. 62), so that one can scratch the surface by pushing aside stacks of atoms with a fingernail (which is itself strong or hard because of its atomic structure).⁴⁰ Again, we have what seems to be good evidence from Theophrastus:

> None of the other sensible qualities has any nature of its own, but all are states of the sense when it is altered so as to give rise to an appearance. For there is no nature belonging to hot or cold, but change in shape [sc. of the thing perceived] brings about alteration in us; a concentrated effect dominates each individual, whereas an effect which is spread out over time is not noticed. The evidence for this is that things do not naturally seem the same to all creatures, but what is sweet to us is bitter to other creatures, sharp-tasting to others, pungent to others, sour to others again, and the same for other cases. Further they [i.e., observers] vary in the judgments according to their different states and to their ages; which makes it clear that their disposition is the cause of how things seem to them.
>
> (*de Sens*. 63–64)

Democritus' insistence that sensory experiences are the combined effect of the states of the perceiver, the medium through which sensation occurs, and the object of sense, is the foundation of his claims that we do not have direct experience of anything, and that perceivers who disagree can all be correct. This earns for him the reputation of having adopted Protagorean subjectivism and skepticism.⁴¹ As he himself says, "In reality we know nothing; for truth is in the depths" (T.D15). This quotation, like most of the other epistemological fragments that we have, comes from Sextus Empiricus, who is happy to try to claim Democritus as a fellow skeptic; but the links with Protagoras go back at least as far as Aristotle. While Democritus' analysis of sensation provides some evidence for this, and while Aristotle insists that Democritus identifies sensation and thought, a case can be made that Democritus distinguishes them. If this is so, Democritus allows for cognition that counts as genuine knowledge, while at the same time claiming that sense-experience is necessary (although not sufficient) for knowing.⁴²

In *De Anima*, Aristotle says that for Democritus soul and mind are the same thing: soul is both the source of motion and the seat of cognition:

> Democritus says that the soul is same as the mind, and is composed of the primary, indivisible bodies, and is a source of motion because of their smallness and shape. He says that the sphere is the most mobile of shapes, and that mind and fire are of the same nature.
>
> (*DA* 405a8–13)

An identity of some sort between soul and intellect or mind is, of course, true even for Plato and Aristotle. Both allow for different parts or aspects of soul and both acknowledge a rational part; yet Aristotle suggests that Democritus has a more radical view. Testimonia from Lucretius (68 A108) and Sextus Empiricus (DK69

A107) suggest that Democritus thought of the soul as a web of very fine atoms spread throughout the body, and this view, while not universally accepted, is plausible.[43] The mechanism of thought in Democritus is not clear: thoughts must be some kind of atomic movement (as is everything else). It is possible that thinking is the result of the finest atomic effluences (εἴδωλα) penetrating the entire body and proceeding immediately to the web-like system of soul atoms spread throughout the body; the more coarse-grained sensory εἴδωλα are channeled through the sense organs before they affect the soul (and this would explain the Aristotelian claim that thought and sensation are the same since the same mechanism is at work). If soul atoms are like fire, then Democritus' view would be consistent with other Presocratic views that make thinking at least partly a matter of the relevant part of the body being in a hot and dry state (Heraclitus DK22 B117 and B118, and Parmenides DK 28 B16 on which, see above pp. 46–48).

Despite his claim that '*in reality* we know nothing; truth is in the depths,' it seems clear that Democritus supposes that some thinking can lead to the truth. He presents his own atomic theory using the same sort of language: "By convention sweet and by convention bitter, by convention hot, by convention cold; yet *in reality* atoms and void" (DK68 B9; B125). The same Greek word (translated as *in reality*) appears in both fragments. As Lee has argued, 'by convention (*nomos*)' here should not be taken as meaning something like 'general established agreement' in the way that a group can agree (implicitly or explicitly) on what name to use for a thing ('the trunk' as opposed to 'the boot' of 'a car' or 'a motor'). Rather, 'by convention' refers to "the subjectivity of the fact that things appear sweet."[44] Sextus and Galen both offer explanations of Democritus' claim and while there are some differences between their views, they agree that Democritus is contrasting how things themselves are (that there are really only atoms and void as genuine realities) and appearances at the level of the mixtures of atoms and void that we (as atomic mixtures ourselves) experience. If such a distinction is actually possible, then there must be a way for us to reach the conclusion that there are atoms and void even if we do not have direct experience of them as such. That way must be through abstraction and thought, even though thought itself can be affected by the state of the body. That Democritus is committed to the possibility of coming to understand how things are in themselves through thought seemed odd and even inconsistent to ancient commentators. Summarizing the case for Democritus as skeptic, doing away with the possibility of knowledge, Sextus recognizes that Democritus' own words could suggest that view. Yet even Sextus acknowledges that Democritus does not accept universal skepticism. Sextus distinguishes the roles of perception and thought in Democritus, and introduces the notion that genuine knowledge is grounded in thinking and reasoning rather than only in the evidence of sense perception:

> In *On Ideas* [Democritus] says, "it is necessary that a person know by this rule that he is separated from reality" [68B6]. . . . But in the *Rules* he says that there are two kinds of knowing, one through the senses and

the other through the understanding. The one through the understanding he calls genuine, witnessing to its trustworthiness in deciding truth; the one through the senses he names dark, denying it steadfastness in the discernment of what is true. He says in these words, "There are two forms of knowing, one genuine and the other dark. To the dark belong all these: sight, hearing, smell, taste, touch. The other, the genuine, has been separated from this" [68B11]. Then preferring the genuine to the dark, he continues, saying, "Whenever the dark is no longer able to see more finely nor hear nor smell nor taste nor perceive by touch [other things in the direction of greater fineness]." Therefore according to him, too, reason is a criterion, which he calls 'genuine knowing' [68B11].
(Sextus Empiricus, *Adv. math.* VII 135–139)

In B11 Democritus uses the word *gnōsis* (γνῶσις), knowing or cognizing, and contrasts them: one kind is genuine or legitimate; the other is dark or bastard.[45] The latter is clearly identified with sensation/perception, and it cannot get at the way things are in themselves; the claim is that the dark kind of cognition gives out as it attempts to grasp things "of greater fineness." If we note that Democritus seems to identify thinking with the finest atomic εἴδωλα or effluences, then it is reasonable that only cognition/reasoning could grasp the real nature of things: atoms and void.

Aristotle himself seems to recognize that Democritus has a role for thinking to play that is independent of sensation. In *On Generation and Corruption* he praises Democritus for having thought carefully about the real problems in accounting for coming-to-be and passing-away, and says that while others of his predecessors gave no detailed account of these, Democritus and Leucippus were able to do so because they "posited the shapes" (i.e., the atoms). They, says Aristotle, explained alteration by appeal to the order and arrangement of the atoms, and coming-to-be and passing-away "by separation and joining together." He then adds:

> And because they supposed that truth was in appearance, and the appearances are opposed and infinite, they made the shapes infinite, so that on account of changes in the underlying the same thing seems opposite to one and to another, and changes around as the result of a small added ingredient and appears entirely different on account of the alteration of one thing; for tragedy and comedy come to be from the same letters.
> (*Gen et. Corr.* 315b9–15 = DK68 A35)

While the discussion is shaded by Aristotle's own concerns, the claim that the atoms have an infinite number of shapes is presented as the result of reasoning from evidence. What could explain the differences in sensory reports given that Democritus seems to think that reports of sensation as sensation are always true?[46] It must be that minute changes below the level of appearances must be causing the different sensations, and this is something that one could not determine by sensation alone. It takes thought about the way things must be in order to explain the nature and the subjectivity of appearances. The testimonia attribute explanations of all sorts of things to Democritus; the enormous list of his works in Diogenes Laertius covers everything from astronomy to zoology with ethics, embryology, and epistemology included, in addition to treatises on physics and proper farm management (even if we acknowledge that some of these are spurious attributions, it is still a large list covering many topics). According to Eusebius (B118; T. D2), "Democritus himself, so they say, asserted that he would prefer to discover a single causal explanation (αἰτιολογία) rather than gain the kingdom of the Persians." These explanations could not all be based only on immediate sensory evidence. Like the other Presocratic thinkers, Democritus had an important place for thinking and reasoning in his account of how we come to understand the world as it genuinely is. Yet he did not think that mind alone could have direct intellectual apprehension of the truth. Human cognition must begin with perception; in this he agrees with Xenophanes, Heraclitus, Anaxagoras, and Empedocles. As Democritus has the senses exclaim in 68B 125 (from Galen), "Wretched mind! From us you get your evidence, yet you overthrow us? The overthrow is a fall for you!"

Notes

1 Wright 1990 and Laks 1999 provide good introductions to the question.
2 The interpretation of Parmenides has always generated disagreement and debate. Here I am presenting an account of Parmenides that I have argued for elsewhere (Curd 1998/2004, 2011, and 2015).
3 The classic discussions of *nous* and *noein* in early Greek thought are in von Fritz 1943, 1945, 1946, and 1964. Lesher 1981 and 1984 provide a necessary refinement and revision of von Fritz. (In the dialect used by Heraclitus and Parmenides, the spelling is νόος; in Anaxagoras and Democritus it is νοῦς.)
4 Thus in DK22 B40, Heraclitus charges Hesiod, Pythagoras, Xenophanes, and Hecataeus with "much learning" but no "understanding (νόος)"; in B104 he asks of the crowd, "What understanding (νόος) or intelligence (φρήν) do they have?"
5 Alcmaeon DK24 B1; Homeric *Hymn to Apollo* fragments 131 and 132 West. See especially Lesher 1994 on this.
6 Lesher 2008, Curd 2013a, Tor 2015.
7 Lesher 1983, Curd 2013a.
8 Both the text and the translation of the last lines are disputed.
9 Here I follow Tor 2015 in his translation.
10 Other useful discussions of the fragment are Laks 1990, Schofield 1987, Bredlow 2011, Dilcher 2006, Hussey 2006.
11 Hussey (2006, p. 26) argues that B16 is evidence that Parmenides adopted what he calls an 'inner model' view of mind, in which any state of mind with content consists "in having, inside the mind, a scale model of the situations that are perceived or imagined or planned."
12 The original statement of the routes of inquiry shows that the options are "is or is-not?" Is-not is ruled out as impossible, leaving only what is and must be. The modalities here are not those of modern logic; see especially Mourelatos 1971/2008. Dilcher (2006) develops an interpretation of Parmenides on thought and insight that is broadly

compatible with what I have suggested, although we differ in many details of analysis and interpretation.

13 Dilcher (2006, p. 46) is quite correct in noting that *noos* in humans "is present in man as having some intrinsic contact with the limbs' mixture, while on the other hand not being restricted to it."

14 On this, see Hussey's comment (2006, p. 18): Presocratic theories "take those aspects of things that we might distinguish as 'physical/material' and as 'mental,' as both equally fundamental in ontology and explanation, and as found everywhere entwined together."

15 In DA I Aristotle surveys earlier views of soul as an introduction to his own views in Books II and III. Evaluating Aristotle's accounts is complicated by the fact that few of the Presocratics actually spoke of soul as such. They have things to say about sensation and about knowledge, but the idea of a human soul as the seat of motion, perception, and knowledge is in its developing stages. While a number of important fragments of Heraclitus use the term, and he develops a complex theory of soul, the word does not appear in the extant fragments of Parmenides, and in Empedocles appears only in B138. Anaxagoras mentions 'soul' twice; and the atomist texts present their own difficulties (see discussion of Anaxagoras and Democritus).

16 The most famous version of this is the Protagorean claim that all perceptions are true; DK80 B1, "man is the measure of all things, of things that are that they are, of things that are not that they are not" was taken to assert that things indeed are as they appear to any perceiver; thus all perceptions are true. Aristotle uses this phrase several times in discussing earlier views of sensation and thought, and links it with his claim that for almost all the Presocratics, perception and cognition are "the same."

17 B3 has been subject to many interpretations; Long 1996 gives clear discussions of the options (see also MacKenzie 1982, Cherubin 2001, Crystal 2002, and Robbiano 2006).

18 Plato uses the arguments at the end of *Rep.* V to show that the lovers of beautiful sights and sounds, relying on perception, cannot have knowledge and so are unfit to rule in the ideal city. The status of the assertions of *Doxa* has been much discussed recently. Among those attributing legitimacy to the claims of *Doxa* (although they have disagreements with one another) are Cordero 2010, Graham 2006, Palmer 2009, Sisko and Weiss 2015; but see also Cosgrove 2014.

19 The claim here is a counterfactual: There would have been no observers at this point, but even if there had been, nothing could have been observed.

20 B12 is the longest extant piece of pre-Platonic philosophical prose (if we do not count early medical writings as Presocratic).

21 As the exchange between Socrates and Meletus in Plato's *Apology* (26e) makes clear.

22 See the texts translated in A93 on p. 120 of Curd 2007; the report about pores is not included in DK.

23 That some perceptions (the taste of honey, for instance) are pleasant is not mentioned or explained in any text that we have.

24 See Laks (1993, 1999, 2002) on *nous* and the links between separation and discrimination; on B12 see also Lesher 1995; Curd 2007, ch. 4.

25 The language in B12 has direct echoes in Plato's accounts of non-sensible immaterial Forms (especially in the *Phaedo*).

26 Marmodoro (2015) discusses powers in Anaxagoras. Curd (2016) considers the Empedoclean roots and Love and Strife as powers.

27 Xenophanes DK 21 B23, 24, 25, 25; Heraclitus DK 22 B1, B30, B41.

28 See Sedley (2007, pp. 11–12 and 20–25) on the importance of distinction between ingredients and *nous* in Anaxagoras.

29 I shall speak of Democritus throughout as we have no independent evidence about Leucippus' views on these questions. I also concentrate on the evidence from Aristotle

and Theophrastus, to avoid as far as possible, attributing post-Aristotelian atomic views to Democritus.
30 Taylor (1999) provides a clear and thorough account.
31 For discussions about the possible sizes of atoms, see Taylor 1999.
32 On void, see Sedley 1982 and Berryman 2002.
33 Simplicius, quoting Aristotle's *On Democritus*, discusses entanglement; DK68 A37 Taylor 44a.
34 Are we immediately aware of the inner state of our own sensory apparatus? It is not clear whether that too is part of what is transferred further into the body.
35 For Empedocles on sensation, see Curd 2015, Ierodiakonou 2005, Inwood 1992, Wright 1990.
36 Where do perceptions go? Burkert (1977, p. 101) discusses the difficulty of determining this from the evidence that we have.
37 Theophrastus raises a number of questions about Democritus' story; like modern readers he found Democritus' view quite unclear. Lee's (2005) explanation of Democritus' account of vision is very helpful, as is Burkert's (1977), who usefully compares Democritus and Empedocles.
38 See the account in O'Keefe 1997.
39 A classic statement of the problem is in O'Brien 1981.
40 Theophrastus describes and criticizes Democritus' color theory in *de Sensibus* sections 73–83 (DK68 A135 = T113).
41 See Lee (2005, chs. 8 & 9) for a thorough discussion of Democritus and Protagoras.
42 The same is true of Empedocles.
43 Taylor 1999, pp. 200–208.
44 Lee (2005, p. 226): "as Theophrastus puts it, things are sweet only insofar as they appear sweet to us; they are not sweet in themselves." Lee has a clear and subtle analysis of the differences between Sextus' and Galen's interpretations.
45 End of B11: following Lee (2005, p. 229) following Sedley's version of the emended text; for the variations, see Taylor 1999. While the word 'dark' here can mean 'bastard' and Democritus' use could be connected with the idea that sense perceptions are not legitimate: they are (apparently) generated by complex objects, which themselves are not genuinely real (see Curd 1998/2004 and Morel 1998). Lee (2005) argues that 'dark' is a better translation, allowing a wider range of references for the term (including the sense of 'bastard').
46 That is, if it appears green to me, then it is true that I am appeared to greenly.

Bibliography

Baldes, R. W. (1975) Democritus on visual perception: Two theories or one? *Phronesis* 20: 93–105.

Berryman, S. (2002) Democritus and the explanatory power of the void. In Caston, V., and Graham, D. W. (eds.) *Presocratic Philosophy: Essays in Honour of Alexander Mourelatos*. London: Ashgate.

Bredlow, L. A. (2011) Aristotle, Theophrastus, and Parmenides' theory of cognition (B16). *Apeiron* 44: 219–263.

Burkert, W. (1977) Air imprints or Eidōla: Democritus' aetiology of vision. *Illinois Classical Studies* 2: 97–109.

Cherubin, R. (2001) Λέγειν, Νοεῖν and τὸ 'Εόν in Parmenides. *Ancient Philosophy* 21: 277–303.

Cordero, N. (2010) The 'Doxa of Parmenides' dismantled. *Ancient Philosophy* 30: 231–246.

Cosgrove, M. (2014) What are true Doxai worth to Parmenides? Essaying a fresh look at his cosmology. *Oxford Studies in Ancient Philosophy* 46: 1–31.

Crystal, I. (2002) The scope of thought in Parmenides. *Classical Quarterly* 52: 207–219.

Curd, P. (2001) Why Democritus was not a skeptic. In Preus, A. (ed.) *Before Plato*. Albany, NY: State University of New York Press, pp. 149–169.

———. (1998/2004) *The Legacy of Parmenides: Eleatic Monism and Later Presocratic Thought*. Princeton: Princeton University Press. Corrected paperback edition with new introductory chapter, Las Vegas: Parmenides Publishing, 2004.

———. (2007) *Anaxagoras of Clazomenae: Fragments, Text and Translation with Notes and Essays*. Toronto: University of Toronto Press.

———. (2011) Divinity and intelligibility in Parmenides. In Riggiu, L., and Natali, C. (eds.) *Ontologia Scienza Mito: Per una Nuova Lettura di Parmenide*. Milan: Mimesis Edizione.

———. (2013a) The divine and the thinkable: Toward and account of the intelligible cosmos. *Rhizomata* 1 (2): 217–247.

———. (2013b) Where are love and strife? Incorporeality in Empedocles. In McCoy, J. (ed.) *Early Greek Philosophy: The Presocratics and the Emergence of Reason*. Washington, DC: Catholic University Press of America, pp. 113–138.

———. (2015) Thinking, supposing, and Physis in Parmenides. *Études Platoniciennes* (12): 1–17.

———. (2016) Powers, structure, and thought in Empedocles. *Rhizomata* 4: 55–79.

Dilcher, R. (2006) Parmenides on the place of mind. In King, R. A. H. (ed.) *Common to Body and Soul: Philosophical Approaches to Explaining Living Behaviour in Greco-Roman Antiquity*. Berlin: de Gruyter, pp. 31–48.

Graham, D. W. (2006) *Explaining the Cosmos*. Princeton. Princeton University Press.

Hussey, E. (2006) Parmenides on thinking. In King, R. A. H. (ed.) *Common to Body and Soul: Philosophical Approaches to Explaining Living Behaviour in Greco-Roman Antiquity*. Berlin: de Gruyter, pp. 13–30.

Ierodiakonou, K. (2005) Empedocles on colour and colour vision. *Oxford Studies in Ancient Philosophy* 29: 1–37.

Inwood, B. (1992) *The Poem of Empedocles: A Text and Translation with an Introduction*. Toronto: University of Toronto Press.

Laks, A. (1990) 'The more' and 'the full': On the reconstruction of Parmenides' theory of sensation in Theophrastus, 'De Sensibus', 3–4. *Oxford Studies in Ancient Philosophy* 8: 1–18.

———. (1993) Mind's crisis: On Anaxagoras' NOUS. *The Southern Journal of Philosophy* 31 (Supplement): 19–38.

———. (1999) Soul, sensation, and thought. In Long, A. A. (ed.) *The Cambridge Companion to Early Greek Philosophy*. Cambridge, MA: Cambridge University Press, pp. 250–270.

———. (2002) Les fonctions de l'intellect à propos, derechef, du *Nous* d' Anaxagore. *Methodos* 2: 7–31.

Lee, M. K. (2005) *Epistemology After Protagoras: Responses to Relativism in Plato, Aristotle, and Democritus*. Oxford: Clarendon Press.

Lesher, J. H. (1981) Perceiving and knowing in the Iliad and the Odyssey. *Phronesis* 26: 2–24.

———. (1983) Heraclitus' epistemological vocabulary. *Hermes* 111: 155–170.

———. (1984) Parmenides' critique of thinking: The 'poludêris elenchos' of Fragment 7. *Oxford Studies in Ancient Philosophy* 2: 1–30.

———. (1992) *Xenophanes of Colophon: Fragments*. Toronto: University of Toronto Press.
———. (1994) The emergence of philosophical interest in cognition. *Oxford Studies in Ancient Philosophy* 12: 1–34.
———. (1995) Mind's knowledge and powers of control in Anaxagoras DK B12. *Phronesis* 40: 125–142.
———. (2008) The humanizing of knowledge in Presocratic thought. In Curd, P., and Graham, D. (eds.) *The Oxford Handbook of Presocratic Philosophy*. New York: Oxford University Press, pp. 458–484.
Long, A. A. (1996) Parmenides on thinking being. *Proceedings of the Boston Area Colloquium in Ancient Philosophy* 12: 125–151.
Mackenzie, M. M. (1982) Parmenides' dilemma. *Phronesis* 27: 1–13.
Mansfeld, J. (1999) Parménide et Héraclite avaient-ils une théorie de la perception? *Phronesis* 44: 326–346.
Marmodoro, A. (2015) Anaxagoras's qualitative gunk. *British Journal for the History of Philosophy* 23: 402–422.
Morel, P. M. (1998) Démocrite: Connaissance et Apories. *Revue Philosophique de la France et de l'Étranger* 188: 145–163.
Mourelatos, A. P. D. (1971/2008) *The Route of Parmenides*. New Haven: Yale University Press. Second, expanded edition: Las Vegas: Parmenides Publishing, 2008.
O'Brien, D. (1981) *Democritus, Weight and Size: An Exercise in the Reconstruction of Early Greek Philosophy*. Leiden: Brill.
O'Keefe, T. (1997) The ontological status of sensible qualities for Democritus and Epicurus. *Ancient Philosophy* 17: 119–134.
Palmer, J. A. (2009) *Parmenides and Presocratic Philosophy*. Oxford: Oxford University Press.
Robbiano, C. (2006) *Becoming Being: On Parmenides' Transformative Philosophy*. Sankt Augustin: Academia Verlag.
Schofield, M. (1987) Coxon's Parmenides. *Phronesis* 32: 349–359.
Sedley, D. (1982) Two conceptions of vacuum. *Phronesis* 27: 175–193.
———. (2007) *Creationism and Its Critics in Antiquity*. Berkeley and London: University of California Press.
Sider, D. (2005) *The Fragments of Anaxagoras: Edited with an Introduction and Commentary*. 2nd edn. Sankt Augustin: Academia Verlag.
Sisko, J. E., and Weiss, Y. (2015) A fourth alternative in interpreting Parmenides. *Phronesis* 60: 40–59.
Taylor, C. C. W. (1999) *The Atomists: Leucippus and Democritus: Fragments and text*. Toronto, University of Toronto Press.
Tor, S. (2015) Parmenides' epistemology and the two parts of his poem. *Phronesis* 60: 3–39.
von Fritz, K. (1943) NOOS and NOEIN in the Homeric poems. *Classical Philology* 38: 79–93.
———. (1945) NOOS, NOEIN, and their derivatives in presocratic philosophy (excluding Anaxagoras) I. *Classical Philology* 40: 223–242.
———. (1946) NOOS, NOEIN, and their derivatives in presocratic philosophy (excluding Anaxagoras) II: The post-parmenidean period. *Classical Philology* 41: 12–34.
———. (1964) Der *NOUS* des Anaxagoras. *Archiv für Begriffsgeschichte* 9: 87–102.
Wright, M. R. (1981) *Empedocles: The Extant Fragments*. New Haven: Yale University Press.
———. (1990) Presocratic minds. In Gill, C. (ed.) *The Person and the Human Mind: Issues in Ancient and Modern Philosophy*. Oxford: Clarendon Press, pp. 207–225.

3

SOUL, PERCEPTION AND THOUGHT IN THE HIPPOCRATIC CORPUS

Hynek Bartoš

> Do we think with our blood, or air, or fire, or none of these, and does the brain provide our senses of hearing and sight and smell, from which come memory and opinion, and from memory and opinion which has become stable, comes knowledge?
> – (Plato, *Phaed.* 96b2–8, tr. Grube.)

Socrates in Plato's *Phaedo* mentions these theories within a brief reflection upon his early years when he was engaged in the "inquiry into nature" (περὶ φύσεως ἱστορία). He himself adheres to none of the theories, which only represent the intellectual background against which he introduces his own dualistic conception of soul and body and philosophical care of the soul. There is no doubt that questions concerning the physiological explanations of thought and perception were commonly discussed already before Plato, although our evidence of the debate is considerably limited. On the one hand, we have a number of fragments attesting that some of the most prominent Presocratic philosophers took part in the discussion (see the previous chapter by P. Curd). The main disadvantage of this body of evidence rests in the fact that it is only fragmentary, detached from the original contexts, often contaminated with later terminology and sometimes even misrepresented for the specific purposes of those who transmitted it. On the other hand, there are several anonymous texts in the Hippocratic corpus which elaborate upon the topics mentioned by Socrates and thus provide us with a relatively rich source of information. In comparison with the fragments of the philosophers, the medical texts provide non-fragmentary and first-hand evidence, within their original contexts and in the original wording, which makes them unique and especially valuable. I shall confine my attention to selected passages from the five most relevant Hippocratic texts, namely *On Flesh*, *On Regimen*, *On Diseases I*, *On Winds* and *On the Sacred Disease*,[1] assuming that even such a limited evidence is sufficient (a) to show that these medical texts perfectly correspond to the tradition reflected in the *Phaedo* and (b) to illustrate one particular feature of the medical tradition which played an important role in the formation of philosophy as a therapeutic discipline.

There are various ways to handle the pre-Platonic evidence in general and the Hippocratic in particular; some scholars (e.g. Manuli and Vegetti 1977) for instance distinguish between the encephalocentric, cardiocentric and hematocentric view on the seat of the mind. Although such a classification captures some of the most important features of the discussion, it does not cover the whole spectrum: some accounts do not fit these categories and some fit into more than one. As we shall see, some Hippocratic authors were indeed preoccupied with the project of identifying the seat of mind, others rather focus on processes which take place within the whole body or its complex parts (such as the chest, belly, head, limbs), on relations between various substances, and on numerous other issues which played, according to their view, an important role within faculties we would call "psychic" or "mental". Accordingly, instead of focusing solely on the question concerning localization of thought, I shall ask more generally in which terms the Hippocratic authors thought about matters related to cognition and perception, which types of arguments they used to substantiate their views, and for what purposes (cf. van der Eijk 2005, p. 125). With regard to the philosophical tradition starting with Democritus and Socrates, in which philosophy is often introduced as a specific therapy of the soul which surpasses the medical care, it is necessary to ask whether the Hippocratic authors under discussion have any definite concept of mind or soul and in which terms they make a distinction between mental and bodily processes. As for the bodily aspect, I shall also pay attention to the varying levels of anatomical knowledge they exhibit and to the role which anatomy plays in their accounts.

1. *On Flesh*

I start with the Hippocratic *On Flesh*, which is, as Jouanna remarks, "a unique, entirely preserved example that gives some idea of what the Greeks of the fifth and sixth centuries meant by 'inquiry into nature'" (Jouanna 1999, p. 392). Nevertheless, it is also important to highlight that the author makes a considerable effort to specify the limited focus of his account: he aims only at discussing those natural phenomena that are relevant to his specifically medical concern. This effort can be illustrated with the opening paragraph of the treatise:

> In this treatise I shall employ assumptions that are generally held – both those of my predecessors and my own – since it is necessary to establish a common starting point (κοινὴν ἀρχήν), if I wish to compose a treatise about medicine. About what is in the heavens (περὶ δὲ τῶν μετεώρων) I have no need to speak, except insofar as is necessary in order to explain how man and the other animals are formed and come into being, what

the soul is (ὅ τι ψυχή ἐστι), what health and sickness are, what in man is evil and what good, and where his death comes from.

(Carn.1 (Joly 188,1–10), tr. Potter)

The author announces here several important methodological guidelines that deserve our attention. First, he makes clear that he aims at writing a treatise in the field of medicine, which already implies some limitations. When he mentions "what is in the heavens", he not only sets boundaries to the relevance of astronomical and meteorological discussions for his own purposes (cf. Deichgräber 1935, p. 27), but also and more importantly he specifies the extent to which cosmological issues will be taken into consideration, for cosmology indeed plays an eminent role in his embryologic account (chapters 2–14). Second, he clearly differentiates between the ideas held by his predecessors and his own considerations. And third, he holds that it is necessary to build his account on one common principle or "starting point", which he announces as a general methodological requirement demanded in the field of medicine.

Of the topics announced in the second sentence of our passage, only the first one, i.e. the question of origins of men and other animals, is explicitly discussed later in the text (cf. Gundert 2000, p. 16; Craik 2015, p. 44). As for ψυχή, the author clearly indicates that it is one of the key notions he aims at explaining and it is therefore rather surprising that he never uses the term again. It seems that he exploits the term in a very broad, traditional sense, according to which ψυχή means simply "life", or perhaps "the principle of life".[2] One can therefore reasonably conclude that the animating principle is identified with the heat (θερμόν), which is introduced in the first sentence of chapter 2 (188,12–14): "I believe that what we call heat is in fact immortal, that it perceives all things, and sees, hears and knows (εἰδέναι) all that is and all that will be". In addition, the cold (ψυχρόν) is introduced in chapter 6 (192,9–193,9) as the counterpart and nutrition of the heat. All processes involved in embryology are directly or indirectly reducible to the effects of the heat (it burns the fatty, bakes the gluey, dries the moist and melts the cold stuffs) and the cold (it congeals the liquid stuffs), and especially to the relation between the two opposite qualities. Although both elements are distributed across the whole body, the greatest amount of heat is located in blood vessels and in the heart, which is said to be the hottest part in the human body (*Carn*.6 (192,12–14)). The brain, on the other hand, is singled out as "the *metropolis* of the cold and gluey" (*Carn*.4 (190,20–22)). Thus the concept of the heat (or more precisely the heat together with the cold as its nutritive counterpart) serves the Hippocratic author as the common starting point (κοινὴν ἀρχήν) of his complex embryologic account and stands, roughly, for the principle of life.

The claim that the heat "perceives all things, and sees, hears and knows all that is and all that will be" clearly indicates that the heat should also play some role in cognition, although no details are provided on this role. More attention is paid to sense perception, namely to hearing, smell, vision and speech, albeit this account focuses exclusively on the physical qualities of the related structures and the concept of heat is of little relevance there. For instance hearing is ascribed to the bone in the ear, which echoes the sounds coming from outside. The bone is "hard and dry like a stone" (*Carn*.15 (197,18)), which secures its acoustic qualities. The author explicitly denies that it would be the brain which echoes, for the brain, as he argues, is moist and moist things do not resonate: "There are many proofs that what is driest echoes best; and when a thing echoes best, we hear best" (*Carn*.15 (197,24–26)). Nevertheless, there is another role which he ascribes to the brain in his account of perception: "The brain, being itself moist, perceives the smell of dry things, by drawing the odour along with air through the bronchial tubes which are dry" (*Carn*.16 (198,2–4)).

The functioning of the eye is explained with reference to the transparent membranes that reflect the visible things. Even though the author is well aware of the connection between the eyes and the brain (*Carn*.17 (198,24–26)), he does not assign any specific role to the brain in the process of vision. As in the case of hearing, his explanation is based on purely mechanistic grounds: "it is in this transparency that light and all bright things reflect; through the agency of this reflection, then, the person sees" (*Carn*.17 (199,5–7)).

The account of speech in chapter 18, although highly original,[3] is no less mechanistic. In short, sounds are produced through the resonance of the head as the flow of breath comes out of the body, and articulated speech depends on the tongue which "encloses the air in the throat and touches the palate and the teeth" (*Carn*.18 (200,1–3)). There is no hint towards a relation between the articulated speech (which he calls διαλέγεται or διάλεξις) either with intelligence (not to say specifically human intelligence) or with the heat announced at the outset of the account as the bearer of intelligence.[4]

To conclude, the author has an extraordinary sense for methodological exposition, he makes remarkable claims concerning the specification and limitation of his topic, and distinguishes between the ideas he accepts from other authorities and his own opinions. He frequently uses first-hand empirical evidence and attests a considerable level of anatomical knowledge (cf. Craik 2015, pp. 45–46). Soul (ψυχή) seems to be identified with the heat (θερμόν), which serves as the main explanatory principle in the embryologic part of the account, but it is only vaguely connected with cognition and plays practically no role in sense perception. The capacities of hearing, smelling and seeing depend on the structure of the particular sense organs and its condition, especially in terms of dryness and moistness. The brain plays a considerable role in smelling but not in hearing, as the author explicitly argues, which suggests that there were also authorities who ascribed a more prominent role to the brain.

2. *On Regimen*

My second example is the Hippocratic *On Regimen*, which provides by far the richest evidence for using the term ψυχή in the medical literature of the Classical period and represents the most elaborated account of cognition and perception in all extant pre-Platonic literature. Before I turn to the concept of soul and related topics in the treatise, a few words must be said about its scope and methodological framework.

The treatise is devoted to dietetic therapy and prevention, and despite the remarkable variety of the topic it covers across its four books, it displays a strong unity in structural composition matched by "striking consistency and coherence in theoretical stance" (Craik 2015, p. 270). At the beginning of book I, the author posits that "whoever aspires to treat correctly of human regimen must first acquire knowledge and discernment of the nature of man in general" (*Vict*.I.2 (Joly-Byl 122,22–23)). He builds his account of the nature of man on two basic assumptions: (a) there are two essential factors of life, which stand in opposition, although they are complementary, namely the movement and the nutrition; and (b) health as the optimal condition of human organism depends on a balanced mixture of four elemental qualities: moist – dry – hot – cold. While the latter assumption is a commonplace in the dietetic as well as philosophical tradition (cf. Aristotle, *PA*.648b4–6), the first notion seems to be an original discovery of the author and his main contribution to the field of dietetics. These two assumptions are combined in the author's theory of fire and water introduced in chapters 3–4: fire represents the motion and is characterized by the hot and dry qualities, the water stands for nutrition and has moist and cold qualities, although "mutually too fire has the moist from water, for in fire there is moisture, and water has the dry from fire, for there is dryness in water also" (*Vict*.I.4 (126,21–23)).

This elemental theory has close parallels in *On Flesh*: on both accounts the heat and the cold are the principle opposites; the heat (fire) is nourished by the cold (water); and the most significant process in the embryonic development is the solidification and shaping of the moist and cold materials by the work of the heat (fire). "In a word, all things were arranged in the body, in fashion comfortable to itself, by fire", summarizes the author of *On Regimen*. A few lines later he specifies: "the hottest and strongest fire, which controls all things, ordering all things according to nature, imperceptible to sight or touch, wherein are soul, mind, thought, growth, motion, decrease, mutation, sleep, waking" (*Vict*.I.10 (5–6 and 17–19)). Yet, in contrast to *On Flesh* where the connection between the soul, the heat and capacities of thought and perception is only vague and underdeveloped, *On Regimen* offers a remarkably complex and particularized account of these topics, which is nevertheless in some details unparalleled, puzzling and even obscure.

The term ψυχή has a broad semantic range in the treatise. In general it can represent the principle of life which differentiates living beings from artificial objects (*Vict*.I.21 (140.5–10)). In the accounts on embryology and procreation (chapters 6–10 and 25–31) the term corresponds to the capacity of the seed and embryo to grow and develop, and from this point of view the relationship between the soul and the body is remarkably similar to the one between fire and water. In this context soul and body are inseparable from each other and it is often even difficult to see the difference between the two. In other contexts, in which the physiology of fully developed individuals is at focus, the soul denotes a kind of life-stuff which travels around the body and participates in various processes and activities, including locomotion, perception, cognition, imagination and dreaming. The difference between the soul and body is especially evident during sleep, as we can read in the opening chapter of book IV, in which the author explains why the "signs in sleep" (i.e. dreams) can be helpful in diagnosing health condition of the dreamer:

> For when the body is awake the soul is its servant, and is never her own mistress, but divides her attention among many things, assigning a part of it to each faculty of the body – to hearing, to sight, to touch, to walking, and to acts of the whole body; but the thought never enjoys independence. But when the body is at rest, the soul, being set in motion and awake, administers her own household, and of herself performs all the acts of the body. For the body when asleep does not perceive, but the soul when awake perceives all: sees what is visible, hears what is audible, walks, touches, feels pain, ponders, in her limited space. All the functions of body and of soul are performed by the soul during sleep.
> (*Vict*.IV.86 (218.4–12), tr. Jones – modified)

This passage has caused serious misunderstandings in modern scholarship, for often it has been read in isolation from the rest of the treatise and interpreted as evidence of a kind of dualism between the soul and body, akin to the accounts in Plato's *Phaedo* or Pindar's fragment 131b. Nonetheless, as a number of studies published recently reveal, there is no ontological dualism between the soul and body either in this passage or in the rest of the treatise (cf. Cambiano 1980, Bartoš 2009, van der Eijk 2011). The author aims here at explaining why a dietician should pay attention to images that are "seen" in dreams, although the eyes are shut. He neither suggests that the dreaming soul would leave the body, nor that dreams in general provide more relevant source of knowledge than the sense perception and wakeful thinking, nor that the activities performed by the soul in dreams would be more valuable or more actual than what the soul does together with the body in waking life. His point is that the dreaming soul, as it travels through the sleeping body, detects various pathological conditions at various places in the body and expresses this experience in the form of a dream (cf. *Vict*.II.71 (202.34–204,8)). Accordingly, anyone who can identify the relations between particular dream images and the condition of the body can also use the evidence of dreams for a dietetic diagnosis and accordingly also for an appropriate dietetic therapy. But this is only one way, among many, to diagnose the health condition and the specific account of soul and body presented here is evidently based on a more general analysis of the nature of man, which is presented in book I.

In brief, the author advocates a mereological approach to the human organism: each whole can be divided into parts and each part is a whole in respect to its constitutive parts. From the dietetical point of view it is essential that each individual organism (and each of its parts) can be viewed as a mixture of fire and water and accordingly diagnosed in terms of the four elemental qualities (all dietetic factors, no matter whether it is a foodstuff, an exercise, climate or weather condition, can be classified according to the capacity to dry, moisten, heat or cool the human body). Both body and soul are said to "have" a mixture of fire and water, the soul also has "parts of the body" and each part of the body has the mixture (cf. *Vict*. I,7 (130.18–19), and I,25 (124,6–7)). In terms of treatment, it does not make much difference whether the author diagnoses an imbalance in a particular part of the body or "a disturbance" of the soul (e.g. *Vict*. IV.88 (220.5–10); IV.93 (228,27 and 230,2)). As a rule the author recommends treatment of the whole organism and there is no difference between the therapy of the body and of the soul.[5] The continuity between the various bodily structures and processes and the capacities which can be ascribed to the soul is an essential presumption underlying all parts of the account.

Although the dreaming soul is said to enjoy some kind of independence during sleep, it should be recognized that this state is considerably different from awake cognition and perception. First, the individual sense organs[6] are inactive during sleep, which clearly indicates that dreaming is a state of sensory deficiency. And second, when describing dream images the author frequently speaks about the beliefs or assumptions of the one who dreams (e.g. *Vict*.IV.89 (220.23); IV.90 (228.3); IV.93 (228.26)), which can be opposed to the waking mind of "a wise man" (τὸν φρονέοντα) who reflects upon his dreams and uses them in the diagnosis of his healthy condition (*Vict*.II.71 (204.8–10); cf. IV.86 (218.3–4)). During the waking state the soul actively cooperates with the body, and if we want to learn more about this cooperation, we should focus on passages in which the author gives instructions on how to achieve the best possible condition of the soul.

The author provides two different (though complementary) typologies of human constitutions. In chapter 32 he introduces six bodily constitutions classified according to six different kinds of mixture of fire and water and different liabilities to various kinds of diseases. In a similar vein, in chapter 35 he attempts to discuss "what are called the intelligence of the soul (φρονήσιος ψυχῆς) and the want of it (ἀφροσύνης)" (*Vict*.I.35 (150.29)).[7] The author introduces seven types of soul that are defined by the quality of fire and water in the mixture. The classification is perfectly symmetrical: there is one ideally balanced and accordingly the most intelligent mixture (1), as well as two extreme mixtures which represent two kinds of madness, one dominated by water (4) and the other dominated by fire (7). In between these two extremities and the ideal constitution there are four intermediate compositions, two influenced by the predominance of the water (2 and 3) and two by the fire (5 and 6).

The numerous details given in chapter 35 clearly indicate that the soul dwells in and travels around the body and that its capacities depend on the condition of the body in two ways. First, the soul nourishes from the moisture of the body: for instance an inflammation of the blood can cause madness of the soul (*Vict*.I.35

(154.21–156.3)). And second, the activity of the soul depends on the condition of the passages through which it travels (*Vict*.I.35 (152.8–24)). As it moves through the passages, it falls upon the sensibles and *vice versa:* the sensibles fall upon the soul (*Vict*.I.35 (152.30–31)). Speed matters in both cases: various kinds of sense particles travel at different speed according to their nature (those of sight and hearing are quicker, those of touch slower) (*Vict.* I.35 (152.30–154.3)), and the speed of soul is different in each individual and at different conditions. When the sense particles and the soul come into collision, the soul is shaken and thus the act of sensation takes place (cf. *Vict*.I.35 (154.1)). The proportionality between the speed of the soul and the speed of the particles is the key parameter for the mental processes under discussion: it must be high enough to be able to register the sensory particles as they enter our sense organs, but slow enough to devote due attention to each of the sense stimuli (cf. *Vict*.I.35 (154.7–13)). The speed of the soul depends on two parameters: on the mixture of the soul (to which fire provides motion and swiftness and water provides nutrition and, at the same time, slows the motion down) and the condition of the passages (namely their throughput). If the movement of the soul is impaired by residue of nourishment or other substances blocking the passages, it is possible to improve this condition by appropriate moderation of the lifestyle.

In chapter 36, which closes the account of the nature of man in book I, the author introduces an additional factor concerning the passages of the soul which influences our psychic functions but cannot be moderated by dietetic means. He lists three pairs of opposite characteristics (irascibility and indolence, craftiness and simplicity, quarrelsomeness and benevolence) and claims that these dispositions of the soul do not depend on the soul's mixture but rather upon (a) "the nature of the vessels through which it (i.e. the soul) passes", (b) "that of the objects it encounters" and (c) "that of the things with which it mixes" (*Vict*.I.36 (156.25–26), cf. Jouanna 2012, 207). "It is accordingly impossible to change the above dispositions through regimen", he concludes, "for invisible nature (φύσιν . . . ἀφανέα) cannot be moulded differently" (*Vict*.I.36 (156.27–28)). It is unclear to what the "invisible nature" refers: some scholars (Heidel 1914, p. 162; Kapferer 1933–1940 (vol. I.3), p. 58, n. 122) suggest that it is the soul, while Joly (1967, p. 35, n. 1) opts for the passages of the soul; on both readings the argument unfortunately remains rather obscure. Nevertheless, it is obvious that the author's aim in chapter 36 is to make clear that there are some limits to the suggested dietetic care of soul, namely that dietetics cannot influence certain dispositions of individual character. As I discuss elsewhere (Bartoš 2015, pp. 217–222), in this and several other passages the author seems to deliberately avoid ethical and moral issues. Thus he represents medical dietetics, an approach that can be contrasted with other therapeutic approaches to the soul, such as the philosophical ethics of Democritus or Plato.

As for the anatomy in *On Regimen*, the author is extremely vague in his descriptions of the inner bodily structures, some vital organs are never mentioned, such as the heart or lungs, others are mentioned only as an edible part of animal bodies, such as the brain (*Vict*.I.49 (172.7 and 10)). It even seems that the author does not presuppose any interest in anatomy among his readers and, after all, anatomical details are of little importance for his holistic dietetic approach. It is therefore not surprising that it is extremely difficult, if not impossible, to identify the various passages (πόροι), circuits (περίοδοι) and outlets (διέξοδοι) mentioned in chapters 35 and 36, through which the soul travels and on which the soul capacities depend, with any specific anatomical structure. Nevertheless, at least some clues can be found within the embryological discussion in chapters 9–10. Outlets are mentioned for the first time in chapter 9, where we read that fire, which arranges the body according to nature, is enclosed in the central cavity and cannot make lasting outlets through the hard and dry parts of the body (*Vict*.I.9 (132.23)), but it can do so through the soft and moist parts. First the "greatest outlet" (μεγίστην διέξοδον) from the cavity is made by fire (*Vict*.I.9 (132.27), and then other outlets are made "for the breath and to supply and distribute nourishment" (*Vict*.I.9 (132.29)). Shortly after this claim the fire, shut up in the body, is said to make "three circuits (περιόδους τρισσάς)".[8] A few lines later (*Vict*.I.10 (134.13–16)) the same idea is repeated with an additional specification that the circuit towards "the hollows of the moist" relates to the power of the moon, and that the one towards the outer circumference and solid enclosure relates to the power of the stars. The middle circuit is bounded both within and without, and from the parallel passage in chapter 89 it can be deduced that this circuit relates to the power of the sun. We can conclude that the soul most probably moves around the body through the passages made by fire in three circuits (as mentioned in chapter 10), and if not through all of them, the middle circuit seems to be the best candidate to be identified as the circuit of soul (cf. Jouanna 2012, p. 205), as suggested by its middle position and its relation to the orbit of sun.[9] This arrangement evidently does not arise from anatomical investigations but it rather works on the general assumption that macrocosmic structures, and those of the human body in particular, correspond to the structure of the whole cosmos.[10]

3. *On Diseases I*

In the list of the possible causes of thinking in *Phaedo* we find blood at the prominent first place, which corresponds with the popularity of the blood hypothesis at that time. A well-known philosophical proponent of the theory is Empedocles, who wrote that "the blood around the heart in human is thought" (DK.31.B.105) and a number of Hippocratic authors also attests that similar theories were relatively widespread. Already in the two Hippocratic texts just discussed there is some link between blood and thinking: in *On Regimen* there are indications that the circuit of the soul can be related to the flow of blood (e.g. *Vict*.IV.90 (226,14)) and the "inflammation of blood" mentioned in chapter 35 (154,31) is the most obvious point of reference for such a link.[11] In *On Flesh* we read that the greatest amount of the heat is located in blood vessels and in the heart. Yet neither of the authors puts much weight on the role of the blood, for they draw on other explanatory principles (namely the heat and the fire) to which the condition of blood is subordinated. But there are other texts in the corpus that ascribe a more prominent role to the blood and deserve special attention, such as *On Winds*, which I discuss shortly, and *On Diseases I*.

The Hippocratic *On Diseases I* opens with a brief but dense methodological introduction into the art of medicine, presupposing that the most important medical question is: "whence all diseases in man arise" (*Morb*.I.1 (ed. and tr. Potter 98,3–4)). The author distinguishes between the diseases arising from internal factors, which are identified with bile and phlegm, and those arising from external factors, such as exertions, wounds, heat or cold. In chapter 30, within the discussion of a peculiar disease called "phrenetis", the author introduces blood as the cause of thought: "The blood in man contributes the greatest part to his intelligence (σύνεσις), some people say everything" (*Morb*.I.30 (176,23–178,1). Drawing on this assumption, he explains that, when bile is mixed with blood, it heats the blood and thus alters its normal consistency and motion. This may result in a state in which one "loses his wits (παρανοέει) and is no longer himself (οὐκ ἐν ἑωυτῷ ἐστιν)" (178,5–6). The author also remarks that these patients are similar to melancholics "in their derangement (κατὰ τὴν παράνοιαν)", "for melancholics too, when their blood is distorted by bile and phlegm, have this disease and are deranged – some even rage (μαίνονται)" (176,23–178,16).

The connection between blood and various forms of insanity is clearly suggested in this passage, although the topic is rather isolated within the treatise. No other passage speaks about intelligence (σύνεσις), and it is obvious that the author alludes here rather *ad hoc* to a common opinion in order to explain a particular "mental" disease. Nevertheless, this assumption obviously helps him in leading the causal chain up to the bile and phlegm, the principle causes of all internal diseases, as he aims to demonstrate. On one occasion (*Morb*. I.5 (106,23–25)) the author also uses the term *psuchē* in the Homeric meaning which has no "psychological" connotations and little to do with perception and cognition as such.

4. *On Winds*

Besides the blood and the heat, Socrates also mentioned the air as a strong candidate for the physiological explanation of thinking, which we have not discussed yet.[12] The idea that air is the chief cause of various vital functions, including cognition and perception, belonged to the most discussed hypotheses in the philosophical tradition preceding Plato (Anaximenes and Diogenes of Apollonia are the most remarkable proponents of the idea), and it was no less important in the medical discussions. The most eloquent medical exponent of the theory is the author of *On Winds*, who attests a strong commitment to the search for causal explanations and forcefully argues in favour of air as the most significant condition of life and the most important pathological factor.

In the opening paragraphs the author declares that "knowledge of the cause of a disease will enable one to administer to the body what things are advantageous"

(*Flat*.1 (Jouanna 104,1–2)) and promises to show in the consequent discourse "what this cause is" (*Flat*.2 (105,7–11)). In order to pave the way for his main thesis that the air (or "wind" or "breath")[13] is this cause, he introduces a remarkable argument based on common experience:

> So great is the need of wind for all bodies that while a man can be deprived of everything else, both food and drink, for two, three, or more days, and live, yet if the wind passages into the body be cut off he will die in a brief part of a day, showing that the greatest activities of a man are intermittent, for life is full of changes; but breathing is continuous for all mortal creatures, inspiration and expiration being alternate.
>
> (*Flat*.4 (107,12–108,7), tr. Jones)

This is, I believe, a convincing argument for establishing the air as a prerequisite for life, though it certainly cannot rule out other vital conditions. The author's aim is not only to substantiate that air "is the cause of life" but also and more importantly that it is "the cause of disease in the sick" (*Flat*.4 (107,11–12); cf. *Flat*.5 (108,14–109,2)). In the consequent chapters he draws on this assumption and suggests explanations of a number of "familiar maladies" in which, as he proudly announced at the end of his account, "the hypothesis has shown itself correct" (*Flat*.15 (124,16–17)).

Of these aetiologies the most significant for our discussion is the explanation the so-called sacred disease, commonly identified in modern scholarship with epilepsy. It is significant namely because it reveals some details about the author's view of cognition and perception, and because it exploits the theory of blood as the cause of *phronēsis* and thus provides valuable information (absent from other extant sources) about particular aspects of the notion. The key passage reads:

> To the same cause I attribute also the disease called sacred. . . . Now I hold that no constituent of the body in anyone contributes more to intelligence (ἐς φρόνησιν) than does blood. So long as the blood remains in its normal condition, intelligence too remains normal; but when the blood alters, the intelligence (ἡ φρόνησις) also changes. There are many testimonies that this is the case. . . . When sleep comes upon the body the blood is chilled . . . the eyes close; the intelligence alters (ἡ φρόνησις ἀλλοιοῦται), and certain other fancies (δόξαι) linger, which are called dreams (ἐνύπνια). Again, in cases of drunkenness, when the blood has increased in quantity, the soul (αἱ ψυχαί) and the thoughts in the soul (ἐν τῇσι ψυχῇσι φρονήματα) change; the ills of the present are forgotten, but there is confidence that the future will be happy. I could mention many other examples of an alteration in the blood producing and alteration of the intelligence.
>
> (*Flat*.14 (121,6–122,12), tr. Jones)

There are two remarkable issues in this passage to be highlighted: First, in connection with *phronēsis* the author refers to the concept of *psuchē*, which appears in no other part of his account. And second, despite his initial hypothesis according to which the air is the cause of life, he does not advance that the air is also the imminent cause of human thought. Instead, he introduces a version of the hematocentric theory, which he testifies with several examples. Then he turns back to his initial goal (i.e. to show that the air is the cause of the sacred disease) and explains that when an abundant portion of air mixes with all the blood throughout the body, the veins are blocked and the blood is prevented from passing on. "So greatly does a disturbance of the air disturb and pollute the blood", concludes the author and adds a recommendation for a therapy: one should take warming exercises which warm up the blood, the blood heats the air inside (τὰς φύσας) and accordingly the congestions of the blood are resolved. The disease ends "when the blood has re-established itself, and calm has arisen in the body" (*Flat*.14 (122,16–124,10)).

There is a causal chain in this account which connects the air with human intelligence: the air influences everything and is the main pathogenic factor in all diseases. Among other things, air influences the condition of the blood, and the blood has the power to influence our thoughts. Thus the hematocentric hypothesis is auxiliary to the main thesis in explanation of the sacred disease,[14] for which it is significant that it disturbs thought localized to the soul.

5. *On the Sacred Disease*

The aetiology of epilepsy, which plays only a cameo role in *On Winds*, it is the main topic in *On the Sacred Disease*, the only Hippocratic text entirely devoted to a disease which manifests itself in specifically psychic or mental dysfunctions. The primary aim of the author is to prove that the so-called sacred disease is no more divine than other diseases, that it has a natural cause and, accordingly, it is curable by the same means as other diseases. For our purposes it is important that in *On the Sacred Disease*, like in *On Winds*, the explanation of epilepsy also includes an outline of a general 'psychology'. Although the author never mentions the term *psuchē* or any equivalent of it, he has a complex theory which comprises the cognitive and perceptive capacities as well as emotions and localizes them into a single organ: the brain.

Other Hippocratic authors occasionally mention the connection between the brain and individual sense organs,[15] some presuppose that motor functions and speech are correlated to the brain,[16] but apart from *On the Sacred Disease* there is little extant evidence for a developed encephalocentric theory in the Hippocratic corpus as well as in other pre-Platonic documents.[17] This Hippocratic treatise is therefore a unique and extremely important document of a view, which Plato's Socrates counted, obviously not without reason, among the most valuable hypotheses explaining the nature of mental processes.

The complexity of the account of brain in *On the Sacred Disease* can be most conveniently illustrated in the following passage in chapter 14:

> Men ought to know that from the brain, and from the brain only, arise our pleasures, joys, laughter and jests, as well as our sorrows, pains, griefs and tears. Through it, in particular, we think and ponder (τούτῳ φρονεῦμεν μάλιστα καὶ νοέομεν), see, hear, and distinguish the ugly from the beautiful, the bad from the good, the pleasant from the unpleasant.... It is the same thing which makes us mad or delirious (μαινόμεθα καὶ παραφρονέομεν), inspires us with dread and fear, whether by night or by day, brings sleeplessness, inopportune mistakes, aimless anxieties, absent-mindedness, and acts that are contrary to habit. These things that we suffer all come from the brain, when it is not healthy, but becomes abnormally hot, cold, moist, or dry, or suffers any other unnatural affection to which it was not accustomed. Madness (μαινόμεθα) comes from its moistness.
>
> (*Morb.Sacr.*14 (Jouanna 25,12–26,13), tr. Jones (modified))

According to this passage, the brain is the only source of human emotions and the main organ by means of which sensation and cognition come about. Functioning of this organ depends on qualities like hot, cold, moist and dry. As long as the brain is still and undisturbed by a surplus of any of these qualities, it fulfils its task properly (*Morb.Sacr.*14 (27,3–4). If these conditions are lost, various pathological processes can occur, including epileptic seizures. The author operates on the assumption that there are two basic bodily constitutions (the phlegmatic and the bilious) and that these two prominent bodily humours can disturb the brain most significantly: the phlegm can make the brain excessively cold and the bile can bring to it excessive hotness.[18] As for the sacred disease, it is presupposed that it "affects the naturally phlegmatic, but does not attack the bilious", from which the author infers that this disease, like the two bodily constitutions, is hereditary and, accordingly, it is "no more divine than any other" (*Morb.Sacr.*2 (10,4–11,5)). These observations also indicate that the disease can be related with the phlegm and the corresponding qualities, i.e. coldness and moistness. The author therefore suggests that the diseased brain is "unnaturally moist, and flooded with phlegm" (*Morb.Sacr.*11 (21,10–11)), a claim which can be hardly demonstrated directly. But the author develops a sophisticated argument based on comparative anatomy and animal dissection. First, he makes the cases that human and animal brains have the same structure and position in respect to other organs (*Morb.Sacr.*3 (11,6–12,9)), and then he shows that other animals suffer from the same disease and that their brain is excessively moist (*Morb.Sacr.*11 (21,15–22,2)).

The author applies to this specific disease a widely shared concept of health, commonly defined as a balance of opposite elementary qualities. Its application has important therapeutic consequences, which are summarized in the concluding chapter of the treatise:

> So the physician must know how, by distinguishing the opportune moment for individual things, he may assign to one thing nutriment and growth, and to another diminution and harm.... Whoever knows how to cause in men by regimen moist or dry, hot or cold, he can cure this disease also, if he distinguish the opportune moments for useful treatment.
> (*Morb. Sacr.* 18 (32,7–33,3))

The opportune moment for the cure is important especially with regard to the changes of winds. The time when one wind ceases and another commences is of crucial importance, for at that time epileptic attacks occur most frequently (*Morb. Sacr.*13 (23,6–9)), which is explained by the effects of the winds to the elemental qualities in the human body (23,9–25,11) and thus fits perfectly to the dietetic framework of the treatise and its therapeutic aims.

Apart from the power to cool, heat, dry and moisten, there is another essential capacity of the air, which is less consensual in the dietetic tradition and, after all, has little relevance to the therapeutic goals, though it plays an important role in the encephalocentric theory. The author presupposes that air is the original source of "consciousness" (φρόνησις), a concept which he presupposes in chapter 4, clearly spells out in chapter 16 and fully exploits in his argumentation against the rival views in chapter 17. In chapter 4 he asserts that a greater part of our breath is inhaled by the veins which distribute it all over the body; the body is thus cooled and the air is exhaled. How this intake and outtake of breath into veins happens is not specified, apart from the laconic claim that "the breath cannot rest, but moves up and down" and that veins are the "vents" (ἀναπνοαί) of our body (*Morb.Sacr.*4 (12,11–12)). The author is more concerned with the consequent distribution of the air around the body and pays special attention to the situation when the distribution is suspended. When a man is lying or seated so that his veins are compressed, "a numbness immediately seizes him" in that part of the body where the veins were blocked. Although this phenomenon on its own right can be explained in various ways, most obviously with reference to blood,[19] our author claims that the loss of sensitivity is caused by the stoppage of the air (*Morb.Sacr.*4 (12,18–19): "the air cannot pass through the vein").[20] This indicates that the author ascribes to the air a special function, which is nevertheless remarkably different from what we find in *On Winds*.

A full-blown account of the pneumatic theory, including its relevance to the encephalocentric thesis, is introduced in chapter 16:

> For these reasons I believe that the brain is the most powerful part in a human being. So long as it is healthy, it is the interpreter (ἑρμηνεύς)[21] of what comes to the body from the air. Consciousness (φρόνησιν) is provided by the air. The eyes, ears, tongue, hands and feet carry out what the brain knows (γινώσκῃ), for throughout the body there is a degree of consciousness (φρονήσιος) proportionate to the amount of air which it receives. As far as understanding (σύνεσιν) is concerned,[22] the brain

is also the part that transmits this, for when a man draws in a breath it first arrives at the brain, and from there it is distributed over the rest of the body, having left behind in the brain its best portion and whatever contains consciousness (φρόνιμόν) and thought (γνώμην). For if the air went first to the body and subsequently to the brain, the power of discerning thinking (διάγνωσιν) would be left to the flesh and to the blood vessels; it would reach the brain in a hot and no longer pure state but mixed with moisture from the flesh and from the blood so that it would no longer be accurate. I therefore state that the brain is the interpreter of consciousness.

(*Morb.Sacr.*16–17 (29,4–30,4), tr. van der Eijk 2005, p. 126)

This passage is extraordinarily rich in terminology related to cognition and it is questionable whether all the expressions used here are taken as more or less synonyms, as Jones (1923, p. 179, n. 1) and Jouanna (2003, pp. LVI and 121–122) believe, or whether there is some further distinction among them. Van der Eijk (2005, p. 127) suggests, and I follow him in this, that the author at least differentiates between consciousness (φρόνησις), which is provided by the air and which can be found throughout the body, and "understanding (σύνεσις)", which is restricted to the brain and related to the "discerning thinking (διάγνωσις)".

More can be learned about the distinction between the processes in the brain and in the rest of the body from the author's polemic against two rival views which localize thinking and consciousness either to the diaphragm or to the heart. The first view is rejected as a superficial etymology, and although the author admits that some kind of a sudden reaction happens in this organ when an unexpected emotion occurs, this has nothing to do with thought and intelligence (φρονεῖν τε καὶ νοεῖν) (*Morb.Sacr.*17 (30,4–10)). As for the second notion, "some people say that the heart is the organ with which we think, and that it feels pain and anxiety". "But it is not so", objects the author, for the heart "is merely convulsed (σπᾶται), as is the diaphragm, only more so" (*Morb.Sacr.*17 (30,17–31,1)). What happens in both organs is a simple mechanical reaction to an excitement, tension or pain in the body. Due to the specific anatomic features of the two organs (the diaphragm has a wider extent than any other organ, it is thin and contains no cavities; the heart has direct connection with the rest of the body via the veins which extend to it), the author concludes that these organs "are best endowed with feeling (αἰσθάνεταί τε μάλιστα)". Nevertheless, "neither of them has any share of intelligence (φρόνησις), but it is the brain which is the cause of all these things" (*Morb.Sacr.*17 (30,6–8)).

The claim that neither heart nor diaphragm has any share of intelligence is a bit surprising with regard to the view that "throughout the body there is a degree of consciousness". There are various degrees of consciousness, depending on the quality as well as quantity of the air, for instance if the air becomes hot and mixed with moisture, thinking can "no longer be accurate". The point of the author's argumentation is that brain receives the air first, still in its pure state and containing "its best portion". Accordingly, the degree of consciousness is at maximum in the brain, and therefore this is the organ in which we think "in particular" or "for the most part" (μάλιστα). What singles out brain as the chief cause of all cognition and perception is the most prominent access to the air and the capacity called φρόνησις which can be understood as a kind of notification (or conscious reflection, cf. Hüffmeier 1961, p. 60) of the processes which take place in our body.

The brain in the author's conception plays both an active and a passive role. On the one hand, some kind of intelligence pre-exists in the air before it enters our body (and the brain in particular): it is the source of human thinking and from this point of view brain only passively receives what the air brings in. On the other hand, the brain is also said to be the "interpreter" (ἑρμηνεύς) and distributor of the understanding (σύνεσις) over the body, which certainly is a distinguished activity ("the eyes, ears, tongue, hands and feet carry out what the brain knows").

In summary, there are several remarkable features of this particular Hippocratic account relevant to our discussion. First, the author suggests a complex physiological explanation of capacities and processes (such as thinking, perception, emotions, motor functions) which other authors, especially in the philosophical tradition, associate with the soul. Second, he singles out the brain as the organ responsible for *all* these capacities and thus provides a unique evidence of a complex encephalocentric theory.[23] Third, he displays a remarkable anatomical knowledge which plays a crucial role in his expositions, even though some notions, especially on the courses of the veins in the body, "were evidently neither based on, nor checked by, dissection" (Lloyd 1979, p. 157). In any case, the author seems to believe that his readers will pay special attention to notions presented as anatomical facts derived from first-hand experience. And lastly, his explanation of the functions of brain is based on a theory of air as the source of intelligence, which is accepted as initial hypothesis and never put in question.

6. Conclusion

The Hippocratic evidence on the nature of cognition and perception closely corresponds with the picture presented in the *Phaedo* passage. Moreover it provides a number of details which are unattested in the philosophical doxography and can be thus helpful in reconstructing the pre-Platonic history of the discussion. As a matter of fact, there is no common theory of the cognitive processes in the medical evidence: some authors put stress on the role of breath, or blood or heat, others accent some specific organ or bodily structure; some draw on a profound knowledge of anatomy, others are relatively careless to anatomical details; some cover the cognition and perception with a concept of *psuchē* while others use the term unspecifically or not at all. Nevertheless, there is an important common feature present in all these accounts which should not be overlooked, especially when discussing the relevance of the medical tradition to philosophy.

Therapy is the chief goal of the Hippocratic accounts and all authors (possibly except *On Flesh*) express their views on the nature of thought and perception within a debate of specific pathological states which are in principle curable. As a rule, they presuppose that the same perceptive qualities, according to which patients are diagnosed and by means of which patients can be cured (for instance the wet-dry-hot-cold), are also relevant to the theories of human thought and perception (for instance in terms of the qualities of the blood, air or brain). Their particular theories bridge the gap between the symptoms of the psychic disorders and the suggested therapy, which was in principle dietetic and applicable to body as well as soul, if this polarity was distinguished at all. They all take for granted a kind of continuity between mental processes on the one hand and the bodily states on the other. This continuity, including the continuity between thought and perception, is a fundamental presupposition in the medical tradition (which was centuries later eloquently advocated by Galen in *The Powers of the Soul Follow the Mixtures of the Body* – see Chapter 13 by J. Hankinson).

Against this tradition, which had respect and authority throughout antiquity, it was the task of philosophy to elaborate such a conception of soul (and accordingly cognition and perception), which would not only supersede in consistency and detail the accounts of previous physicists and physicians but also vindicate the superiority of philosophy over medicine, especially in questions concerning the therapy of soul. There is no doubt that there were philosophers who faced this challenge (most notably Plato and Aristotle) and handled it each in his peculiar way.[24]

Notes

1 For the purposes of this chapter it is, I believe, justified to rely on the suggestions made by recent authorities and assume that all the texts I am going to discuss were written during Plato's life or shortly before. See Jouanna (1999) and Craik (2015).
2 Modern scholars usually translate ψυχή in this passage as "soul" (Jones), "l' âme" (Littré, Joly), "Seele" (Deichgräber), although Craik's (2015, p. 44) "animation" is probably a more appropriate rendering.
3 Jouanna (1999, p. 281) praises this chapter as "the earliest account of the physiology of voice".
4 It is noteworthy that also speech is ranked among the senses. Cf. *Vict*.I.23 (mentioned previously).
5 There is one remarkable exception from this rule: in ch. 61 (184.8–14) the author suggests that a certain kind of dream indicates "a disturbance of the soul arising from thinking (ψυχῆς τινα τάραξιν σημαίνει ὑπὸ μερίμνης)" and recommends to "have a rest" (or "leave off work", ῥᾳθυμῆσαι) and to turn the soul "to the contemplation (πρὸς θεωρίας) of comic things, if possible, if not, to such other things as will bring most pleasure when looked at". This therapeutic suggestion represents a genuine piece of psychotherapy unprecedented in other Hippocratic treatises. Cf. Gundert 2000, p. 25, n. 69; Bartoš 2015, pp. 199–201.
6 Individual sense organs are enumerated in ch. 23 (140,17–23), in which the author aims at illustrating that number seven is especially important in understanding human cognition and sensation. First he says that there are seven figures (σχημάτων), probably the seven vowels of the Greek alphabet, by means of which men acquire

knowledge (γνῶσις), and "seven figures (σχημάτων)" by which men receive sensations (αἴσθησις): there is hearing by which we receive sounds, sight for the visible, nostril for smell, tongue for pleasant or unpleasant tastes, mouth for speech, body for touch, and "passages outwards and inwards" for hot or cold breath (πνεύματος). "Through these", concludes the author, "comes knowledge (γνῶσις)".

7 The expression *phronēsis* is used here in a rather broad sense, for it stands, as we shall see shortly, for a complex psychological agenda including cognition, perception, imagination and memory.
8 According to the manuscript reading we should speak more literally about three "groups of circuits" (*Vict*.I.9 (134,13–16): περιόδους τρισσάς... αἱ μὲν... αἱ δὲ... αἱ δέ). But Jouanna (1998, pp. 163–164) convincingly argues that only three circuits should be presupposed here, in which I follow him.
9 Thinkers like Heraclitus (DK.22.B.67a) and Alcmaeon (DK.24.A.1) have been reported to draw an analogy in their accounts between sun and soul.
10 The text of *On Regimen* provides the most detailed pre-Platonic account of the micro-macrocosm analogy, which is based on the concept of *mimēsis* and has close parallels (as well as dissimilarities) both with Plato's account (cf. Sisko 2006) and with the fragments and testimonies of the early Pythagoreans (cf. Bartoš 2015, pp. 111–164).
11 Cf. Hüffmeier (1961), p. 76.
12 It is noteworthy that on the list of the seven ways "by which men receive sensations (αἴσθησις)" in *Vict*.I.23 (140,17–23) we also find "the passages for hot or cold breath", which suggests that also the breath has some function in perception, although this idea is not further elaborated elsewhere in the text.
13 Although in ch. 3 (105,14–106,2) he defines that πνεῦμα in the living bodies should be called φῦσαι, while the wind outside the bodies ἀήρ, this distinction is not maintained throughout the treatise. Moreover, other expression for wind and air are also occasionally used (e.g. ἄνεμος and ἀτμός). Cf. Craik (2015), pp. 98–99.
14 Cf. *Flat*.15 (124,11–13) where the author summarizes that winds are the most active agents during all diseases, while "all other things are but secondary and subordinate causes".
15 E.g. *Carn*.16 and 17 (mentioned previously); *Loc.Hom*.2; *Salubr*.8.
16 Cf. *Coac*.489 (ed. and tr. Potter 226,24–27): "Persons whose brain is shaken and who suffer pain, either as the result of blows or otherwise, immediately fall down, loose their speech, can neither see nor hear, and in most cases succumb".
17 The most famous proponent of the view is Alcmaeon of Croton, who is also often mentioned as the authority which influenced our Hippocratic author (Jouanna 2003, pp. LXII–LXX).
18 Accordingly, two kinds of mental disturbances can be distinguished and diagnosed (*Morb.Sacr*.15 (27,7–10)).
19 Cf. Empedocles DK.31.B.105; the Hippocratic *Flat*.14 (mentioned previously), and *Virg*.1 (Littré VIII,466–470).
20 It is noteworthy that one of the main manuscripts (θ) reads αἷμα instead of πνεῦμα.
21 Lo Presti (2010, pp. 147–180) makes the case that in the fifth century BCE the verb ἑρμηνεύειν means "to express" rather than "to interpret", and accordingly it should be thus understood also in our passage.
22 For a considerably different reading of this phrase see Solmsen 1961, p. 156, n. 39.
23 The author is probably the first who claimed that brain is the organic centre of not only cognition and sensation (cf. Alcmaeon DK.24.A 5 and A 8) but also of emotions and motivity (cf. Miller 1948, p. 179).
24 I am grateful to Ján Országh and John Sisko for valuable comments on previous drafts of this chapter, which is an outcome of a research project GAČR 13–00800S.

Bibliography

Bartoš, H. (2009) Soul, seed and palingenesis in the Hippocratic 'De Victu'. *Apeiron* 42 (1): 1–31.

———. (2014) The Concept of 'Mimēsis' in the Hippocratic 'De Victu'. *The Classical Quarterly* 64 (2): 542–557.

———. (2015) *Philosophy and Dietetics in the Hippocratic on Regimen: A Delicate Balance of Health*. Leiden and Boston: Brill.

Byl, S. (2002) Le vocabulaire de l'intelligence dans le chapitre 35 du livre I du traité du Régime. *Revue de philologie* 76: 217–224.

Cambiano, G. (1980) Une interprétation 'matérialiste' des rêves: Du Régime IV. In Grmek, M. D. (ed.) *Hippocratica: Actes du Colloque hippocratique de Paris (4–9 septembre 1978)*. Paris: CNRS, pp. 87–96.

Craik, E. M. (2015) *The 'Hippocratic' Corpus: Content and Context*. London and New York: Routledge.

Deichgräber, K. (1935) *Hippokrates Über Entstehung und Aufbau des menschlichen Körpers*. Leipzig and Berlin: Teubner.

Eijk, P. J. van der (2005) *Medicine and Philosophy in Classical Antiquity: Doctors and Philosophers on Nature, Soul, Health and Disease*. Cambridge, MA: Cambridge University Press.

———. (2011) Modes and degrees of soul-body relationship in 'On Regimen'. In Perilli, L., Brockmann, C., Fisher, K. D., and Roselli, A. (eds.) *Officina Hippocratica*. Berlin: Walter de Gruyter, pp. 255–270.

Grube, G. M. A. (tr.) (1997) Plato: Phaedo. In Cooper, J. M. (ed.) *Plato: Complete Works*. Indianapolis: Hackett, pp. 49–100.

Gundert, B. (2000) Soma and psyche in Hippocratic medicine. In Wright, J. P., and Potter, P. (eds.) *Psyche and Soma: Physicians and Metaphysicians on the Mind-Body Problem from Antiquity to Enlightenment*. Oxford: Clarendon Press, pp. 13–35.

Heidel, W. A. (1914) Hippocratea I. *Harvard Studies in Classical Philology* 25: 139–203.

Hüffmeier, F. (1961) Phronesis in den Schriften des Corpus Hippocraticum. *Hermes* 89: 51–84.

Joly, R. (1960) *Recherches sur le traité pseudo-hippocratique Du régime*. Paris: Les Belles Lettres.

———. (ed. and tr.) (1967) *Hippocrate: Du régime*. Paris: Les Belles Lettres.

———. (1978) *Hippocrate: Des lieux dans l'homme; Du système des glandes; Des fistules; Des hémorroïdes; De la vision; Des chairs; De la dentition*. Paris: Les Belles Lettres.

Joly, R., and Byl, S. (eds. and tr.) (2003) *Hippocrate: Du régime*. 2nd edn. CMG 1.2.4. Berlin: Akademie-Verlag.

Jones, W. H. S. (ed. and tr.) (1923) *Hippocrates*. Vol. 2. LCL 148. Cambridge, MA: Harvard University Press.

———. (ed. and tr.) (1931) *Hippocrates*. Vol. 4. LCL 150. Cambridge, MA: Harvard University Press.

Jouanna, J. (1988) *Hippocrate: Des vents; De l'art*. Paris: Les Belles Lettres.

———. (1998) L'interpretation des rêves et la théorie micro-macrocosmique dans le traité Hippocratique 'Du Regime': semiotique et mimesis. In Fisher, K. D., Nickel, D., and Potter, P. (eds.) *Text and Translation*. Leiden: Brill, pp. 161–174.

———. (1999) *Hippocrates*. Translated by M. B. DeBevoise. Baltimore: Johns Hopkins University Press.

———. (ed. and tr.) (2002) *Hippocrate: La nature de l'homme*. CMG 1.1.3. Berlin: Akademie-Verlag.
———. (2003) *Hippocrate: La maladie sacrée*. Paris: Les Belles Lettres.
———. (2012) *Greek Medicine from Hippocrates to Galen: Selected Papers*. Translated by N. Allies. Edited with a preface by P. van der Eijk. Leiden: Brill.
———. (2013) The typology and aetiology of madness in ancient Greek medical and philosophical writing. Translated by C. Wazer. In Harris, W. V. (ed.) *Mental Disorders in the Classical World*. Leiden: Brill, pp. 97–118.
Kapferer, R. (tr.) (1933–1940) *Hippokrates: Sämtliche Werke*. 3 vols. Stuttgart, Germany: Hippokrates Verlag Marquardt and Cie.
Littré, E. (ed. and tr.) (1839–1861) *Oeuvres complètes d'Hippocrate*. 10 vols. Paris: J. B. Baillière.
Lloyd, G. E. R. (1979) *Magic, Reason and Experience*. Cambridge, MA: Cambridge University Press.
Lo Presti, R. (2010) The matter of sense, the sense of matter: What does the Brain-hermeneus perform according to On the Sacred Disease. *Rhizai* 7: 147–180.
Manuli, P., and Vegetti, M. (1977) *Cuore, sangue, cervello: biologia e antropologia nel pensiero antico*. Milan: Episteme Editrice.
Miller, H. W. (1948) A Medical Theory of Cognition. *Transactions and Proceedings of the American Philological Association* 79: 168–183.
———. (1959) The Concept of Dynamis in De victu. *Transactions and Proceedings of the American Philological Association* 90: 147–164.
Potter, P. (ed. and tr.) (1988) *Hippocrates*. Vol. 5. LCL 472. Cambridge, MA: Harvard University Press.
———. (ed. and tr.) (1995) *Hippocrates*. Vol. 8. LCL 482. Cambridge, MA: Harvard University Press.
———. (ed. and tr.) (2010) *Hippocrates*. Vol. 9. LCL 509. Cambridge, MA: Harvard University Press.
Sisko, J. E. (2006) Cognitive circuitry in the Pseudo-Hippocratic 'Peri Diaites' and Plato's 'Timaeus'. *Hermathena* 180: 5–17.
Solmsen, F. (1961) Greek philosophy and the discovery of the nerves. *Museum Helveticum* 18: 150–197.

4

PLATO'S GUIDE TO LIVING WITH YOUR BODY

Russell E. Jones and Patricia Marechal

1. Soul, with and without body

Plato famously partitions the soul. In the *Republic*, the soul is divided three ways, into reason, spirit, and appetite. When the soul is in its best condition – when it is virtuous – reason is in charge, using spirit as its ally to direct and control appetite. When the soul is disordered, though, appetite comes to dominate the soul, usurping reason's proper role. Now, there are many things that tend to perish when disordered: organs and even whole bodies fail because of disease, artifacts made of metal are destroyed when rust disorders them. Plato uses this observation, together with his conception of what it is for a soul to be disordered, to construct an argument that the soul is immortal.[1] Disease and rust are the proper evils of bodies and metal artifacts, respectively, the things that disorder and destroy them. Likewise, vice is the proper evil of the soul. But souls respond differently to their proper evil than do bodies and metal artifacts, for souls that have been disordered by vice appear no closer to perishing than souls that are well ordered. Since even the proper evil of the soul does not destroy it, Plato has Socrates conclude that it is likely that the soul is indestructible.

Suppose we agree at this point that Socrates has given us a good reason to think that souls are indestructible.[2] Still, we will want an *explanation* of this fact. What makes souls different from other composites that are subject to decomposition? Socrates' answer is that souls aren't really composite, at least not in their "truest nature" (611b1). But how can he think such a thing, given that he's spent much of the dialogue developing an account of the tripartite soul? Socrates tells us quite clearly: Earlier, he and his companions were not studying the soul "as it is in truth" (611b10) and "as it is when pure" (611c2), but as it is "when it is mutilated by its partnership with the body and by other evils" (611b11–c1). They gave an account of its condition and parts as it is "in a human life" (612a5). But being in a human life is not essential to the soul and examining the soul as it is in human life will not supply an explanation of its immortality. For that, we need to examine its essential nature. And when we do, Socrates thinks, we'll find that the soul doesn't admit of "great variety and dissimilarity and differences from itself" (611b2–3). In other words, we'll discover that the soul in its true nature is simple.³

Socrates doesn't pursue this line of thought in the *Republic*; he is content to have given an account of the embodied soul. But he does indicate where we should begin if we are going to give a fuller account of the true nature of the soul: We must look to "its love of wisdom, and consider what it grasps and longs to associate with, because it is akin to what is divine, deathless, and always is, and we must consider what sort of thing it would become if, putting in all its effort, it lifted itself by its desire out" of its present condition (611d8–e3). Moreover, it is clear enough, in broad outline at least, how the account will go. The soul, in its pure form, apart from the body, is simple and unchanging, akin to those things that are most real and are, most properly speaking, the objects of knowledge. And what the soul, in its pure form, wants is to grasp those things, to know them. When, however, the soul is embodied, the body changes the soul, dividing it and posing other ends than knowledge to it. The embodied soul is complex, is attracted to diverse and sometimes incompatible ends, and so can be diverted from the single-minded pursuit of its proper end of knowledge. When an embodied soul is in excellent condition, it imperfectly approximates the soul's true nature, minimizing the force of the attractions that result from its embodiment. The account of virtue in the *Republic* is an account of this very condition, the approximation of the embodied soul to its true nature as a pure soul. But the embodied soul can only ever approximate to that nature.

A similar picture emerges in the *Phaedo*, though of a bipartite rather than tripartite soul. Here, however, the partition in the soul may be less obvious. Socrates often speaks as if he were simply contrasting the soul with the body. In fact, in this context, he is contrasting experiences that are proper to the soul in its own right with those that it has because it is embodied. So when Socrates describes the true philosopher as someone who turns away from the body towards the soul – in so doing turning away from pleasures of food, drink, sex, and the like – he explains that such a person does not care about those pleasures that come "through the body" (65a7). Socrates is not saying that some pleasures, pains, and desires are experienced by the soul, and others by the body, but rather that some of the pleasures experienced by the soul are experienced because of its association with the body.[4]

As in the *Republic*, Socrates insists in the *Phaedo* that one part of the soul must rule, at least if the soul is to be well ordered. Though he sometimes talks only of "the soul" ruling, he has in mind the "wise soul" (94b5), the soul considered most properly in its own nature.

> Well then, doesn't it now seem to us that the soul . . . takes command over all those elements of which it is said to be composed and opposes nearly all of them throughout the whole of life, lording it over them in every way, sometimes disciplining them more harshly and painfully,

following the prescriptions of the crafts of physical training and medicine, and other times doing so more gently, whether by threatening or admonishing, speaking with desires or impulses or fears as if it were one thing and they another? Surely it's just as Homer wrote in the Odyssey, where he says of Odysseus:

> Beating his breast, he reproved his heart, saying:
> "Steady, my heart; you once bore worse than this."
> (94c9–e1)[5]

The *Phaedo* is strikingly different from the *Republic* in one crucial respect, though. In the *Republic*, Plato remained content to have Socrates gesture towards the true nature of the soul, briefly mentioning a few of its qualities. It is largely left to us to piece together how the excellent state of the embodied soul – the topic that dominates the discussion – is in fact the best approximation in this life of the soul's true nature. Certainly we have resources for doing so, especially in the character of the philosopher-rulers. But Socrates doesn't linger on the matter. In the *Phaedo*, by contrast, Socrates takes up the matter of the soul's true nature in detail, contrasting it with the embodied soul. His explicit recommendation is that we aim, even while embodied, to make our souls approximate their own true nature to the greatest possible degree. And so he here focuses much more on that true nature at which we should aim.

This focus is evident throughout the *Phaedo*, but nowhere more so than in the so-called Affinity Argument (78b4–84b8). There Socrates argues for what he claims in the *Republic*: that the soul, taken on its own, is "akin" to "what is pure, ever existing, deathless, and the same" (79d2). He carries on his list of characteristics: "The soul is most like the divine, deathless, intelligible, simple, indestructible, always the same as itself" (80b1–3). As such, these are the things it desires to be in contact with:

> being akin to [what is pure], it always comes to be with it whenever it is by itself and can do so; then it ceases from its wandering and is always the same as itself, being in contact with things of the same kind; and its experience is called "wisdom," isn't it?
> (79d3–7)

While the argument is complex and difficult, we want to emphasize two points that are relatively clear: first, that he thinks that the soul, just taken on its own, is simple in the way suggested by the *Republic*, lacking parts which differ from one another; and second, that wrapped up with this conception of the soul is the view that it has a single proper end, which is to know the things that are akin to it.

If the soul has a single proper end, then *we* have a single proper end, for we, strictly speaking, are our souls. Socrates memorably suggests that he is his soul and not at all his body, saying to Crito:

"You might [bury me] however you like," he said, "if, that is, you manage to take hold of me, and I do not escape you." And laughing softly while he gazed at us, he said: "I am unable to persuade Crito, my friends, that I am this Socrates here, the one who is now talking with you, arranging each of the things being said; he thinks instead that I am that corpse which will shortly appear before his eyes, and so he asks how he should bury me.

(115c4–d2)

Socrates is the thing engaged in rational activity, talking and directing, not the body that will soon be a corpse.[6] If he is his soul, then his proper end just is to know the things that are most akin to him, those things that are pure, always the same, immortal, simple. Those who recognize that they are their soul come to see the body as somehow external. They organize their life around attaining the proper end of the soul, rather than fulfilling the needs of the body. They "care for their own soul and don't live sculpting their bodies . . . believing that they mustn't do anything contrary to philosophy and to their release and purification" from the body (82d2–6).

This set of commitments about the true nature of the soul, its proper end, and its divergence from its true nature when embodied forms the backdrop to the *Phaedo*'s recommendations for living a philosophical life, especially regarding the philosopher's attitudes and behavior concerning bodily pleasure, pain, and desire. These recommendations have been the subject of quite a bit of interpretive controversy, especially of late. There are two broad families of interpretation. On one view, in the *Phaedo* Socrates recommends avoiding bodily pleasure to the extent possible. This is the "ascetic" reading.[7] On the other view, Socrates recommends not the avoidance of bodily pleasure, but proper evaluation of it as worth little or nothing. This is the "evaluative" reading.[8] Each of these families of interpretation highlights an important aspect of the philosophical life. Philosophers must both avoid and properly evaluate bodily pleasure, pain, and desire. But it is a mistake to make one or the other of avoidance and evaluation *foundational*. The interplay between behavior and judgment is complex, and sweeping generalizations about one or the other being more fundamental tend to obscure facts about psychology that must be appreciated by anyone who is going to successfully follow Socrates' recommendations. What is crucial is to recognize the foundational role of Socrates' conception of the soul and its proper end.[9] Proper evaluation and actual avoidance of bodily pleasures (and pains, and desires) are necessary, insofar as they are, because of the way they affect the embodied soul's ability to approximate its true nature and attain its proper end of knowledge.

Bodily pleasures, pains, and desires pose three obstacles to attaining knowledge. First, pleasures and desires can *divert* us from the pursuit of knowledge by enticing us to pursue them instead. For a soul that has fallen prey to this sort of diversion, experiencing bodily pleasures and satisfying bodily desires appears to be a goal worthy of all or most of our time, energy, and attention, excluding the serious pursuit of our proper goal. Second, bodily pleasures and pains can *distract* us by pulling our attention away from knowledge. A distracted soul may be totally convinced that she must pursue and develop knowledge as her primary goal, but the experience of strong pleasures and pains can nevertheless be so salient as to impede her proper and optimal engagement with intellectual activities. Finally, bodily pleasures, pains, and desires can *deceive* us about what is real and true, causing us to form false beliefs. A deceived soul will hardly count as approaching knowledge or being on the right track to developing her proper end as a knower.

These three obstacles, which result from letting the body rule over the soul, are importantly related to one another, as we'll discuss later. Nevertheless, different strategies may be required for overcoming different obstacles. Distinguishing among both the obstacles and the particular ways of avoiding them will show that *both* the avoidance of pleasures, pains, and desires *and* the proper evaluation of them play an important role in the life of the philosopher, roles that are equally important for the successful pursuit of our true end of attaining knowledge.

2. Diversions

The most obvious of these obstacles is that bodily pleasure *diverts* us from the pursuit of knowledge by enticing us to pursue it instead. Because of its connection to the body, the soul forms desires for many things: tasty food, delicious and intoxicating drink, sex, fancy clothes, and accessories top the list for Socrates (64c–d).[10] To acquire these goods directly, or to amass the wealth needed to purchase them, requires tremendous energy, time, and attention. As Socrates colorfully puts the point: "[t]he body keeps us busy in countless ways because of its need for nurture" (66b8). We are "enslaved to its service," and so "it leaves us no time for philosophy" (66d1–2). Those of us who have lived our lives giving in to diversion, "having always been associated with the body, serving and loving it," end up irremediably "bewitched by its desires and pleasure, to the point that nothing else seems to be real other than bodily things, which one might touch and see, drink and eat, and use for sexual enjoyment" (81b2–6). We, then, relegate the pursuit of wisdom – our proper end – to an afterthought at best, and all our time and efforts are diverted to serving the body. Our capacity for pursuing objects of desire, and even for cultivating different kinds of desires, is finite, as Socrates vividly emphasizes to Glaucon in the *Republic*:

> When the desires someone harbors incline strongly toward one thing, surely we know that his desires for other things are weakened, just like a current of water that has been diverted elsewhere.
> Naturally.
> Now, when someone's desires flow toward learning and that sort of thing, I believe they would be for the pleasure of the soul by itself, and they would cease to be for those pleasures experienced through the body.
> (485d6–12)

To avoid such diversion, we ought to refrain from actively pursuing bodily pleasures as far as possible. Bodily pleasures compete for limited time, energy, and attention with the only end that really matters, and thereby impede our progress towards knowledge. Instead of pursuing pleasure, we should allocate those resources to pursuing the soul's (i.e., our own) proper end.

As far as possible is a crucial qualification, which Socrates repeats for emphasis. It must be understood in the context of pursuing the soul's proper end. We must free our soul from association with the body "as much as it is possible" (64e5), but this leaves room for indulging in bodily pleasures "insofar as one cannot do without them" (64e1). Indeed, we all require food and drink. We also need to preserve our bodies from diseases and pains for basic functioning. Satisfying the basic needs of the body and indulging in some pleasures may prove indispensable for maximizing the time, energy, and attention available for inquiry. Surely the need to eliminate diversion demands that one not spend a lot of time satisfying one's basic needs for food by seeking out the richest and most delicious dishes. But suppose you are hungry, and someone offers you a plateful of rich and delicious food. Should you refuse? Perhaps refusal would mean that you would have to devote time and attention to seeking out some alternative or else struggle to ignore the gnawing pangs of hunger. Actively avoiding the pleasure of delicious food may in some circumstances prove more diverting than simply indulging. Unless there is some further reason to abstain, beyond the avoidance of diversion, there will be certain circumstances in which you should willingly allow yourself to experience bodily pleasure.

Even this pleasure will likely be tempered, though. If you conceive of food quite generally as valuable just for its ability to maintain your body in a good condition, allowing you to engage your mind fully with intellectual inquiry, then you are unlikely to attend to the gustatory qualities of your food in the same way as someone who takes the taste of the food to be important. You are thus likely to experience the food differently than someone who attends to it. Consider, by way of example, an experience of ours that is fairly common. Good wine is best appreciated as good wine if one pays attention to it, lingers over the bouquet, and rolls it around in one's mouth, separating and reintegrating in one's mind the various flavors contained in it. When we drink good wine, we often notice these qualities. But when we drink good wine while engaged in a particularly stimulating conversation, we tend to experience less pleasure from the wine, because it is the content of the conversation that occupies us. The wine is pleasant enough while it goes down our gullets, of course, but the pleasure of it is diminished by our attention to (and pleasure in) intellectual matters. Now, suppose we were to add in the background belief that wine and its pleasures are completely unimportant, that they don't matter *at all*. Surely someone with this belief, who is attending to intellectual matters and who drinks the wine, will have a different experience of it than someone who sets out to explore the wine itself. But it is exactly this person, who finds no value in the pleasures of wine, who is most like the philosopher Socrates describes.

Avoiding diversion is often a matter of simply refraining from pursuing pleasures, but for some pleasures, active avoidance may be necessary. Some pleasures have the power, when we encounter them, to change our values, leading us to pursue them even if prior to the encounter we would have affirmed that these very pleasures were hardly worthwhile. You may now affirm that chocolate cake is not to be pursued, yet also know that if you walk past the bakery window and get a look at one, your judgment will tend to shift.[11] You may now recognize that sex has no value, yet also suspect that if you are around someone who seems both attractive and available, you are likely to adjust your values. The best strategy in such cases is to chart a course that steers you around such temptations altogether. By such means you can maintain your correct judgments about what really is good for you. But when avoidance is impossible, you must find ways to tie yourself to the mast, so that even if your judgment is swayed in the moment, your original, clear-headed resolve can win the day. Our sirens may be different from yours, so that some self-awareness is necessary to design and implement effective plans for avoiding diversion.

Thus different strategies are required for avoiding diversion: sometimes we must actively avoid, sometimes simply refrain from pursuing, and sometimes even willingly experience bodily pleasure. But each of these strategies is designed to maximize the attention and energy we have for intellectual pursuits. Of course, as these examples illustrate, avoiding diversion will, for all practical purposes, require that you properly evaluate bodily pleasures. If you don't recognize them as worthless in comparison with your true end, you will have no reason to refrain from pursuing them and you will likely want to experience them again. If you have not tasted the fruits of intellectual inquiry, you will be unlikely to maintain the proper comparative judgment between the value of knowledge and the value of bodily pleasures. Only if you value bodily pleasures properly – that is, little or not at all – will you be able to maintain your focus on the pursuit of knowledge. But the *goal* isn't to avoid bodily pleasure or to refrain from pursuing it, nor even to properly evaluate it (at least not directly; more later); the goal is to clear as much space as possible for the pursuit of knowledge.

3. Distractions

It is crucial to keep in mind, though, that it is not just bodily pleasure that poses a problem for the properly intellectual life, but also bodily pain. Of course, bodily pain won't divert us from our proper goal by replacing it, but it can nevertheless pull our attention away from that goal. Though it doesn't divert, it may *distract*. Notice that in the case of distraction, unlike diversion, the danger is not that we may adopt a life goal other than the pursuit of knowledge. We may be wholly devoted to pursuing knowledge, but intense pains may still interfere with our otherwise full commitment to that goal.

Imagine, for example, being deep in thought, focused entirely on the object of your inquiry. (Perhaps you already find yourself in such a state as you read this chapter. We hope self-reflection doesn't break the spell!) Now imagine some sudden pain, perhaps a bee sting, or a muscle cramp. Such a pain has the power to break your train of thought, to snap your attention away from intellectual inquiry. The same may be true of more chronic pains: it is difficult to think in a clear and sustained way when one has a headache, or a sore throat, or a pulled muscle, or persistent hunger or thirst. Such things have the power to distract us from inquiry, even though they do not displace knowledge as a goal. As Socrates says: "if certain diseases befall [the body], they hinder our pursuit of what's real" (66c1–2).

Given this fact, it is worth making some effort to avoid such pains. If you sit under a tree to contemplate, and then find yourself surrounded by a swarm of bees, you should take the time to find a new location. If you ride the subway to work, you should take the time to wash your hands when you arrive. You should make some effort to maintain your body in basic condition, not letting your muscles or bones weaken severely, and maintaining basic nutrition and hydration. Failure to do these things puts you at risk of experiencing pains that may distract you from advancing intellectually.

Likewise, some pleasures may be intense enough to distract one from intellectual inquiry, though a more nuanced discussion is required in the case of pleasure. While intense pain may come upon you all of the sudden, completely unanticipated and catching you unaware, pleasure rarely does that. When Socrates speaks of intense pleasures, he is probably thinking of the pleasure of sex as a paradigmatic case. But this pleasure is not the sort of thing (at least normally) that just happens to one, unanticipated and unsought. Rather, it is the result of a decision to pursue it, or at least to participate in the sorts of activities that tend to lead to it. So, it seems like this is the sort of thing one won't experience unless one actively seeks it; normally, when sexual pleasure hinders our intellectual progress, it is because our attention has been diverted to its pursuit, not because it comes on us unawares as a distraction.

However, insofar as we have sexual desires, these desires can be aroused all of the sudden, in unanticipated ways. Imagine, for example, that you are reading your Plato, pursuing knowledge, when an extremely attractive person walks by. The sight of such a person may be enough to turn your attention from knowledge to sex. Thus you have succumbed to distraction. And of course the point needn't be limited to the paradigmatic case of sex; the aroma of a favorite food may arouse one's appetite, causing a shift of focus from intellect to appetite.

The problem of distraction requires a solution that goes beyond merely avoiding the pursuit of bodily pleasure. Here, active avoidance is required. In the case of pain, we need to avoid, to the extent we reasonably can, the conditions in which intense pain tends to arise. Likewise, we need to avoid the conditions in which intense pleasure tends to arise – a simpler task, perhaps, than with pain. But we also need to avoid the conditions in which our desire is likely to be aroused. There are two ways to effect such avoidance: we can stay away from places where the objects of our desires are likely to make an appearance, and we can take measures to lessen the strength of our desires.

Now, if we don't recognize that bodily pleasures lack value, we won't successfully avoid them, or control and moderate our desires. We will avoid circumstances in which distracting pleasures tend to arise only if we are already convinced that these pleasures don't really matter. As in the case of diversion, to avoid distraction we must properly evaluate bodily pleasures. If we don't already recognize them as worthless, we will have no reason to avoid them, or to control and moderate our desires. Again, the goal isn't to avoid pleasure, pain, and desire, nor is it (at least directly) to properly evaluate them. The goal is to maintain our full attention on the pursuit of knowledge. Proper evaluation and avoidance together serve to support that end.

4. Deceptions

Besides diverting and distracting, bodily pleasure *deceives* us about what is real and important, causing us to form false beliefs. Shortly after concluding the Affinity Argument, Socrates identifies the "greatest and most extreme evil" that we face during our embodied life:

> The soul of the true philosopher . . . reckons that whenever someone experiences intense pleasure, fear, pain, or desire, he doesn't suffer some minor harm from them of the sort someone might think – for example, falling ill or wasting money to fulfill his desires – but that in fact he suffers the greatest and most extreme harm of all, without even realizing it.
> What is that, Socrates? asked Cebes.
> That the soul of every human being, at the same time that it experiences intense pleasure or pain at something, is compelled to believe that *this* – which pleases and pains it most of all – is most clear and most true, though it isn't. These things are, mainly, visible things. Aren't they?
> Certainly.
>
> (83b5–c10)

Such a consequence is a great evil indeed. Having knowledge involves recognizing what is most "clear" and "true." Such things are not sensible, but intelligible. Insofar as a person thinks that sensible things are most clear and true, she suffers a major setback in her proper goal of attaining knowledge. This is not simply a case of diverted aims or distraction. Here we have false content being introduced into her soul, false content that necessarily excludes the fundamental truths that would constitute her knowledge.

What, exactly, is going on here? Unfortunately, Socrates doesn't elaborate much, but the idea seems to be as follows. When we experience intense pleasure and pain, they command our attention, crowding out other thoughts. (This is why the problem of distraction requires avoiding such experiences.) Imagining or remembering a moment of intense pain or pleasure is sufficient for recognizing this: the pain or pleasure becomes the dominating aspect of our consciousness.

If it is intense enough, there really is little or even no competition at all for our attention. And so the objects that cause these experiences, the things that these experiences are *about*, seem to us at that moment most "clear" and "true." We are talking about *bodily* pleasure and pain, which are caused by material objects. These experiences make us think that material objects are the most clear and true things, the things that are most real and matter most. Intense pleasure and pain make us believe both that these things exist, and that they deserve our concern and attention, when, in fact, they do not. Of course, in later, soberer moments, we might upon reflection revise those judgments. But nevertheless such experiences make their mark on us, causing us to tend to rate their causes as more important than they are. Repeated experiences of this sort will reinforce that tendency, so that, with enough reinforcement, we overrate material objects not just at the moment but all the time. Therefore, we must actively avoid these experiences.

Is this as far as the view goes, or might Socrates add to this the recommendation to actively avoid *all* pleasure and pain, as some commentators have thought?[12] After all, in the so-called Riveting Argument, Socrates says that "*each* pleasure or pain" rivets the soul to the body (83d4–5). We read this in the context of the immediately preceding lines (quoted previously), where Socrates clearly identifies the experiences he has in mind as *intense*. Moreover, if Socrates here means to indicate that *every* experience of pleasure, pain, or desire is harmful, he risks making a fetish out of avoiding pleasure.[13] But such a fetish – allowing the avoidance of pleasure to occupy a central place in our lives – would, as we have seen, risk diverting us from our proper end, taking our focus from the pursuit of knowledge to the avoidance of pleasure. Barring some account (not forthcoming in the *Phaedo*) of how every pleasant or painful experience has significantly harmful effects, such an overriding focus on avoiding pleasure risks being counterproductive. Better to understand Socrates as focusing here on those intense pleasures that are especially prone to deceive us into thinking that material things are most real and important.

5. Solutions

As we suggested earlier in the chapter, the problems of diversion, distraction, and deception do not arise fully independently of one another, nor are the solutions to them to be applied piecemeal. The solutions involve a combination of behavioral change and revaluation. Simply adopting asceticism in any of its varieties, or solely changing our evaluative outlook, won't successfully overcome these obstacles. Both behavioral restraint and proper evaluative attitudes are necessary. On the one hand, we should refrain from making bodily pleasure any sort of aim. For all we learn from the *Phaedo*, at least, there may well be some bodily pleasures that do no harm when they come to us of their own accord. But once we begin to aim at experiencing them, we divert our precious resources of time and attention from our proper aim of pursuing knowledge. Now, if we are to refrain consistently from pursuing bodily pleasure, we must recognize it as unimportant and, in some sense, alien to us: the soul doesn't experience bodily pleasures *by itself*; rather, these pleasures are the result of the soul's (temporary) association with the body. However, when it comes to intense pleasures, it is not enough to refrain from pursuing them. If they come upon us, they can distract our efforts at inquiry, and they can deceive us into thinking that the material world and our relationship to it are, respectively, the most real thing and the most important aspect of ourselves. So these must be actively avoided.

These prescriptions may sound simple enough (even if difficult to follow), but the real world and real psychologies are complicated things. There is no *one-size-fits-all* rule-book, and even ordinary, milder pleasure may require active avoidance if inquiry is to proceed at full speed. For example, suppose you are convinced that you ought to pursue knowledge and you formulate a plan to read Plato all morning to advance your aims. You recognize that pursuing bodily pleasure has no place in your morning. Where should you read? Perhaps in a coffee shop, where you can have bland fare (oatmeal and water) to sustain your body while you inquire. That's a great plan, unless you are the sort of person (as we are) who, when sitting near a pastry counter and smelling roasted coffee beans, slowly finds her appetite for macchiatos and scones awakened. Of course, you may successfully resist the urge to partake. But the point is not to resist for the sake of abstaining, but for the appetite never to fight for your attention in the first place. Macchiatos and scones are not (normally) the sources of intense pleasure but, if you are like us, it may nevertheless be advisable for you to avoid the coffee shops where they are to be found. As we've pointed out, the strength and sources of desire may vary from person to person; someone may find that they can sit in coffee shops all day without the slightest urge to indulge, and someone else may find the temptation strong. The former need only continue to set knowledge, rather than macchiatos and scones, as the object of their pursuit; for the latter, this may not be enough. But the concern to avoid pleasure should not dominate their attention. Rather, they must recognize that *bodily pleasure is insignificant*, while remaining aware of its potentially significant effects. Avoiding pleasure is not the goal; pursuing knowledge at full throttle is.

Similar considerations go for the avoidance of pain. As with pleasure, bodily pain is itself insignificant, though it may have significant effects. Avoiding intense pain will surely require active measures. When we do inevitably experience some pain, we must do our best to retain a proper evaluation of it as insignificant. Only by reminding ourselves that bodily pain is insignificant with respect to our true nature can we combat the tendency of pain to fix our minds on the material and sensible, and away from the immaterial and intelligible. Even with our best efforts at proper evaluation, though, intense pain may overwhelm our ability to think properly, forcing our attention to the pain and its material sources. Socrates never says anything to suggest that even the most fervent and experienced philosophers could succeed in inquiry while being tortured on the rack.[14] It is not entirely within our control to avoid intense pain, but we should do what we can to minimize our experience of it. Again, the goal is to maximize the attention we can devote to inquiry, not to maximize our efforts at avoiding pain.

6. Living with your body and dying without it

Mightn't this all be much ado about very little? Surely if *embodiment* is the obstacle preventing the soul from attaining its true end, this obstacle will be removed soon enough and with no special effort. We are all destined to die and death, according to Socrates, is just the separation of the soul from the body (64c5–6). The time we have remaining as embodied humans appears quite slight in the context of the immortality of the soul. Moreover, Socrates seems to think that we can't possibly overcome the ill effects of embodiment entirely; the best we can do in this life is to mitigate the body's influence as far as possible. Perhaps, then, it's not worth making so much of a fuss over, and organizing so much of our lives around, the effort to free our soul from the body to maximize its pursuit of knowledge while embodied. Any gains come at a steep price and amount to only partial and temporary advantages over non-philosophical, hedonistic lifestyles.

Socrates rejects this characterization. Central to his recommendation of the philosophical life is the idea that the effects of embodiment can outlast embodiment itself. Consider the Riveting Argument again, where Socrates speaks of the experience of intense pleasure or pain.

> Then isn't it in this experience that the soul is most of all bound by the body?
> How so?
> Because each pleasure and pain brings along, as it were, a nail and rivets the soul to the body and fastens it and makes it bodily, such that it believes to be true whatever the body asserts. And it's because it shares the beliefs of and takes pleasure in the same things as the body that it is compelled, I think, to share in the same lifestyle with the body and to feed at the same table. And so it is never able to arrive in Hades pure; instead it always sets out filled to the brim with the body, so that it quickly falls again into another body and is implanted into it like a seed sown in a field. As a result, it is bereft of association with the divine and pure and simple.
>
> (83d1–e3)

Obviously, the passage is metaphorical; there are no actual nails connecting body and soul. But how far does the metaphor extend? Is Socrates here identifying *something* that literally connects body and soul? It would be odd if he were: it doesn't seem that people who frequently experience intense pleasure or pain are thereby further from the separation of body and soul – further from *death*. Moreover, Socrates tells us in the passage what he means by saying that the body and soul are bound together and that the soul becomes "bodily." He means that the soul adopts the lifestyle of the body, that it takes on bodily concerns and pursuits. The soul thus adopts certain attitudes, cultivates certain desires, and pursues certain ends because of its association with the body. But these attitudes, desires, and adopted ends are, properly speaking, characteristics of the soul, not of the body, despite the fact that they are produced as a result of the body's influence. There is thus no impediment to these "bodily" conditions of the soul outlasting its association with the body. Indeed, these conditions exert a pull, according to Socrates, back to body, leading souls to "fall again" into a new body and thus to be reincarnated.

The point is significant enough that Socrates makes it repeatedly. At 80d5–81e4, Socrates contrasts those souls that have purified themselves from the body from those that haven't. Those that remain contaminated by the body, that think that the physical, and in particular what can be used for bodily pleasure, is all that exists, cannot, even after death, attain the knowledge that is the most proper goal of the soul. Indeed, Socrates tells us (surely playfully), such souls are so bodily that they sink to the earth and wonder around graveyards as shadowy figures that are on occasion seen by the living (81c9–d4). These bad souls remain in such a state until their desires again imprison them in a body. By contrast, the purified souls leave the body behind upon death, arriving at the place where they can attain their one true desire and thus be happy.

The upshot of all of this is that if we fail to organize our embodied life around the effort to free our soul (i.e., *ourselves*) from the body, thus maximizing the pursuit of knowledge, we stand to lose a very great deal. We will depart this life being not at all akin to those things that our true self longs to have intercourse with. A "bodily" soul fails to be pure, simple, always the same as itself; rather, it is complex and disordered, since it harbors desires different in kind to the philosophical wants that define its true nature. Such a soul does not have a single end. This soul's proper end (i.e., knowing those things that are akin to its true self) has been occluded by ends adopted during its human existence due to its close association with the body. This is a striking suggestion: what makes a soul simple or complex in the way relevant for a philosophical life is connected with, and determined by, the pursuit of a *single* end. And the pursuit of this end is, in turn, linked with the soul's harboring a single kind of motivation. A soul – even a disembodied one – that is not motivationally unified by its quest towards the right sort of end is disordered, complex, and vicious.[15]

We have emphasized that, according to Socrates' recommendations in the *Phaedo*, our lives should be guided by the quest for knowledge. That is, indeed, our soul's true and proper end. And we are but only our soul. Nevertheless, it should be clear by now that Socrates' claims in this dialogue do not entail that we should refrain from engaging in ordinary human activities, or even attempt to transcend our human existence by denying our embodied condition. If we ignore the fact that we are embodied, we will hinder the pursuit of our true goal. Being aware of our embodied condition, navigating and negotiating the body's needs by sometimes avoiding them and sometimes giving in to them, is absolutely necessary and fundamental to the optimal pursuit of our goal. We must be aware of our embodied selves to live our lives well and approach purity as far as possible. Thus, we cannot and should not ignore human activities. We must, of course, engage in them wisely, but Socrates doesn't call for the denial of our (temporary) humanity, and he doesn't ask us to turn away from human life *tout court*; that would actually hurt us. After all, whatever the body suffers and undergoes is registered by the soul. There are not different subjects of experience here. What happens to the body happens to *us*. Or rather, nothing happens *to* the body as a subject of experience; the only subject of experience is the soul, though its experiences may come *through* the body. In fact, as we have said, the consequences of what happens to the soul through and because of its association with the body are dangerously lasting and difficult to erase. So we must, to an important extent, care for what happens to the body, and partake of those human activities that best preserve and keep in line its needs, affording us the time, energy, and attention to pursue wisdom.[16]

Notes

1. The argument here is really the first part of a two-stage argument. First, we get an argument *that* the soul is immortal (608d–611a) and then an explanation of *how* the soul can be immortal, given that other composite objects tend to decompose (611a–612a, discussed in the following paragraph).
2. In fact, commentators have been largely unimpressed by this part of Socrates' argument. Julia Annas goes so far as to refer to it as "a ridiculous little argument" and claims that "this is one of the few really embarrassingly bad arguments in Plato" (1981, p. 344). In any case, our interest here lies in the explanation of the soul's immortality (the second stage), not the initial attempt to demonstrate that it is so. Clearly Socrates conceives of the soul as immortal; given that he also seems to conceive of it as composite, how can he explain its immortality?
3. Unattributed translations are ours, based on the texts of Slings (*Republic*) and Duke et al. (*Phaedo*).
4. Socrates explicitly makes a parallel point about desire at *Philebus* 34d–35d. Some interpreters have defended the view that bodily pleasures, pains, and desires are experienced by the body as subject. Irwin (1977), for example, says that "[l]ike the *Gorgias*, the *Phaedo* recognizes conflicts of desires rejected by Socrates; but, unlike the *Gorgias*, it ascribes them, *not to two parts of the soul, but to the soul and the body*" (p. 160; emphasis added). See, also, Price (1995), pp. 35–42; Bobonich (2002), pp. 28–30; and Bailly (2010), pp. 290–296. For a defense of the view that Socrates recognizes only one subject of psychological states – *viz.* the soul – see Rowe (2007), pp. 96–121; Beere (2010); and Butler (2017).
5. The very same Homeric lines (*Odyssey* XX. 17–18) are used by Socrates as evidence in favor of the partition of the soul in the *Republic* (441b5).
6. Socrates is not always so careful as he pointedly is here. See, for example, 79b1–2, where Socrates asks: "Isn't one part of us body, and another part soul?" The "us" in this quote refers to our embodied selves and may misleadingly suggest that the self is the whole complex of body and soul. That, however, is not Socrates' considered view in the *Phaedo*.
7. For "ascetic" readings of the *Phaedo*, see especially Butler (2012) and Ebrey (2017), but also Hackforth (1955), pp. 48–49; Gallop (1975), p. 88; Bostock (1986),

p. 30; Pakaluk (2003), pp. 99–102; and Sedley and Long (2010), p. XXIV. For an argument that Socrates advocates for asceticism only in the sections of the dialogue that follow the Affinity Argument, see Apolloni (1996), p. 32, and Woolf (2004), p. 116 ff.

8 For "evaluative" readings of the *Phaedo*, see especially Woolf (2004) and Russell (2005), ch. 3; also Bluck (1955), pp. 2–5 and pp. 46–47; Tenkku (1956), p. 111 and 118; Dorter (1982), pp. 26–27; Weiss (1987), pp. 58–59; Gallop (2001); and Jansen (2013), p. 343. (The labels "ascetic" and "evaluative" trace back to Woolf (2004).)

9 Some recent commentators have recognized this point. For example, Ebrey (2017) makes the proper condition and activity of the soul a central aspect of his interpretation. And Butler (2012), while strongly emphasizing the importance of behavioral avoidance of pleasure, makes the effective pursuit of philosophy the goal by which we judge whether some pleasure is or is not permitted, even going so far at one point (p. 113) as to suggest that "drinking alcohol with fellow philosophers" may be permissible. We cannot quite see on what grounds Butler can allow for social drinking among philosophers (unless it is mere wishful thinking, with which we sympathize greatly), but we agree with the impulse to let the effective pursuit of philosophy arbitrate questionable cases. The interpretation we offer thus belongs in the same family as Butler's and Ebrey's, though we find the label "ascetic" to be potentially misleading about what is most important in Socrates' account.

10 Socrates refers to these as "so-called pleasures" (64d3), hinting at the possibility and superiority of non-bodily pleasures, which are related to the proper activity of the soul. These intellectual pleasures or "pleasures of learning" are introduced at the end of the dialogue (114e3–4).

11 Such a phenomenon is utterly familiar. The mechanism underlying it is less clear. While we don't explore the mechanism here, we do note that the phenomenon is compatible with the view that all ethical failure is the result of some failure to apprehend what is best. Pleasures, desires, and appetites can affect our cognitive capacity to grasp what is good, thus leading us to choose and act incorrectly. See, for example, Brickhouse and Smith (2010) and, on the *Phaedo* specifically, Butler (2017).

12 See, for example, Butler (2012), especially pp. 110–111, and Ebrey (2017).

13 See Woolf (2004, p. 104): "[Socrates] has more important things to do than make an idol or fetish out of withdrawal of bodily activity."

14 This is true even when Socrates argues that just people who are severely tortured will be happier than unjust people, as he does in the *Republic* (rejecting Glaucon's characterization at 361e3–362a3). This is not a judgment that people can be well off, or that they can succeed in inquiry when tortured, but only that they are nevertheless better off than the wicked. There are times when Socrates suggests that pain would be good for someone, as at *Gorgias* 473d7–e1. But such a verdict is limited to cases of people whose desires and beliefs are *already* severely skewed, where painful treatment may limit the further development and full expression in behavior of these misguided values.

15 Ebrey (2017) usefully emphasizes that the soul can be in better or worse condition after death due to the lingering effects of embodiment, but a central aspect of his explication of this idea is, in our view, untenable. Ebrey appeals to an allegedly Socratic distinction at 64c4–8 between death and being dead: *death* (ὁ θάνατος) is the separation of the soul and body; *being dead* (τὸ τεθνάναι) requires in addition to separation that each of the soul and the body is "itself according to itself". A soul may thus experience death without being dead but being dead (not death) is what the philosopher desires. Now, even given the unusual context, in which Socrates is claiming that philosophers want to die, that distinction would be a strange one for him to make: these

two Greek terms would not ordinarily be sharply distinguished. (For nice Socratic examples of their juxtaposition, see the final pages of Plato's *Apology* and Xenophon's *Apology*.) But even aside from its strangeness, the distinction seems to appear in the passage Ebrey quotes only because of where he marks the passage. Preceding the passage as Ebrey marks it (c2), Socrates asks, "Do we think that death (τὸν θάνατον) is something?" (This is a standard way for Socrates to introduce a topic (compare 65d4–5).) And following the passage (c8), Socrates asks, "Is death (ὁ θάνατος) anything other than that?" This frame makes clear that there is only one subject under consideration at 64c4–8, namely death, and that the verbal expression 'τὸ τεθνάναι' is used only in the service of clarifying the basic concept.

16 We are grateful to Willie Costello, David Ebrey, and John Sisko for generous comments.

Bibliography

Annas, J. (1981) *Introduction to Plato's Republic*. Oxford: Oxford University Press.

Apolloni, D. (1996) Plato's affinity argument for the immortality of the soul. *Journal of the History of Philosophy* 34: 5–32.

Bailly, J. (2010) Commentary on Beere. *Proceedings of the Boston Area Colloquium in Ancient Philosophy* 26: 289–300.

Beere, J. (2010) Philosophy, virtue, and immortality in Plato's *Phaedo*. *Proceedings of the Boston Area Colloquium in Ancient Philosophy* 26: 253–288.

Bluck, R. S. (1955) *Plato's Phaedo*. London: Routledge and Kegan Paul.

Bobonich, C. (2002) *Plato's Utopia Recast*. New York: Oxford University Press.

Bostock, D. (1986) *Plato's Phaedo*. Oxford: Oxford University Press.

Brickhouse, T., and Smith, N. (2010) *Socratic Moral Psychology*. New York: Oxford University Press.

Butler, T. (2012) A riveting argument for asceticism in the *Phaedo*. *History of Philosophy Quarterly* 29: 103–123.

———. (2017) Bodily Desire and Imprisonment in the *Phaedo*. *Logical Analysis and History of Philosophy* 20: 82–102.

Dorter, K. (1982) *Plato's Phaedo: An Interpretation*. Toronto: University of Toronto Press.

Duke, E. A. (1995) *Phaedo*. In Duke, E. A., Hicken, W. F., Nicoll, W. S. M., Robinson, D. B., and Strachan, J. C. G. (eds.) *Platonis Opera, t. I. Tetralogias I-II continens*. Oxford: Oxford University Press.

Ebrey, D. (2017) The Asceticism of the Phaedo: Pleasure, Purification, and the Soul's Proper Activity. *Archiv für Geschichte der Philosophie* 99: 1–30.

Gallop, D. (1975) *Phaedo*. Oxford: Clarendon Press and Oxford University Press.

———. (2001) Emotions in the *Phaedo*. In Havlíček, A., and Karfík, F. (eds.), *Plato's Phaedo: Proceedings of the Second Symposium Platonicum Pragense*, pp. 275–286.

Hackforth, R. (1955) *Phaedo*. Cambridge, MA: Cambridge University Press.

Irwin, T. (1977) *Plato's Moral Theory*. New York: Oxford University Press.

Jansen, S. (2013) Plato's *Phaedo* as a pedagogical drama. *Ancient Philosophy* 33 (2): 333–352.

Pakaluk, M. (2003) Degrees of separation in the *Phaedo*. *Phronesis* 48: 89–115.

Price, A. (1995) *Mental Conflict*. New York: Routledge.

Rowe, C. (2007) *Plato and the Art of Philosophical Writing*. New York: Cambridge University Press.

Russell, D. (2005) *Plato on Pleasure and the Good Life*. Oxford: Oxford University Press.

Sedley, D., and Long, A. (2010) *Plato Meno and Phaedo*. Cambridge, MA: Cambridge University Press.
Slings, S. R. (2003) *Platonis Respublica*. Oxford: Oxford Classical Texts.
Tenkku, J. (1956) The evaluation of pleasure in Plato's ethics. *Acta Philosophica Fennica* 11.
Weiss, R. (1987) The right exchange: *Phaedo* 69a6–c3. *Ancient Philosophy* 7: 57–66.
Woolf, R. (2004) The practice of the philosopher. *Oxford Studies in Ancient Philosophy* 26: 97–129.

5

PLATO AND TRIPARTITION OF SOUL[1]

Rachel Singpurwalla

According to a standard interpretation, Plato's conception of our moral psychology evolved over the course of his written dialogues. In his earlier dialogues, notably the *Protagoras*, *Meno*, and *Gorgias*, Plato's Socrates maintains that we always do what we believe is best. Many commentators infer from this that Socrates holds that the psyche is simple, in the sense that there is only one ultimate source of motivation: reason. By contrast, in the *Republic*, *Phaedrus*, and *Timaeus*, Socrates holds that the psyche is complex, or has three distinct and semi-autonomous sources of motivation, which he calls the reasoning, spirited, and appetitive parts. While the rational part determines what is best overall and motivates us to pursue it, the spirited and appetitive parts incline us towards different objectives, such as victory, honor, and esteem, or the satisfaction of our desires for food, drink, and sex.

Many of Plato's readers think his views evolved for the better, at least in so far as the tripartite theory of the psyche seems better suited to explain the experience of motivational conflict, or the experience of believing that some course of action is best overall and yet feeling simultaneously inclined to do something else. According to the tripartite theory, we can have this experience because we have distinct and semi-autonomous sources of motivation, each with its own distinctive way of assessing and responding to the world. More specifically, reason is oriented towards what is best overall, but spirit is solely focused on the pursuit of victory and honor, and the appetitive part is single-mindedly attuned to the satisfaction of bodily desires.

Socrates's tripartite psychology seems intuitive enough, at least in broad outline; but in fact, it is more puzzling than it might first appear. While it is obvious that Socrates primarily characterizes and distinguishes the parts in terms of what each desires and pursues, what is less often brought to the fore is that he also characterizes and distinguishes the parts in terms of how they think. More specifically, he claims that the rational part forms its beliefs on the basis of rational calculation, while the spirited and appetitive parts form their beliefs on the basis of how things appear, without scrutinizing those appearances.

Socrates's dual characterization of the parts of the soul raises a question: why does he characterize each part as having the particular desires and cognitive abilities that he does? While it is perhaps reasonably clear why Socrates might think that the part that desires what is in fact best overall is also the part that engages in rational calculation, it is less clear why he would think that the part that desires victory, honor, and esteem, and the part that desires food, drink, and sex, are also parts that form their beliefs on the basis of appearances alone. As long as Socrates attributes to the spirited and appetitive parts the capacity to form beliefs at all, then why not attribute to them the capacity to form their beliefs using more sophisticated ways of reasoning? In general, how do facts about what a part desires relate to facts about how it thinks?

In this chapter, I suggest an answer to this question, one that I hope sheds light on the nature of the parts of the soul and so on Plato's theory of tripartition more generally. I begin in the first section by presenting the evidence that Socrates distinguishes and characterizes the parts of the soul along two dimensions: in terms of what they desire and in terms of how they think. In the second section, I consider and reject one possible account of the relationship between what a part desires and how it thinks. In the third section, I present an account of the parts of the soul which highlights the fact that each part of the soul has a specific function or capacity, and I show how this account suggests an answer to the question of why Socrates thinks that only the rational part forms its beliefs on the basis of calculation, while the spirited and appetitive parts form their beliefs on the basis of appearances alone. In the conclusion, I show that Socrates's theory bears a notable resemblance to contemporary dual process theories of judgment, according to which we have two distinct processes for forming judgments, one which is broadly akin to reflection and another to intuition.

1. Two characterizations of the parts of the soul

Perhaps Socrates's most well-known argument for the view that the soul has three parts occurs in *Republic* IV. Socrates begins by noting that it is obvious that we can do and desire different things. For example, we can love learning and acquire knowledge, we can get angry, and we can have appetites for the pleasures of things like food and sex. What is less obvious, he claims, is whether we do these things with the whole soul once we feel the impulse, or whether we do them with some distinct aspect or part of the soul (435e–436b). Socrates wants to know, then, whether the soul has distinct parts that can function independently and so by themselves lead the person to act, while the other parts of us play no role in desiring and pursuing that action, or even positively resist.

Socrates thinks that the experience of a certain kind of psychological conflict shows that the soul does contain distinct sources of desire and motivation. More specifically, he thinks that the fact that we can simultaneously desire and be averse to the very same object or course of action shows that we must have distinct parts of the soul. Socrates begins by pointing out that sometimes people determine through reasoning that they should not drink and so are averse to drinking, and yet are thirsty and so desire to drink. He claims that this shows that there are two parts of the soul: the rational part, which determines what is best and gives rise to motivations to act accordingly, and the irrational and appetitive element, which feels passion, hungers, thirsts, and is stirred by other appetites (439a–e). Socrates goes on to argue that there is a third part of the soul, the spirited part. He presents the case of Leontius, who has an appetitive desire to look at some recently executed corpses, but is simultaneously disgusted at the thought of acting this way. Socrates claims that it is Leontius's appetitive part which gives rise to the desire to look at corpses, while his spirited part gives rise to his disgust and is averse to the very same action (339e–440a). To show that the spirited part is distinct from the rational part, Socrates presents the case of Odysseus, who returns home from a long journey to find that his maids are flirting with his enemies in his own home. He is angry and shamed at this insulting behavior and desires to retaliate immediately; at the same time he is opposed to this action and struggles to restrain himself from retaliating (440b–c). According to Socrates, Odysseus's spirit is the source of the desire to retaliate, while his reason urges him to wait, presumably on the grounds that it is best overall not to act on his anger at this point in time.

Socrates thinks, then, that these experiences of motivational conflict show that we can experience and assess the same situation from radically different and even opposed perspectives. This suggests in turn that within each of us there are distinct parts of the soul, each with its own aims and desires. Socrates's examples identify three such parts: the rational part, which cares about what is best overall; the spirited part, which is attuned to honor and esteem; and the appetitive part, which is solely interested in satisfying desires for things like food, drink, and sex.

But motivational conflict is not the only type of conflict that Socrates uses to show that the soul has parts. In *Republic* X, during the course of his critique of the imitative arts, and in particular, tragedy, Socrates draws on the experience of cognitive conflict to show that our souls have distinct parts, each with its own characteristic way not of desiring, but of thinking. Socrates begins by noting that sometimes the same object appears larger when viewed from nearby but smaller when viewed from a distance, or sometimes the same object can appear straight when seen out of the water but bent when seen in the water. In these cases, we use calculation (i.e. measuring, counting, weighing) to assist us. Nonetheless, sometimes, even when we have calculated that something is larger or smaller than others, or the same size, the opposite simultaneously appears to hold of these same things. According to Socrates, this shows that we have distinct parts of the soul, each with its own way of forming judgments about the world: the rational part, which forms its beliefs on the basis of calculations, and 'the inferior part,' which forms its beliefs on the basis of how things appear alone (602c–603a).

This alternative characterization of the parts of the soul poses a puzzle for commentators, for it is not clear how, if at all, this characterization of the parts of the soul relates to Socrates's earlier characterization. In the first place, in *Republic* X, Socrates claims that there are two parts of the soul, while earlier he had claimed that there were three. In addition, in book X, Socrates characterizes the parts in terms of how they form beliefs, while earlier he characterized them in terms of what they pursue. These differences have led some scholars to conclude that, in book X, Socrates is referring to a different division of the soul. Specifically, he is highlighting a division within the rational part into its superior and inferior elements.[2]

There is sufficient evidence, however, to reject this conclusion, and to think instead that the so-called inferior part is or includes the spirited and appetitive parts.[3] Immediately following his division of the soul into the rational and inferior element, Socrates presents yet another characterization of the parts of the soul. He claims that just as we can be conflicted in matters of sight, we can be conflicted in matters of action. When someone loses a son or something else he values highly, he may be tempted to give himself over to grieving and do many things he would not want anyone else to see him doing, and yet at the same time he might resist excessive lamentation and try to have a more measured response in the face of his pain. According to Socrates, it is the rational part that deliberates about what is best given the circumstances and motivates the person to arrange his affairs accordingly, while it is the irrational, idle part that leads us to recollections of our suffering and lamentation (603c–604d). But Socrates then goes on to equate the part that experiences strong emotions with the part that believes on the basis of appearances. Specifically, he claims that imitative poetry, in particular, tragedy, should not be allowed in the city, since it gratifies this lamenting element, which he then describes as "the element in it that lacks understanding and cannot distinguish bigger from smaller, but believes the same thing to be now large, now small"[4] (605a–c). Thus, Socrates thinks that the part that experiences strong feelings and desires is also the part that forms its beliefs on the basis of appearances alone. Socrates then goes on to loosely equate this part of the soul with the spirited and appetitive parts, for he claims that imitative poetry nurtures and waters the anger, sexual desires, and appetites, pleasures, and pains that accompany all of our actions (606d). Thus it is reasonable to conclude that the 'inferior' part of the soul, the part that believes on the basis of appearances, is or includes the spirited and appetitive parts.

The general psychological picture, then, is compatible with the picture presented in the *Phaedrus*, where Socrates likens the soul to the union of a charioteer and two winged horses, one noble and obedient, and the other unruly (246a–b). The charioteer represents reason, the good horse represents the spirited part, and the bad horse represents the appetitive part. In this image, Socrates depicts the rational part as importantly distinct from the spirited and appetitive parts, and he suggests that the rational part is more closely tied to what makes us human. The passages we have been examining in the *Republic* tell us why Socrates depicts the parts in this way: the rational part of the soul is the only part that is capable of scrutinizing appearances and using calculation to figure out the truth. The spirited and appetitive parts, on the other hand, are different from one another in so far as they desire different things (victory, honor, esteem, and things like food, drink, sex, respectively), but they are similar to one another in so far as they think in similar ways; more specifically, both form their beliefs on the basis of appearances alone.

But all of this raises a question: why would Socrates argue that the spirited part, the part that gets angry, forms its beliefs on the basis of appearances? And similarly, why would he claim that the appetitive part, the part that thirst, hungers, and feels desires for sex, also forms beliefs on the basis of appearances? I should stress here that I am not asking why Socrates attributes to each part the capacity to both desire certain things and to form beliefs about the world. I am not, that is, asking why he characterizes the parts as agent-like in this way. Instead, I am asking why he characterizes each part as having the particular motivational and cognitive capacities that he does. More specifically, I am asking why he associates certain desires with certain ways of thinking. While it is reasonable to hold that the part that desires what is best overall is associated with the part that is capable of calculating, it is less clear why the spirited and appetitive parts should be associated with forming their beliefs on the basis of how things appear alone. Why does Socrates deny them the ability to scrutinize appearances? And why does he deny them the ability to weigh, measure, and calculate?

2. Appetitive and spirited desires and appearances

Surprisingly, commentators have paid scant attention to this question, perhaps on the grounds that there is no principled reason for Socrates to think that the spirited and appetitive parts must form their beliefs on the basis of appearances. A recent commentator sums up this thought sharply: "Plato presumably fails to see that his argument will not work, that desire has nothing to do with optical illusions, because he thinks of the lower part of the soul as being merely the trashy and reason-resisting part."[5] Other commentators, however, have ventured a solution. They have argued that, for Socrates, the fundamental difference between the parts of the soul is the one expressed in *Republic* X: the rational part forms its attitudes, its beliefs and desires, on the basis of calculation, while the non-rational, inferior parts form attitudes on the basis of how things appear. In the case of forming desires, the rational part forms its desires on the basis of calculating about what is good and bad, while the non-rational parts form their desires solely on the basis of what *seems* or *appears* good or bad, without subjecting those appearances to scrutiny. These commentators argue, then, that it *is* reasonable for Socrates to associate certain desires with a certain way of thinking. More specifically, it is reasonable to think that the part that desires what is best overall is the part that calculates about what is best, since desiring what is best overall is a response to having a belief about what is best overall. And it is reasonable to claim that the part that seeks victory, honor, and esteem and the part that desires food, drink, and sex are also the parts that form attitudes on the basis of appearances, for these desires just are responses to things appearing good and bad. Indeed, the cognitive character of the parts explains the motivational character of the parts: it is *because* the rational part forms its attitudes on the basis of calculation that it desires the things that it does, and it is *because* the appetitive and spirited parts forms their attitudes on the basis of what merely appears good or bad that they desire the things that they do.[6]

What is the evidence for this view? It is difficult to deny that Socrates holds that the rational part forms its desires on the basis of calculation. In the argument for soul division in *Republic* IV, where Socrates first distinguishes the rational from the appetitive part, Socrates explicitly claims that the impulse to prevent the thirsty person from drinking arises from calculation, presumably about whether it is good or bad to drink (439c). But why think that Socrates holds that the spirited and appetitive parts form their desires on the basis of what appears good? The evidence is twofold. First, there is evidence that Socrates holds that spirited and appetitive desires involve cognizing the object of desire as good. Second, there is evidence that he thinks these evaluations are based on the fact that the object appears good or bad. I consider each piece of evidence in turn.

While many commentators have thought that only the rational part desires 'under the guise of the good,' there is strong evidence for thinking that the desires that emanate from the spirited and appetitive parts also involve cognizing the object of desire as good.[7] First, in *Republic* VI, Socrates claims that everyone pursues the good and does everything for its sake (505d–e); this suggests that even when an individual is motivated by spirited or appetitive desires, he or she pursues those objects thinking that they are good. Second, in *Republic* VIII, Socrates criticizes the individual who controls his appetitive desires by force instead of "persuading them that they had better not" or taming them with arguments (554c–d). It is reasonable to think that persuading and taming our desires through argument involves showing that the object of desire is not worth pursuing, and this in turn suggests that appetites crucially involve representing their objects as good. Finally, also in *Republic* VIII, Socrates describes how appetites can shape the beliefs of someone who does not have knowledge. He says,

> they [his appetites] seize the citadel of the young man's soul, since they realize that it is empty of . . . fine studies and practices. . . . Then, I suppose, beliefs and arguments that are lying imposters rush up and occupy this same part of him in place of the others.
>
> (560b–c, my brackets)

Socrates is clear here that appetites can affect one's beliefs about value, and this suggests that appetites involve cognizing the objects of desire as good. Thus, there is evidence for thinking that spirited and appetitive desires involve cognizing their objects as good. But how, then, do the spirited and appetitive parts arrive at these evaluations?

It is reasonable to think that while the rational part forms its desires on the basis of calculating about what is good and bad, the non-rational parts form their desires solely on the basis of what appears good and bad. As we have seen, *Republic* X explicitly states that the non-rational part of the soul forms its attitudes on the basis of how things appear alone. Moreover, in another dialogue, the *Protagoras*,

Socrates explicitly claims that things can appear good or bad and that desires are responses to those appearances. In a passage that bears a striking resemblance to the passage we have been discussing in *Republic* X, Socrates says that just as things can look bigger than they really are when seen from close-by and smaller when seen from a distance, so pleasures can seem greater than they really are when near at hand, and smaller than they really are when in the future. While knowledge, understood in this passage as the art of measurement, can show us the truth about what is good and bad, the 'power of appearance' can make us wander around confused, regretting our choices and actions (352b–357e). This passage suggests, then, that there are two ways of forming ideas about value and so desires: we can reason and calculate, or we can go with the way things appear. Of course, there are crucial differences between the moral psychology presented in the *Protagoras* and the *Republic*. Perhaps most importantly (at least for our purposes), the *Protagoras* is silent on the issue of whether we have distinct parts of the soul and thus on whether desires based on reasoning and desires based on appearances emanate from different parts of the soul. Nonetheless, the passage makes clear that Socrates holds that things can appear good or bad, better or worse, and that some desires are responses to those appearances.

To reiterate, then, recent scholars argue that it is reasonable for Socrates to think that the part that desires victory, honor, and esteem and the part that desires food, drink, and sex are also parts that form their attitudes on the basis of appearances, since their desires just are responses to things appearing good. Indeed, the tendency to form attitudes on the basis of appearances explains the motivational character of these parts: it is *because* spirited and appetitive parts form their attitudes on the basis of appearances that they desire the things that they do.

While I agree with this view in broad outline, I do not think it captures the full story. We can begin with the most obvious problem for this view. This view holds that the fundamental difference between the parts of the soul is how they form their attitudes: the rational part forms its attitudes on the basis of calculations, while the non-rational parts form their attitudes on the basis of appearances. But of course throughout most of the *Republic*, Socrates argues that the soul has *three* parts; indeed, there is a suggestion that there may be more than three parts (443d). How, then, can the difference between two tendencies – forming attitudes on the basis of calculation versus forming attitudes on the basis of how things appear – fully explain why there are three parts of the soul?

Defenders of the view we have been considering hold that the non-rational part of the soul, the part that forms its attitudes on the basis of how things appear, includes the spirited and appetitive parts. Perhaps the most obvious way to respond to this question, then, is to argue that the distinction between spirit and appetite is made on the basis of the different things that appear good to each. More specifically, victory, honor, and esteem appear good to the spirited part and so it forms it attitudes on the basis of these appearances. But things like food, drink, and sex appear good to the appetitive part and so it forms its attitudes on the basis of these appearances.

If, however, we assume, quite reasonably, that for something to appear good just is or at least includes being attracted to that thing, then it seems there is something about each part that is already positively attuned to and attracted to the relevant objects, *independently* of the tendency to form beliefs and desires on the basis of appearances.[8] And if this is true, then we cannot conclude that the tendency to form attitudes on the basis of appearances explains the tendency to desire certain things. The tendency to be attracted to and so ultimately desire certain things seems fundamental to the spirited and appetitive parts of the soul. And indeed this makes sense: it seems that we are creatures who find victory, honor, and esteem, as well as food, drink, and sex, attractive and good, independently of whether we also have a tendency to form beliefs and desires on the basis of how things appear. Whatever else the purposes of the tripartite theory, it certainly seems designed first and foremost to highlight this human tendency to find certain things attractive in order to explain common motivational patterns.

If all this is correct, then we still do not have an answer to our original question. We cannot say that Socrates associates the desire for victory, honor, and esteem, and the desire for food, drink, and sex, with forming beliefs on the basis of appearances since this cognitive tendency explains why we have these desires. Instead, we have seen that the tendency to be attracted to these things is fundamental to the parts of the soul. Thus, we still need an explanation for why Socrates associates the desire for victory, honor, and esteem, and food, drink, and sex, with the tendency to form beliefs on the basis of appearances alone.

3. The parts of the soul, function, and value

I propose that to answer our question we should look more carefully at the nature of the part. Most commentators have sought to illuminate the nature of the parts by focusing on the distinct things they desire and pursue.[9] But in fact Socrates also characterizes the parts as capable of *doing* distinct things.[10] Indeed, throughout the *Republic*, Socrates characterizes the parts in two main ways: in terms of what they do, their capacity or function, and in terms of what sort of thing each values and pursues. In what follows, I discuss the parts in turn, with an emphasis on highlighting their unique capacity or function, their unique object of pursuit, and the relationship between them. More specifically, I argue that each part of the soul is the source of a capacity that is uniquely suited to attain a certain end or goal, one which we are disposed to value.

3.1 The rational part

Socrates claims that the rational part of the soul has the capacity to calculate. Thus, in the argument for soul division in *Republic* IV, Socrates distinguishes the rational from the appetitive element by holding that the rational element is "the element in the soul with which it calculates, the rationally calculating element" (439d). Throughout most of the *Republic*, Socrates emphasizes the rational part's capacity to reason about what is best for the soul as a whole. Thus, in *Republic* IV, he argues that the rational part is wise and "exercises foresight on behalf of the whole soul" (441e); he claims that the rational part, in virtue of its capacity to deliberate, would do the finest job guarding the soul (442b); and he claims that the rational part makes pronouncements and "has within it the knowledge of what is advantageous – both for each part and for the whole, the community composed of all three" (442c). This conception of reason's capacity to calculate about what is best for the whole soul is reiterated in book IX, where Socrates likens the soul to the union of a human being (reason), a lion (spirit), and a many-headed beast (the appetites). He holds that when the human being (reason) rules, it takes care of the many-headed beast like a farmer, nurturing the gentle heads and preventing the savage ones from growing, while making the lion's nature his ally, with the result that they are friends with one another and with himself (589a–b). This suggests that reason scrutinizes the desires of the other parts, encouraging some and discouraging others, with the aim of harmonizing these desires and ensuring that the desires of one part do not grow too large and overwhelm the soul. We should stress, though, that Socrates does not think that reason only calculates about what is best for the person. In book IX, he characterizes reason as that with which a person learns in general (580d), and he claims that the person who is ruled by reason is a philosopher (581b–c), someone who strives for all kinds of knowledge and, in particular, knowledge of the forms (474bff).

But Socrates does not characterize the rational part only in terms of what it can do. He also characterizes it in terms of what it loves and values. Thus, in book IV, Socrates suggests that reason is the source of the love of learning found in those who live in Athens (435e–436a). In *Republic* IX, he describes the rational part as the part that loves to learn and that is always wholly straining to know the truth (581b). And, as we just saw, he describes the individual who is ruled by reason as a lover of wisdom, or a philosopher, an individual whose dominant value and greatest pleasure is thinking, learning, and trying to understand the world (581bff).

In sum, then, Socrates characterizes the rational part in two main ways: in terms of what it can do (namely, calculate) and in terms of what it loves and values (which is learning, understanding, and knowing the truth, including the truth about what is best). We can synthesize these characterizations in the following way: reason is the source of a certain capacity, calculating, that enables us to attain a certain end, knowing and acting in the light of the truth, which we desire and value. Socrates holds that a person who is ruled by reason makes exercising her ability to calculate in pursuit of the truth the dominant value in her life.

3.2 The spirited part

Socrates first explicitly introduces the spirited part as that with which we feel anger (439e) and his subsequent illustrations of spirit highlight its capacity to get angry and fight. Thus, Socrates describes Leontius's spirit as angry at and struggling against his desires for moving him to act in a way he does not approve (439e–442b). He claims that when a noble man is treated unjustly, his spirit boils and grows harsh and fights as an ally of what he holds to be just (440c–d). And he claims that Odysseus's spirit grows angry and wants to retaliate against his maids for flirting with his enemies (441b–c). Socrates also highlights spirit's ability to fight in his description of its normative roles. So, he claims that reason and spirit should rule the soul and guard it against unruly appetites and external enemies: reason by deliberating and spirit by fighting, following the ruler, and using its courage to carry out the things on which the former has decided (442a–b). Indeed, Socrates defines courage as spirit's ability to preserve through pains and pleasures the pronouncements of reason about what should and should not inspire terror, presumably so it can enable the individual to stay strong against an enemy and carry out what reason deems best (442b–c).

It is reasonable to think that spirit gets angry and fights when it perceives some kind of threat to the self. Socrates seems to think that this can manifest in a variety of ways. Surely spirit enables one to get angry and fight against physical threats to oneself or one's own. Thus, Socrates says that animals have spirit and that this is what enables their courage and ability to fight against an enemy, and he claims that spirited individuals are best suited to guard the city against enemies (375a–b). In other cases, however, Socrates stresses that spirit gets angry at threats to one's honor and self-worth. Thus, Leontius is angry at his desires for moving him to act in a way he does not approve, the noble man is angry at the person who treats him unjustly, and Odysseus is angry at the disrespect he receives from his maids. We can conclude from all this, then, that the spirited part is the source of the ability or capacity to get angry and to use this energy to fight and win against an enemy, someone or something that poses a threat to one's self, ranging from a threat to one's basic life to a threat to one's sense of honor and self-worth.

As in the case of reason, however, Socrates does not just characterize spirit in terms of what it can do, but also in terms of what it loves and values. In *Republic* IX, Socrates says that the spirited part loves mastery, victory, and high repute, and thus that it is appropriate to describe it as victory loving and honor loving (581a–b). He describes an individual who is ruled by spirit as victory loving (581c) and as someone who wants to be honored for his courage (582c). In *Republic* VIII, Socrates describes the individual who is ruled by spirit as a proud and honor-loving man (550b). He claims that such a person loves ruling and honor, but bases his claims to rule on exploits in war and things having to do with war; and he describes him as a lover of physical training and hunting (549a).

In sum, Socrates describes the spirited part in two ways: in terms of what it can do, namely, get angry and fight, and in terms of what it loves and values, victory, honor, and esteem. Again, then, we can synthesize these features of spirit in the following way: spirit is the source of a capacity, to get angry and fight, that enables us to attain a goal, victory, honor, and esteem, which we desire and value. When an individual is ruled by the spirited part of the soul, he or she makes exercising this capacity to get angry and fight in pursuit of victory and honor his or her dominant goal. This explains why the person who is ruled by spirit is interested in competitive arenas – war, athletics, hunting – since these are arenas where one's courage, one's ability to fight against both external and internal enemies (e.g. fear), are on display.

3.3 The appetitive part

Socrates primarily characterizes the appetitive part of the soul as the source of the capacity to feel desires for things that satisfy bodily needs, though clearly the appetitive part's desires go beyond what is necessary for bodily survival and well-being. Thus, in book IV, he introduces the appetitive part as the part that feels passions, hungers, and thirst, as well as that is stirred by other appetites, "friend to certain ways of being filled and certain pleasures" (439d). He also describes the appetitive part as the part that aims to be filled with the so-called pleasures of the body (442a). In book IX, he claims that the appetitive part is multi-form, but that it is reasonable to name it after the biggest and strongest things in it, its appetites for food, drink, sex, and all the things that go along with them (580d–e). In book VIII, Socrates discusses the difference between necessary and unnecessary desires, and this discussion also stresses the relationship between appetitive desires and the body. Socrates claims that necessary desires include those that are required for life and those whose satisfaction benefits us. Bread (here understood more generally as food), for example, is both necessary for life and beneficial, while relishes, though surely not necessary for life, are beneficial and conducive to well-being. Unnecessary desires are those that we can get rid of if we practice from childhood on and whose presence does not do any good but may do harm. Appetites that go beyond bread and relishes, for example, and seek other sorts of foods (which are neither beneficial nor conducive to well-being), are harmful to the soul's capacity for wisdom and temperance (558d–559c). Interestingly, Socrates also repeatedly characterizes the appetitive part as desiring money (442a, 580e–581a), but it is reasonably clear that it does so, at least initially, because it associates money with the satisfaction of bodily desires (580e). In sum, then, the appetitive part is the source of the capacity to desire things that can be consumed by and gratify the body.[11]

As in the other cases, Socrates characterizes the appetitive part not just in terms of what it does, but also in terms of what it loves and values, though his characterization in this respect is not quite as straightforward. As we have seen, in *Republic* IX, Socrates claims that the appetitive part is multi-form but that for the purposes of argument it is reasonable to call it the money-loving and profit-loving part, since its appetites for things like food, drink, and sex are most easily satisfied by money (580d–581a). In books VIII and IX, Socrates claims that being ruled by the appetitive part of the soul can take different forms: some people who are ruled by this part love and value money more than anything else (553a–555); others seem to value the freedom to satisfy whatever desires they happen to have (558c–561e); and in the worst case, someone ruled by the appetitive part is simply driven to satisfy his strongest desires, no matter how outrageous (571a–580c). Perhaps we can conclude that the appetitive part loves and values gratifying (or having the ability to gratify) its desires, whatever those desires may be.

So, in sum, Socrates characterizes the appetitive part in two ways: it is the source of our capacity to desire things that can be consumed by and satisfy the body, and it is at the same time the source of our interest in gratifying those particular desires. We can synthesize by saying that the appetitive part is the source of our capacity to desire, to signal that one should seek something in the environment that can be consumed by the body, which then motivates the person to pursue it, thereby enabling him or her to gratify the desire.

Let us, then, sum up the results of this examination of the nature of the parts of the soul. We have seen that Socrates holds that each part of the soul is dedicated to performing a certain function in pursuit of a certain end which it is positively oriented towards and values. More specifically, the rational part is the source of the capacity to reason and thereby attain truth and understanding; the spirited part is the source of the capacity to get angry and fight against threats to the self and thereby attain victory and honor; and the appetitive part is the source of the capacity to desire, to signal that there is something in the environment that can gratify the body, thereby moving the person to pursue the object and attain satisfaction. Socrates's tripartite psychology claims, then, that as humans we are fundamentally oriented towards certain ends and have parts of the mind that have the unique ability to attain them. Because we are, by nature, positively oriented towards these ends, Socrates seems to think that it is not uncommon for individuals to take one of them and elevate it to their dominant value in life. Thus, Socrates claims that to be ruled by a certain part of the soul is to take the relevant end to be one's dominant end or value.

But why does Socrates think that we have these parts of the soul in particular? In *Republic* X, Socrates suggests that tripartition is due to the soul's partnership with the body.[12] While reason is clearly essential to the soul, the spirited and appetitive parts are somehow a result of or related to embodiment (611b–612a). Thus, one reasonable answer to the question of why we have the non-rational parts in particular is that each part positively orients us towards something that we need given the fact that we are embodied and is uniquely suited to help us attain it. So, our body needs to be nourished, it needs certain things in order to survive and to be satiated; the appetitive part is the source of the capacity to desire those things, to positively orient us towards things in the environment that satisfy the body. But the fact that we have a body also means that we need to be protected, both from external threats, such as individuals who want to harm us, and internal threats that arise from the body, such as appetites, which are prone to go to excess in ruinous ways. Thus, the spirited part of the soul is the source of the capacity to get angry at those threats and fight against them, seeing victory over them as good.

The *Timaeus* provides some confirmation for this view. While a full discussion of the *Timaeus* is outside the scope of this chapter, some passages stress that the appetitive and spirited parts of the soul are tied to embodiment and are geared towards attaining things that we need because we are embodied.[13] Thus, Socrates claims that when the demi-gods created mortals, they had to create a different type of soul as well, a mortal type of soul, which he describes as containing the desires characteristic of appetite and spirit (69c–d). When he describes where the gods placed each aspect of the mortal part of the soul in the body, he highlights their particular role in preserving and caring for the body. So, he says,

> The part of the soul that has appetites for food and drink and whatever else it feels a need for, given the body's nature, they settled in the area between the midriff and the boundary toward the navel. In the whole of this region they constructed something like a trough for the body's nourishment. Here they tied this part of the soul down like a beast, a wild one, but one they could not avoid sustaining along with the others if a mortal race were ever to be.
>
> (70d–e)[14]

Thus, Socrates is clear that the appetitive part of the soul is oriented, at least in part, towards getting the body what it needs to survive. He goes on to say that gods settled the part of the soul that exhibits manliness and spirit nearer the head, so that it could listen to reason and constrain by force the appetitive part if it refuses to obey the commands of reason. Thus, they settled it near the heart, which causes the blood to course through all the bodily members (69e–70b). He continues:

> That way, if spirit's might should boil over at a report from reason that some wrongful act involving these members is taking place – something being done to them from outside or even something originating from the appetites within – every bodily part that is sensitive may be keenly sensitized to the exhortation or threats and so listen and follow completely.
>
> (70b)

As in the *Republic*, then, we see Socrates highlighting spirit's role in safeguarding the person from threats, both external and internal.[15] Both the *Republic* and the *Timaeus*, then, suggest that Socrates might think that we have appetitive and spirited parts of the soul in particular since they enable us to attain things – food, drink, and sex, and victory over enemies – that we need as embodied humans.[16]

In sum, Socrates thinks that the purpose of the appetitive and spirited parts of the soul is to positively orient us towards food, drink, and sex, and victory, honor, and esteem respectively, since these things are important for our survival as embodied creatures. Recall that earlier we said that the appetitive part of the soul is responsible for the fact that instances of food, drink, and sex consistently appear good to us, and the spirited part of the soul is responsible for the fact that threats to the self appear bad and winning out over them appear good. This account explains why: as embodied creatures food, drink, and sex, as well as victory, honor, and esteem, are necessary for our survival and so highly salient to us; instances of such things are, in other words, likely to appear good to those parts of the soul whose job it is to attain those things.

We should stress, however, that the fact that we have a tendency to find instances of food, drink, and sex, as well as victory, honor, and esteem, good does not mean that every instance of these will appear good to us, for our other experiences and beliefs can affect the way things appear. If, for example, someone has been habituated to think that dessert is unhealthy or revenge small-minded, then instances of those things may not appear good to him or her. Moreover, the fact that we have a tendency to find food, drink, and sex, as well as victory, honor, and esteem, good does not mean that we will act on every appearance of goodness. Even if a particular instance of food or victory appears good to us, reason can intervene, scrutinize, and if necessary critique the appearance, and so prevent us from forming a full-fledged desire on its basis. This is why Socrates thinks it is crucial for reason to rule in the soul.

We are now in a position to suggest a line of response to the question with which we began: why does Socrates think that the parts that desire food, drink, and sex and victory, honor, and esteem are also the parts that form their beliefs on the basis of appearances? We have seen that the parts are fundamentally distinguished by what they do and value. Reason calculates, which enables it to pursue the truth. Spirit gets angry and uses this energy to fight, which enables it to attain victory, honor, and esteem. And the appetitive part desires, it positively orients the person to objects that can gratify the body, which enables us to pursue those objects and attain satisfaction. This account suggests an answer to our question. Socrates seems to think that each part of the soul has a specific job to do in the life of the person; perhaps, then, he thinks that each part only has the cognitive resources it needs to do its job. It is the rational part's role to discover the truth; thus, it is the part that has the ability to scrutinize how things appear and to use more sophisticated methods of reasoning to arrive at the truth. Spirit's role is to identify threats and move the person to win out over them, and the appetitive part's role is to identify things that can satisfy the body and move the person to pursue them. In both of these cases, forming judgments on the basis of appearances is enough to get the person in motion to go after these things and, in typical cases, get them. Perhaps Socrates thinks, then, that these parts simply do not need greater cognitive resources in order to attain their ends.

Of course one potential problem for this line of thought is this: there may be occasions where we do need to distinguish between, say, real and apparent food (e.g. between nutritious versus poisonous mushrooms) or between real and apparent threats. Thus perhaps these parts do need to scrutinize appearances and engage in calculations in order to attain their ends. However, while it is true that there may be occasions where we need to distinguish between real and apparent food or threats, this need not entail that the appetitive and spirited parts must have their own ability to scrutinize appearances. Instead, it could entail that the appetitive and spirited parts must have the ability to be responsive in various ways to reason, that part of the soul whose specific job is to scrutinize appearances and intervene should the need arise. Indeed, it might be better in some respects for the spirited and appetitive parts to be merely responsive to reason as opposed to having their own sophisticated cognitive abilities. For scrutinizing appearances and performing calculations is effortful and may in certain circumstances – say circumstances of material scarcity and threat – slow down the operation of the parts in unnecessary and potentially detrimental ways.

In sum, I have suggested that thinking about the parts of the soul in terms of their functional role suggests a possible line of response to the question of why Socrates associates certain desires with certain cognitive tendencies: the spirited and appetitive parts have a specific role to play in the life of the person, a role which does not require that they have their own ability to scrutinize appearances and perform calculations; it is enough for these parts to be responsive to reason, the part of the soul whose specific job is to uncover the truth using sophisticated forms of reasoning should the need arise. Of course more needs to be said to fully articulate and defend this line of thought, but I hope to have shown that it is a promising route to explore.

4. Conclusion: tripartition and dual process theories of judgment

In closing, I would like to highlight some similarities between Plato's theory of tripartition and a theory championed by many psychologists today, dual process theories of judgment. Many contemporary psychologists hold that there are distinct processes by which human beings make judgments about the world. These processes are often referred to as 'system one' and 'system two,' and the operations of each correspond very roughly to the distinction between intuition and reflection.[17] While there is debate about how to characterize the necessary or defining features of each system, it is generally agreed that system one processes are often quick, automatic, and intuitive, while system two processes are often slow, deliberate, and sequential.[18] The judgments of system one, then, are not a result of the person deciding to determine whether something is, for example, large or small, good or bad. Instead, something just *appears* large or small, or good or bad, with little or no sense of voluntary control. Many contemporary psychologists think there are multiple system one processes; that is, there are multiple distinct and autonomous processes in the psyche which are responsible for generating our automatic, intuitive judgments. The judgments of system two, on the other hand, are a result of something more akin to conscious deliberation. Psychologists hold that, in general, system one processes yield default responses to a variety of situations. But these judgments can be intervened on by the distinctive higher-order reasoning processes of system two. Thus, system two is responsible for scrutinizing the intuitive judgments generated by system one and controlling its impulses if necessary.

Since both Plato and contemporary psychologists advance theories according to which there are distinct 'parts' of the mind, it is reasonable to wonder if they are gesturing at the same basic distinctions and so positing theories with the same basic shape. I think that they are.[19] Just as contemporary theories hold that there are, broadly speaking, two ways of forming judgments, so Socrates thinks there are, broadly speaking, two ways of forming judgments: one that is deliberate and reflective and another that is automatic and intuitive. Moreover, like many contemporary psychologists, Socrates holds that there are numerous distinct and autonomous systems responsible for yielding our automatic and intuitive judgments. Socrates is keenly interested in motivation and value. Accordingly, he highlights the spirited and appetitive parts of the soul, which are the parts responsible for two kinds of very typical quick, intuitive judgments, those revolving around the value and pursuit of victory, honor, and esteem, as well as food, drink, and sex, respectively. As we mentioned earlier, however, there is evidence that Socrates is not committed to the thought that there are only three parts of the soul (443d–e).

In highlighting and characterizing the appetitive and spirited parts in the way that he does, Socrates tells us why we are prone to make quick, intuitive judgments about the value of victory, honor, and esteem or food, drink, and sex. In short, we have parts of the mind that are uniquely suited to positively orient us towards and attain instances of victory, honor, and esteem, as well as food, drink, and sex. In other words, we have parts of the mind that automatically see instances of these things as attractive and so are prone to form quick judgments about their value. And we have these parts of the mind in turn because they are uniquely suited to help us get what we need as embodied creatures. Socrates is clear, however, that in order to *flourish*, we often need to use our reason to scrutinize and intervene on the impulses of the spirited and appetitive part, which, without such supervision, can lead us astray and threaten to overtake our lives.

Notes

1 Many thanks to David Bronstein, Peter Carruthers, Rachana Kamtekar, Whitney Schwab, Clerk Shaw, Christopher Shields, and John Sisko for comments on an earlier version of this chapter.
2 Adam, Murphy, Nehamas.
3 Lorenz, Moss, Singpurwalla (2011).
4 All quotations are from Reeve (2004).
5 Annas, pp. 337–338.
6 Moss, Singpurwalla (2010, 2011). As is evident from the argument of this chapter, I would no longer say that the cognitive capacities of the parts fully explain the motivational capacities.
7 For commentators who hold that Socrates thinks that appetitive desires at least are independent of our beliefs about goodness, see Irwin, Penner, Reeve. For those who hold that he thinks appetites involve cognizing the object of desire as good, see Bobonich, Carone, Lesses, Moss, Singpurwalla (2010).
8 See Singpurwalla (2006, 2010, 2011) for a more precise account of the relationship between appearances, attraction, and desire.
9 For one of the best papers exemplifying this approach, see Cooper.

10 Kamtekar (2008, 2018) is a notable exception. She focuses on the function, or as she calls it, the capacity, of each part to illuminate the nature of the parts of the soul.
11 In book VIII, Socrates claims that the 'democratic character' – one of the personality types that is ruled by the appetitive part – desires things like politics, military training, and philosophy (561c–d). These do not seem to be desires that gratify the body. Scott argues that the democratic person has a shifting character: at one time he is ruled by the spirited part, at another time the rational part, at another time by the appetitive part. If he is right, then we need not think that the appetitive part is the source of the desire to engage in military activity or philosophy.
12 Burnyeat also claims that the spirited and appetitive parts are somehow a result of embodiment.
13 Johansen and Kamtekar (2018) argue that the *Timaeus* stresses the positive function of the parts of the soul. Kamtekar (2018) argues that each part of the soul is teleologically oriented towards the good.
14 All translations of the *Timaeus* from Zeyl.
15 See Brennan for an interesting account of spirit's functional role as 'policing' the appetites in others and ourselves.
16 In the *Phaedrus*, Socrates suggests that the gods have spirited and appetitive parts of the soul; this poses a challenge for the view that those parts are somehow tied to embodiment, since the gods (as Socrates conceives of them) are never embodied. However, the context for the claim that the gods have spirited and appetitive parts is complicated, for it is made during the course of a speech which is designed both to display Socrates's oratorical skills and move his interlocutor, Phaedrus, towards a more philosophical way of life. Socrates describes the soul of both gods and humans as the union of a charioteer (reason) and two horses (spirit and appetite); the gods' horses, however, are good and obedient, while humans have at least one bad and unruly horse (appetite) (246aff). It is possible that Socrates depicts the gods as having spirited and appetitive parts simply to inspire Phaedrus (and us, Plato's readers) to make our spirited and appetitive parts fully obedient to reason, so that we can be as god-like as possible.
17 For a recent overview, see Kahnemann; see also Evans and Stanovich.
18 See Evans and Stanovich, who argue that the defining feature of what they call type one processes is that they are autonomous, in so far as they do not require controlled attention and make minimal demands on working memory, while the defining feature of type two processes is that they make use of working memory, which enables us to engage in hypothetical thinking and consequential decision-making. Carruthers argues for a similar characterization.
19 In a recent paper, Tamar Gendler has suggested that Plato's theory is missing the insights crucial to dual process theories of judgment. While she lauds Plato for noting that the mind contains distinct and autonomous sources of motivation, and while she agrees that the parts he cites might indeed be the source of our felt experiences of conflict, she thinks that he fails to highlight a distinct source of error: our capacity to make quick, intuitive judgments, many of which are a result of culturally encoded stereotypes. Referring to Socrates's image of the soul in the *Phaedrus*, she argues that Socrates fails to note that there is 'a third horse,' namely, the part of us that is responsible for making quick, intuitive judgments. I hope to have suggested in this chapter, however, that Gendler's critique is at least somewhat misguided, since Plato's theory of tripartition and dual process theories of judgment have more in common than might first appear. More specifically, Socrates *is* aware that there are parts of us that are prone to make quick, intuitive judgments, and he has identified two of those parts: spirit and appetite. Moreover, he is aware that the fact that these parts form beliefs on the basis

of appearances makes them particularly susceptible to cultural influences of a certain kind, as his critique of art in *Republic* X makes clear. If, then, Socrates's famous image of the soul requires a third horse (or more), it is not to acknowledge our tendency to make quick, intuitive judgments, but rather to identify additional sources of those judgments.

Bibliography

Annas, J. (1981) *An Introduction to Plato's Republic*. Oxford: Oxford University Press.

Bobonich, C. (2002) *Plato's Utopia Recast: His Later Ethics and Politics*. New York: Oxford University Press.

Brennan, T. (2012) The nature of the spirited part of the soul and its object. In Barney, R., Brennan, T., and Brittain, C. (eds.) *Plato and the Divided Self*. Cambridge, MA: Cambridge University Press, pp. 102–127.

Burnyeat, M. (2006) The truth of tripartition. *Proceedings of the Aristotelian Society* 106: 1–22.

Carone, G. (2001) Akrasia in the 'Republic': Does Plato change his mind? *Oxford Studies in Ancient Philosophy* 20: 107–148.

Carruthers, P. (2015) *The Centered Mind: What the Science of Working Memory Shows Us About the Nature of Human Thought*. Oxford: Oxford University Press.

Cooper, J. (1984) Plato's theory of motivation. *History of Philosophy Quarterly* 1 (1): 3–21.

Evans, J., and Stanovich, K. (2013) Dual process theories of higher cognition: Advancing the debate. *Perspective on Psychological Science* 8: 223–241.

Gendler, T. (2014) The third horse: On unendorsed association and human behaviour. *Proceedings of the Aristotelian Society Supplementary Volume* 88: 185–218.

Irwin, T. (1995) *Plato's Ethics*. Oxford: Oxford University Press.

Johansen, T. (2000) Body, soul, and tripartition in Plato's 'Timaeus'. *Oxford Studies in Ancient Philosophy* 19: 87–111.

Kahneman, D. (2011) *Thinking, Fast and Slow*. New York: Farrar, Straus and Giroux.

Kamtekar, R. (2008) The powers of Plato's tripartite psychology. *Proceedings of the Boston Area Colloquium in Ancient Philosophy* 24: 127–150.

———. (2018) *Plato's Moral Psychology: Intellectualism, the Divided Soul, and the Desire for the Good*. Oxford: Oxford University Press.

Lesses, G. (1987) The divided soul in Plato's 'Republic'. *History of Philosophy Quarterly* 4: 147–161.

Lorenz, H. (2006) *The Brute Within: Appetitive Desires in Plato and Aristotle*. Oxford: Oxford University Press.

Moline, J. (1978) Plato on the complexity of the psyche. *Archiv für Geschichte der Philosophie* 60: 1–26.

Moss, J. (2008) Appearances and calculations: Plato's division of the soul. *Oxford Studies in Ancient Philosophy* 34: 34–68.

Murphy, N. (1951) *The Interpretation of Plato's Republic*. Oxford: Oxford University Press.

Nehamas, A. (1982) Plato on imitation and poetry in 'Republic' X. In Moravscik, J. M. E., and Temko, P. (eds.) *Plato on Beauty, Wisdom and the Arts*. Towata: Rowman and Littlefield, pp. 47–78. Reprinted in his (1999) *Virtues of Authenticity: Essays on Plato and Socrates*. Princeton: Princeton University Press, pp. 251–278.

Penner, T. (1971) Thought and desire in Plato. In Vlastos, G. (ed.) *Plato: A Collection of Critical Essays Volume 2*. New York: Anchor Books, pp. 96–118.

———. (1990) Plato and Davidson on parts of the soul and weakness of the will. *Supplementary Volume of the Canadian Journal of Philosophy* 16: 35–74.

Reeve, C. D. C. (1988). *Philosopher-Kings: The Argument of Plato's Republic*. Princeton: Princeton University Press.

———. (tr.) (2004) *Republic*. Indianapolis: Hackett.

Scott, D. (2000) Plato's critique of the democratic character. *Phronesis* 45 (1): 19–37.

Shields, C. (2010) Plato's divided soul. In McPherran, M. (ed.) *Plato's Republic: A Critical Guide*. Cambridge, MA: Cambridge University Press.

Singpurwalla, R. (2006) Reasoning with the irrational: Moral psychology in the 'Protagoras'. *Ancient Philosophy* 26: 243–258.

———. (2010) The tripartite theory of motivation in Plato's 'Republic'. *Blackwell Philosophy Compass* 5 (11): 880–892.

———. (2011) Soul division and mimesis in book X. In Destrée, P., and Herrmann, F. G. (eds.) *Plato and the Poets*. Leiden: Brill.

Zeyl, D. (tr.) (1997) *Timaeus*. In Cooper, J. (ed.) *Plato: Complete Works*. Indianapolis: Hackett, pp. 1224–1291.

6

COSMIC AND HUMAN COGNITION IN THE *TIMAEUS*[1]

Gábor Betegh

1. Cosmic intellects

Many early Greek philosophers thought that higher level cognitive functions are not the prerogatives of human beings and the gods of the traditional pantheon. The orderly functioning of the cosmos, the regularity and constancy of its cyclical processes, were in need of explanation. Where does this order stem from and how is it maintained, if not for eternity, at least for immensely long periods of time? One possibility was to refer to some form of cosmic law or necessity. Another was to posit a cosmic intelligence, which is in some way akin to human intelligence, yet immensely more powerful, capable of governing and steering the entire cosmos and rendering physical processes regulated and orderly. We find different expressions of this latter model, possibly in combination with the first model, in the fragments of Xenophanes, Heraclitus, Parmenides' *Doxa*, Anaxagoras, Diogenes of Apollonia, and Archelaus of Athens. There is good evidence that such ideas were current also in Athens around the time of Socrates. Hecuba in her prayer in Euripides' *Trojan Women* (884–7) lists human intelligence, alongside necessity and Zeus, as one possible identification of the supreme cosmic god. More important for our present topic, Xenophon presents Socrates approvingly giving voice to such a theory (*Mem.* 1.4.8).

Earlier Platonic dialogues, which are supposed to more closely reflect the ideas of the historical Socrates, do not elaborate on the idea of a cosmic intelligence – overall, the Socrates of these dialogues shows little concern for cosmological questions. There are, moreover, good reasons why such an immanent cosmic intelligence is absent from the dialogues of Plato's middle period as well. In these texts the physical world is presented as possessing very limited orderliness and inherent rationality; if there is any order and rationality in it, it comes not from an immanent cosmic intellect, but from its relation to the transcendent Forms, even if the precise nature of this relation, as Plato candidly acknowledges, remains an open question.

In his later period, and most prominently in the *Timaeus*, Plato appears to allow more intrinsic value and orderliness to the physical world, and, correspondingly, shows more interest in the source of these features. Yet even in the *Timaeus*, Plato remains committed to the idea that the ultimate origin of anything that is rational and orderly in the corporeal world must be transcendent to it. In order to account for the relationship between the physical world and the eternal and changeless, and hence inactive, transcendent realities, he posits a similarly transcendent yet active divine craftsman who creates order in the inherently disorderly corporeal realm by moulding it, as far as possible, on the model of eternal, perfect, and intelligible transcendent entities. With the introduction of the divine craftsman, we get a partial answer to the question concerning the ordered structure of the cosmos.

Yet, even if he is the ultimate origin of rationality and structure in the physical world, the divine craftsman does not seem to be directly involved in maintaining the everyday functioning of the cosmos. Timaeus, the spokesman of the dialogue, calls the cosmos itself a living god, constituted of a rational soul and a physical body, both created from preexisting stuffs by the divine craftsman (34b).[2] The orderly motions of the heavenly bodies, which in turn guarantee the regularity of other physical processes, are described as being only the visible manifestations of the regular motions of the soul of the cosmos. The rational soul of the world, similarly to the Presocratic cosmologies mentioned previously, is at the same time the cosmic counterpart of the individual rational human souls.

Interestingly enough, the transcendent divinity – as his job title, 'craftsman', also indicates – is the divine paradigm of practical rationality. His activity in creating the orderly cosmos exemplifies how a rational agent can achieve the best results given certain initial limiting conditions and constraints inherent in the features of the raw material one has to work with.[3] On the other hand, as we shall see in a moment, the immanent soul of the cosmos is the paradigm of higher, and indeed the highest, forms of cognitive activities, which include not only forming correct opinions about the physical world, but also gaining genuine knowledge about eternal realities. This is a new development not only compared to Plato's previous dialogues. Timaeus' description of the cognitive functioning of the soul of the cosmos, and its relation to the highest cognitive functions of human beings, contains significantly novel elements compared to the Presocratic accounts as well. For beyond some rather vague pronouncements about the supreme cognitive abilities of their respective cosmic gods and intelligences, the Presocratics – as far as we can judge from their extant fragments – said next to nothing about the actual cognitive processes that characterise these cosmic intelligences and, just as important, how their cognitive processes are related to the cognitive functions of human beings.

In what follows, I shall approach Plato's account of the relationship between cosmic and human rational soul not by comparing it to its Presocratic predecessors, but by showing how the views put forward in the *Timaeus* can be conceived as offering solutions to a number of problems raised, but left unanswered, in Plato's earlier dialogues.

2. The Affinity Argument of the *Phaedo*

There are many ways in which the *Timaeus* appears to be directly related to the *Phaedo*, which on a standard chronology was written considerably earlier, around the beginning of Plato's middle period. It is in the *Phaedo* that Socrates expresses most explicitly his discontent with the explanatory accounts of those of his predecessors who engaged in 'inquiry into nature', and it is in this context that he formulates the need for a cosmology that explains the structure and functioning of the cosmos with reference to a cosmic rationality aiming at the best (96a–99c). In important respects, the *Timaeus* fulfills precisely this project.[4] This much seems to be relatively obvious and uncontested. I would like to maintain, however, that in developing his conception of the cosmic soul and its relation to individual human souls in the *Timaeus* Plato was also reflecting on a number of problems of great consequence that remained unresolved in the *Phaedo*, and, in particular, in that part of the dialogue which is customarily called the Affinity Argument (77a–84b).

The Affinity Argument, the last of the three initial arguments for the immortality of the soul, has received bad press. In his classic commentary on the *Phaedo*, Kenneth Dorter maintained that we should appreciate it not for its logical consistency, but rather for its emotive value and elevated massage (Dorter 1982: 76). One recent interpreter even claimed that Plato introduced it

> precisely in order to illustrate how not to argue the case for immortality, and, more generally, how not to argue the case for any thesis. The affinity remarks, then, form part of an object lesson in how not to do good philosophy.
> (Elton, 1997: 313)

It seems to me however that we arrive at a significantly different assessment of this section of the *Phaedo* if we recognise that it has a somewhat different agenda than simply arguing for the immortality of the soul. After all, Socrates himself acknowledges in the conclusion of the argument that he hasn't in fact presented a watertight proof. As he says, 'If all this is the case, isn't the body the sort of thing to be quickly disintegrated, but soul, on the other hand, the sort to be altogether incapable of being disintegrated, ***or nearly so***?'[5] (80b; my emphasis). Indeed, what does it mean that the soul is 'nearly' incapable of being disintegrated?

On the face of it, the Affinity Argument purports to show that the soul is indestructible because it shares more features with the transcendent immutable Forms than with the ever-changing composite physical bodies. Yet, as we have just seen, it is able to do so only with some serious caveats. So what is the function of the Affinity Argument, if it avowedly does not provide a cogent proof for the immortality of the soul? I would like to maintain that the primary purpose of this section of the text is to return to a previous part of the dialogue, customarily called Socrates' Defence (57a–69e), and to give a new formulation of the Defence with the help of the metaphysical framework developed in the intervening section of the dialogue, and in particular in the Recollection Argument (72e–77b). In the

Defence, Socrates tries to convince his friends that in so far as death is the separation of soul and body, and the philosophical life consists in separating the soul from the body as far as it is possible in our earthly life, the philosopher is practicing for death already during his embodied existence, and has therefore nothing to fear when biological death approaches. The Recollection Argument in turn argues for and solidifies the fundamental metaphysical division between transcendent and intelligible Forms on the one hand and perceptible physical bodies on the other, and presents the theses about the immortality of the soul and the existence of the Forms as standing or falling together (76d–77a).[6] Then, the Affinity Argument picks up the central themes of the Defence, such as the relationship between body and soul, and the normative ideal of the purification of the soul from the body, and provides a new formulation of these theses, already equipped with the much more robust and philosophically well-articulated dualist metaphysical framework as developed in the Recollection Argument.

Accordingly, at the outset of the Affinity Argument, Socrates distinguishes between these two kinds and gives them the following characterisation. Members of the first kind are 'divine, immortal, intelligible, uniform, and incapable of being disintegrated, and . . . always stay in the same condition and state' (80b). Moreover, being divine, there are 'naturally the kind to rule and lead' (80a). The clearest examples of this kind are the Forms (78d), even though it is not explained in exactly what the ruling and leading function of the Forms consist. Members of the other kind are 'mortal, resistant to intelligence, multiform, able to disintegrate, and never in the same state' (80b). It is to this latter kind that everything bodily, and consequently the human body itself, belongs.

Interestingly, although he has his interlocutors' consent that they will assume that only these two kinds of beings exist (79a), Socrates never actually says that the human soul squarely belongs in the first kind. Or, for that matter, that it belongs in the second kind. The soul shares certain key features with members of the first kind, whereas there are other features in respect of which it is unlike them and more like members of the second kind. For instance, it is surely not true of the soul that it would always be in the same state as the members of the first kind emphatically are. Bodily pleasures and pains, as well as perceptions stemming from bodies, can affect the soul – and as we have learnt in the Defence they can affect it very negatively – whereas *bona fide* members of the first kind are completely immune to any such deleterious influences from the bodily. Indeed, death, as the ultimate separation of the soul from the body, is beneficial precisely because as long as the soul is attached to the body, the body keeps disturbing the soul. Referring back to his earlier claims made in the Defence, Socrates explains in the Affinity Argument that whenever the soul uses sense perception through the body

> it is dragged by the body into things that never stay in the same state, and the soul itself wanders and is disturbed and giddy as if drunk, because the things it is grasping have the same kind of instability.
>
> (79c)

Sense perception causes disorder, instability, and confusion in the soul.

What is more, the souls of those who are constantly preoccupied with bodies and bodily desires and pleasure can even become tainted with the physical characteristics of the body such as weight and visibility (81c). Socrates however adds that on the other hand, when the soul focuses on the divine, immutable Forms, and

> considers them alone by itself, it gets away into that which is pure, always in existence, and immortal, and which stays in the same condition; that the soul because it is akin to this, always comes to be with it whenever alone by itself and able to do so; that the soul is then in the same state and condition, because the things it is grasping have the same kind of stability; and that this state of the soul is called 'wisdom'.
>
> (79d)

Thus, even though the soul does not squarely belong in the first kind, it is similar and akin (συγγενής 79d; 79e) to the members of the first kind. By concentrating on these divine beings, the soul avoids and rectifies, as far as possible, the confusion, wandering, and giddiness caused by perception and corporeal desires and pleasures, and becomes more stable. These disturbing desires are not restricted to drink, food, and sex, but include the love of money, power, and honour (82c). Giving a new formulation to the central tenet of the Defence, Socrates expresses his normative ideal in the Affinity Argument in the following terms: we can achieve the best life during our embodied, earthly existence when we focus on those beings which our soul is akin to, or συγγενής with, and thereby approximate the stable state that characterises the Forms. In this way, we distance our souls from the confusion and instability that characterises bodies and, at the same time, secure for ourselves the best possible post-mortem existence in which we can continue our quest for truth.

Notably, this characterisation of the relationship between soul and the Forms, and the normative ideal this relationship bestows on the human beings, is not limited to the *Phaedo*. Plato's language is strikingly similar when he describes the characteristic activities and natural motivations of the philosophical nature in Book 6 of the *Republic*. Socrates explains that such a nature has a passionate love for that kind of study which reveals to it the Forms and those features which have complete stability, not being subject to becoming and destruction (485a–b). In addition to possessing a set of natural cognitive endowments including good memory and quickness of mind, the philosophical nature is akin (συγγενής) to 'truth, justice, courage, and moderation' (487a). For this reason,

> the genuine lover of learning naturally strives for what is. He does not linger over each of the many particulars that are subject of opinion, but keeps on striving towards it [i.e. what is], without losing or lessening his passion, until he grasps what the nature of each thing itself is with the

part of his soul that is fitted to grasp a thing of that sort because of its kinship (συγγενεῖ) with it.

(490a–b, trans. Reeve, modified)

Moreover, through an enduring study of the rational order of these realities, the soul of the philosopher gets assimilated to them, and becomes orderly (κόσμιος) and divine, as far as possible:

> as he looks at and contemplates things that are orderly and always the same, that neither do injustice to one another nor suffer it, being all in a rational order, he imitates them and tries to become as like them as he can. Or do you think there is any way to prevent someone from associating with something he admires without imitating it? . . . Then the philosopher, by associating with what is orderly and divine, becomes as divine and orderly as a human being can.
>
> (500c, trans. Reeve, modified)

This last passage further emphasises that the most important feature in respect of which the soul gets assimilated to the Forms is rational order – the 'cosmos' of the Forms – without however detailing what that order is. Moreover, having introduced the thesis of the tripartite soul in Book 4, Socrates now intimates that it is not the entire soul that is akin to the Forms, but only a part or aspect of it – in all probability only the rational part.[7]

In sum, although we do learn a great deal about the soul's relationship to the Forms in these texts, at the end of the day it remains unexplained what it means exactly that the soul is akin to the divine Forms. Moreover, we do not get a straightforward answer to the question concerning the soul's place in the twofold metaphysical framework. It remains unclear how the soul can have this dynamic middle status and become more like the divine and stable Forms or the disorderly always-changing bodies depending on which of the two it focuses on. It remains unclear whether the soul constitutes a third kind ultimately irreducible to the two other kinds, or whether it occupies this intermediary position between the two realms by some other way. And, further, it remains unexplained how the body can affect the soul, whereas it cannot affect the *bona fide* members of the first kind. For although the disturbances and negative effects caused by the body are central to Socrates' claim that it is the greatest benefit for the philosopher to die, we do not in the end hear anything about the actual way in which the body can exert all its harmful effects on the soul.[8]

3. The kinship of individual and cosmic soul in the *Timaeus*

As stated at the outset, I would like to suggest that the *Timaeus* picks up and answers some of these issues left open in the *Phaedo*.[9] Let us start with the question of the middle position of the soul. By the description of the ingredients out of which the divine craftsman formed both the soul of the cosmos and the rational souls of individual human beings, Timaeus finds a way to state very clearly that although the soul does not belong in either of the two kinds, it is not a third independent kind either. For he relates that the soul is a mixture of the two kinds, or more precisely of the Being, Same, and Different pertaining to the two kinds:

> In between the Being that is indivisible and always changeless, and the one that is divisible and comes to be in the corporeal realm, he [i.e. the divine craftsman] mixed a third, intermediate form of being, derived from the other two. Similarly, he made a mixture of the Same, and then one of the Different, in between their indivisible and their corporeal, divisible counterparts. And he took the three mixtures and mixed them together to make a uniform mixture, forcing the Different, which was hard to mix, into conformity with the Same. Now when he had mixed these two together with Being, and from the three had made a single mixture, he redivided the whole mixture into as many parts as his task required, each part remaining a mixture of the Same, the Different, and of Being.
>
> (35a)[10]

This chunk of text, constituting a single syntactically very complex sentence in the Greek, presents a great number of interpretative puzzles that I cannot discuss in the present context. What is nonetheless clear is that the two types of Being, Same, and Different are characterised by the centrally important oppositions of the two kinds that we find in the *Phaedo*: indivisibility and changelessness on the one hand, and divisibility and corporeality on the other. These contrasting characteristics are thus in some way inherent to soul, both cosmic and human. Admittedly, one would still have many questions to ask from Timaeus at this point; yet his description at least goes some way to account for the fact that the soul cannot be classified in either of the *Phaedo*'s two kinds.[11]

Just as important, Timaeus agrees with the Socrates of the *Phaedo* and the *Republic* that the soul is a dynamic entity that gets assimilated to what it is primarily concerned with:

> Now, if someone got absorbed in his appetites or his ambitions and takes great pains to further them, all his thoughts are bound to become mortal. And so far as it is possible for a human being to thoroughly become mortal, he will not fall short of it, since it is this aspect of himself that he has strengthened all along. On the other hand, if a man has seriously devoted himself to the love of learning and to true wisdom, if he has exercised these aspects of himself above all, then there is absolutely no way that his thoughts can fail to be immortal and divine, should truth

come within his grasp. And to the extent that human nature can partake of immortality, he can in no way fail to achieve this: constantly caring for his divine part as he does, keeping well-ordered the guiding spirit that dwells within him, he must indeed be supremely happy.

(90b–c)

What is more, just a few sentences earlier, Timaeus had made clear that the divine, on which the soul should focus, is akin (συγγενής) to the soul (90a). So far we are stunningly close to what we have seen in the *Phaedo* and the *Republic*. Yet, in Timeaus' account – and this is the first momentous difference compared to the earlier texts – the divine counterpart of the individual human soul on which it should focus, and to which it is akin, is not the Forms, but rather the soul of the cosmos. Indeed, in his description of the happiest human life, which constitutes the crescendo of his long speech, Timaeus explicitly calls the relationship between the individual human soul and its divine heavenly counterpart it ought to emulate 'kinship' (συγγένεια 90a). Moreover, he uses the same term when he states that the teleological cause of eye sight is to observe the heavenly motions, which are akin (ξυγγεῖς, 47b) to the motions of our rational soul.

The nature of the kinship that remained unexplained in the earlier texts becomes entirely obvious in the *Timaeus*. The cosmic soul and the individual rational soul are made by the same maker – the divine craftsman – of the same, although less pure, ingredients, mixed in the same way (41d), divided according to the same complex mathematical and harmonic ratios, and finally fashioned into concentric circles in the same manner (43d). The spherical human rational soul housed in our skulls are isomorphic miniature replicas of the spherical cosmic soul.[12]

All this however means a considerable shift from the original framework as formulated in the Affinity Argument and echoed in the *Republic*. For it turns out that what the human soul is akin to, and what it has to emulate by making it the object of cognition, are no longer the eternal, immutable, uniform Forms, but rather the generated, moving, composite cosmic soul.

This shift might seem fatal to the core of the Affinity Argument conceived as an argument for the indestructibility of the soul. If as both the soul and its divine counterpart turn out to be generated composites – indeed composed by the divine craftsman of very different and contrasting ingredients hard to combine – it would follow that just like any other generated composite entity, the soul can be subject to destruction. In fact, Timaeus fully acknowledges that anything that has been generated and composed is not immune to destruction and decomposition (41b). However, Timaeus at this point introduces a consideration which is entirely lacking from the Affinity Argument but is introduced as the ultimate explanatory desideratum at a later point of the *Phaedo*: the reference to the best. Qua composites, both the cosmic soul and the individual human souls are prone to disintegrate, just like any bodily composite. Nonetheless, they will *not* disintegrate because the *demiurge* made them good – indeed to be the best possible – so it is **good** that they remain in existence, and the *demiurge* will therefore not let them disintegrate. By introducing teleology into the picture, Timaeus can thus maintain both the principal premises of the Affinity Argument, i.e. (i) that generated composites are destructible and (ii) that the human soul is like its divine counterpart in terms of indestructibility, while still maintaining that both the human soul and its divine counterpart will never in fact disintegrate because they are protected by the good will of the *demiurge*.[13] In this new framework, even the puzzling expression of the *Phaedo* makes much better sense: 'soul [is] the sort to be altogether incapable of being disintegrated, *or nearly so*'.[14]

Note also that the cosmic soul is a much better role model for the individual soul than the Forms. After all, the Forms are immobile and devoid of any activity, whereas the soul, as Plato emphasises in his later works, has an essential, inherent relationship to motion, or can even be characterised as motion as such (*Phaedrus* 245c–246e; *Laws* 10 895c–896c). However, the cosmic soul, created as the moving image of eternity, can provide us with a paradigm of a motion that is as orderly as possible, and shows as much constancy as possible. Moreover, as we shall see in the final section of this chapter, the cosmic soul is not only intelligible like the Forms but – as is appropriate for a divine soul – also performs cognitive activity at the highest level. It is active, in constant motion, and due to its constant and fully regular motion, keeps cognising both the Forms and physical particulars.[15] According to the new framework introduced in the *Timaeus*, it is the constant and orderly divine cognitive activity, expressed in terms of regular circular motions, that we ought to replicate in our individual rational souls, and not the frozen perfection of the Forms.[16]

4. Soul-body interaction

On the list of issues raised but left unanswered in the *Phaedo* there is a centrally important item that I haven't broached as yet: how can corporeal processes, perception, pleasure, and pain cause all the confusion that we ought to counter by focusing on the divine counterpart of our soul? Can the new way of conceiving the individual human rational soul and its divine kin as introduced in the *Timaeus* help us to understand better how the body can exert its effects on the soul? In other words, to what extent can the psychology and physics of the *Timaeus* deal with the question of body-soul interaction – an issue that has been almost completely left unexplained in the *Phaedo*, or for that matter in other dialogues. Indeed, it might very well be that Plato simply did not think that the interaction between body and soul is problematic. In the *Timaeus*, however he does seem to consider this relationship worthy of consideration and provides at least the outlines of an account of it. Of course, I will not suggest that Plato in this dialogue solved the problem of body-soul interaction. Nonetheless, I think it is worthwhile to try to identify, as precisely as possible, the limits of this new explanatory framework, and to see at which point, and for what reasons, the explanation breaks down.

Prima facie, the *Timaeus* offers a strikingly simple answer to this question: the soul can interact with and be affected by the bodily because of its ontological constitution. As we have seen, the soul has a share of the bodily in so far as the 'stuff' out of which the soul is constituted contains not only indivisible Being, Different, and Same, but also divisible Being, Different, and Same, which belong in the realm of the bodily.[17] By virtue of its ontological makeup, the soul can have cognitive access to both realms; but it can also interact with and be affected by entities belonging to both realms. Surely, this goes some way towards answering the puzzle of body-soul interaction. Nonetheless, this is still not a causal explanatory account of how exactly the body can affect the soul. In fact, we can formulate this question in another way as well: What does it actually mean that the soul contains something of the bodily? What are the properties that the soul acquires by virtue of having a share of the bodily in its ontological makeup? What are the properties that it shares with bodies, without however becoming a body?

In so far as divisibility is singled out by Timaeus as the most important characteristic of the bodily components of the soul (35a), it is reasonable to think that it is the very divisibility of soul that stems from its bodily aspect. The divine craftsman can divide up the mixture of soul ingredients by mathematical and harmonic proportions, and can construct out of them a complex structure, precisely because the mixture contains something of the bodily and hence divisible. Nonetheless, although divisibility and internal complexity are certainly crucial features in Timaeus' account of the soul, these will still not account for the soul's ability to be affected by the body. It is not by being divisible, or by having a complex internal structure, that the soul can interact with the body.

We might get one step closer to an answer by concentrating on another feature of the rational soul which appears to be a novelty of the *Timaeus* and which might very well be connected to the bodily. For one might argue that the cosmic soul and the individual human souls can have spatial extension, whether in one, two, or three dimensions, precisely because they have a share in the nature of the bodily. In this vein, Thomas Johansen has suggested that by making the soul spatially extended and in motion, Timaeus can consider the problem of body-soul interaction solved.[18] At the same time, Johansen argues that, in contrast to bodies, the circles of the soul do not have depth and solidity.[19]

Although I find Johansen's solution highly attractive, I would like to question this last contention. Solidity, as we shall shortly see, means in this context precisely that entities show resistance to each other, so that when they get into contact spatially, there is some mechanical, causal interaction between them. It is exactly in this sense that we need to attribute at least some type of solidity at least to the circle of the Different. When it comes into contact with bodily particles it can be affected by them, precisely because it shows some resistance to them, so that these particles cannot simply travel through it.[20]

It will be worthwhile to have a close look at Timaeus' description of the way in which sense perception reaches and affects the soul of human beings, and the way in which the cosmic soul comes into contact with perceptible bodies so as to formulate true opinions about them.

Let us start with Timaeus' account of human perception.[21] In brief, we become aware of a sensation when a motion originated by an external object reaches the human body, and then this motion gets propagated through the body by the corporeal particles of the body moving one another in a chain, so that the last particles at the end of the chain exert some effect on the circles of the rational soul, and more specifically on the circle of the Different.[22] This is how Timaeus gives his preliminary description of this process:

> For mighty as the nourishment bearing billow was in its ebb and flow, mightier still was the turbulence produced by the disturbances caused by the things that struck against the living things (προσπιπτόντων παθήματα ἑκάστοις). Such disturbances would occur when the body encountered and collided with external fire (i.e., fire other than the body's own) or for that matter with a hard lump of earth or with the flow of gliding waters, or when it was caught up by a surge of air-driven winds. The motions produced by all these encounters would then be conducted through the body to the soul, and strike against it (διὰ τοῦ σώματος αἱ κινήσεις ἐπὶ τὴν ψυχὴν φερόμεναι προσπίπτοιεν). That is no doubt why these motions as a group came afterward to be called 'sensations' (αἰσθήσεις), as they are still called today.
>
> (43b–c)

What is particularly noteworthy in this paragraph is that Timaeus uses the very same verb, προσπίπτω, to describe the way in which external bodies reaching the human body cause affections (παθήματα) in it, and the way in which the motions transmitted through the organism finally affect the soul. We find the same verbal stem, this time with a different prefix, in the concluding general description of how external impacts reach the soul:

> When even a minor disturbance affects (ἐμπίπτῃ) that which is easily moved by nature, the disturbance is passed on in a chain reaction with some parts affecting others in the same way as they were affected, until it reaches the mind (τὸ φρόνιμον) and reports what produced the reaction.
>
> (64b)

The general picture we get from these passages is confirmed, even at the level of vocabulary, by the more detailed description of vision:

> Now whenever daylight surrounds the visual stream, like makes contact with like (τότε ἐκπῖπτον ὅμοιον πρὸς ὅμοιον) and coalesces with it to make up a single homogeneous body aligned with the direction of the eyes. This happens whenever the internal fire strikes and presses against an external object it has connected with (τὸ προσπῖπτον ἔνδοθεν πρὸς ὃ τῶν ἔξω συνέπεσεν). And because this body of fire has become uniform

throughout and thus uniformly affected, it transmits the motions of whatever it comes in contact with (ἐφάπτηται) as well as of whatever comes in contact with it, to and through the whole body until they reach the soul.

(45c–d)

All physical processes leading to perceptions, in all sense modalities, are thus ultimately explainable by, and reducible to, the mechanical interactions of the elementary particles. Physical bodies are perceptible in so far as their component elements can causally affect the particles composing the body by dislocating them and thereby triggering off a chain of motions.[23] At the end of the day, perception depends on, and is explained by, the fact that when two particles meet they don't travel through one another but hit one another like two billiard balls. In other words, all these interactions are dependent on the fact that elementary particles are impenetrable to one another; they have solidity in the sense of showing resistance to one another.[24]

It is worthwhile to compare this account of the mechanical basis of sense perception with the way in which Timaeus first characterises the bodily towards the beginning of his speech:

> Now that which comes to be must have a bodily form, and be both visible and tangible, but nothing could ever become visible apart from fire, nor tangible without something solid, nor solid without earth.
>
> (31b)

Visibility and tangibility, and their dependence on fire and earth, constitute the premises from which Timaeus deduces his theory of four elements. We need fire and earth to account for visibility and tangibility, and we will need another two, air and water, to create bonds between fire and earth. Yet the account of perception, and in particular the description of vision, necessitates a reinterpretation, and in fact some significant modifications, of these initial assumptions. When one first reads the sentence quoted previously, one could easily have the impression that fire makes things visible in so far as these things contain some measure of fire. Yet later parts of the text rectify this assumption. Timaeus explicitly says that all four bodies are visible in and of themselves, even if individual particles of them are not visible due to their smallness (46e; 56b–c). On the other hand, the description of the physics and physiology of vision makes clear in what sense fire is indeed a necessary condition for seeing. There would be no vision if the eye did not contain fire and if the sun did not emit the fire of daylight, so that the two can jointly form the cone-shaped visual body stemming from the eye, and which can then be effected by external bodies and can transmit to the soul the motions triggered by them (45b–46a). This is, by the way, also why individual particles of the elements are not visible: individually they do not possess sufficient power to induce motion in the visual body.

Even more interesting for us is Timeaus' claim about tangibility and solidity being dependent on earth. Once again, a first reading of the sentence might suggest that only those objects which have some measure of earth in them can possess solidity. All we have seen so far about the mechanics of perception – and more generally about solidity being the criterion of any mechanical causal interaction – shows clearly that earth has no role in providing solidity to elementary particles or composite bodies. All four elements, and in fact every individual particle of all four elements, have to possess solidity, i.e. be resistant to other particles, in order to participate in any kind of physical interaction.

In so far as all the bodily interactions, and in particular the transmission of motion, depend on touch and solidity, we could expect that the bodily motions can be transmitted to the motions of the circles of the soul on the basis of the very same property. This assumption is further reinforced by the fact that, as we have seen, Timaeus uses the same language of 'striking against' to describe the interaction among elementary bodily particles within the chain of transmission of motion on the one hand and the interaction between the elementary particles at the end of the chain and the circles of the soul on the other. The emerging picture is that the rational soul is not only spatially extended and moving but, by the bodily element in its ontological make-up, can interact with bodily particles by showing some measure of resistance to them.

There is further evidence to substantiate this conclusion. The younger gods, who had the task of creating the human body, started their work by fashioning the spherical skull – similar in its shape to the spherical cosmos – to house the circles of the rational soul (44d). This hard shell provides precious protection for the rational soul in so far as bodily motions can reach it not from every direction, but only through the sense organs and the appropriately narrow tube of the neck.[25] However, the skull not only envelopes the soul, but is also affected by it. For as Timaeus explains, the sutures on the skull are produced in the early stages of human life by the struggle between the circular motions of the soul and the linear motions due to nutrition:

> the sutures varied considerably, owing to the power of the revolutions and of the nutriment: the greater the conflict among these powers, the more numerous the sutures – the lesser the conflict, the less numerous they were.
>
> (76a–b)

This admittedly curious account of the observable fact that different people have different sutures shows that the circles of the soul are powerful enough to carve even the hard bone of the skull. This description of the physical effects of the circles of the soul on the hard bodily structure of the skull once again suggest that the circles of the soul possess some sort of solidity; they need to push and rub the skull to be able to mould it and carve sutures in it. Together with divisibility, spatial extension, and motion, this might then be a property that the soul receives by having a share of the bodily.[26] Indeed, because soul has something of the bodily, it cannot avoid causally interact with bodies when it gets into contact with them spatially. It is on the basis of this feature that bodies can affect the soul and the soul can affect bodies.

5. The cosmic soul as a role model

Up until now, I have focused on the way in which Timaeus describes body-soul interaction in the case of the human soul. Yet, as we can see from Timaeus' account about the cognitive operations of the cosmic soul, such interactions occur at that level as well:

> Because the soul [of the cosmos] is a mixture of the Same, the Different, and Being, these three components, and because it was divided up and bound together in various proportions, and because it circles round upon itself, whenever it comes into contact (ἐφάπτηται) with something whose being is scatterable or else with something whose being is indivisible, it is moved throughout its whole self and tells what exactly that thing is the same as, or what it is different from, and in what respect and in what manner, as well as when, it turns out that they are the same or different and are characterised as such, this applying both to the things that come to be, and to those that are always changeless. And when the account (λόγος) that is equally true whether it is about what is different or about what is the same, and is borne along without utterance or sound within the self-moving thing, then, whenever the account concerns anything that is perceptible, the circle of the Different goes correctly and proclaims it throughout its whole soul, and this is how firm and true opinions and convictions come about, whenever on the other hand, the account concerns any object of reasoning, and the circle of the Same, running smoothly, reveals it, the necessary result is understanding and knowledge; and if anyone should ever call that in which these two arise not soul, but something else, what he says will be anything but true.
>
> (37a–c)

The construction, translation, and interpretation of these two long sentences are open to debate.[27]

To some extent, the passage can be illuminated by the account of true and false sentences and beliefs in the *Sophist* (260a–263e), even if that account itself is vexed. According to the *Sophist*, formulating a sentence (λόγος) that is capable of being true or false consists of three operations. (1) The speaker has to pick out an object by 'naming' it; in order for the sentence to be truth-apt, the speaker has to pick out a real entity.[28] (2) The speaker also has to pick out a 'verb', which can either consist of a single verb or of a predicate phrase. (3) The speaker has to 'weave' the 'name' and the 'verb' together determining the relation between the two. False sentences are then defined as 'different things said as being the same' (263d), i.e. such combinations of 'names' and 'verbs' which say about the object thus picked out that it is same as something which in reality it is different from.[29] Finally, thought (διάνοια) is characterised as the soul's inner conversation with itself and belief (δόξα) as affirmation or denial resulting from that inner conversation, which may also involve perceptual data (263d–264b). The successive steps of this discussion can be mapped on the elements of the passage quoted previously.[30] In particular, we can see that sentences produced in the cosmic soul are never false in so far as the soul never mistakes difference for sameness or sameness for difference.

While the *Sophist* primarily focuses on the general logical conditions of forming true declarative sentences, the *Timaeus* concentrates on the processes in the soul that lead to the formation of such sentences. The core of the account in the *Timaeus* is at the same time analogous to what we have seen in the description of sense perception in the human rational soul: the soul gets into contact with an object which causes some motion in the circles of the soul – or more precisely, which causes a modification of the motions of the circles of the soul – and this motion has a mental correlate. In the case of sense perception, the mental correlate is the awareness of the sense object, whereas in the case of the cognitive process described in the sentences quoted previously, the mental correlate is the formation of a statement about the cognised object, establishing the different respects in which it is the same as, and the different respects in which it is different from, any other given entity. Even if this much appears relatively clear, a great deal is still in need of explanation.

First, it is far from evident how we are to conceive the contact between the circles of the soul and the objects cognised. It is surely not by accident that Timaeus uses the same verb, ἐφάπτηται, that he will use in a later part of the text to describe the way in which the external visual body composed of the fire of daylight and the fire pouring out of the eye comes into contact with an external visual object (45d, see the text quoted previously on pp. 130–131). In that context, the verb refers to the mechanical contact and interaction between two bodies. In our passage, however, the same term covers the ways in which the circles of the soul come into contact with both physical bodies and Forms. Even if, as I have suggested above chapter, the soul is capable of interacting with physical bodies in so far as it has some measure of solidity, and hence is capable of some sort of corporeal contact, this feature of the soul is certainly not relevant for its interaction with incorporeal entities such as Forms. We should therefore construe the verb generously enough so that it encompasses both types of encounters. Moreover, it is crucial to note that although the customary English rendering of the verb in this passage is 'to come into contact with', this translation conceals an important aspect of the meaning of the Greek verb, which has a clearly active connotation, including senses such as 'reach' and 'lay hold of'. In fact the verb ἅπτω, with or without the prefix, occurs in a number of Platonic dialogues to describe the way in which the soul reaches and grasps the truth as a result of a conscious and systematic engagement with intelligible objects.[31] This strongly suggests that the soul in our passage does not passively and randomly happen to get into contact with these entities, but actively seeks them out. The cosmic soul constantly searches and explores the relationships among these corporeal and incorporeal entities. This reading is fully borne out by the use of the same verb in the account of vision: we don't only happen to see things, but we also actively and purposefully scan and monitor our environment.

One intriguing further outcome is that the cognitive activity of the cosmic soul appears to show variation. The description strongly suggests that it is not the case that the soul would constantly be cognising, and formulating statements about, the same objects, nor even simultaneously cognising, and formulating statements about, all the entities belonging to both ontological realms. Note also that the soul is formulating statements about the temporal aspects of the relations obtaining about changing corporeal entities ('*when* it turns out that they are the same or different'). If the cosmic soul were also to simultaneously entertain all true sentences also about changing objects, it would possess complete foreknowledge of all future events. This view would commit Timaeus to fatalism about all events, including the ethically relevant actions of humans. Besides the fact that Timaeus' formulations do not recommend this reading, there are strong philosophical reasons why he – and Plato – would reject fatalism. It is better to conclude then that even though the cosmic soul is a divine intellect and its mental life shows high-level constancy, it does show temporal variation.

Prima facie, this conclusion might create some tension with the emphatic orderliness and the closely related astronomical function of the world soul as the cause and guarantor of the regular revolutions of the celestial bodies. For the contacts with the objects cognised cause motions in the soul and, as I have argued, such contacts and the concomitant motions are temporally distinct events. Thus, if the contacts with different entities and the concomitant motions are temporarily distinct events, shouldn't these events disrupt the orderliness of the revolutions, in such a way that the perturbations might even become visible through the motions of the heavenly bodies?[32] I wish to suggest that the active connotation of the verb ἐφάπτηται becomes crucial at this point as well. As I have argued in this chapter, it is not the case that the soul would encounter, and be affected by, all kinds of entities in a haphazard way; rather, it seeks out the objects of its cognition in an active manner. To this, we can now add that the soul makes these various entities the objects of its cognition, and formulates thoughts about them, in a systematic and orderly way. Although in our passage Timaeus only emphasises that the statements formulated by the cosmic soul are true whether they are about eternal changeless entities or about changing bodies, we must realise that, just as importantly, these true statements are not unconnected, but are formulated in a systematic and methodical way. The mark of a good thinker is not merely to formulate true statements randomly and independently of each other, but to formula them in a well-ordered, systematic way.

Timaeus explains that after the birth of human beings their rational souls get bombarded and overwhelmed by the irregular motions stemming from perception and nutrition. The circles of the soul become deformed and their motions irregular and sometimes even reversed, which results in severe cognitive deficiency:

> Whenever they happen to encounter (περιτύχωσιν) something outside of them characterisable as same or different, they speak of it as 'the same as' something, or as 'different from' something else when the truth is just the opposite, so proving themselves to be misled and unintelligent.
> (44a)

We can recognise here the echoes of both the *Phaedo*'s description how through perception the bodily drags about and disturbs the soul, and the account of false statements as mistaking difference for identity. Moreover, the verb that is used in this sentence to describe how the soul comes into contact with external objects emphasises the haphazard way in which these encounters occur, creating a meaningful contrast with the methodical and orderly way in which, as I have suggested, the cosmic soul encounters the objects of its cognition. So, it is starting from this disorderly state that the human soul should reorganise itself by assimilating itself to its divine kin, first by observing and understanding the complex but regular motions of the celestial bodies. Through advanced studies in astronomy and mathematics, the motions of the soul become increasingly orderly and, as a result, will formulate true statements more and more reliably. Just as important, it will conduct its enquiry more and more methodically, so that it will not merely 'happen to encounter' the objects of its cognition, but it will examine them and analyse what they are the same as and what they are different from in a more and more systematic manner.

The Socrates of the *Phaedo* argued that we should separate our souls, as far as possible, from the body by concentrating exclusively on eternal and changeless objects, and thereby preparing ourselves to an unimpeded search for the truth, which will be available to us in a post-mortem disincarnate existence. For Timaeus, the primary objective will still be to acquire 'understanding and knowledge' of eternal objects, similarly to the cosmic soul. Yet, in his account both the divine cosmic soul and its miniature replicas are forever attached to a body – the cosmic soul to the same body and its replicas to a succession of different bodies. If so, both the divine cosmic soul and the human souls are, and will remain to be, in constant contact with changing bodies and these encounters inevitably have an impact on their motions. As we have seen, for the cosmic god, these encounters unfailingly result in true beliefs and do not disrupt the orderliness of the revolutions of its soul. Contact with bodies do not 'drag about' the cosmic soul and do not cause any 'giddiness' in it.

This is surely unachievable for human beings. Their souls are not only inherently inferior by being composed of second- and third-rate leftover ingredients, but they are also constantly subject to bodily affections coming from the outside. By contrast, the divine craftsman made sure that there is nothing left outside of the cosmos, so that the cosmic god, and its soul, will never have to deal with such hostile external impacts. Given that contact with the bodily is inevitable, the best human souls can do is to try to minimise the negative, disruptive effects of the bodily. Fortunately, the cosmic soul can serve as a role model in that as well. But for this, humans have to emulate not only the way in which the cosmic soul formulates true statements about the eternal and changeless Forms, but also the way in which 'firm and true opinions and convictions' about changing bodies emerge in it as a result of a systematic examination of corporeal entities and their interrelations. This is the best way for the soul not to be 'dragged about' by the bodily motions triggered by encounters with bodies, but regulate and make these contacts orderly, as far as possible.

Notes

1 I had the opportunity to present an earlier version of this chapter at the Symposium Platonicum Pragense, at the University of Florence, at the Collegio Ghislieri in Pavia, and in Cambridge. I am grateful for helpful remarks by Mariapaola Bergomi, István Bodnár, Luc Brisson, Nick Denyer, Silvia Gastaldi, Máté Herner, Chad Jorgensen, Filip Karfík, Curie Virág, Robert Wardy, and James Warren. I have benefited most from long discussions with David Sedley.
2 I use 'stuff' here in the loosest possible sense, without any metaphysical specification, to capture both the three-dimensionally extended disorderly *khôra*, in which, or out of which, the body of the world is formed, and the incorporeal ingredients of the world soul, the two kinds of Being, Same, and Different, on which see more later. On Timaeus' cosmos as a corporeal god, see Broadie (2016).
3 On the point that the *demiurge*'s reasoning is (primarily) practical and not theoretical, see Burnyeat (2005). Obviously, the *demiurge*'s activity in creating the cosmos presupposes the knowledge of the intelligible paradigm, which in turn involves theoretical knowledge.
4 On the criticism of the physicists, see Menn 2010. On the relationship between the desideratum of a teleological cosmology in the *Phaedo* and its relation to the *Timaeus*, see Sedley 1988–9 and Betegh 2009.
5 Translations from the *Phaedo* are from Sedley and Long 2014 with occasional modifications.
6 Cf. Dimas 2003.
7 Reeve's translation of 490a3–4 ('the part of his soul that is fitted to grasp a thing of that sort') is more explicit than the Greek, which only uses a genitive, which would literally translate 'that of it which is fitted'.
8 Cf. Dillon 2009: 350: 'In general, I think we may agree that, while the body is seen as a serious problem for the soul in the *Phaedo*, the problem of just how the one entity acts on the other is not even raised.'
9 In establishing the connection between these two texts, I owe much to the inspiring discussions I have had with Máté Herner.
10 Translations from the *Timaeus* are from Zeyl (2000) with occasional modifications.
11 The most important discussion of the status and function of the 'ingredients' of the soul is in D. Frede 1996, who relates them to the 'common concepts' of the *Theaetetus*. While I agree with Fronterotta 2007a that the soul does not become a body in the *Timaeus* as Carone 2005 claims, I don't agree with him that the soul according to the *Timaeus* would be a third distinct kind. To my mind, the point is precisely that Plato has not become a trialist, but retains his Form – body dualism, while allowing that the soul can share certain properties with both kinds. Importantly, when and in so far as

Timaeus distinguishes three kinds, he lists the Forms, their generated (and destructible) copies, and the *khôra* (52a–c).

12 Timaeus does not make explicit how far the isomorphism goes. It is clear that the major structural parts of both the cosmic soul and the human rational soul are the circles of the Same and the Different (on which see more later). It is equally clear that the circle of the Different in the cosmos is further divided into seven concentric circles which are responsible for the revolutions of the Sun and the Moon and the planets, attached to their respective circles at a later stage of the creation. Timaeus never mentions that the circle of the Different in the rational human soul also has a corresponding seven-fold division. However, the teleologic role of the observation of heavenly motions and astronomical phenomena at 47a–b, which emphatically includes the motions of Sun and Moon, strongly suggests that the circle of the Different in our rational soul has the same structure as its cosmic counterpart, including the division into seven concentric circles.

13 Commentators usually do not sufficiently appreciate this aspect of the *Timaeus* (see, e.g. Lorenz (2008, p. 253)).

14 Socrates in his Final Argument in the *Phaedo* (99d–102a) argues that the soul is *essentially* indestructible and immortal. The conception of the (rational) soul as a generated composite, and the concomitant recognition that at least in principle it could disintegrate, is obviously incompatible with the core tenet of the Final Argument. The fact that the *Timaeus* effectively invalidates the Final Argument of the *Phaedo* and offers a completely new explanation for the immortality of the soul, cannot in itself decide the vexed question whether Plato at the time of composing the *Phaedo* meant the Final Argument to be recognisably invalid.

15 On the point that we do not need to choose between what he calls the cognitive and the kinetic readings of the cosmic soul, see the cogent arguments in Johansen (2004, p. 139). Cf. also Lee 1976.

16 The Friends of Forms in the *Sophist* seem to be pressed to accept that what really is cannot be devoid of soul and motion (248e–249a). Nonetheless, neither the *Phaedo*, nor the *Republic*, nor again the *Timaeus* appear to subscribe to the view that the Forms would perform cognitive functions.

17 Commentators and translators often seem to take too lightly Timaeus' circumspect formulation περὶ τὰ σώματα by translating it as 'in bodies' as e.g. Cornford does. Clearly, Timaeus does not want to ascribe being, even divisible being – as opposed to becoming – to bodies.

18 Johansen 2004, p. 141: 'we can understand why Timaeus seems to see no ontological problem in soul-body interaction. Both soul and body are spatially extended and move in space. Because both body and soul move in space we can see how the motions of the soul may affect the motions of the body and vice versa. Body and soul may have different spatial properties . . . but there is no fundamental ontological difference between the two.'

19 Johansen 2004, p. 141: 'In contrast [to the three-dimensional bodies showing solidity], there is no indication that the material out of which the soul is made itself has depth or solidity. . . . [T]he important point is that for Timaeus body is differentiated from soul by having *specific* spatial attributes (such as depth and solidity) rather than by the possession of spatial attributes as such.'

20 Aristotle in *Met.* 3.2 998a11–15 claims that the Platonic theory involves the absurdity that ontologically separable geometrical solids can spatially coincide with physical bodies. ('Further, it follows from this theory that there are two solids (*sterea*) in the same place, and that the intermediates [i.e., geometrical solids] are not immovable, since they are in the moving perceptible things'; cf. *Met.* 13.2 1076a38–b3.) What Aristotle attributes to Plato amounts to saying that spatial extension in itself is not sufficient to bridging the metaphysical gap and that it is possible for two extended

entities to occupy the same place, or be in contact in space, without (a physical type of) causal interaction between them. I am of course not suggesting that we need to accept Aristotle's interpretation of Plato. Yet the fact that Aristotle can even formulate such an interpretation shows that such a scenario is not inconceivable within the Platonic framework.

21 This topic has been dealt with in considerable detail in the literature. See in particular Brisson 1997 and 1999; Johansen 2004, ch. 8 and Lautner 2005. In the confines of the present chapter I cannot provide either a detailed analysis of the relevant passages or a fully argued defence of what I take to be the most likely interpretation.

22 For a defence of this latter point, see Lautner 2005.

23 In rare cases, the affection coming from the outside not only triggers off a chain of motions, but also brings about a transformation of the elementary bodies composing the tissues of the organism. Certain substances, such as soda, instantiating the perceptible quality of acridity, have the power to dissolve some particles composing the tongue (65d).

24 For a more developed defense of this interpretation and the broader historical context of the emerging view, see Betegh (2016).

25 Cf. also the explanation of bones providing protection to marrow at 73e–74b.

26 Timeaus specifies that the gods created a special type of body, the brain-marrow, which is particularly refined and can therefore interact with the revolutions of the soul without disturbing them.

27 These difficulties notwithstanding, there has been surprisingly little written on this passage. Apart from some rather trivial remarks in the systematic commentaries by Taylor 1928 and Cornford 1935 *ad loc*, see Fronterotta (2007b), who, however, offers a markedly different grammatical construal and interpretation of the text.

28 Cf. e.g. Frede (1992, p. 417).

29 For a vindication of this interpretation and a systematic discussion of alternative interpretations, see Crivelli (2011, ch. 6).

30 It is undisputed that the list of the ingredients of the soul in the *Timaeus* is derived from the discussion of the 'largest kinds' in the *Sophist*; thus a comparison recommends itself. Nonetheless, I haven't been able to find a sustained comparative analysis of the two passages.

31 See e.g. *Symp.* 212a4–5; *Phaedo* 65a9; *Rep.* 572a7–b1; *Rep.* 608a6–b2; *Tht.* 186d2–3.

32 Zeyl's translates the verb κινουμένη, describing the causal effect of the contacts, as 'is stirred'. It seems to me however that the more neutral 'is moved by' is not only closer to the Greek but is also philosophically preferable.

Bibliography

Apolloni, D. (1996) Plato's affinity argument for the immortality of the soul. *Journal of the History of Philosophy* 34 (1): 5–32.

Betegh, G. (2008) Tale, theology, and teleology in the Phaedo. In Partenie, C. (ed.) *Plato's Myths*. Cambridge, MA: Cambridge University Press.

———. (2016) Colocation. In Bucheim, T., Meißner, D., and Wachsmann, N. C. (eds.) ΣΩΜΑ: *Körperkonzepte und körperliche Existenz in der antiken Philosophie und Literatur*. Hamburg: Felix Meiner.

Brisson, L. (1997) Perception sensible et raison dans le Timée. In Calvo, T., and Brisson, L. (eds.) *Interpreting the Timaeus-Critias*. Berlin: Akademia Verlag.

———. (1999) Plato's theory of sense perception in the Timaeus: How it works and what it means. *Proceedings of the Boston Area Colloquium in Ancient Philosophy* 13: 147–176.

Broadie, S. (2016) Corporeal gods, with reference to Plato and Aristotle. In Bucheim, T., Meißner, D., and Wachsmann, N. C. (eds.) *ΣΩMA: Körperkonzepte und körperliche Existenz in der antiken Philosophie und Literatur*. Hamburg: Felix Meiner.

Burnyeat, M. (2005) Εικως μυθος. *Rhizai* 2: 143–165. Reprinted in Catalin, P. (ed.) *Plato's Myths*. Cambridge, MA: Cambridge University Press.

Carone, G. R. (2005) Mind and body in late Plato. *Archiv für Geschichte der Philosophie* 87 (3): 227–269.

Cornford, F. M. (1935) *Plato's Cosmology: The Timaeus of Plato*. London: Routledge.

Crivelli, P. (2011) *Plato's Account of Falsehood: A Study of the Sophist*. Cambridge, MA: Cambridge University Press.

Dillon, J. (2009) How does the soul direct the body, after all? Traces of a dispute on the mind – body relations in the Old Academy. In Frede, D., and Reis, B. (eds.) *Body and Soul in Ancient Philosophy*. Berlin: Walter De Gruyter.

Dimas, P. (2003) Recollecting forms in the Phaedo. *Phronesis* 48 (3): 175–214.

Dorter, K. (1982) *Plato's Phaedo: An Interpretation*. Toronto: University of Toronto Press.

Elton, M. (1997) The role of the affinity argument in the 'Phaedo'. *Phronesis* 42 (3): 313–316.

Frede, D. (1996) The philosophical economy of Plato's psychology: Rationality and concepts in the Timaeus. In Frede, D., and Striker, G. (eds.) *Rationality in Greek Thought*. Oxford: Oxford University Press.

Frede, M. (1992) Plato's Sophist on false statements. In Kraut, R. (ed.) *The Cambridge Companion to Plato*. Cambridge, MA: Cambridge University Press.

Fronterotta, F. (2007a) Carone on the mind-body problem in late Plato. *Archiv für Geschichte der Philosophie* 89 (2): 231–236.

———. (2007b) Intelligible forms, mathematics, and the soul's circles: An interpretation of Tim. 37a-c. *Les études platoniciennes* 4: 119–127.

Johansen, T. (2004) *Plato's Natural Philosophy: A Study of the Timaeus-Critias*. Cambridge, MA: Cambridge University Press.

Lautner, P. (2005) The Timaeus on sounds and hearing with some implications for Plato's general account of sense-perception. *Rhizai: A Journal for Ancient Philosophy and Science* 2: 235–253.

Lee, E. N. (1976). Reason and rotation: circular movement as the model of mind (Nous) in later Plato. In Werkmeister, W. H. (ed.) *Facets of Plato's Philosophy*. Assen: Van Gorcum.

Lorenz, H. (2008) Plato on the soul. In Fine, G. (ed.) *The Oxford Handbook of Plato*. Oxford: Oxford University Press.

Menn, S. (2010) On Socrates' first objections to the physicists (Phaedo 95 E 8–97 B 7). *Oxford Studies in Ancient Philosophy* 38: 37–68.

Sedley, D. (1989) Teleology and myth in the Phaedo. *Proceedings of the Boston Area Colloquium in Ancient Philosophy* 5: 359–383.

———. (1999) The ideal of godlikeness. In Fine, G. (ed.) *Plato 2 Ethics, Politics, Religion, and the Soul*. Oxford: Oxford University Press, pp. 309–328.

Sedley, D., and Long, A. (eds.) (2014) *Plato: Meno and Phaedo*. Cambridge, MA: Cambridge University Press.

Taylor, A. E. (1928) *A Commentary on Plato's Timaeus*. Oxford: Clarendon Press.

Zeyl, D. (2000) *Plato: Timaeus*. Indianapolis: Hackett Publishing.

7

THE POWER OF ARISTOTLE'S HYLOMORPHIC APPROACH

Kelsey Ward and Ronald Polansky

> For the starting-point of every demonstration is the statement of what the subject is, and definitions that do not enable us to know the attributes, or that fail to facilitate even a conjecture about them, must obviously, one and all, be dialectical and futile.
> – (*De anima* I.1.402b25–403a2)

Scientific understanding for Aristotle requires apprehending principles appropriate to the subject matter. Such principles should enable derivation of what follows from them. Form, matter, and privation of form serve as the principles that account for the possibility of change in natural science (*Physics* I). These principles enlisted for explaining becoming also support Aristotle's elucidation of natural being. Natural beings, living and nonliving, all possess a nature that is the inner principle of motion and rest (*Phys*. II.1.192b10–16). This nature is primarily the being's substantial form and secondarily its matter (*Phys*. II.1). The nature of living things is the soul, which is the principle and cause of the life of the living being as form, mover, and end (DA II.4.415b8–12; cf. *Phys*. II.7.198a24–33). Moreover, it accounts for multiple living capacities, including nutrition, perception, thought, and progressive motion, with the body of the living being subserving the soul as matter or substratum. Aristotle insists that soul and body, or form and matter, are united and one in living beings (DA II.1.412b6–9). This position regarding the unity of soul and body or form and matter has in recent times been called "hylomorphism". It is Aristotle's key conception of the functional relationship of soul and body.[1]

Hylomorphism, as elaborated in Aristotle's accounts of the soul and its functions, has in our time received two prominent sorts of criticism. Ackrill (1972–1973) raised questions about the consistency of the definition of soul and the relation of soul and body based on the hylomorphic view. Burnyeat (1992) doubts the credibility of Aristotle's account of sense perception deriving from the hylomorphic approach. Each of these attacks has received many responses, but usually separately. We seek a combined response to both in order to verify Aristotle's consistency in his own terms and to suggest that his hylomorphic approach can still have some appeal in its definition of soul and account of the functions following from it. We thus aim to determine Aristotle's success in his "most common account of soul" (DA II.1.412a3–6) and how far his definition assists in explaining sense power in animals.

1. Soul as form, mover, and end of the living being in unity with the body

In developing the common account of soul in DA II.1, Aristotle aspires to cover any soul of any kind of mortal living being.[2] It is crucial that he clarify the sort of being that soul is in order that his account work with the observed operations of living beings. He purposefully offers several definitions of the soul. He first defines it as the substantial form of a natural body having life in potentiality (II.1.412a19–21). This means that soul is in the category of substance, but as the form rather than composite substance.[3] Some of Aristotle's predecessors had instead tried to view the soul as a highly mobile body, as a *harmonia*, or a self-moving number (see I.2.403b28–31 and I.4). Aristotle supposes viewing soul as substantial form to be much more promising and more suited for clarifying the operations of living beings. Therefore, the *first* definition of soul is "substance in the sense of the form of a natural body having life in potentiality" (II.1.412a19–21). If soul is the substantial form, the body is matter only having life *in potentiality*. Matter, nothing determinate in virtue of itself, is only the potentiality for determination by form. The material body then has life merely in potentiality even when the living being is alive.

That matter in virtue of itself is not determinate and "a this", as is the composite being and its form, is Aristotle's standard position (see II.1.412a6–9; cf. *Phys*. I.7.191a8–15). Though the ensouled body is nothing determinate in virtue of itself, it can be viewed as already composed of lower levels of determinate matter. In PA II.1, Aristotle suggests three levels of matter pertinent to living beings. At the lowest level of composition are the simple elemental bodies – or more precisely, composition out of the powers characteristic of them. These elemental bodies or powers compose the second level, homoeomerous materials such as flesh, blood, and bone. From these arise the third level of composition, the anhomoeomerous parts such as limbs, heart, and eye. Hence the body of a living being is already a composition of lower levels of formed matter, the lower levels being for the sake of that which can perform the operations of the living body. This is one of the insights to be gained from Aristotle's several definitions of the soul. A natural body having life in potentiality might be taken to be lower or higher-level matter, but Aristotle works to ensure that it is the higher-level matter, proximate to the soul as form.

As the form of the natural body, the soul is the actuality of the body analogous to knowledge not yet put to use, that is, the soul is actuality comparable to a developed disposition (II.1.412a21–23). Thus the *second* definition of soul, exploiting this disambiguation of actuality regarding form, is the first sort of actuality (i.e., like knowledge) of the natural body having life in potentiality. The natural body having life in potentiality due to the first actuality form is instrumental (ὀργανικόν) for the operations of the living being. With this qualification comes the *third* definition of soul as the first sort of actuality of the natural instrumental body (II.1.412b5–6).[4] The succession of definitions of soul, besides clarifying the status of soul as substantial form and actuality, makes evident that the body informed by the soul is highest-level *proximate matter*.

Since there are the different levels of matter, Aristotle should be indicating at which level he locates the matter for the soul. By the natural body having life in potentiality and the natural instrumental body, Aristotle intends the body to be the highest-level matter closest to soul and therefore most in unity with it. The natural instrumental body, when informed, is that already fully capable of supporting the functions of the soul. Hence Aristotle insists that soul and body are one: "That is why we can dismiss as unnecessary the question whether the soul and the body are one: it is as though we were to ask whether the wax and its shape are one, or generally the matter of a thing and that of which it is the matter" (II.1.412b6–8). He can compare the relation of soul and body in a living being to the relation of form and matter in an artifact, as an ax, or to a part of a living being, as sight and the eye (II.1.412b10–25). In the case of an artifact, matter seems to have independence from the form, for there can be wax before something is shaped from it or metal before an ax is made from it. With a living being, however, there can only be the living body entire when ensouled, though the homoeomerous and anhomoeomerous constituents of the living body in a way can and in a way cannot be other than ensouled.[5]

The body for a mortal living being has received the different levels of formation to serve appropriately as the proximate matter for the living being. This body requires the soul and Aristotle says of this natural body having life in potentiality, "We must not understand by that which is potentially capable of living what has lost the soul it had, but only what still retains it" (II.1.412b25–26). Since this body can only be such when ensouled in actuality, this seemed problematic to Ackrill, who wished it to be possible to have the matter of living beings apart from the living being, as the iron that can compose an ax can be apart from it.

If the proximate matter of the living being, the living body, cannot be without being ensouled, Ackrill (1997, p. 173) asks whether the lower homoeomerous matter, such as flesh and bone, has the desired separability. He points to passages in which "flesh and bone are defined by the work they do, and that therefore in a dead body they are only homonymously called flesh and bone" (e.g., *Meteorology* IV.12.390a14–15). When the body no longer supports life functions, the soul cannot continue to maintain the life of the living being. Yet in the corpse for some time the lower levels of matter that went into composing the body having life in potentiality can continue, in a condition that would permit reutilization, though these too deteriorate more or less quickly (see Mirus 2001, pp. 370–372 and Dowd 2015, p. 103).[6] Since homoeomerous bodies have their own form as such homoeomerous bodies (i.e., there are forms determining the matter to be flesh and bone), both flesh and bone can be defined apart from the soul, even if they are only fully functional when ensouled. There are ways, then, in which the homoeomerous components can have some independence of the composite living being. Ackrill expected too strict a separation of form and matter, and failed to appreciate why Aristotle appeals to the analogy with an artifact. Ackrill may be relying on a modern conception of matter, identifying it with body and magnitude. For Aristotle, however, matter unlike body is always in relation to its form as potentiality for determination by that form. Hence his concept of matter never quite has the independence for which Ackrill searches and this lack of independence does not become a problem for Aristotle.[7]

The way in which Aristotle takes the soul to animate the natural body having life in potentiality also fits the basic phenomena. Death turns out to be due to the body's inability to support nutritive functioning. Death results when the heat vital to the soul's being able to employ the body to serve nutritive needs is lost, resembling the burning out or extinguishing of fire (see *De juv*. 5.469b21–470a1). Similarly, loss of power to think effectively or loss of visual capacity with aging comes from bodily incapacity to support the soul (I.4.408b18–31). Aristotle supposes that the soul never becomes incapacitated, but any loss of perceptive ability of the living being results from the body or some organ that serves the soul becoming dysfunctional. Replacement with a suitable organ for the soul's operation could restore full functionality. Similarly thinking is impaired due to drunkenness, disease, or fatigue, which are incursions upon bodily organs' abilities to function. When and if the physical apparatus is restored, thinking and mental life resume their proper activity. Evidence of this is readily seen in recovering from being drunk, waking up, and so on. Healing of parts of the body and return to full functioning prove that impairment is bodily and pertains to the composite rather than soul. All disability for Aristotle is in effect physical disability. When the instrument ceases to serve the soul suitably, the soul can no longer utilize it for operations in the living being.

The splitting of certain plants and animals that Aristotle often refers to further demonstrates this point (I.5.411b19–27 and II.2.413b16–29). These experiments show that each divided part gains a whole soul and may continue to survive at least for a time. This means the soul only comes as a unity. Any lack of functioning is due to absence of the requisite bodily instruments, which some plants or animals can regrow. Ancient experience of plant grafting would support that all incapacity is bodily incapacity with the soul always unmoved and whole. Contemporary organ transplantation also fits with Aristotle's view. In these cases the body and living being is clearly divisible and capable of being functional or dysfunctional in whole or in part, but the soul or life principle only remains intact or whole. The common account of soul that Aristotle provides thus seems to accord with the experience of living things and his own view of principles of being and becoming.

Aristotle has been defining soul in DA II.1 before even determining that soul is needed.[8] When he declares that the faculties of soul are in succession, starting with nutritive capacity, the only life faculty of plants and presupposed for animal life, the nutritive capacity becomes the necessary and sufficient condition of all mortal life.[9] He can then show that soul is needed for mortal life by the inadequacy of bodies and their powers alone to explain nutritive functioning. He argues that the orderly growth and decline found in living things, for example consistent production of oak leaves, requires nutritive capacity in soul (II.4.415b23–416a18). While heat and fire enter into sustaining life, fire naturally goes upward and grows without internal limit. Living beings, however, grow in all directions in a characteristic way because the life principle of soul directs heat and fire to do the needed work. Thus growth in living beings is ordered and limited due to soul as cause and form or *logos* (esp. II.4.416a16–18). Heat is a contributing cause (*sunaition*) or instrument utilized by the soul for nutrition, but there must be soul directing this.

In fact the nutritive faculty is a faculty of subfaculties, for it comprises nutrition (θρεπτική), reproduction (γεννητική), and growth and decline (αὐξητικόν, see II.4.416b11–20). The conversion of what is ingested as food in potentiality into food in actuality supports the living being in its continuing living, its growth to maturity, and reproduction by the ultimate development of seed. Aristotle likens nutritive functioning to governing a ship to clarify the different roles of causal factors:

> The expression 'wherewith it [the living being] is fed' is ambiguous just as is the expression 'wherewith the ship is steered'; that may mean either the hand or the rudder, i.e. either what is moved and sets in movement, or what is merely moved. All food must be capable of being digested, and what produces digestion is warmth; that is why everything that has soul in it possesses warmth.
>
> (II.4.416b25–29)

In this comparison, the soul that moves the hand to move the rudder to control the ship is analogous to the nutritive capacity that directs the fire to work on the food to maintain the life of the living being and to make it grow and to enable it to reproduce. We expect that the nutritive soul is here an unmoved mover utilizing a moved mover to assimilate the food, which is merely moved. As the person steering the ship controls the movements of the hand and the rudder, the nutritive soul controls the use of heat to operate on the food (see *Meteorology* IV.2.379b33–380a3 and PA II.3.650a2–9).

The hylomorphic account looks well suited to explicate the relation of soul and body in general and to account for the basic life principle, nutritive capacity. If we are not much discomfited by the common account of the soul and its applicability to nutritive functioning, we may turn to consider whether sense perception in fact raises any insurmountable difficulties for hylomorphism.

2. Soul as cause of perception

Aristotle surrounds or frames his accounts of each of the five senses (DA II.7–11) with his common or universal account of sense perception (see II.5.416b32–33 and II.12.424a17).[10] In DA II.5.418a3–6 the sense power is said to be in potentiality what sort of thing the sensible object is already in actuality (τὸ δ' αἰσθητικὸν δυνάμει ἐστὶν οἷον τὸ αἰσθητὸν ἤδε ἐντελεχείᾳ), while in DA II.12.424a17–19 the sense is what is receptive to sensible forms without the matter (ἡ μὲν αἴσθησίς ἐστι τὸ δεκτικὸν τῶν αἰσθητῶν εἰδῶν ἄνευ τῆς ὕλης). These accounts differentiate what happens in perceiving in actuality from what occurs in the sense medium and sense organ. Aristotle holds that only the sense power or sense receives action from the sensible object *already in actuality*. By contrast bodily magnitudes, including the sense medium or sense organ, only receive action from the sensible object *in potentiality*.

Most of Aristotle's predecessors explained perception by the action of like upon like. Thus Empedocles proposed, "For 'tis by Earth we see Earth, by Water Water" (I.2.404b13, DK 31.B.109). But Aristotle disputes that like simply acts on like (see *On Generation and Corruption* I.7.323b29–324a2–9 and DA II.5.417a17–20). Explaining perception so directly by having like acting on like raises the question why the animal perceives anything beyond its own bodily composition and ever makes perceptual errors (DA III.3.427a26–b6). Rather than having like act directly on its like, Aristotle has what is in the same genus or class but only in potentiality like acted upon by what is in potentiality like it and able to move it. In the case of bodies that undergo alterations, some body having a sensible quality, which Aristotle in *Categories* 8.9a28–29 names "affective qualities and affections" (παθητικαὶ ποιότητες καὶ πάθη), is acted upon to take on a new affection, the previous one being destroyed or replaced (see *Phys.* IV.9.217a20–26 and DA II.5.417b2–3). Such a standard sort of alteration occurs when a body gains a new sensible or affective quality by the action of a different sensible quality in the same class, as a hot body is cooled, or a surface of one color is changed to a different color.

Yet sense media and sense organs are not thus so straightforwardly changed. Whereas the ordinary body has definite sensible features that undergo alteration from one perceived quality to another in its genus, the sense media and organs that serve for the distance senses, vision, hearing, and smell, and in a way even taste, are predominately air and/or water. These do not serve in their role as medium or organ just as air or water, but as being colorless, soundless, odorless, and tasteless (see, e.g., II.7.418b26–419a1, II.8.419b33–420a9, II.10.422a15–31). Lacking these sensible qualities, air and water as media can be acted upon by sensible objects, but unusually since, lacking any definite quality, no previous quality of their own is destroyed. Aristotle has thus prepared for saying that sense media and sense organs are acted upon in non-standard alterations.[11] In an instance of such non-standard alteration, DA II.12.424b14–16 illustrates that odor can act quickly on indeterminate air. Were the medium and sense organ undergoing a standard alteration (e.g., taking on the odor as a lasting quality), there would be very little flexibility in the sense power, for the result of the alteration would dominate for a long time.

Not only does this non-standard sort of alteration apply for the sense media and organs of the distance senses and taste, but also even for touch. The flesh that enters into touch doubles as medium and organ. Hence Aristotle readily concedes that tangibles and flavors act on bodies (see II.12.424b12–13), but though flesh as body can undergo ordinary alterations by tangibles, as being warmed or cooled, overmuch ordinary alteration incapacitates it for any additional perception. While the flesh has some temperature of its own and its own hardness, and therefore only tends to feel contrasting temperature and hardness, we expect that merely a small portion of the flesh need be affected and just with some of what is in the sensible object for the animal to perceive the contrasting sensible object. Too much heating or cooling would be destructive. So we must say that flesh can be heated or cooled and undergo an ordinary alteration, as any other bodily magnitude, but the action it undergoes to enable perception of a tangible is not a standard alteration. The way the flesh is heated, cooled, or compressed in perception differs from the way a plant's body is heated, cooled, or compressed since the plant does not feel any of these (II.12.424a32–b3). Thus perception by touch is possible not simply because of some standard alteration, but only through this non-standard alteration in the medium and organ for contact sense.[12]

We have considered the non-standard alteration of the sense medium and sense organ caused by the sensible object when the medium and organ are acted upon by the sensible object in potentiality. But Aristotle hardly stops here, for his accounts of sense aim further to treat what can be said about the power of the sense to perceive. The sense, unlike the bodily apparatus acted upon by the sensible object in potentiality, receives action from the sensible object already in actuality, which enables the animal to perceive the sensible object in actuality. In other words used by Aristotle, in perception the sense of an animal, unlike any body, is receptive to sensible forms without the matter. This means especially that the sense of an animal does not re-enmatter the sensible form even as it is non-standardly re-enmattered in the sense medium and sense organ, since the sense itself, or the animal by its means, will perceive the sensible object. The sense organ is a body part, and so it can only receive the action of the sensible object in its own matter, though as we have argued this is not a standard alteration, for the organ originally was colorless, soundless, odorless, or flavorless. The sense by contrast is acted upon immaterially, that is, by the sensible object as it is already in actuality.[13] Reception of sensible forms without the matter is a way of saying that the sense in actuality and the object in actuality can be and are one (see DA III.2.426a6–26). Bodily magnitudes can receive the action of the sensible object in potentiality, but only a sense can receive the action of the sensible object in actuality. Aristotle in DA II.5 considers not merely the action on the sense medium and sense organ non-standard alterations, but also the transition from having the sense ready to perceive to perceiving in actuality.

The case of the sense medium and organ are non-standard since what is colorless, soundless, odorless, or tasteless quickly takes on, in a way, an affective quality. Sensing, too, involves a non-standard alteration, for here there is the transition to the actuality of what the sense is in potentiality rather than an ordinary change, as a carpenter using that very craft does not change but does in actuality what the craft prepares him for doing. Much of Aristotle's account of the perceptive faculty has been designed to compare and contrast the way bodies and bodily organs are acted on with the way that the sense is acted on. The way the sense medium and sense organ are acted on by the sensible object in potentiality moves the sense to be acted upon by the sensible object in actuality. The animal then perceives the sensible object as it is in actuality.

What Aristotle's hylomorphic account of perception manages differs from what both "literalist" and "spiritualist" interpretations of Aristotle have supposed, and even perhaps from the "structuralist" interpretations. Literalist interpreters try to keep Aristotle with a strictly physicalist account in which perception is merely or largely the going red (i.e., literally becoming what is perceived). It looks as if they limit their interpretation to what Aristotle has going on in the sense organ. The spiritualist account, by contrast, holds that little or nothing is supposed to happen in the sense organ, but instead the animal simply perceives when the situations of the organ and sensible object are suitable. This does a better job with what transpires in the sense itself, but the action upon sense medium and sense organ gets short shrift. We have pointed out, however, that DA, despite its main focus on the soul, hardly ignores the correlated action upon the sense organ (and see *De somno* 1.454a7–11). So the spiritualist interpretation that discounts Aristotle's "philosophy of mind" for giving no really plausible role to the sense organs is unpersuasive as an interpretation of Aristotle. He does allow physical change in the sense organ, though it is a non-standard alteration, along with a different kind of non-standard alteration of the sense. The structuralist interpretation has some homologous change going on in the sense organ in some opposition to both the literalist and spiritualist accounts.[14] Allowing such a homologous change does well for the non-standard alteration of the sense organ, but perhaps still with commitment to a largely physicalist explanation of perception. The structuralists may not sufficiently recognize that a different sort of non-standard alteration occurs in the sense when sensing. On the view we have been presenting, Aristotle does not quite fit with any of these interpretations. There is alteration of a sort (i.e., non-standard alteration) occurring in the sense medium and sense organ, and this is causing the sense to perceive the sensible object as that is in actuality, which is again a non-standard alteration that is the very perceiving. In the way the sense receives sensible forms without the matter, it is perceiving, for sensible forms are the perceptible correlates of the activity of perceiving (DA III.2.425b26–426a26). By perceiving the sensible object in actuality, the perceiving animal has somehow become one with its object and so secondarily becomes aware of itself in perceiving (DA III.2 and *De insom*. 2). Aristotle's account avoids strict physicalism while capturing much of what physicalists seek in an account of perception.

What has been emphasized regarding non-standard alterations in sense perception could be extended to the connate *pneuma* that Aristotle holds exists in all animals (see *De motu* 10.703a9–10). This sort of subtle body, with respect to progressive motion of animals, readily undergoes expansion and contraction due to perceiving, imagining, or thinking, which cause desiring to pursue or avoid pleasant or painful objects. This is Aristotle's intermediary between the soul as unmoved mover and the large bodily movements brought about by this subtle moved mover. Small and imperceptible alterations from heating and cooling lead to significant expansion and contraction of the connate *pneuma*, and hence it much more importantly causes locomotion in major limbs of the body rather than producing alterations in these parts (see 10.703a20–28). The *pneuma*, heavier than fire and lighter than water, and thus quite airy, like the sense medium air is colorless, soundless, odorless, and tasteless (see, e.g., GC I.3.318b29, GA II.3.736a1, 736b37–737a1, III.11.762a19–21). Hence it is prepared to undergo non-standard alterations and to serve as tool and intermediary for the soul in many operations of the animal.

3. Soul as principle rather than subject

The soul as substantial form of the living being is substance in a different way from the composite living being. Aristotle is careful to deny that the soul is subject or substratum for motion. In fact the soul for him cannot undergo any motion at all, except accidentally, as when a plant grows or an animal changes location, the soul is then moved along with the body as a passenger in a ship. Despite our usual way of predicating things of the soul, for example, passions of the soul and virtues of the soul, or saying the soul engages in activities, such as perceiving or thinking, and Aristotle himself speaks in these ways, he really does not intend for the soul to be supposed the proper subject. In DA I.4 he says,

> Yet that it [the soul] can be moved incidentally is, as we said above, possible, and even that it can move itself, i.e. in the sense that the vehicle in which it is can be moved, and moved by it; in no other sense can the soul be moved in place. More legitimate doubts might remain as to its movement in view of the following facts. We speak of the soul (φαμὲν γὰρ τὴν ψυχήν) as being pained or pleased, being bold or fearful, being angry, perceiving, thinking. All these are regarded as modes of movement, and hence it might be inferred that the soul is moved. This, however, does not necessarily follow. We may admit to the full that being pained or pleased, or thinking, are movements (each of them a being moved), and that the movement is originated by the soul. For example we may regard anger or fear as such and such movements of the heart, and thinking as such and such another movement of that organ, or of some other; these modifications may arise either from changes of place in certain parts or from qualitative alterations (the special nature of the parts and the

special modes of their changes being for our present purpose irrelevant).
Yet to say that it is the soul which is angry is as if we were to say that it
is the soul that weaves or builds houses. It is doubtless better to avoid
saying that the soul pities or learns or thinks, and rather to say that it is
the human who does this with his soul. What we mean is not that the
movement is in the soul, but that sometimes it terminates in the soul and
sometimes starts from it, sensation e.g. coming from without, and reminiscence starting from the soul and terminating with the movements or
states of rest in the sense organs.

(408a30–b18; slightly modified trans.)

What this passage decisively states and aims to make clear is that the soul itself strictly undergoes no motion, for motion really belongs to bodies. But we have been insisting that operations such as perceiving, experiencing emotions, and thinking are not exactly ordinary motions, so is Aristotle brought back to the question of something possibly taking place in the soul itself? Most definitely we should take very seriously Aristotle's emphasis in this passage on denying these for the soul. Though we inevitably speak of affections of the soul, actions common to soul and body (see *De sensu* 1.436a7–8), and things arising in the soul (e.g., *De mem.* 1.449b22–23), for Aristotle these are just ways of speaking (cf. Charles 2008, p. 19). What Aristotle suggests in the passage is that it is the plant or animal, the living being, which does whatever the living being does by means of the soul and any cooperating bodily instrument. Surely this is the way we must understand the role of soul as principle and cause of the life of the living being. The soul is always the principle as unmoved mover of the living being. In its causal role it serves as form, mover, and end of the living being while itself being unmoved. This is so, even if, as Aristotle suggests, motion terminates or originates in the soul (e.g., I.4.408b15–18). Whichever of these applies, this only indicates that the soul is the principle of what occurs actively or passively in the living being, but not the subject.

The passage regarding the soul and motion should not be discounted on the grounds that it occurs quite early in DA I, since even though some of this book is aporetic or exploratory, this first book is the principal argument against the soul itself being in motion. In *De motu animalium* 6.700b4–6 Aristotle asks whether or not soul undergoes motion, and he refers to DA as if for the definitive treatment of the question. So we should take DA I as definitely denying locomotion or any other sort of motion for the soul, except accidentally. Only in light of this denial of the soul as suitable subject for motion can Aristotle subsequently in DA comfortably speak of the soul as undergoing alteration or motion of a sort (see, e.g., II.4.415b24, II.5.416b34, and III.3.428b11). We find Aristotle asserting strikingly in II.2.414a12–14, "since it is the soul by which primarily we live, perceive, and think: – it follows that the soul must be an account and essence, not matter or a subject". Here he makes clear that the soul is cause and principle, but definitely not as matter or substratum. As form, mover, and end, the soul will not be substratum for any operations, but it is the cause of these in the composite plant or animal. The soul as principle enables nutritive, perceptive, and intellective functioning, but nutritive life and perceiving and thinking are activities of the plant or animal engaged in them.

DA aims to treat the soul as much as possible within natural science. We have already observed that non-standard alterations in perception, mixing to constitute homoeomerous tissue material, and retention of the "motions" that are *phantasmata* force Aristotle to refine his positions to maintain key lines of natural science. And this is hardly all, for Aristotle admits that the treatment of soul cannot be kept tightly within natural science. Complete containment is impossible because humans can think all things, so that if mind falls within physics, it looks as if physics is first philosophy or the highest theoretical philosophy (see PA I.1.641a32–b10). Nonetheless, despite the limitations of natural philosophy, Aristotle tries to consider the soul within the context of natural science since within this science the four causes evidently apply and they may be used to clarify the unity of soul and body.

Physics treats nature as the inner principle of motion and rest. Many of the operations of the ensouled being take place as motions in parts of the body or involve such motions, and so they seem to fit conveniently within natural science. For instance, in nutrition heat works on nutriment and in animal locomotion there are motions in joints and limbs giving rise to the animal's larger-scale progressive motion (see *De motu* 6–9). Yet the most characteristic life functions of animal life are not straightforwardly the sorts of motions elucidated in the *Physics* (i.e., changes in quality, quantity, or place). We have seen that Aristotle has non-standard alterations going on in the sense medium and sense organ, and he also speaks of sensing itself as non-standard alteration.

In fact we suggest that he speaks this way in his effort to stay within natural science as much as possible. Sense-perceiving that takes place through the transition from sense power to its utilization is an even more unusual non-standard alteration than what takes place in the sense organ and medium. The most crucial life functions according to Aristotle, unlike motions, have their ends in themselves, and they are therefore complete at the very moment of their onset and at each moment of their entire duration. Passages in the ethical works, and a disputed passage at *Metaphysics* IX.6.1048b18–35, distinguish motion from a kind of actuality that is complete in itself.[15] Aristotle often differentiates these activities from motions by appealing to the possibility of conjoining present and perfect tenses simultaneously. Whereas we do not say I am walking and I have walked, except retrospectively, we say I am perceiving x and have perceived x at once. This appeal to conjoining present and perfect tenses intends to point to the way activities have their ends within themselves and so are always complete. By contrast for Aristotle motions other than the revolutions in the heavens are on their way to an end that they only reach on their termination.[16]

At least the cognitive, affective, and action-directed (*praxis*) functions of animals eventuate in operations that are such activities distinguished from motions. In *Metaphysics* IX.8 in a passage that Burnyeat does not dispute, Aristotle states,

> And while in some cases the exercise (ἡ χρῆσις) is the ultimate thing (e.g. in sight the ultimate thing is seeing, and no other product [*ergon*] besides this results from sight), but from some things a product follows (e.g. from the art of building there results a house as well as the act of building), yet none the less the act is in the former case the end and in the latter more of an end than the mere potentiality is. For the act of building is in the thing that is being built, and comes to be – and is – at the same time as the house. Where, then, the result is something apart from the exercise, the actuality is in the thing that is being made, e.g. the act of building is in the thing that is being built and that of weaving in the thing that is being woven, and similarly in all other cases, and in general the movement (*kinesis*) is in the thing that is being moved; but when there is no product (*ergon*) apart from the actuality (*energeian*), the actuality is in the agents (ἐν αὐτοῖς), e.g. the act of seeing is in the seeing subject and that of theorizing in the theorizing subject and the life is in the soul (and therefore well-being [*eudaimonia*] also; for it is a certain kind of life). Obviously, therefore, the substance or form is actuality. From this argument it is obvious that actuality is prior in substance to potentiality; and as we have said, one actuality always precedes another in time right back to the actuality of the eternal prime mover.
>
> (1050a23–b6)

Aristotle's instances of activities complete at every moment conform with the classes we have elicited, which include those seemingly crucial for DA. Nonetheless, Aristotle is not at all explicit about this distinction of activity from motion in DA, as illuminating as it might be. The reason appears to be that he wishes to keep the investigation of soul largely within natural science, for the soul is the nature of the natural living being. Activity, as distinguished from motion, does not fit the account of nature, since nature is a principle of motion and rest. If the nature is also a principle of activity as distinct from motion, this has not been explicated in the *Physics*.

Where Aristotle has to speak of non-standard motions in DA, he tends to speak of motion of a sort (κίνησίς τις) or alteration of a sort (ἀλλοίωσις τις), which may do well enough for what occurs in the sense medium and sense organ. But sensing and thinking look to be activities rather than motions despite needing to speak of them still in this context as motions of a sort (see, e.g., DA II.5 and III.3). This amounts to an indirect or subtle way to speak of activity, while holding a place for it outside natural science.

Though Aristotle is rather coy regarding activity in DA, we may occasionally find evidence of its presence. In one notable passage he says,

> In the case of sense clearly the sensitive faculty already was potentially what the object makes it to be actually; the faculty is not affected or altered. This must therefore be a different kind of movement; for movement is an activity of what is imperfect, activity in the unqualified sense, i.e. that of what has been perfected is different.
>
> (DA III.7.431a4–7)

Here Aristotle comes closest in DA to stating that perceiving is not a motion at all but instead an activity (i.e., a complete actuality). He denies that perceiving is undergoing an alteration; rather it is simply an actuality, the actuality of what is complete (i.e., an activity). And there is an even more explicit statement along these lines in *De sensu* where he observes,

> Now, even if every perceiver at once hears and has heard – and, in general, perceives and has perceived – and these acts do not come into being but occur without coming into being – yet, just as, though the stroke which causes the sound has been already struck, the sound is not yet at the ear.
>
> (6.446b2–6)

In this passage Aristotle is contrasting the way that hearing is an instantaneous and complete activity with the way that sound travels and takes time to reach the ear. The conjunction of present and perfect tenses is his usual way of referring to activity in contrast with motion. We thus find that Aristotle does occasionally in these theoretical works that generally remain within the confines of natural science nonetheless speak fairly openly of activity as differentiated from motion.

Whereas motion can be in a body or part of a body, activity should always be said to be in the composite substance.[17] The plant lives and the animal perceives and thinks. Activity cannot just involve the soul since soul is not a suitable subject for either motion or activity. The soul always remains an unmoved mover. Hence Aristotle insisted in DA I.4 that it is better to say that the *human* perceives, fears, or thinks, rather than the soul, part of the soul, or merely parts of the human. An advantage of activity over motion is that in pertaining to the composite plant or animal, it does not strictly have a body as its direct substratum. Hence activity is not strictly localized, as is motion, which is in what is moved. The animal does not in fact perceive in its sense organs or its heart or its soul. The animal in perceiving is in the world of and with its sensible objects. Even when Aristotle says "in the soul", as he sometimes does, this is shorthand for saying the ensouled being undergoes or does the operation in question due to the soul as agent.

Some of the best evidence that the living being engages in activity rather than the soul is to be found by considering plants. In *Metaphysics* IX.8.1050a30–b1 Aristotle is not hesitant to say that life, along with perceiving and thinking, is activity. Plants live, and so they may have activity. In the discussion of nutritive capacity in DA II.4, Aristotle keeps insisting that the operations of the nutritive soul are *saving* the sort of faculty and these operations. This saving is perhaps a way of speaking of activity, for saving is a way of retaining completeness. Aristotle surely would not wish to say the living activity of the plant pertains merely to its soul. The soul, as mover, form, and end, is the principle directing and causing the plant's life. Thus plants may provide evidence that activity takes place in the living being with soul as its principle. Aristotle similarly speaks of the subject for perceiving and thinking as the animal rather than just its soul. This concurs with what we have seen in the insistence in DA I.1.403a3–25 that "affections of the soul" truly pertain to the composite and I.4.408a30–b18 that the animal perceives or thinks. This must be Aristotle's considered view.

In DA II.4 Aristotle seems to have nutrition utilizing food to maintain the life of the living being, to lead the living being to grow to its mature size, and to prepare the living being to reproduce itself. Each of these saves the life of the living being since each keeps the being's life or contributes to generating another life such as its own. Each of the other leading life functions belonging to animals beyond nutrition is also somehow saving that kind of life. Perceiving is the exercise of the potentiality for perception, and so the realization of this perfection. And in perceiving there is self-awareness as the sense becomes cognitively what sort of thing it perceives. And the same applies analogously with intellection and its objects.

Aristotle must suppose that speaking of things as "in the soul" will not result in serious misunderstanding. In *Categories* 2 he speaks of literacy and knowledge being in a subject and in the soul (1a20–b3); in DA II.5.417b23–24 he says, "what knowledge apprehends is universals, and these are in a sense within the soul itself". "In the soul" here seems to mean available for use by the soul so that the ensouled being undergoes or does it. In *De memoria* 1.449b23, for example, Aristotle says that the animal "says in the soul" when it remembers that it remembers. Surely he speaks this way to mean that the animal is aware of remembering and his indicating here that it is aware "in the soul" rather than the animal should not be misleading, for were he to claim that it says "in the animal", this could mean merely in the body (as a broken bone occurs in the body).

A most helpful discussion regarding states or dispositions of the soul is *Physics* VII.3. Here Aristotle denies that such states are alterations or that their coming to be is an alteration. These are instead relations connected with perceptions. Even virtues of character have to do with pleasure and pain, which pertain to perception. So coming to have these states is to gain a perfection natural for humans, and exercising these states is activity. And even the more intellectual attainment of getting universals derives from sense experience, since a human "knows in a manner the universal through the particular" (VII.3.247b5–6). Because the soul is the principle directing active or passive activities engaged in by the plant or the animal, it seems harmless to say that these activities or the states that cause them are "in the soul", though the states and their activities truly belong to the living being. It seems useful to speak this way since we are quite aware of these affections "in us", while we are hardly so aware of them as located in our body.[18] When called upon to reject the supposition that the soul is itself the subject, Aristotle as we have seen will do so. Even when he seems to say that things pertain to the soul, besides its being the principle, it is clear from the quoted passages that he often adds qualifying words to express reservations.

We might be ready enough to accept that operations pertaining to the nutritive capacity, sensitive capacity, and the capacity for progressive motion pertain to the composite living being. But there remains the question whether the mind and its operations might belong exclusively to soul. After all, Aristotle himself raises this issue more than once (see I.1.402a8–10, 403a3–11, III.4.429a10–13). And in *De somno* 1.454a8 he says, "for of which there is the potentiality of this is also the actuality". Hence, if mind is a potentiality merely proper to soul in humans, then the activity would pertain exclusively to soul. But even though mind lacks a specific organ, as the five senses have, and this enables the thinking of all things, in fact it is we humans who think. The capacity for thinking must pertain to the human being and the actuality of thinking does so as well. This is because perception gives rise to all possibility for human thinking and *phantasia* and the *phantasma* must always come into play in the thinking. With the deactivation of sense due to sleep in humans, thinking also generally ceases, which shows that thinking is psychophysical. Yet Aristotle acknowledges that we sometimes even think during our sleep (*De insomn.* 3.462a27–31). This he can still allow because waking and sleep are not exclusive contraries (3.462a25–27) and because while asleep we still have the possibility that *phantasmata* are operative, which opens the possibility for some thinking during sleep. Perhaps surprisingly, the seeming shut down while asleep with its lingering availability of *phantasmata* may serve as compelling evidence of the need for *phantasmata* for thinking, and hence that thinking is engaged in by the person rather than just the soul.

Now if all or most of the primary life functions result in operations that are activities rather than merely motions, plants and animals have these operations. And these can only occur in ensouled beings, among perishable beings, since non-living bodies only permit motions. The ensouled beings support activities as their operations. If motion and change exhausted the capacities of all living beings, it would be permissible and plausible to insist that they undergo these merely as bodily beings. Having a body suffices for motion. But if living beings have activities as their most characteristic operations, and these have to pertain to the composite of soul and body as their substrata, then we should be inclined to embrace the hylomorphic view of the perishable living being. Moreover, we have seen that Aristotle's definitions of soul cohere with his thinking of form and matter as principles that are in a unity. And his accounts of nutrition, perception, and thought follow well from his definition of soul. His explication of perceiving manages to give prominent roles to the sense media and sense organs, while not reducing the activity of perceiving to what goes on in the organ, a strict physicalism, or making it merely psychical. He finds a way to stake out a position that avoids extremes. Perhaps there is yet power and beauty in his delineation of concepts and the hylomorphic approach.[19]

Notes

1 Williams 2006, p. 218 says, "I take hylomorphism to be the view that the relation of soul to body bears some illuminating resemblance to the relation of form to matter". Keeping "hylomorphism" merely in reference to soul-body relations is too narrow. Soul-body relations are only a set of the possible form-matter relations, though they are clearly the most important and most characteristic, since for Aristotle among perishable, living beings, plants and animals are most strictly substantial beings (see esp. *Metaphysics* VII.16.1040b5–16).
2 For Aristotle a "common" account intends to give a single account covering all the kinds generally on the same level, as all sorts of plants and animals are ensouled, and the common account of soul should apply similarly to all. In some contrast to this, a "universal" account covers things on quite different levels and may have to take account of wide differences. In *De motu* Aristotle seeks a common cause of all animal motion (1.698a4–5), whereas he also develops a universal reflection (1.698a11–14) upon the motion of the heavens and of non-living things in order to facilitate his account of animal motion.
3 And though it is true that the soul as form is the form of the living composite being, Aristotle carefully defines the soul as the form of the matter at II.1.412a6–10.
4 *Organikon* in II.1.412a28–b1 is here understood to mean "instrumental" rather than "organized" or composed of instruments or organs (cf. III.9.432b18). Aristotle is making the general point, consistent with his top-down approach to explanation, that the body of the living being is instrumental to its functioning and so used as an instrument by the living being's soul.
5 In generation, for Aristotle, parts can precede the entire living being since he has observed, probably with chicken eggs, that the heart emerges early and then leads to the development of the rest of the animal (see *De juv.* 3.468b28–469a2, and PA III.4.665a33–b2).
6 In recent times we have the experience of resuscitation and transplantation of body parts to support this. Aristotle himself hypothetically entertains the possibility of an eye transplant (see DA I.1.408b18–31) and speaks of asexual reproduction of plants by divisions and the grafting of plant parts (see *De juv.* 3.468b16–28).
7 Charles 2008 accuses most recent commentators of Aristotle of making Cartesian assumptions since they begin trying to relate the physical to the psychological. Charles instead assigns Aristotle a version of hylomorphism with formal and material components so inseparable they cannot even be known apart. Yet form and matter's being one still allows the priority of form, distinct accounts, and some separability. In DA II.1 Aristotle gives accounts of soul involving form and matter, but in II.2.413b11–13 he offers a purely formal account of soul. There must be some separability of psychical function and body type inasmuch as different sorts of bodies in different kinds of animals support similar operations, e.g., nutrition, perception, and passions. See Caston 2008 for further critique of overly strong hylomorphism.
8 The discussion of method in *Posterior Analytics* II.1 would lead us to expect the determination *that* the soul is prior to seeking *what* it is, but Aristotle does not quite go in this order in DA. Yet that the predecessors allow soul to account for motion and perception (see DA I.2.403b20–27) is some evidence for this method, even if their tendency to conceive the soul as a mobile body and perception as due to like by like awareness casts doubt on the genuine need for soul as anything beyond a kind of bodily magnitude.
9 Aristotle indicates that the capacity of touch is required for *animal* life, for loss of this sense destroys the animal (DA III.13.435b4–21). A general loss of touch likely removes all other perceptive capacity, which is the defining capacity of an animal, since touch might only be ended when the bodily organ supporting all sensitivity, i.e., the heart or its analogue, ceases to support perception (see III.12.434b9–27 and *De*

somno 2.455a12–b13). Perhaps where there is such overall loss of capacity for touch this is due to lethal disease or injury impacting the crucial body part, but even if the animal could survive briefly in a kind of vegetative condition, with loss of touch the animal loses its ability to pursue and avoid, and hence is exposed to further destruction and cannot locate and take in any nutriment, ensuring death.

10 While we earlier emphasized the distinction between common and universal, Aristotle need not mean "universal" in DA II.12 as pertaining across vastly different genera. He instead speaks universally of all sense in II.12.424a17 to set up a contrast with that which is "according to each" or "particular", which immediately precedes his point here. DA II.11 ends with this line: καθ' ἑκάστην μὲν οὖν τῶν αἰσθήσεων εἴρηται τύπῳ. Chapter 12 begins thus: καθόλου δὲ περὶ πάσης αἰσθήσεως δεῖ λαβεῖν ἡ μὲν αἴσθησίς ἐστι τὸ δεκτικὸν τῶν αἰσθητῶν εἰδῶν ἄνευ τῆς ὕλης. Since the chapter breaks are not Aristotle's, we here have *men-de* structure. He then has the standard contrast, "particular-universal", which works better than "particular" vs. "common". Aristotle contrasts particular and universal at I.1.402b7, II.5.417b23, III.11.434a16–17 and 434a20, but never particular with common in DA. Thus the distinction between common and universal, though significant, can be outweighed by the "particular" and "universal" contrast, as in II.11–12.424a15–18.

11 Burnyeat 2002 introduces the terminology "non-standard alteration". Frey 2007, pp. 187–190 argues pertinently that Aristotle's account of chemical change by mixture also goes outside his treatment of the kinds of motions in the *Physics* (cf. Ackrill 1997, pp. 176–177). We might wonder as well how Aristotle is comfortable with long-term continuation of *phantasmata* as alterations of a sort, perhaps analogous to projectile motions, if he insists that all motion requires a mover. His answer is that *phantasmata* may be lasting as motions in potentiality (see *De insom*. 2.459a24–b7 and 3.461b12–13). As potentialities to be reinvigorated in imagining, deliberating, remembering, recollecting, or dreaming, the "motions" last for long periods.

12 Burnyeat 1992, pp. 20–21 misses how the organ of touch undergoes some limited compression when it touches something hard. Hence some of his evidence for the "spiritualist" interpretation of perception – that feeling something hard does not require any hardening of the flesh – seems quite mistaken. The slight compression we feel in lightly touching a hard object can convince us of its hardness, as slight and rapid contact with something very hot or cold convinces us that it is very hot or cold.

13 For a fuller account of receptivity to sensible form without the matter, see Polansky 2007, pp. 338–349.

14 "Structuralism" is our coinage based on the claim in Miller 1999, p. 191 that "The eye could thus replicate the formal structure of the colored object without itself having to exhibit color literally." Tending to this position are Ward 1988, Shields 1995, Bradshaw 1997, Caston 1998 and 2005.

15 Burnyeat 2008 argues that this passage does not really belong in its context in the *Metaphysics*, nor does it fit within theoretical sciences. Yet even if 1048b18–35 does not belong in its present location, Burnyeat himself acknowledges that Aristotle appeals to the distinction of activity and motion in *Metaphysics* IX.8, so activity is hardly out of place in theoretical contexts.

16 Adding to the possible difficulty of the activity-motion distinction is that activity often encompasses motions. If we are correct in our account of perception, perception is an activity arising on the basis of motion, at least non-standard alteration, in the sense organ. And the sensible object may be something temporally extended, such as locomotion, and hence the activity of perceiving is presumably complete at each moment though its object is not. Ackrill (1965) supposed this presented an insuperable problem for Aristotle since one could only say at its end rather than each moment during a performance that I am enjoying and have enjoyed the play. Activities with temporally

extended objects, such as enjoying a play or choosing to go to war, must have the enjoyment or choice complete throughout the play or the war in a way in which the play or war is only complete when it ends. Aristotle manages this since the activities of enjoying or choosing are built upon cognition, and cognition is by way of sensible or intelligible forms that are as forms always a unity and complete.

17 That the body can undergo motion rather than solely as an ensouled body should be clear from Aristotle's account of involuntary motion in NE III.3. When a human is compelled violently, the body is moved without any direction by the person's desire or soul. Yet when Aristotle says that "life is in the soul" in *Meta.* IX.8.1050a36–b1, this must mean the living being lives *due* to its soul, for in the case of things engaging in activity, the actuality is in what engages in the activity (1050a34–36).

18 This is especially evident for the case of memory, in which something past and absent is remembered by way of something present. So in *De memoria* Aristotle speaks repeatedly of what occurs as in the soul (see 1.450a27, 450b9–11, 450b27–29, 451a2–5, 2.451a22–24).

19 Our greatest discomfort with Aristotle may be his arguments for the location of the primary organ of the soul in the heart or its analogue so that nutrition, perception, and progressive motion would have great unification, at least they would have a single organ in actuality though this organ would be capable of supporting these different powers (see *De juv.* 1.467b25–27 on the one central organ supporting multiple operations). Unification of the soul in the heart explains why all the senses tend to deactivate together in sleep, sensible objects of different senses can be discriminated, animal motion is coordinated and closely connected with perception, and death shuts down all life functions. If we wonder what empirical evidence Aristotle has for not also making the heart the organ for thought, it is his contrasting the way humans can think *all* things with the way each sense has only a restricted range of sensible objects due to the sense's dependence on a peculiar bodily organ, such as eye or ear (see DA III.4.429a13–27). We wish to thank John Sisko for his helpful suggestions.

Bibliography

Ackrill, J. L. (1965) Aristotle's distinction between 'Energeia' and 'Kinesis'. In Brambrough, R. (ed.) *New Essays on Plato and Aristotle*. London: Routledge and Kegan Paul, pp. 121–141 [pp. 142–162 in Ackrill 1997].

———. (1972–1973) Aristotle's definitions of 'Psuche'. *Proceedings of the Aristotelian Society* 73: 119–133 [pp. 163–178 in Ackrill 1997].

———. (1997) *Essays on Plato and Aristotle*. Oxford: Clarendon Press.

Barnes, J. (ed.) (1984) *The Complete Works of Aristotle*. 2 vols. Princeton: Princeton University Press.

Bradshaw, D. (1997) Aristotle on perception: The dual-logos theory. *Apeiron* 30: 143–161.

Burnyeat, M. F. (1992) Is Aristotle's philosophy of mind still credible? A draft. In Nussbaum, M., and Rorty, A. (eds.) *Essays on Aristotle's De Anima*. Oxford: Oxford University Press.

———. (2002) De Anima II 5. *Phronesis* 47: 28–90.

———. (2008) 'Kinesis' vs. 'Energeia': A much-read passage in (but not of) Aristotle's 'Metaphysics'. *Oxford Studies in Ancient Philosophy* 34: 219–292.

Caston, V. (1998) Aristotle and the problem of intentionality. *Philosophy and Phenomenological Research* 58: 249–298.

———. (2005) The spirit and the letter: Aristotle on perception. In Salles, R. (ed.) *Metaphysics, Soul, and Ethics in Ancient Thought: Themes from the Work of Richard Sorabji*. Oxford: Clarendon Press, pp. 245–320.

———. (2008) Commentary on Charles. *Proceedings of the Boston Area Colloquium on Ancient Philosophy* 24: 30–49.
Charles, D. (2008) Aristotle's psychological theory. *Proceedings of the Boston Area Colloquium on Ancient Philosophy* 24: 1–29.
Dowd, J. (2015) Does Aristotle believe in essentially-ensouled matter? *Ancient Philosophy* 35: 97–111.
Frey, C. (2007) Organic unity and the matter of man. *Oxford Studies in Ancient Philosophy* 32: 167–204.
Miller, J. R. F. (1999) Aristotle's philosophy of perception. *Proceedings of the Boston Area Colloquium in Ancient Philosophy* 15: 177–213.
Mirus, C. (2001) Homonymy and the matter of a living body. *Ancient Philosophy* 21: 357–373.
Shields, C. (1995) Intentionality and isomorphism in Aristotle. *Proceedings of the Boston Area Colloquium in Ancient Philosophy* 11: 307–330.
Ward, J. (1988) Perception and Λόγος in 'De anima' ii 12. *Ancient Philosophy* 8: 217–234.
Williams, B. (2006) Hylomorphism. In Williams, B., and Burnyeat, M. (ed.) *The Sense of the Past: Essays in the History of Philosophy*. Princeton: Princeton University Press.

8

ARISTOTLE ON THE INTELLECT AND LIMITS OF NATURAL SCIENCE

Christopher Frey

Most present-day philosophers of mind are *physicalists*. When it comes to determining the world's ontology, physicalists privilege the position of those who study the inanimate world and refuse to countenance what is utterly mysterious (i.e., seemingly brute and arbitrary) from the physicist's point of view. This orientation leads to a version of the "mind-body problem." For the concepts we employ to describe thought, conscious perception, and the other states and activities Descartes indelibly marks with the label "mental" do not belong to physics' basic conceptual repertoire. So, assuming that the physicalist doesn't wish to eliminate the mental altogether, she must find a way to effect an explanatory continuity between the world that the contemporary (or future, or perfect) physicist describes and the mental life of living organisms. At a minimum, this continuity consists in a restricted form of the global logical supervenience of mental properties upon physical properties. That is, the mental ceases to be mysterious to the physicist if and only if the totality of our world's true physical facts entails the totality of our world's true mental facts.[1] Though the goal is easily stated, and many physicalists take it for granted, establishing this supervenience claim is no easy task.

Aristotle, unlike the present-day philosopher of mind, faces no special mind-body problem. For according to Aristotle, mental capacities are simply to be placed, with equal footing, alongside other vital capacities (δυνάμεις τῆς ψυχῆς) (e.g., respiration and digestion). At most, Aristotle faces a "life-body problem." This life-body problem is not without its obstacles and several of these challenges mirror difficulties that the mind-body problem raises. But Aristotle's framework allows him to sidestep the one obstacle we have already mentioned: he does not have to establish that vital capacities and their activities are intelligible to those who study the inanimate world. For according to Aristotle, the science that studies the inanimate world is the science of nature (φυσικὴ ἐπιστήμη) and the individual who practices this science, the student of nature (φυσικός), examines that which "is by nature or according to nature" (φύσει καὶ κατὰ φύσιν) (*Phys*. II.1, 193a1–2).

The vital activities of living organisms are "by nature" in the relevant sense; their source (ἀρχή) and cause (αἰτία) is an internal principle of movement and rest and such a principle *is* a nature (φύσις) (192b21–33). If this is correct, that is, if the set of facts the student of nature investigates includes the totality of vital facts, then vital facts, including mental facts, supervene trivially on natural facts.

But there is one vital capacity that complicates this picture significantly, namely, the intellect (νοῦς). The intellect occupies an exalted position among the vital capacities. Its possession distinguishes human beings from all other terrestrial organisms, its operation is central to a flourishing human life, and its status as divine is ensured by its being god's sole activity. One would expect it to be among the most important things for us to understand. But it is a curious capacity. On numerous occasions, Aristotle isolates the intellect for special consideration and what he does say about it often differs from what he says about the other vital capacities (see *DA* I.1, 403a27, 413a5–7 and *PA* I.1, 641a17–18, a23). For example, Aristotle maintains that the intellect is alone among our vital capacities in not being realized physiologically in a proprietary organ (see *DA* III.4, 429b26–27, 430a17–25; I.5 411b15–18; II.1, 413a4–9, b24–27; and *GA* II.3, 736b28). More often than not, Aristotle raises questions about the intellect only to leave them unanswered. Given this peculiar status, it is unclear whether we ought to employ the methods of natural science when we investigate the intellect. To which science, if any, does the intellect's study belong?

We already have the resources to provide a strong argument on Aristotle's behalf for the intellect's inclusion in natural science's domain. Natural science studies natures and Aristotle is clear that (i) the principle and cause of a living organism's vital activities, including its intellectual activities, is its form, viz. its soul (ψυχή), and that (ii) souls are natures.

But at one point Aristotle says explicitly that the intellect is *not* to be studied by the student of nature (PA I.1, 641a32–b10). In what has come to be known as *the correlatives argument*, Aristotle argues that if the student of nature were to study the intellect, she would be forced to study not only that which is by nature but everything that is intelligible and we should therefore exclude the intellect from natural science's domain. Aristotle goes on to argue that this exclusion is not problematic because the intellect is not really a principle of movement at all. If this is correct, then it looks like the intellect falls outside the student of nature's ken. But this exclusion comes at a cost; it throws Aristotle into the same position as the present-day physicalist insofar as it renders a central aspect of our mental lives utterly mysterious from the student of nature's point of view.

This is an uncomfortable impasse and my aim in this chapter is to reconcile these opposed strains within Aristotle's thought. I will begin with a thorough presentation and critical examination of the case against the intellect's inclusion in natural science's domain. Three principal considerations drive this exclusion. First, the way in which the intellect is related to the body (or, better, the ways in which it *isn't* related to the body) precludes its naturalistic study. Second, the correlatives argument shows that the student of nature can't study the intellect without corrupting natural science's boundaries. And third, natural science studies movements and their principles and the intellect is not a principle of movement and rest. I will argue that this third consideration is ultimately the most important for Aristotle and that it is the most difficult for those in favor of a naturalistic examination of the intellect to accommodate. I will then defend the view that the student of nature can (and ought to) study the intellect *despite* its not being a principle of movement and rest. More specifically (and more controversially), I will argue (i) that, strictly speaking, the only principle of an organism's vital activities is their specific soul considered as a unitary whole; (ii) that this unitary soul is an organism's nature; (iii) that the student of nature must concern herself with whatever activities are involved in the coming to be, development, and full realization of these natural forms; and (iv) in doing so, the student of nature does not slip into first philosophy (i.e., metaphysics or theology). My positive interpretation depends on two central aspects of Aristotle's philosophy: his account of organic hylomorphism and his account of natural teleology. In addition to answering our guiding question, I hope the following discussion sheds light on these pivotal topics.

1. The case against the intellect's inclusion in natural science's domain

1.1 The intellect and matter

The first reason to exclude the intellect from natural science's domain concerns the way in which the intellect is separable from an organism's body (χωριστὴ τοῦ σώματος). Aristotle recognizes a variety of ways in which one thing is separable from another: in account, in being, in function, in place, in magnitude, in thought, *simpliciter*, and perhaps others as well. What each of these means precisely and the ways in which they relate to each other spark intense debate.[2] But even before these issues are settled, it is important to note that Aristotle thinks the intellect is, in some sense, separable from body. For the intellect is alone among vital capacities in not being realized physiologically in a proprietary organ or organ system. Sight is realized in the eye, digestion is realized in several organs, primarily the heart, but there is no single organ or dedicated system of organs that comes to be for the sake of the intellect's operation (*DA* III.4, 429a24–27, cf. *DA* II.1, 413a5–7).[3]

This difference between the intellect and the other vital capacities has consequences for determining which science one ought to employ when one investigates the soul and its activities. For Aristotle divides the theoretical sciences into three main branches – natural science, mathematics, and first philosophy (*Met.* VI.1, 1026a18–20) – and he grounds this taxonomy on the extent and respect in which the objects these sciences investigate are separable from matter. The objects first philosophy studies are separable from matter. The objects mathematics studies are not separable from matter but the mathematician studies them as if they were by means of a kind of abstraction in thought. The objects natural science studies differ from those of both first philosophy and mathematics: they are not separable from matter and the student of nature studies them as enmattered (*Phys.* II.2 193b31–35, 194b13–14; *DA* I.1, 403b12–16; *Met.* I.3, 995a15–20; VI.1, 1025b27–8, and 1025b30–1026a17).

So, if the student of nature is to study the intellect, it must not be separable from an organism's body in a way that would place it in either mathematics' or first philosophy's purview. As Aristotle says, "it belongs to the student of nature to study soul to some extent, i.e. so much of it as is not separable from matter" (see *Met.* VI.1, 1026a5–6, cf. *DA* I.1, 403a27–28). Does the fact that the intellect requires no specific, dedicated physiological realization entail that it is separable from an organism's body in a way that places it beyond the student of nature's ken?

There are two considerations that suggest we answer this question negatively. First, the human intellect cannot function without a body. For the intellect's operation depends upon the operation of imagination and imagination is necessarily realized materially (see *DA* I.1, 403a8–12, III.7, 431a14–15, b2, III.8, 432a8; and *De Mem.* 1, 449b31). So the human intellect is always "with body (μετὰ σώματος)" (DA I.1, 403a16–17).

Second, the student of nature cannot succeed in understanding living organisms if she ignores the intellect altogether. Aristotle argues that one cannot explain completely several characteristics of an organism's tissues and organs if one does not explain them as coming to be as they are for the intellect's sake. Several characteristics have been suggested as being inexplicable without an appeal to the intellect. It is because of humans' intellect that (i) their lips and tongues are well suited to the formation of articulate speech (i.e., their lips are moist and their tongues are the most detached, soft, and broad), (ii) their blood is conducive to intelligence (i.e., their blood is comparatively thin, cold, and pure), (iii) they possess hands that are particularly useful as instruments in various productive endeavors, and (iv) they possess an upright posture and are therefore bipedal.[4]

The ineliminable appeal to the intellect in the explanation of humans' upright posture is the least controversial of these examples.[5] Aristotle argues as follows (*PA* IV.10, 686a25–b2). The human intellect, the most divine capacity of soul that humans possess, could not be exercised successfully (i.e., it would be exercised sluggishly) if there were too much weight in the upper region of the organism's body pressing down upon the body's lower region. So in order for a human to come to be and exercise its intellect successfully, it cannot have much bodily weight pressing down in this way. And anything that does not have much bodily weight pressing down in this way has an upright posture. So humans' posture comes to be as it is because it must come to be this way if the human is to function properly and thereby realize its form completely.

So it is wrong to say that "man is as complete and explainable a thing as other animals are, without taking account of intellect" (Balme 1992, 89). Upright posture and the features it entails, such as our unique form of bipedalism, are among humanity's differentiae – they are features that distinguish humans from all other living organisms – and if the student of nature were to prescind from the intellect altogether, she could not explain either the presence of these features or the physiological happenings that bring them about.

1.2 The correlatives argument

We have shown that the intellect cannot function without, and is therefore not absolutely separable from, body and that the student of nature cannot neglect the intellect altogether. However, even though these two considerations are powerful, they do not settle whether the student of nature is to study the intellect. The student of nature may, and occasionally must, appeal to the intellect in her explanations, but whether she is to investigate theoretically the intellect itself remains unanswered. Aristotle addresses this further question directly in *the correlatives argument*.

In the *Parts of Animals*' introductory chapter, Aristotle argues that the student of nature ought to study a living organism's soul more than its matter (*PA* I.1, 641a15–31). In the course of this argument, he raises (though does not immediately endorse) the possibility that it is not the soul in its entirety, but only some part of the soul, that is an organism's form and nature (641a17–18, 28). He then turns to the intellect and appears to use this possibility to argue directly for the intellect's exclusion from natural science's domain. He says,

> In view of what was said just now, one might puzzle over whether it is up to natural science to speak about *all* soul, or some <part>, since if it speaks about all, no philosophy is left besides natural science. This is because intellect is of intelligible objects, so that natural science would be knowledge about all things. For it is up to the same science to study intellect and its objects, if they truly are correlative and the same study in every case attends to correlatives, as in fact is the case with perception and perceptible objects.
>
> (641a32–b4)

This argument reduces the assumption that natural science studies all of the soul to absurdity by showing that it entails the patently false claim that natural science is the only variety of philosophical inquiry. We can reconstruct the argument as follows.

I   Assumption for *reductio*: Natural science studies all of the soul.
II   The intellect is a part of the soul.
III   So natural science studies the intellect.
IV   The same science studies correlatives.[6]
V   The intellect's correlative (i.e., what intellect is of) is intelligible objects.
VI   So natural science studies intelligible objects.

VII But the objects of every philosophical investigation, viz. "all things," are intelligible.
VIII So natural science studies the objects of every philosophical investigation.
IX So no philosophy is left besides natural science.

The correlatives argument brings two key premises together: the claim that the same science studies correlatives and the claim that the intellect is *of* all things. Few would now endorse the former premise, but Aristotle maintains this view throughout his corpus (for example, at *Cat.* 7, 8a36–b15 and *DA* II.4, 415a14–22). And the latter premise is a central feature of Aristotle's account of the intellect. For the intellect "thinks all things" (*DA* III.4, 429a18) and through its exercise "the soul is in a way all the things that are" (III.8, 431b21). Everything that is can be thought of and everything that can be known is intelligible (or can be derived from that which is intelligible). So if natural science studies the intellect, it will study the objects of mathematics, first philosophy, ethics, politics, rhetoric, and every other variety of philosophical inquiry that yields knowledge.

One sign that this argument is off track is that it justifies a position much stronger than its stated conclusion. For we could substitute any philosophical investigation for natural science in the initial assumption without altering the remainder of the argument. So if first philosophy studies the intellect there is no philosophy left besides first philosophy and if ethics studies the intellect there is no philosophy left besides ethics, etc. If the correlatives argument is sound, there is no means by which we could investigate the intellect scientifically that would not be an investigation into everything that is.

Fortunately, the argument fails by Aristotle's own lights. Aristotle allows for more than one science to study the same objects as long as they treat the objects differently. We have already seen that natural science and universal mathematics study the same objects; natural science studies them *qua* enmattered and mathematics studies them *qua* separable from matter.[7] This same move allows Aristotle to countenance sciences with domains that comprise everything that is; a science can study everything that is, as long as it considers only one aspect of the things that are. In fact, Aristotle already accepts that there is such a science. Aristotle describes first philosophy as the science of being *qua* being; it is a science of everything that is but, when it studies something, it restricts its focus to "both what it is and the attributes which belong to it *qua* being" (*Metaph.* E.1, 1026a23–32; cf. Γ.1). First philosophy's scope is universal, but this does not, nor should it, lead Aristotle to worry that it precludes other varieties of philosophical inquiry.

Similarly, Aristotle can maintain that the science that studies the intellect, whatever it turns out to be, will indeed study everything that is. But it does not follow that there will be no philosophy besides this science. For the intellect's correlative is being *qua intelligible*. This leaves plenty of room for other varieties of inquiry and other kinds of knowledge. So if the theoretical investigation of the intellect belongs to natural science, natural science will indeed study each and everything that is. But when it does so, it will consider what they are and the attributes that belong to them *qua* intelligible.[8]

1.3 The intellect as principle of movement

The correlatives argument does not establish that natural science cannot study the intellect. But the case for the intellect's exclusion from natural science's domain is not complete. Immediately after Aristotle presents the correlatives argument, he gives another, much simpler, argument for the same conclusion. He says,

> Or <one could argue that> it is not the case that all soul is an origin of change, nor all its parts; rather, of growth the origin is something present even in plants, of alteration the perceptual capacity, and of locomotion something else, and not the intellectual capacity; for locomotion is present in other animals too, but thought in none. So it is clear that one should not speak of all soul; for not all of the soul is a nature, but some part of it, one part or even more.
>
> (*PA* I.1, 641b4–10)

According to this argument, natural science studies natural movements and their principles or origins. The explanations of a living organism's natural movements (i.e., the explanations of the natural changes in quantity, quality, and location that are characteristic of living organisms) need not (and often do not) include the intellect.[9] So the student of nature need not study the intellect.

One could push back against this conclusion by arguing that it conflicts with the explanations of human locomotion Aristotle provides elsewhere.[10] Aristotle says that the intellect, in the form of practical reason, conceives an object as a practical good and thereby brings about a desire that moves the reasoner. Unfortunately, even in these discussions, Aristotle appears to relegate the intellect's contribution to a secondary status. The possibility of irrational action implies that the intellect is not *necessary* for human locomotion. More importantly, the intellect's primary role is to serve as an aid to desire, so it is not *sufficient* for human locomotion either. "There is one thing which produces movement," says Aristotle, namely

> the faculty of desire. For if there were two things which produced movement, intellect and desire, they would do so in virtue of some common form; but as things are, the intellect does not appear to produce movement without desire ... and desire produces movement even contrary to reasoning.
>
> (*DA* III.10, 433a21–25)

As Balme notes correctly, the intellect is not "a moving cause of man except indirectly, in the way that the universe's prime mover moves it, by arousing desire" (Balme 1992, 89).

So the intellect is neither necessary nor sufficient for an organism's vital movements. And since the student of nature studies a part of the soul only if it is an internal principle or origin of movement, she will not study the intellect.[11]

2. The case for the intellect's inclusion in natural science's domain

2.1 A "simple" argument

So there is a significant obstacle to the intellect's inclusion in natural science's domain: the intellect is not a principle of movement and natural science studies only that which is "by nature or according to nature" (*Phys.* II.1); that is, natural movements and the internal principles of movement that are their source. But there seems to be an equally compelling argument that the intellect *is* to be studied theoretically by the student of nature.

Victor Caston offers "a simple (perhaps simple-minded) argument for thinking the intellect *is* part of the form of the human body" (Caston 1996, 180). He says,

I   The intellect is part of the human soul.
II The human soul is identical with the form of the human body.
III [So t]he intellect is part of the form of the human body.

(*ibid.*, 180)

This argument is clearly sound. The human soul comprises three principal parts – the nutritive, the perceptual, and the rational – and the intellect belongs to the rational part of the human soul. And Aristotle maintains that a living organism's soul *is* its form. So a human's form comprises the intellect.[12]

We can extend this argument to the conclusion that the student of nature studies the intellect.

IV   A living organism's form is a nature.
V   So a human's nature comprises the intellect.
VI   Natural science studies natures.
VII So natural science studies something that comprises the intellect.
VIII If a science studies something, it studies all that it comprises.
IX   So natural science studies the intellect.

According to Aristotle, the "form indeed is nature more than the matter" (*Phys.* II.1, 193b6–7) and an organism's form, its soul, is life's principle (i.e., it is the formal, final, and efficient cause of those activities that exhaust what it is for the organism to live).[13] So if the intellect belongs to an organism's form, it will also belong to an organism's nature.

But this argument is question begging in at least two places. Against premise IV, one can maintain that an organism's soul is not a nature; only some parts of the soul are natures or compose a nature. That is, the soul's nutritive part is an internal principle of an organism's threptic and reproductive movements and the soul's perceptual part is an internal principle of an organism's locomotive and perceptual movements, but the soul's rational part is not an internal principle of any movements at all. And even if one grants that the student of nature studies the soul and that the soul comprises the intellect, one can maintain, against premise VIII, that natural science need not study every part of soul, but only those parts that are sources of movement. So if we are to include the intellect in natural science's domain, it will require a better argument.

2.2 *The unity of soul and the soul as nature*

If the student of nature is to study the intellect, there must be something wrong with the claim that she can study only some part or parts of the soul. I will argue against this position in two stages. First, I will argue that the student of nature's ultimate focus is not natural movement but those beings who have internal principles of movement and rest (§II.2.1). Second, I will argue that the principle of each of an organism's vital movements and activities is the organism's unitary soul considered as a whole (§II.2.2).

2.2.1 *What natural science studies*

Aristotle offers numerous descriptions of what the student of nature studies:

(i) what is or exists by nature (*Phys.* II.1, 192b8, 12, 193a1–2, b3, 6)
(ii) what is or exists according to nature (192b35, 193a1–2, 32–33)
(iii) what is constituted naturally (192b13)
(iv) natural objects (193a10)
(v) the natural (192a32–33)
(vi) natural compounds (193a36)
(vii) magnitude, motion, and time (III.4, 202b30; *DC* I.1, 268a1–4)
(viii) the qualities and forms of things insofar as they are inseparable from perceptible matter (II.2, 194b13–14; *Metaph.* VI.1, 1025b27–1026a17; *DA* I.1, 403b12–16)
(ix) what is capable of movement (I.2, 185a12–13; *Metaph.* VI.1, 1025b27–1026a17)
(x) "some genus of being, namely that substance which has the principle of change and rest in itself" (*Metaph.* E.1, 1025b18–21)

Some of these descriptions are meant to fix natural science's domain; others are meant merely to describe salient and important characteristics of that which belongs to natural science's domain. Nevertheless, this list brings two features into relief as being of special interest to the student of nature: (i) those changes that things are capable of by virtue of being enmattered – qualitative movement, quantitative movement, and locomotive movement – and (ii) that which can change in these ways by virtue of an internal principle of movement and rest. But which of these is natural science's primary focus? The answer, it turns out, makes no small difference to our guiding question.

On the one hand, if we take natural movements to be primary, the following procedure for determining natural science's domain seems plausible. First, list all the natural movements, and second, list all the natural capacities that, when exercised, result in these movements. If this procedure fixes natural science's domain, the intellect will be absent. For, as we have already seen, all the natural movements an organism undergoes by virtue of its soul – vital quantitative change (growth), vital qualitative change (perceptual alteration), and vital locomotive change – can be explained without an appeal to the intellect.

On the other hand, if we take natures to be primary, that is, if natural science studies natural movement only because natural science studies a specific class of beings, namely, beings who possess internal principles of movement and rest, it remains an open question whether the intellect belongs to natural science's domain. Perhaps the student of nature must study the intellect if they are to study the human soul even if the intellect, when considered as a part of soul, does not itself issue in any proprietary movements.

We can determine which is the correct orientation if we consider the significance of the oft-repeated methodological precept with which Aristotle begins the *Physics*: we ought to begin our inquiries with what is obvious, especially with what can be known simply through perception, and only then proceed to discover that which is comparatively unclear but is ultimately explanatorily fundamental and constitutes the basis of genuine knowledge (*Phys*. I.1, 184ab16–21. Cf. *DA* II.2, 413a11–12; *Metaph*. VII.3, 1029b3–12; *EE* I.6, 1216b26–35, and I.7, 1217a19–20). What is comparatively clear to us is that there is movement and that some movement has a source that is internal to what moves. But the knowledge to which we aspire concerns the principles of this movement. As Aristotle says, "systematic knowledge of nature must start with an attempt to settle questions about principles" (*Phys*. I.1, 184a14–15). We will possess this knowledge if we come to understand both the principles by virtue of which movement in general is possible and if we come to understand the primary cause and principle of natural movement in particular (i.e., natures).

So the student of nature concerns herself with movement and ought to begin her inquiry by focusing her attention upon movement. But what is prior with respect to the explanations of a completed natural science are natures and those substances whose movements arise from them. It remains an open possibility, then, that the intellect is included in natural science's domain. That is, if the study of a human's nature demands that we study the intellect, then the intellect will be included in natural science's domain even if the totality of humanity's vital activities are the exercises of sub-intellectual capacities that we share with other animals.

2.2.2 The soul as unitary nature

I contend that the soul's unity entails that the study of human nature does indeed require the study of the intellect. Aristotle raises questions about the unity of soul in the opening book of *De Anima*. He asks,

> since knowing, perceiving, opining and further desiring, wishing, and generally all other modes of appetition, belong to soul, and the local movements of animals, and growth, maturity, and decay are produced by the soul, we must ask whether each of these is an attribute of the soul as a whole, i.e. whether it is with the whole soul we think, perceive, move ourselves, act or are acted upon, or whether each of them requires a different part of the soul?
>
> (I.5, 411a26–b2)

Though there is a sense in which it is appropriate to speak of the soul as comprising parts, Aristotle is clear that "the soul is one" and that this unitary soul considered as a whole is the source of each of an organism's vital activities (411b5–14). To do otherwise, that is, to think of the soul as being fundamentally a collection of parts or capacities, is to render unintelligible how the soul could ever serve as the principle and cause of an organism's bodily and functional unity. Moreover, the entire soul is present as a unity throughout the body (411b14–27). Even though our capacity to see is localized in the eye, "in each of the parts is present all the parts of soul" (411b25). That is, the entire soul is present as the principle and cause of those movements that are the exercises of capacities that are localized in an individual's diverse organs and organ systems.

This is a somewhat surprising answer. Why invoke the notion of parts at all if an organism's vital activities and movements have the entire soul as their principle? The parts of soul are a privileged subclass of our vital capacities. Isn't it right to say that our digestive movement is the exercise of our nutritive capacity and that our perceptual movement is the exercise of our perceptual capacity?

The answer to this last question is, of course, yes. But an affirmative answer does not preclude there being a single internal principle of our vital movements. It would be a mistake not to attribute nutritive *capacities* to animals. But when an animal exercises its nutritive capacity, this activity does not have a nutritive soul as its principle. *The principle of an animal's nutritive activities is a perceptual soul*. Everything an animal does has its one and only soul as its principle and end. So feeding is one of the ways in which the animal's single soul, a perceptual soul, is actualized. Similarly, it would be a mistake not to attribute both nutritive and perceptual capacities to humans. But when a human exercises her nutritive and perceptual capacities, these activities do not have nutritive or perceptual souls as their respective principles. *The principle of a human's nutritive and perceptual activities is a rational soul*.[14]

This fits well with Aristotle's general understanding of teleology with respect to beings with natures. The soul is the internal principle and cause of those movements and activities that are the manifestation of a living organism being what it is (*DA* II.4, 415b12–14). Since "for living beings, to be is to live" (415b13), the soul is the principle of those activities that are the exercises of an organism's vital capacities. And as it is with most natural unities, the final, formal, and efficient causes of a living organism's vital movements coincide. For,

> the soul is the cause and first principle of the living body . . . the soul is cause as being that from which the movement is itself derived, as that for the sake of which it occurs, and as the essence of bodies which are ensouled.
>
> (415b9–12)

So insofar as a soul is a nature, one can't understand the soul's activities without understanding them as occurring for the sake of a form, namely, the soul itself.

There is one and only one internal principle of movement and rest within living organisms. Strictly speaking, the only principle of an organism's vital movements and activities is their specific soul considered as a unitary whole. And Aristotle says that, "it is for the same science to know that for the sake of which and the end as well as what is for the sake of these" (*Phys*. II.2, 194a27–29). So the student of nature must concern herself with whatever activities are involved in the coming to be, development, and full realization of this natural form. Every vital movement of a human being is a partial realization or perpetuation of their human (i.e., rational) soul. For the student of nature to neglect the intellect is for her to misconstrue the formal end of a human's natural movements. These movements are not all for the sake of the intellect, but they are for the sake of a unitary soul that comprises intellect. Aristotle is correct when he says that "our reason and intellect are the end of our nature" (*Pol*. VII.15, 1334b15). But this is because reasoning and intellection are the distinctive activities that mark our specific way of living and our natural end is to live (and therefore be) in precisely this way.

3. Conclusion

The interpretation I have defended, that the student of nature is to study the intellect insofar as she studies the unitary form for the sake of which a human comes to be as it is and act as it does, fits well with many of the claims made in our presentation of the case against the intellect's inclusion in natural science's domain. Given our preferred interpretation, it is no surprise that there are characteristics of an organism, say, upright posture, that cannot be explained without an appeal to the intellect as part of the form for the sake of which man's generation and natural development occur. And it is equally unsurprising that the correlatives argument is, in numerous respects, a resounding failure.

But Aristotle does give the correlatives argument. What are we to make of the several arguments Aristotle provides in *Parts of Animals* I.1 against the natural scientific study of intellect? I contend that these arguments, like many other arguments Aristotle advances, are not put forward as arguments Aristotle himself endorses.[15] They are challenges to the position he ultimately wishes to maintain.

This becomes clear once we note that, immediately after he presents these arguments, he offers the key to their dismissal.[16] He says,

> But we say "this is for the sake of that" whenever there appears to be some end towards which the change proceeds if nothing impedes it. So it is apparent that there is something of this sort, which is precisely what we call a nature.
>
> (*PA* I.1, 641b23–26)

I have argued that it is this very invocation, the invocation of a variety of teleological explanation that is only applicable to natural unities, that allows Aristotle to view the totality of an organism's vital movements as arising from a single, internal, principle of movement and rest and as occurring for the sake of a specific, unitary form. Aristotle makes the strongest case he can for the intellect's exclusion from natural science. But given his view that souls are natures and that these unitary natures are the ends for the sake of which all of an organism's vital movements occur, we must, and Aristotle does, reject these arguments.

So Aristotle's account of how natural teleology is operative in living organisms allows our intellectual activities and the soul that is their principle to be intelligible to those who study the inanimate world. The intellect may be difficult to understand, but it is not utterly mysterious to the student of nature.

Notes

1 More precisely, the claim is true if and only if for any logically possible world *W*, if all and only the positive physical facts true of our world are the physical facts true of *W*, then all and only the positive mental facts true of our world are the mental facts true of *W*. Chalmers aptly calls explanations that establish such a supervenience claim "*mystery-removing* explanation[s]" (Chalmers 1996, p. 48). He says, "logical supervenience removes any *metaphysical* mystery about a high-level phenomenon, by reducing any brutality in that phenomenon to brutality in lower-level facts." (*ibid.*, p. 50; cf. Jackson 1993).
2 Corcilius and Gregoric (2010) contains a nice discussion of these varieties of separability.
3 Victor Caston emphasizes these Aristotelian claims, but goes on to argue that the intellect is realized in the organism's body considered as a whole in Caston (2000). As we will see, there is a sense in which this claim is correct. But the sense in which it is correct is applicable equally to the perceptual souls of animals and the nutritive souls of plants; we can correctly view each of these types of soul as being realized in their respective organisms' bodies considered as wholes.
4 Sarah Broadie provides this list of features in Broadie (1996, p. 168). On lips and tongue, see *PA* II.16, 659b34–660a8 and II.17, 660a17–27; on blood, see *PA* II.2,

648a2–11 and *HA* III.19, 521a2–3; on hands, see *PA* IV.10, 687a8–23; on upright posture, see *PA* IV.10, 686a25–b2, 687a2–5 and II.7, 653a28–32.

5 Lennox (1999) offers strong arguments against the suitability of the first three examples. (i) Though articulate speech is required for humans to participate in those cultural and political practices necessary to develop their essentially social intellects (*Pol.* I.2, 1253a9–15), the passages in the biological works that explain the characteristics of the lips and tongue that facilitate articulate speech do not refer to the intellect explicitly and employ a notion of human vocalization that is continuous with that of other animals. (ii) Though human blood is thin, cold, and pure because these characteristics are conducive to perception and intelligence, Aristotle does not mention human intellect explicitly and the principle example he gives is bees – they are bloodless creatures that are nevertheless more intelligent than many blooded creatures given the character of their blood-analogue. (iii) Though humans' hands enable them to execute their practical intelligence, the sort of practical intelligence at issue in the biological works is one that numerous animals possess.

6 Correlatives are interdependent opposites that are what they are by virtue of standing in a relation with reciprocation. As examples, Aristotle mentions double/half, larger/smaller, master/slave, perception/the perceptible, and knowledge/what is known (*Cat.* 7, 6b27–37).

7 Universal mathematics does not restrict its domain to a particular kind of mathematical objects as, say, geometry and astronomy do, but rather "applies alike to all" (*Met.* VI.1, 1026a24–27).

8 According to Aristotle, every science is concerned with a determinate and proprietary subject genus (*An. Post.* I.28, 87a38, I.9, 76a12; *Met.* VI.1, 1025b18–21) and cannot prove conclusions concerning another science's subject genus (*An. Post.* I.7, 75b3–14). A science's subject genus is what the science is about (I.10, 76b22). But there are two senses of "what a science is about." In one sense, first philosophy and the science that studies the intellect will be about the same beings, viz. everything that is. In another sense, they will have distinct subject genera, viz. what there is *qua* being and what there is *qua* intelligible, respectively.

9 One could justify the parenthetical claim by invoking Aristotle's precept that "nature does nothing in vain" (*IA* 2, 704b12–705a2). If a living organism's movement could be explained without the intellect, the introduction of the intellect as a further origin of the movement would be superfluous.

10 Charleton does just this in Charleton (1987) and appeals to *De Motu* 6, *EN* VI.1, and *DA* III.9–10.

11 This argument is related to the first reason we canvassed for excluding the intellect from natural science's domain. For there is a close connection between being enmattered and being capable of movement. That is, matter is that aspect of a hylomorphic composite by virtue of which it is capable of undergoing movement. This licenses the transition from "they cannot be defined without reference to movement" to "they always have matter" (*Met.* VI.1, 1026a2–3). And it is why Aristotle's tripartite division of the theoretical sciences can also be cashed out in terms of movement: (i) the objects first philosophy studies are "both separable <from matter> and immovable", (ii) the objects mathematics studies are considered "*qua* immovable and *qua* separable from matter", and (iii) the objects natural science studies "are inseparable from matter and not immovable" (1026a6–17).

12 On the intellect as part of the human soul, see *DA* I.1, 402b9–14, II.2, 413a23–25, III.4, 429a10–11; *PA* I.1, 641b4–10; and *EN* I.7. On the identification of an organism's soul with its form, see *DA* II.1, 412a19–21, a27–28; *PA* I.1, 641a17–18; and *Met.* VII.10, 1035b14–16.

13 On the priority of nature as form over nature as matter, see *Phys.* II.8, 198b8–19, 199a30–32; *PA* I.1 640b29; *GC* II.9, 335b35–336a1; and *Met.* IV.4, 1015a13–15. On

the soul as life's principle, see *DA* I.1402a6–7, II.2, 413b11–13, II.4, 415b8–14, and *Met.* IV.8, 1017b8–11. On the soul (or natures more generally) being formal, final, and efficient causes, see *DA* II.4, 415b8–11 and *Phys.* II.7, 198a25–26.

14 I argue for this position in greater detail in Frey (2015).
15 Mary Louise Gill arrives at a similar conclusion regarding these arguments in her unpublished commentary on Lennox (2009). See p. 15 fn.25 of Lennox's paper for his response. Despite our shared conclusion about these arguments' role, the case I have made up to this point differs significantly from Gill's.
16 There is actually another argument that can plausibly be read as a third argument against the intellect's naturalistic study that comes between the two arguments we have discussed and this statement. This does not alter the present point.

Bibliography

Balme, D. M. (1992) *Aristotle: De Partibus Animalium I and De Generatione Animalium I (with passages from II.1–3)*. Oxford: Clarendon Press.

Broadie, S. (1996) Νοῦς and nature in De Anima III. *Proceedings of the Boston Area Colloquium of Ancient Philosophy* 12 (1): 163–176.

Caston, V. (1996) Aristotle on the relation of the intellect to the body: Commentary on Broadie. *Proceedings of the Boston Area Colloquium of Ancient Philosophy* 12 (1): 177–192.

———. (2000) Aristotle's argument for why the understanding is not compounded. *Proceedings of the Boston Area Colloquium of Ancient Philosophy* 16: 135–176.

Chalmers, D. J. (1996) *The Conscious Mind: In Search of a Fundamental Theory*. Oxford: Oxford University Press.

Charleton, W. (1987) Aristotle on the place of mind in nature. In Gotthelf, A., and Lennox, J. (eds.) *Philosophical Issues in Aristotle's Biology*. Cambridge, MA: Cambridge University Press, pp. 408–423.

Corcilius, C., and Gregoric, P. (2010) Separability vs. difference: Parts and capacities of the soul in Aristotle. *Oxford Studies in Ancient Philosophy* 39: 81–119.

Frey, C. (2015) Two conceptions of soul in Aristotle. In Ebrey, D. (ed.) *Theory and Practice in Aristotle's Natural Philosophy*. Cambridge, MA: Cambridge University Press.

Jackson, F. (1993) Armchair metaphysics. In Hawthorne, J., and Michael, M. (eds.) *Philosophy in Mind*. Amsterdam: Kluwer, pp. 23–42.

Lennox, J. G. (1999) The place of mankind in Aristotle's Zoology. *Philosophical Topics* 27 (1): 1–16.

———. (2009) Aristotle on mind and the science of nature. *Proceedings of the Eight Biennial International Conference of Greek Studies, Flinders University* June: 1–18.

9

ARISTOTLE ON THE PERCEPTION AND COGNITION OF TIME

John Bowin

Aristotle claims that time can be perceived. In *Physics* 4.11 he says we perceive motion and time together and he says that we can perceive instants, or "nows" as he calls them (219a3–4; 219a30–b1). At various places in *De Memoria* 1, he also says that the perception of time is involved in remembering (*Mem*.1.449b29, 450a19, 451a17). Aristotle thinks that by measuring time we can grasp it intellectually as well. He talks of "apprehending time by a measure" in *De Memoria* 2 (452b7), and I shall argue that this is a way of grasping time intellectually.

This chapter will attempt to clarify what is and is not involved in these two modes of apprehending time, and the way in which they interact. I will ultimately argue that, according to Aristotle, one's intellectual grasp of time has an effect on one's perception of time for those beings who have intellect. But first I will establish that, for Aristotle, perceiving time does not presuppose grasping it intellectually. This is important, for Aristotle, because he wishes to credit animals lacking intellect with memory, and he defines memory in a way that presupposes the perception of time: Some animals are sagacious (φρόνιμος) and can be taught, and since they lack intellect, they must rely on memory for this ability (*Meta*.A.1.980a28 ff.). But we remember having learned something only when we recognize that we have learned it *before*, and this requires the perception of time (*Mem*.1.450a14–450a20). Hence, in order to explain animal sagacity without crediting them with intellect, Aristotle must maintain that time can be perceived without intellect.

Still, two things might tempt one to suppose that the perception of time nonetheless requires intellect. First, since Aristotle defines time as "a number of motion in respect of the before and after" (*Physics* 4.11.219b1–2), and since number is a mathematical object, and according to Aristotle, mathematical objects are grasped by the intellect through abstraction[1] and, in the case of numbers, counting, it would appear that time must be grasped in this way. And indeed, Aristotle seems to say in *Physics* 4.11 that it is by a process of counting that we come to know that time exists. Second, in *Physics* 4.14 Aristotle argues that time would not exist in the absence of beings who can count. Since the existence of time depends on

175

counting, one might suppose that the perception of time depends on counting also. I will argue that neither time's status as a number, nor its apparent dependence on mind requires it to be grasped intellectually. In particular, I will argue that commentators, both ancient and modern, have overemphasized the importance of counting in Aristotle's account of time at the expense of time perception.

1. Perceiving time

Albert the Great, for instance, commenting on Aristotle's claim at *De Memoria* 1.449b28–9 that memory is possible only in beings who perceive time says,

> Time is perceived (*sentire*) in twofold fashion. One way is in itself (*in se*), according to a number of motion. Only rational beings perceive (*sentire*) and know (*cognoscere*) time in this manner. In another way time is perceived relationally and not in itself; then it is perceived according to a fixed distinction of time, according to which a time is located near a temporal event.
>
> (B. Alberti Magni 1890, 100)[2]

Themistius, while commenting on Aristotle's claim at *De Anima* 3.11.433b5–11 that a conflict between reason and desire is possible only in beings who perceive time, makes a very similar claim:

> For [a human being] perceives (αἰσθάνεσθαι) time [as time is] in itself, but the other [animals perceive it] incidentally, since they [perceive] not time but [only] the way that they were affected at an earlier time. . . . Only a human being is "at once turned front and back", for it alone has an intellect (νοῦς) by which to count (ἀριθμεῖν) what is before and after, and this number is time.
>
> (Themistius 1899, 120,12–17)[3]

Nothing in the immediate context of the passages that occasion these comments justifies these claims.[4] But the mention of time as a number evidently refers to Aristotle's definition of time as a number of motion. Albert the Great seems to think that merely because time is a mathematical object, grasping it in itself must require grasping it intellectually. Themistius' thought appears to be that perceiving time in itself requires νοῦς[5] because it requires counting and, according to Aristotle, only beings with νοῦς are able to count (*Phys*.4.14.223a26; cf. *Top*.6.5.142b26).[6]

Must, then, time be grasped intellectually because it is a mathematical object? This would clearly be the case if numbers were ontologically constituted by the mind of the mathematician. The extent to which Aristotle thinks this is true of mathematical objects in general is controversial.[7] It is clear that, in Aristotle's view, mathematical objects are sensible objects studied *qua* having certain properties. But it is not clear if or to what extent these properties are actually present in the sensible world independently of the mind of the mathematician. For it is not clear, as Aristotle seems to admit in places (*Metaph*.B.2.997b35–998a6; K.1.1059b10–12), whether ordinary sensible objects supply properties of sufficient quality and variety for mathematical study. And Aristotle does talk, in places, about the construction by geometers of geometrical objects in the course of geometrical proofs, a process by which such objects are brought from potential to actual existence (*Metaph*.Θ.1.1051a21–33; cf. M.3.1078a28–31).

But I think it would be wrong to suppose that just because sensible reality does not supply all of the mathematician's needs, none of the properties that the mathematician is interested in can be found fully actual in the sensible world. And the case of arithmetic is very different from the case of geometry. A geometer studies geometrical objects, which are sensible objects *qua* having geometrical qualities. And it is perhaps plausible to say that sensible objects can only instantiate these properties imperfectly or potentially, and that, as a result, abstraction from their imperfections is required to bring geometrical objects to actuality. But an arithmetician studies numbers, which are pluralities of things studied *qua* indivisible and countable.[8] And there is no reason to suppose that perfect and actual specimens of indivisibles cannot be found among sensible objects and events. A man, for instance, is perfectly and actually indivisible *qua* man. And more importantly in the case of time, as we shall see, instantaneous motion stages are perfectly and actually indivisible insofar as they are instantaneous. No abstraction is required to bring them to actuality.

Does *Physics* 4.11, nonetheless require us to count in order to grasp that time exists? The answer to this question turns on the interpretation of a passage shortly before Aristotle's definition of time as "a number of motion in respect of the before and after" at 219b1–2:

> But time, too, we apprehend when we mark off motion, marking it off by the before and after, and we say that time has passed when we get a perception of the before and after in motion. We mark off motion by taking them to be different things, and some other thing between them; for whenever we conceive of the limits as other than the middle, and the soul says that the nows are two, one before and one after, then it is and this it is that we say time is. (What is marked off by the now is thought to be time: let this be taken as true.)
>
> (*Physics* 4.11.219a22–219a29)[9]

It is clear that "number", here, refers to a number of instantaneous stages of motion, because what are numbered are the bounds or limits of a motion. What Aristotle's definition of time appears to tell us, in the light of this passage, is that time exists just in case there is a number (i.e., two or more, since Aristotle thinks one is not a number) of instantaneous stages of motion limiting something in between (a number of instantaneous stages of motion being just a plurality of instantaneous stages of motion studied *qua* indivisible and countable). What lies between is temporal duration.

We can also gather from this passage that to perceive time and to notice that time has passed, it is sufficient to perceive a number of motion stages. One might take this to mean that we thereby perceive time only indirectly,[10] if at all, but I think this is mistaken. Aristotle is willing on many occasions to simply say that we perceive time (*Phys.* 4.11.219a3–4, *Mem.*1.449b29, 450a19, 451a17), and he says at *Phys.* 4.11.219a30–b1 that we perceive the now as both one and as before and after in a motion. He also says we perceive motion and time together (219a3–4). What Aristotle means by this is that we perceive both time and motion directly because to perceive a number of nows is to perceive a plurality of instantaneous motion stages under a certain description. That is, both the now and time are what are before and after in motion *qua* countable (*Phys.* 4.14.223a28–9, *Phys.* 4.11.219b23–8). So to perceive time and to notice that time has passed, it is sufficient to perceive a number of nows (*Phys.* 4.11.219a30–219b1). That to perceive time in a way *just is* to perceive a number of nows is implied by Aristotle's reformulation of the definition of time at *Physics* 4.14.223a28–9. There he says, "the before and after are in motion, and time is these *qua* countable". Since what are before and after in motion *qua* countable are nows, and in particular, a number of nows ordered as before and after, to perceive time *just is* to perceive a number of nows ordered as before and after.

It is also commonly thought that when Aristotle says "the soul says that the nows are two" at *Physics* 4.11.219a27–8, he is talking about counting nows. One might be tempted to conclude from this that in order to perceive a number of motion stages it is necessary to count them. This seems to be Themistius' interpretation, since he says that the before and after in motion is recognized as a succession whenever it is counted (148,12–13). On the other hand, one might accept that Aristotle is talking about counting nows, here, but deny that counting nows is necessary for perceiving that time has passed.[11] To perceive that time has passed, it is merely necessary to recognize that there are a number of motion stages. But one may wonder, then, why should Aristotle talk about counting nows at all in *Physics* 4.11?

One suggestion has been that nows must be counted because they are brought into existence by the act of counting.[12] This is thought to follow from three assumptions: first, that nows are only potential divisions in time; second, that there are not infinitely many potential divisions in a continuum (hence, they are not already there to be counted even as potential entities); third, that the only way to create potential divisions or mark them off (ὁρίζειν) is by counting them. Aristotle clearly says that the now "divides potentially" (*Phys.* 4.13.222a14), but the second assumption appears to be contradicted by Aristotle's claim at *Physics* 8.8.263a27–8, 263b3–6 that time has infinitely many potential parts.[13] So nows exist potentially, prior to being marked off, and since this is how nows exist in any case, it follows that they already exist prior to being marked off or counted. But even if we reject this interpretation of *Physics* 8.8 and hold that it is necessary to mark off nows in order for them to exist, the third assumption seems unwarranted, since it seems entirely possible to mark off nows by merely perceiving them. Aristotle says that nows can be perceived at *Physics* 4.11.219a30–219b1 and he says that perception is capable of discriminating (*Post. An.* 2.19.99b35; *Top.* 2.4.111a14–20; *DA*.2.11.424a6; 3.2.426b8–21). And if marking off nows means discriminating them as individuals, there is circumstantial though convincing evidence that Aristotelian perception is perfectly able to do this by itself, without the help of intellect. First, incidental perception is the perception of individuals, for example, Diares' or Cleon's son, though not necessarily *as* Diares' or Cleon's son. If Diares' or Cleon's son were necessarily perceived as Diares' or Cleon's son, the perceiver would presumably need to possess the sortal concept *man*, and, therefore, possess intellect as well.[14] But as Cashdollar[15] points out, at *De Anima* 2.6.418a16–17 Aristotle also offers "where" as well as "what" as incidental perceptibles, which seems to imply that one can incidentally perceive, for example, "the thing over there" or "the white thing" as well. Hence, we can perceive individuals incidentally, and while perceiving an individual incidentally sometimes involves the possession of a sortal concept, it does not always require it.[16] The second reason to think that Aristotelian perception can discriminate individuals is that Aristotle appears to talk of perceiving individual φαντάσματα[17] of both objects and events in the *De Memoria*. The account of the way in which φαντάσματα are formed in *De Memoria* 1 seems to imply that they appear as, and indeed *are* fully individuated particulars. Aristotle uses the metaphor of a signet ring (cf. *DA* 2.12.424a19) to describe how a percept gives rise to a φαντάσμα (*Mem.*1.450a27–32), and the mechanical nature of this metaphor, as well as of the ensuing discussion about the causes of defects in memory, suggests that individual sense objects give rise to individual φαντάσματα. And in *De Memoria* 2.452b23 ff. where φαντάσματα take the form of motions instead of images, Aristotle talks of matching motions representing events (e.g., ὅτι ὁδήποτε ἐποίησεν) with motions representing time lapses (e.g., τρίτῃ ἡμέρᾳ), and it seems that this pairing could not proceed unless the motions were individuals. Finally, in *De Memoria* 1, Aristotle talks of φαντάσματα serving as the raw material from which, by a process of abstraction, the intellect grasps essences, which presumably includes sortal concepts (449b31–450a7). So it seems the possession of sortal concepts presupposes the prior perception of individuals rather than the other way around.

In fact, I do not think that when Aristotle says, "the soul says that the nows are two", he is talking about counting nows. Counting (ἀριθμεῖν) is not explicitly mentioned in chapters 10 or 11 until *after* Aristotle's definition of time at *Physics* 4.11.219b1–2, and there in a conjunction with being countable (ἀριθμητόν). He says,

> For that is what time is: a number of motion in respect of the before and after. So time is not motion but in the way in which motion has a number. An indication: we discriminate the greater and the less by number, and greater and less motion by time; hence time is a kind of number. But

number is [so-called] in two ways: we call number both that which is counted and countable, and that by which we count. Time is that which is counted and not that by which we count. (That by which we count is different from that which is counted.)

(*Phys.* 4.11.219b1–9)

Counting, I think, plays a much smaller role in *Physics* 4.10–14 than is often supposed.[18] What is important for Aristotle is that numbers are *countable*, not necessarily that they are counted: time is the before and after in motion *qua countable* (*Phys.* 4.14.223a29) and the now is the before and after in motion *qua countable* (*Phys.* 4.11.219b25; 28). This is borne out by a survey of the text. After the passage quoted previously, the verb ἀριθμεῖν appears eight more times in the remainder of book 4. Of these occurrences, three are concerned only with the possibility of counting (*Phys.* 4.14.223a23–5) and three are concerned with repeating the distinction between the number with which we count and the number which is counted (*Phys.* 4.11.219b6–9; *Phys.* 4.12.220b4–5, 8–9), or *countable*, as we have just seen. The remaining two uses are idiosyncratic.[19]

I suggest, rather, that when Aristotle says "the mind pronounces that the 'nows' are two" at *Physics* 4.11.219a27–8, this need only imply that the mind *perceives* the number of (countable) nows, not that it counts them. Aristotle says that number is perceived directly (καθ' αὑτά) by the common sense in *De Anima* 3.1 (425a16, cf. 2.6.418a7–11), soon after saying that "all the senses are possessed by those animals that are neither imperfect nor maimed" (425a9–10). So the direct perception of number is not limited to beings with intellect. The common sense, in both animals and humans, has the ability to perceive a collection of objects or events and just see (or hear or feel) how many there are without counting them.[20] And in fact, Aristotle credits animals with the ability to perceive numbers even while denying them the ability to count.[21] For how else could birds, for example, keep track of the number of eggs in their clutch, as Aristotle says they do in *HA* 6.6: "The eagle lays three eggs and hatches two of them, as it is said in the verses ascribed to Musaeus: 'That lays three, hatches two, and cares for one'" (563a17–19).

So the soul may perceive that "the 'nows' are two" without counting them. The soul can also, no doubt, perceive that the "nows" are three or four, without much difficulty either, and perceive their order of succession without counting them. In fact, since nows appear in succession, and not in unstructured sets, it is possible to perceptually discriminate relative quantities of motion, and the relative sizes of elapsed durations by perceiving the number as well as the order of the instantaneous motion phases, since later nows bound more of the past than earlier ones. This, I think, is what Aristotle is getting at when, shortly after giving his definition of time he says, "we discriminate (κρίνειν) the greater and the less by number, and greater and less motion by time". As I said, perception is a faculty that discriminates. By perceiving the number and order of successive instantaneous phases of a motion, at least if one perceives more than two of them, we perceptually discriminate whether more or less time has passed. This is not yet time measurement, since it does not involve the application of a standard. It is merely a perceptual grasp of the number and relative magnitude of motion.

2. Measuring time

Perceiving time, then, consists in either perceiving *that* time has passed by perceiving a number (two or more) of nows, or perceiving *how much* time has passed, in purely relative terms, by perceiving the order as well as the number of nows. Perceiving time in no way requires counting. But *measuring* time *does* require counting in a way, and therefore also intellect. In the following passage, the verb ἀριθμεῖν is used in an extended sense to mean measuring:

> Since there is locomotion, and, as a kind of locomotion, circular motion, and since each thing is counted (ἀριθμεῖται) by some one thing of the same kind (units by a unit, horses by a horse), and therefore time too by some determinate (ὡρισμένῳ) time, and since, as we said, time is measured by motion and motion by time (that is, the quantity of the motion and of the time is measured by the motion defined by time) – if, then, that which is first is the measure of all things of the same sort, then uniform circular motion is most of all a measure, because the number of this is most easily known. (There is no uniform qualitative change or uniform increase in size or uniform coming-to-be, but there is uniform locomotion.) This is why time is thought to be the motion of the [celestial] sphere, because the other motions are measured by this one, and time by this motion.
>
> (*Physics* 4.14.223b13–24)

Here, Aristotle says that we measure time by counting units of time (e.g., days) which are determinate because they are marked out by motions that are determinate in time (e.g., celestial motions). The reason that the use of ἀριθμεῖν is extended, here, is that strictly speaking, counting is a type of measurement for Aristotle, not *vice versa*. Counting is the type of measurement that is most exact because the measure that it involves is absolutely indivisible, rather than "indivisible in relation to perception" (*Metaph*.I.1.1053a1, 23). So strictly speaking, nows may be counted, because they are absolutely indivisible, but durations may only be measured. Still, at *Physics* 4.12.220a27–8, Aristotle says that parts of continua can have a "number of a sort" (τὶς ἀριθμὸς) insofar as they can be divided into a number of parts, and this, presumably, is the sense of number here. In fact, it is primarily in counting number in this extended sense, that is, in measurement, that the process of counting has any prominence in these chapters.[22]

It is this, time measurement, that requires νοῦς, and it is this that affords an intellectual grasp of time. The best evidence for this is in *De Memoria* 2, where, in language very similar to the passage quoted from *Physics* 4.14, Aristotle claims that measuring time affords a certain type of cognition of it:

> But the main thing is that one must apprehend (γνωρίζειν) the time, either by a measure (μέτρῳ) or indeterminately (ἀορίστως). . . . Sometimes a person does not remember (μεμνῆσθαι) the time by a measure e.g. that he did something or other the day before yesterday; but sometimes also he does remember the time this way. Nonetheless, he remembers, even if it be not by a measure. And people are in the habit of saying that they remember but don't know (εἰδέναι) when, whenever they do not apprehend the amount of time by a measure.
>
> (*Mem*.2.452b8–9; 452b30–453a4)[23]

Whenever we measure time by counting determinate units of time like days, we apprehend (γνωρίζειν) time and the amount of time determinately. Otherwise, we apprehend time and the amount of time indeterminately (ἀορίστως). Γνωρίζειν is a general term that comprehends both perceiving (αἰσθάνεσθαι) and thinking (διανοεῖσθαι) (cf. *GA*.1.23.731a33–4). The contrast, here, is between grasping time or the quantity of time intellectually (διανοεῖσθαι) by means of a measure (μέτρῳ) and perceiving time (αἰσθάνεσθαι).

Apprehending time by a measure is clearly an achievement of the intellect. Aristotle claims that a measure must be of the same genus as what it measures. For example, spatial magnitudes are measured by a spatial magnitude and times are measured by some definite time (*Phys*. 4.14.223a22–8, *Meta*.I.1053a24–30). And since a measure is that by which a quantity is apprehended, it is clear that one must grasp the genus of the measure and the thing measured in order to measure it. Thus, one must possess what we would call the universal sortal concept of *horse* when counting horses and the sortal concepts of *day* and *hour* when measuring time. Conception is an activity that Aristotle denies beings lacking intellect.[24] Apprehending time indeterminately, on the other hand, seems only to be an achievement of perception. It entails perceiving that time has passed since some remembered event, but not knowing how much. This could be construed, as in *Physics* 4.11, as merely perceiving a number of motion stages ordered as before and after, which, minimally, could be just perceiving that a past event is distinct from what one is now experiencing. To apprehend time indeterminately, according to the account of time perception in *Physics* 4.11, is merely to perceive time.

3. Memory, imagination, the perception of time, and the perception of motion

Aristotle talks of remembering time at *De Memoria* 2.452b30–453a4 rather than perceiving time and this raises a number of questions, the most obvious of which is whether Aristotle recognizes a difference between remembering and perceiving time. For instance, perceiving time might be perceiving time as it is passing while remembering time might be remembering that time has elapsed since a remembered event. Aristotle could not be clearer that it is remembering time, in this sense, that he is concerned with in the *De Memoria*. It is remembering that time has elapsed since a remembered event that makes contemplating a representation of that event remembering something. But he calls *this* perceiving time in *De Memoria* 1: "For, as we said before, when someone is actively engaged in memory, he perceives in addition (προσαισθάνεται) that he saw this, or heard it, or learned it earlier; and earlier and later are in time" (449b29; cf. 450a19, 451a17). Sorabji speculates that Aristotle is using a broader sense of "perceive", here, to emphasize that memory is a perceptual and not an intellectual activity.[25] But I think that Aristotle calls this perceiving time because he does not distinguish between remembering time and perceiving time as it is passing, and I say this for two reasons.

First, I would distinguish between perceiving time as it is passing from perceiving time passing, that is, perceiving the passage of time. In *Physics* 4.11, where the topic is time and not memory, Aristotle speaks of perceiving time as it is passing in terms of perceiving time *having* passed, not perceiving time passing. While temporal passage is mentioned seven times in this chapter, Aristotle nowhere talks about perceiving time passing. Each time he speaks of time *having passed* (γεγονέναι χρόνος) in the perfect tense rather than the present. In each case we are said to think, say or suppose that time *has passed* rather than that time is passing (*Phys.* 4.11.218b23, 32–3, 219a6, 7, 14, 24, 32–3). Aristotle is of course interested in the phenomenon of temporal passage. The puzzle of the ceasing instant at *Physics* 4.10.218a8–21 and his claim in Chapter 11 that the now is always "other and other" (219b9–10) are clearly references to temporal passage. And in *De Memoria* 1, Aristotle speaks of memory as a state or affection of perception whenever time passes (ὅταν γένηται χρόνος, 449b25). But in neither work does he speak of perceiving time passing. The second reason to think Aristotle does not distinguish between remembering time and perceiving time as it is passing is that, according to the account of perceiving time in *Physics* 4.11, perceiving time having passed is just remembering that time has elapsed since a remembered event. According to *Physics* 4.11, to perceive time is to perceive a number of motion stages ordered as before and after. But if as I said, this can be just perceiving that a remembered event is distinct from what one is now experiencing, it is no different from remembering that time has elapsed since a remembered event.

Another question that talk of remembering time raises concerns the relationship between memory and the perception of time, and due to the definitional relationship between time and motion, the relationship between memory and the perception of motion. If to perceive time is to perceive a number of motion stages ordered as before and after, one might think that in order to do this, it is at least necessary to remember the motion stages perceived as before. If to perceive motion is just to perceive a plurality of motion stages, and since only one instantaneous motion stage can be present at a time, it follows that some of the motion stages will need to be remembered. Hence both the perception of time and motion seem to presuppose memory.[26] But since Aristotle claims that memory requires the perception of time, this would imply that memory and the perception of time presuppose each other.

A way to avoid this consequence would seem to lie in Aristotle's discussion of certain memory failures.[27] In *De Memoria* 1, Aristotle explains the notion of perceiving time by saying, "When someone is actively engaged in memory, he perceives in addition that he saw this, or heard it, or learned it before; and before and after are in time" (450a19–22). In Chapter 2 we find out what "perceives in addition" means. Both memory and the perception of time involve φαντάσματα and therefore φαντασία; two φαντάσματα, in fact, one representing the event remembered and one representing the time elapsed since the event.[28] To remember, or to recognize that an event happened before is to have a φαντάσμα of a movement corresponding to the time match a φαντάσμα of a movement corresponding to the event (*Mem*.2.452b31–453a4). If, however, one of these φαντάσματα is missing, one fails to remember. Hence, memory presupposes the perception of time, and both memory and the perception of time presuppose the having of φαντάσματα, but the perception of time does not presuppose memory.

It is clear from this that the perception of time depends on φαντασία.[29] But it is not yet clear that time, after all, does not in some way depend on memory. The problem is that a φαντάσμα of a movement corresponding to a time is itself of a series of events that can be remembered. (The movement corresponding to the time is a φαντάσμα or an *appearance*, not an unconscious internal clock process, as envisaged by modern theories of interval perception.) One could say, perhaps, that these events are not remembered unless there is a further series of φαντάσματα to match the events in the movement corresponding to the time. But then we are off on a regress. Why, however, must the movement corresponding to the time and the movement corresponding to the event be separate? One could concede that they are sometimes or even often separate without requiring that they must always be separate. And when they are not separate we could say that to perceive time and to remember an event is the same activity under different descriptions. This is because, according to *Physics* 4.11, to perceive time is to perceive a number of events ordered as before and after. Since the perception of an event that happened before *as* before must inevitably be a φαντάσμα (Aristotle says we can perceive φαντάσματα at *Mem*.1.450b17–18), then to remember an event is to perceive time and *vice versa*. So memory and the perception of time are interdefined, which is a circularity, but not necessarily a vicious one.

What of the apparent dependence of the perception of motion on memory? Perhaps we could say we perceive motion by perceiving a plurality of motion stages, but none of them *as* having happened before. Or more accurately, since Aristotle talks of "perceiving" φαντάσματα, we perceive a retained plurality of φαντάσματα[30] representing motion stages, but none of them as having happened before.[31] But if the past phases of a motion can be represented by φαντάσματα that are not perceived as before, then perceiving a number of motion stages is not sufficient for perceiving time. According to *Physics* 4.11, in order to perceive time, past phases of a motion must be perceived *as* past. How could past phases of a motion not be perceived as past? Perhaps if they fell within a specious present (though there is little evidence for this concept in Aristotle).[32] Still, it seems plausible that past motion stages could be so recent that they *seem* to be present.

4. The effect of intellect on the perception of time

So according to Aristotle, perceiving time does not presuppose grasping it intellectually, but grasping time intellectually, I will now argue, has an effect on how one perceives time for those beings who have intellect. This idea, I think, is behind the following passage from Pseudo-Philoponus:

> By "time" Aristotle means determinate (ὡρισμένον) time, not indeterminate (ἀόριστον). In this way, at least, he says in the *de Interpretatione* "some simply, some in time",[33] meaning by "simply" indeterminate time, and by "in time" determinate time. Non-rational beings, then, even if they have conscious perception (συναίσθησις) of time, do not have conscious perception of determinate time, but only of winter, say, or summer. Human beings have conscious perception of determinate time because they count (ἀριθμεῖν) days and hours. Counting is proper only to the rational soul (ἡ λογικὴ ψυχή). On this account, then, he says that only man has conscious perception of determinate time, for non-rational beings too have conscious perception of the indeterminate.[34]

The distinction, here, is different from the one Aristotle makes at *Mem.*2.452b8–9 and 452b30–453a4 because it is a distinction between types of perception (αἴσθησις), not apprehension in general (γνῶσις). If we take a "determinate time" to mean, as in *Physics* 4.14, a time used as a measure because it is marked out by a regular motion, Pseudo-Philoponus is saying that only humans perceive, for example, days *as* measures of time. Only humans can do this because only humans can treat days as measures by using them to count. Animals may still perceive a day, but not *as* a day if by "day" we mean a unit of measurement.

Pseudo-Philoponus, like Themistius in the passage quoted earlier, is commenting on *De Anima* 3.10, 433b5–11, where Aristotle claims that perception (αἴσθησις) of time is necessary in beings where reason (ὁ λόγος) and desires (αἱ ἐπιθυμίαι) conflict because "νοῦς bids us hold back because of what is future". Now the perception of time, here, is obviously not of the sort we encountered in *Physics* 4.10–14 or in the *De Memoria*. Perceiving time in those texts amounts to perceiving an ordered series of past or present events. Here, perceiving time is perceiving the future. Strictly speaking, though, one does not perceive the future, as Aristotle points out in *De Memoria* 1, 449b27.[35] But we can perceive φαντάσματα (*Mem.*1.450b17–18), and in *De Anima* 3.7, he says this is very much *like* perceiving the future: "Sometimes by means of the φαντάσματα or thoughts which are within the soul, just as if it were seeing, [the faculty of thinking] calculates and deliberates what is to come (τὰ μέλλοντα) by reference to what is present" (*DA*.3.7.431b6–8). The justification for calling this perceiving, perhaps, is that if contemplating φαντάσματα of past events can be called perceiving time, contemplating φαντάσματα of future events can as well, even if the events may never happen.

The involvement of deliberation, here, is important. The νοῦς that holds us back because of what is future is calculative or deliberative reason (i.e., διάνοια, cf. *DA*.3.10.433a14). And the φαντασία involved in perceiving the future, I suggest, is deliberative φαντασία, which is contrasted with perceptual φαντασία in the following passage:

> Perceptual φαντασία, as we have said, is found in the other animals also, but deliberative [φαντασία] in those which are capable of calculating [ἐν τοῖς λογιστικοῖς] (for the decision whether to do this or that is already a task for calculating [λογισμοῦ ἔργον]; and one must measure (μετρεῖν) by a single standard; for one pursues what is greater (τὸ μεῖζον); hence one has the ability to make (ποιεῖν) one image out of many (φαντασμάτων).
> (*DA*.3.11.434a6–15)[36]

When Aristotle says, "one must measure (μετρεῖν) by a single standard; for one pursues what is greater (τὸ μεῖζον)", what springs to mind is something like Socrates' ἡ μετρητικὴ τέχνη at Plato's *Protagoras* 356d–e, that is, a measure of value. We reckon by some measure of value which of two contemplated actions will result in more, for example, pleasure, wealth, or happiness. But the text is more general than this. It says only that deliberation or calculation about a choice of actions requires a measure with which to calculate what is greater (τὸ μεῖζον); a single unified measure that is synthesized out of many φαντάσματα. I do not think this generality is accidental, because, while deliberation may often culminate in calculations of value, it also typically requires calculating other sorts of quantities as well. In order to maximize the value of a crop, for instance, one must first deliberate about how much seed to plant, how often to water, how long to wait before planting, and how long to wait before harvesting. According to Aristotle, in this case we start our deliberation with the objective of maximizing crop value, and work backward from that in a chain of reasoning that ends in determining the first action towards achieving this goal, for example, buying a certain quantity of a certain type of seed at a certain time. If, indeed, Aristotle is expressing himself with an eye towards this more general idea of measurement and calculation, then one of the many functions of deliberative φαντασία should be to effect a synthesis of φαντάσματα into a unified φάντασμα that we use to reckon time: days, months, and years. If this is accepted, it can support Pseudo-Philoponus' distinction between the perception of determinate and indeterminate time because the former will be a function of deliberative φαντασία while the latter will be a function of perceptual φαντασία.

As we have already noted, Aristotle talks of inner "movements" by which we discriminate greater and smaller times in *De Memoria* 2. Though called "movements", these are also φαντάσματα, as *De Memoria* 1, 451a3 makes clear, and so the representation of time periods is a function of φαντασία. And as already noted, these "movements" are of two kinds. When the "movement" represents a determinate time (cf. *Phys.* 4.14.223b15), for example, a day, we apprehend time and the amount of time determinately. Otherwise, we apprehend time and the amount of time indeterminately. So the suggestion, here, is that "movements" representing determinate time are a product of a synthesis of φαντάσματα undertaken by deliberative φαντασία.

If this is accepted, then Pseudo-Philoponus' distinction will be one between real differences in phenomenal content, not just differences in the way we regard or use phenomenal content.[37] This is because deliberative φαντασία is a sort of φαντασία that is modified by the active involvement of intellect. When Aristotle says that the measure consists in a φάντασμα that is a unity made out of many φαντάσματα, it sounds very similar to what he says about the genesis of experience from memory. In *Posterior Analytics* 2.19.100a3–9, Aristotle says, "From perception there comes memory, as we call it, and from memory (when it occurs often in connection with the same thing), experience; for memories that are many in number form a single experience", and at *Metaphysics* A.1.980b26–981a12, "many memories of the same thing produce finally the capacity for a single experience". A memory, we know, is a special sort of φάντασμα; one in which the φάντασμα is taken to represent an experience of the subject at a prior time. So the relationship between experience and deliberative φαντασία is very close. One difference, I think, is that one who deliberates is said to *make* (ποιεῖν) a unity out of several φαντάσματα, which suggests that deliberative φαντασία is an exercise of active φαντασία as described at *De Anima* 3.3.427b18–20: "[φαντασία] is up to us when we wish (for it is possible to produce something before our eyes, as those do who set things out in mnemonic systems[38] and form images of them)". There is no suggestion in *Metaphysics* A 1 and in *Posterior Analytics* 2.19 that experience requires the active manipulation of images. Another difference is that the synthesis of images involved in deliberative φαντασία is found only "in those which are capable of calculating", while experience is also found in at least some irrational animals (*Meta.*A.1.980b25–7). Deliberative φαντασία, then, would seem to be a sort of experience, but one that occurs only in beings who can calculate, and that characteristically requires the active manipulation of images. Perceptual φαντασία presumably is what is involved in animal perception of time. All animals have perceptual φαντασία (*DA.*3.11.433b31–434a10, 2.2.413b21–3, 3.10.433a9 ff., *Metaph.* A 1, 980b25 ff.), except, perhaps, grubs (*DA.*2.3.415a6–11 and 3.3.428a10 ff.). And humans with no deliberative faculty (e.g., slaves allegedly) or an underdeveloped deliberative faculty (e.g., children) will have only perceptual φαντασία (*Politics* 1.13.1260a12–14).

The suggestion, then, is that the "movements" representing determinate time are a product of the active manipulation of images by deliberative φαντασία in beings who can deliberate. A worry, here, might be that this active manipulation of images is a matter of conception rather than perception, and that Pseudo-Philoponus' distinction is misguided after all. Rather than distinguishing different types of perception, we would have distinguished cognition from perception. But I think it is reasonable to take the view that while intellect has a role in determining the content of the images produced by deliberative φαντασία, the content itself remains non-conceptual. I suggest that while perceiving a day as a day for the purpose of measuring time might employ a sortal concept, the perceptually disambiguated image of a day in one's mind – the normalized image of a day shorn of the rough edges of its particularity such as seasonal variations in length of daylight – may nonetheless be non-conceptual.[39]

While not requiring it, this interpretation would be strengthened if we could establish that Aristotle envisages non-conceptual ἐμπειρία, that is, that many memories may form a single experience in beings not possessed of reason. This is a controversial subject, and one of the key texts on the issue is ambiguous. *Posterior Analytics* 2.19, which describes the genesis of principles of art and science from more primitive mental states, is ambiguous in its description of the transition to these states from a state of experience. In the critical sentence describing this transition, Aristotle says that principles of art and science arise "from experience, or from the whole universal that has come to rest in the soul" (100a6–7). Depending on whether we read the "or" epexegetically or as a corrective meaning "or rather", the sentence will say either that experience involves universals or that it does not.[40]

Still, there are other texts that would seem to favor the existence of non-conceptual ἐμπειρία. Aristotle claims at *Nicomachean Ethics* 7.3.1147b5, that animals "have no universal beliefs (καθόλου ὑπόληψιν) but only imagination (φαντασία) and memory (μνήμη) of particulars". And then in *Metaphysics* A 1, he credits all animals with sensation and only some with memory and ἐμπειρία (980b25–7). So the animals that have experience must have non-universal, which I take to be non-conceptual, ἐμπειρία. And Aristotle seems to say that experience, which some animals possess, does not involve universal concepts when he claims that a single universal is present in the man with art but not in the man with experience (cf. *EN*.6.7.1141b14–21). Humans also possess art and reason, which he contrasts with experience in the respect that art apprehends universals while experience apprehends particulars. Nonetheless, the examples that Aristotle provides are unhelpful in deciding this issue because they represent human cases of experience which clearly presuppose the possession of concepts. Perhaps what Aristotle means is not that the man possessing experience but not art lacks universal concepts altogether, but just that he lacks the universal concept of a particular art, for example, medicine. This does not bar him from having universal concepts altogether.

5. *Physics* 4.14: if there were no νοῦς would there be time?

In the following passage from *Physics* 4.14 Aristotle argues that time would not exist in the absence of beings who can count:

> One might find it a difficult question, whether if there were no soul there would be time or not. For if it is impossible that there should be

something to do the counting, it is also impossible that anything should be countable, so that it is clear that there would be no number either, for number is either that which has been counted or that which can be. But if there is nothing that has it in its nature to count except soul, and of soul [the part which is] intellect, then it is impossible that there should be time if there is no soul, except that there could be what underlies time; as for example if it is possible for there to be motion without soul. The before and after are in motion, and time is these *qua* countable.

(*Phys*. 4.14.223a21–29)

As I said at the outset, this passage might tempt one to think that the perception of time depends on counting since the existence of time depends on the existence of beings who can count.[41] Since perceiving something presupposes its existence, if nows were brought into existence by the act of counting,[42] this would seem to have some plausibility, since acts of perception would depend on acts of counting. And since it also seems plausible to assume that these acts must take place in the same mind, it would have the consequence that no being could perceive time that could not count. But Aristotle is very clear in the *De Memoria* that animals that are unable to count can perceive time.

If, however, nows are already there for us to perceive as suggested by *Physics* 263a27–8, 263b3–6, or it is only necessary to mark nows off perceptually for them to exist, then no such problem arises. Then, if we assume that perceiving something presupposes its existence, the perception of time would depend counterfactually only on the existence of beings who can count, which does not require beings who perceive time to be able to count. In fact, it does not require beings who perceive time, or the before and after in motion *qua* countable, to perceive time *as* countable.

Still, the mind dependence of time implied by this passage has seemed to many a philosophical mistake, either due to a straightforward logical error[43] or a confusion about modality.[44] But, assuming that deliberative φαντασία produces a perceptually normalized image of a day in the perceiver, and only beings with νοῦς have deliberative φαντασία, we can infer a similar conclusion about the measurability of time, that is, that in the absence of beings with νοῦς, time would not be measurable (or countable in the extended sense of time being countable by means of some determinate time discussed at *Physics* 4.14.223b13).

In *Metaphysics* Δ 15, Aristotle says that what are measurable, or knowable, or thinkable, or visible are called relatives, not because they are called just what they are of something else but because something else, that is, a measure or knowledge or thought or sight, is called just what it is of them. I take it that the difference is that a measure is definitionally and intrinsically related to the measurable, while the measurable is not similarly related to the measure, and as a consequence, while the measure cannot be but described as a measure, the measurable admits of other descriptions. *Categories* 7 tells us that the correct way of talking about the measurable in relation to the measure is not to say that the measurable is measurable of the measure, but that the measurable is measurable *by* the measure (6b28–6b36). This use of the instrumental dative is familiar from *Physics* 4: "each thing is counted by some one thing of the same kind (units by a unit, horses by a horse), and therefore time too by some determinate time" (*Physics* 4.14.223b13–15). The measure, then, by being only an instrument of the measurable's measurability, is only incidentally related to the measurable.

Since the measure is only incidentally related to the measurable, this shows that there is another contingency we might consider in connection with the counterfactual in *Physics* 4.14.223a21–29, viz., the absence of the measure by which the measurable is measured. Now clearly, there are some cases where the measure will never be absent. For example, pluralities of horses will always have a measure available to count them because every horse in the plurality will stand in the required relation to the plurality. In general, discrete pluralities of substances are always measurable because their mere existence entails the existence of an intrinsically indivisible measure that they stand in the required relation to.

But continuous magnitudes, however, will not always be measurable in this sense. This is because no part of a continuous magnitude, such as time and motion, is intrinsically indivisible. Continuous magnitudes are only indivisible in relation to perception (*MetA*.I.1.1053a1, 23), which means that they can only be measured by a measure that *appears* indivisible to a being capable of perceiving it. Or perhaps I should say "imagining" since we know from *De Memoria* 2 that the measure by which we have a determinate cognition of the time as being, for example, this or that many days, is an "inner movement" or a φάντασμα; a normalized φάντασμα of a day synthesized from multiple φαντάσματα by deliberative φαντασία. So then, in a world without beings possessing νοῦς, and, therefore, deliberative φαντασία, time would not be measurable because no measure would stand in a measuring relation to it, nor would it be countable in the extended sense of time being countable by means of some determinate time.

Notes

1 *DA* 3.4, 429b18 ff.; *Mem.* 1, 449b31–450a7; *Post. An.* 1.5, 74a32–74b4; *Metaph.* M 3, 1077b17 ff.; *Phys.* 2.2, 193b24–194a7.
2 This translation, with minor modifications, is from Ziolkowski (2002).
3 This translation, with minor modifications, is from Todd (1996). "At once turned front and back" is from Homer, Il. 1.343, 3.109.
4 As Sorabji (2004, pp. XXII–XXIII) points out in the case of Themistius.
5 Here the word νοῦς is being used in Aristotle's broad sense of "that whereby the soul thinks (διανοεῖται) and judges (ὑπολαμβάνει)" (*DA* 3.4, 429a23) rather than in the narrow sense of that whereby the soul grasps the principles of a demonstration (*Post. An.* 2.19, 100b15).
6 For a modern example of this sort of interpretation, see Gregoric (2007, p. 104–5), who seeks to block the inference that the common sense perceives time by claiming that perceiving number and motion is not sufficient for perceiving time. According to Gregoric, one also must be able to count nows in order to perceive time.
7 For a survey of the controversy, see White (1993, pp. 174–182). On Aristotelian arithmetic, see also Mignucci (1987).

8 On number as countable see *Phys.* 4.11, 219b6–7; 4.14, 223a24–25, 223b13–16; *Metaph.* Δ 6, 1016b9–11; K 10, 1066b25–26). On number as a plurality of objects studied *qua* indivisible see *Metaph.* M 3.
9 Translations of Aristotle's *Physics*, in this chapter are, with minor modifications, from Hussey (1983).
10 See Sorabji (2004, p. XXII) and Kahn (1966, p. 53, n. 23).
11 This is Sorabji's interpretation. See Sorabji (2004, p. XXIII).
12 See Coope (2005, pp. 9–13; ch. 5, esp. pp. 89–92).
13 At *Physics* 8.8, 263a27–8, and 263b3–6, Aristotle clearly envisages the traversal of an infinite number of things that exist potentially rather than a potentially infinite number of things. Otherwise, he would not be showing, as he says he is, how in a way it is possible and in a way it is impossible to get entirely through an infinite number of things.
14 Beare (1906, p. 286 ff.), Kahn (1966, p. 46), and Block (1960, p. 94) take this to imply that incidental perception is a performance of intellect.
15 Cashdollar (1973, p. 163).
16 Thus, Caston (1996, p. 42) is right to claim that incidental sensibles may involve the cooperation of intellect in humans, but it is not an essential feature of incidental perception.
17 On perceiving φαντάσματα, see *Mem.*1.450b17–18.
18 For example, by Coope (2005) and by Sorabji (1983, p. 84 ff.).
19 Of the remaining two, one expresses the odd idea that insofar as the now counts, it is a number (4.11, 220a22) and another extends the sense of ἀριθμεῖν to mean time measurement (4.14, 223b13. More on this later).
20 In this, Aristotle recognizes what has been rigorously demonstrated only in the 20th century, that is, that humans and many other animals have a modicum of perceptual numerical competence. In particular, it has been shown by cognitive scientists that both infant and adult humans, as well as many other animals, including birds, fish, and various other mammals, have the ability to accurately and non-verbally assess the cardinality of sets of objects or events of up to about three or four members. This, called "subitizing", is done by keeping track of individual elements in the sets, probably by using discrete perceptual representations. It has also been shown that many animals also have a non-verbal ability to roughly discriminate the relative size of larger cardinalities, and that a few have the ability to grasp ordinal relations within ordered sets of up to about seven items. See Nieder (2005).
21 *Top.* 6.5.142b26 says that only humans are able to count.
22 There are 22 occurrences of the verb μετρεῖν in chapters 12–14, nearly twice as many occurrences as ἀριθμεῖν in the whole of Aristotle's discussion of time.
23 This translation, with minor modifications, is from Sorabji (2004, pp. 57–58).
24 *EN*.7.3.1147b5.
25 Sorabji (2004, p. 70).
26 cf. Irwin (1988, p. 316).
27 cf. Taormina (2002, p. 38); King (2009, p. 65).
28 I assume that, as at *Mem.*1.451a3, the κινήσεις in *Mem.*2.452b8–453a4 are φαντάσματα.
29 *Mem.*1.450a9–11 seems also to point to this conclusion, but the text less clear. Here, the received text says, "Now, one must apprehend magnitude and motion by means of the same thing by which one apprehends time; and τὸ φάντασμα is an affection of the common sense" (*Mem.*1.450a9–11). In the preceding lines Aristotle has implied that magnitudes are apprehended by means of φαντάσματα, so the thought here seems to be that time is apprehended by means of φαντάσματα too. It can also, perhaps, be inferred from Aristotle's remark that we cannot think of anything without a continuum or think of non-temporal things without time that the reason for these two claims is the same, that is, that φαντάσματα must be involved.

30 The following passages characterize φαντασία as a faculty for the retention of perceptual representations: *DA*.3.3.429a1–2; *Insomn*.1.459–a17–18); *Rhet*.1.11.1370a27.
31 Cf. Caston (1996, p. 42), who takes *Mem*. 1, 450a9–11, which implies that magnitudes are apprehended by means of φαντάσματα, to suggest that φαντασία is involved in the perception of common sensibles. Caston also thinks that *De Anima* 3.3.428b18–25 implicates φαντασία in special, common, and incidental perception.
32 The specious present is "the short duration of which we are immediately and incessantly sensible" (James 1905, p. 631). Sorabji (2004, p. 91) tentatively detects the concept of a specious present in Aristotle's use of the aorist ἔπαθε at *Mem*.2.451a31, but this, as Sorabji recognizes, is uncorroborated in any of Aristotle's other discussions of time.
33 The phrase is at *De Int*. 1, 16a18 and is difficult to interpret. Charlton suggests that it distinguishes between untensed and tensed uses of verbs (Charlton 2000, p. 64, n. 30). Ackrill dismisses this as an unsupported conjecture, but offers the even more difficult reading of a distinction between present uses of verbs on the one hand, and past and future uses of verbs on the other (Ackrill 1963, p. 115). Pseudo-Philoponus' reading seems even more improbable.
34 Philoponus, J. 1897, 580,27–37. This translation, with minor modifications, is from (Charlton 2000, p. 31).
35 Aristotle also seems to say that we do not perceive the past either at *Mem*.1.449b27. Taormina makes much of this (Taormina 2002, pp. 46–49), but if this claim is strictly maintained, it will make nonsense of the account of perceiving time in *Physics* 4.11, which requires perceiving at least some motion phases (or *qua* countable, nows) as past.
36 This translation, with minor modifications, is from Hamlyn (1993, pp. 71–72).
37 *Pace* for example, Polansky (2007, p. 530) and Moss (2012, p. 146), who insist that deliberative φαντασία is distinguished from perceptual φαντασία only by the use to which it is put. But I maintain, as I shall explain later, that there is a difference in phenomenal content, though not one that requires deliberative φαντασία to be conceptual.
38 Although these people are called μνημονικοὶ instead ἀναμνηστικοί, the reference is clearly to mnemonic systems used by ἀναμνηστικοί (cf. *Top*. 8.14.163b28; *Mem*.2.452a12; *Insomn*.1.458b20). Recollecting is described in *De Memoria* as a συλλογισμός τίς along with deliberation and is said to belong only to those animals (i.e., humans) possessing a deliberative faculty (βουλευτικὸν) (*Mem*.2.453a5–13).
39 Similarly, Michael Tye argues that while concepts might be involved in perceptually disambiguating a figure with an ambiguous decomposition into spatial parts, such as the two faces-vase figure, the resulting phenomenal content may remain, nonetheless, non-conceptual (Tye 1995, pp. 140–141).
40 For the epexegetical reading, see Sorabji (1993, p. 34). For the corrective reading, and a survey of the interpretative possibilities, see McKirihan (1992, p. 243).
41 Even though the counterfactual contemplated is one where there is no soul *simpliciter*, the argument that there would be no time in this case relies on only the assumption that there is no νοῦς or intellect.
42 As suggested by Coope (2005). See endnote 12.
43 Mignucci (1987, pp. 184–186).
44 Sorabji (1983, p. 89 ff.)

Bibliography

Ackrill, J. L. (1963) *Aristotle: Categories and De Interpretatione*. Oxford: Clarendon Press.
Beare, J. I. (1906) *Greek Theories of Elementary Cognition*. Oxford: Clarendon Press.
Block, I. (1960) Aristotle and the physical object. *Philosophy and Phenomenological Research* 21: 93–101.

Cashdollar, S. (1973) Aristotle's account of incidental perception. *Phronesis* 18: 156–175.
Caston, V. (1996) Why Aristotle needs imagination. *Phronesis* 41: 20–55.
Charlton, W. (2000) *'Philoponus', on Aristotle on the Soul 3.9–13 with Stephanus on Aristotle on Interpretation*. London: Duckworth.
Coope, U. (2005) *Time for Aristotle: Physics IV.11–14*. Oxford: Oxford University Press.
Gregoric, P. (2007) *Aristotle on the Common Sense*. Oxford: Oxford University Press.
Hamlyn, D. W. (1993) *Aristotle De Anima, Books II and III (with Passages from Book I), translated with Introduction and Notes by D.W. Hamlyn, with a Report on Recent Work and a Revised Bibliography by Christopher Shields*. Oxford: Clarendon Press.
Hussey, E. (1983) *Aristotle's Physics III & IV*. Oxford: Clarendon Press.
Irwin, T. (1988) *Aristotle's First Principles*. Oxford: Clarendon Press.
James, W. (1905) *The Principles of Psychology*. Vol. 1. New York: Henry Holt and Company.
Kahn, C. H. (1966) Sensation and consciousness in Aristotle's psychology. *Archiv für Geschichte der Philosophie* 48: 43–81.
King, R. A. H. (2009) *Aristotle and Plotinus on Memory (Quellen und Studien zur Philosophie 94)*. Berlin and New York: Walter de Gruyter.
Magnus, A. (1890) Liber de memoria et reminiscentia. In Borgnet, A. (ed.) *Opera Omnia*, t. IX. Paris: Vives, pp. 97–118.
Mckirihan, R. (1992) *Principles and Proofs: Aristotle's Theory of Demonstrative Science*. Princeton: Princeton University Press.
Mignucci, M. (1987) Aristotle's arithmetic. In Graese, A. (ed.) *Mathematics and Metaphysics in Aristotle: Akten des X. Symposium Aristotelicum*. Bern: Haupt, pp. 175–211.
Moss, J. (2012) *Aristotle on the Apparent Good: Perception, Phantasia, Thought, and Desire*. Oxford: Oxford University Press.
Nieder, A. (2005) Counting on neurons: The neurobiology of numerical competence. *Nature Reviews Neuroscience* 6: 177–190.
Philoponus, J. (1897) In Aristotelis de anima libros commentaria. In Hayduck, M. (ed.) *Commentaria in Aristotelem Graeca*. Berlin: Reimer, p. 15.
Polansky, R. (2007) *Aristotle's De Anima*. Cambridge, MA: Cambridge University Press.
Quine, W. V. O. (1960) *Word and Object*. Cambridge, MA: MIT Press.
Sorabji, R. (1983) *Time, Creation and the Continuum: Theories in Antiquity and the Early Middle Ages*. London: Duckworth.
———. (1993) *Animal Minds and Human Morals: The Origins of the Western Debate*. London: Duckworth.
———. (2004) *Aristotle on Memory*. 2nd edn. London: Duckworth.
Taormina, D. (2002) Perception du temps et mémoire chez Aristote: De memoria et reminiscentia 1. *Philosophie Antique* 2: 34–61.
Themistius (1899) In libros Aristotelis de anima paraphrasis. In Heinze, R. (ed.) *Commentaria in Aristotelem Graeca*. Berlin: Reimer, p. 5.3.
Todd, R. (1996) *Themistius: On Aristotle's on the Soul*. London: Duckworth.
Tye, M. (1995) *Ten Problems of Consciousness*. Cambridge, MA: MIT Press.
White, M. J. (1993) The metaphysical location of Aristotle's Μαθηματικά. *Phronesis* 38 (2): 166–182.
Ziolkowski, J. M. (2002) Albertus Magnus, commentary on Aristotle, on memory and recollection. In Carruthers, M., and Ziolkowski, J. M. (eds.) *The Medieval Craft of Memory: An Anthology of Text and Pictures*. Philadelphia: University of Pennsylvania Press, pp. 118–152.

10

ARISTOTLE ON MIND, PERCEPTION, AND BODY

John E. Sisko

There is significant debate over Aristotle's understanding of the relation between mind and body. Debate centers on interrelated questions concerning Aristotle's views on the mind's distance from the body and its dependence on the body.[1] Scholars ask whether, or to what extent, the mind is, for Aristotle, an immaterial faculty. In addition, scholars ask whether, or to what extent, thought, for Aristotle, relies on material states and changes within the body. We are compelled to ask these questions for two reasons: first, Aristotle seems to mark out mind as being metaphysically disparate from other psychological faculties, like perception, and his treatment of thought does not appear to cohere with his perspective on other psychological states, such as emotion and desire. Nevertheless, Aristotle's overarching approach to explaining the relation of soul to body – hylomorphism – strongly suggests that thought should not differ radically from perception or emotion. So, we are faced with the puzzle of whether Aristotle's theory of mind coheres with the rest of his psychology. Second, while Aristotle's assertions concerning mind and its operations are provocative, these pronouncements are not fully perspicuous and it is not immediately evident that Aristotle's claims on the topic of mind constitute a considered and reasoned account. In key passages, Aristotle's statements seem rather obscure. Yet, even when we are able to gauge the meaning of his claims, it can remain unclear whether Aristotle justifies his assertions. It is possible that Aristotle's declarations on intellect and its operations are expressions of an unsupported prejudice. So, we are faced with a second puzzle: that of whether Aristotle even has a theory of mind.

The project of interpreting Aristotle's views on mind presents numerous challenges. But, progress can be made. In this chapter, I assess Aristotle's claims and arguments, and I offer what I think is the most plausible interpretation of his views on the mind's distance from the body and its dependence on the body. I contend that, for Aristotle, mind is an immaterial faculty: Aristotle holds that thought is neither realized in a dedicated bodily organ nor in any collection of bodily structures. I also show that, for Aristotle, bodily states and changes serve as necessary conditions for mental states, but mental content neither covaries with nor supervenes upon bodily states.

1. Problematizing distance and dependence

Aristotle takes psychology to be a branch of natural science (see *De Anima* (DA) I.1.402a1–10). Accordingly, he brings the conceptual framework of hylomorphism and the theory of the four causes to bear within his analyses of psychological capacities and states. Aristotle claims, "soul is substance as form of a natural body which has life potentially" and "soul is the first actuality of a natural body furnished with organs" (DA.II.1.412a19–20 and 412b4). So, he contends that soul is the form of the organic body and living beings are 'forms in matter': they are hylomorphic compounds. On Aristotle's account, the soul is a set of capacities: capacities that are supported by organic structures.

Since Aristotle holds that psychological capacities are supported by organic structures, it would seem natural for him to suppose both that psychological states have bodily components and that any change in psychological state requires a change in bodily state. Aristotle accepts these conditions for those states or affections that he identifies as being *with the body*. Emotions and desires fall within this category. Aristotle claims, "It seems that all the affections of soul are with the body (μετὰ σώματός), i.e., passion, gentleness, fear, pity, confidence, and joy, as well as loving and hating: for the body undergoes some affection at the same time as these" (DA.I.1.403a16–19). Aristotle posits that psychological states, in the realm of emotion and desire, have bodily components. His account of anger provides a clear illustration of his views on the role of bodily states and changes vis-à-vis the psychological activities that are *with the body*. Aristotle sets out, first, a schematic description of anger and, second, a concrete description. He claims, "anger is a certain sort of change, belonging to this sort of body . . . due to this [cause], for the sake of that [end]" (DA.I.1.403a25–27). Aristotle goes on to state, "anger is desire for retaliation . . . [and] a ferment of the blood or heat which is about the heart" (DA.I.1.403a30–403b1). From the schematic description, we learn that anger has four causes: a formal cause (*a certain sort of change*), a material cause (*belonging to this sort of body*), an efficient cause (*due to this*), and a final cause (*for the sake of that*). From the concrete description, we learn that the material cause of anger is a ferment of blood and its formal cause is a desire for retaliation. In other texts, Aristotle claims that the efficient cause of anger is awareness of insult and its final cause is revenge (see *Nichomachean Ethics* VII.6.1149a29–34 and *Rhetoric* II.2.1378a31–1378b1). Aristotle holds that the four causes of anger are jointly necessary and sufficient for its presence.[2] Aristotle, emphasizing this point, claims,

> at times when there are violent and striking occurrences, no excitement or fear is felt, while at other times we are moved by slight and scarcely noticeable stimulations, when the body is aroused and [already] in a state just as when one is angry.
>
> (DA.I.1.403a19–21)

Here he posits that, when an insult is perceived, but desire for retaliation is not present, the psychological state of anger does not obtain. In such cases desire is impeded or hindered owing to disease, fatigue, or distraction (see DA.III.3.429a5–9 and *De Sensu et Sensibilibus (Sens.)* 7.447a14–17). Aristotle also posits that the state of anger does not obtain, when the blood is boiling, but there is no awareness of insult. This suggests that, under normal conditions (when not diseased, fatigued, or distracted), if an insult is perceived and the blood boils, the psychological state of anger obtains. Generalizing from his account of anger, we see that, for Aristotle, any psychological state that is *with the body* has a concurrent material cause. Further, the transition to the specific bodily state, which serves as the material cause of a given psychological state, is a partial trigger for that psychological state. In order to move from joy to fear, from fear to pity, or from pity to confidence a person must suffer a bodily change: when it comes to affections that are *with the body*, Aristotle holds that changes among positive psychological states require accompanying changes among bodily states.

In the same chapter in which he discusses anger, Aristotle claims, "it seems that mind is peculiar to soul" (DA.I.1.403a8). With this pronouncement, Aristotle suggests that mind is *not with the body*. The claim is offered as an aside, but it is not an isolated declaration. The idea that intellect might be metaphysically disparate from other psychological capacities reappears in a number of asides or caveats peppered throughout early parts of DA. For example, Aristotle states, "as regards intellect ... it would seem to be a distinct type of soul, it alone being separate from the body, just as the eternal is separate from the perishable" (DA.II.2.413b24–27). Further, he states, "it is difficult to conjecture what part [of the body] mind could hold together or how it could hold any part together" (DA.I.5.411b17–19). The later claim suggests that mind lacks its own dedicated organ (i.e., an organ localized in a distinct part of the body), while the former claim suggests that mind is wholly non-bodily. So, Aristotle is willing to consider the thesis that mind is *not with the body*. Nevertheless, the passages (thus far discussed) are located in hypothetical contexts and embedded either in aporetic sections of DA.I or in specialized discussions within which Aristotle is not primarily concerned with the topic of mind. So, alone they do not show that Aristotle is committed to the view that mind is a non-bodily faculty. Plus, insofar as these claims are not supported by argument, they do not signal that Aristotle has theory of mind. The claims could be manifestations of an unsupported prejudice.

By all appearances, Aristotle advances his theory of mind in DA.III.4.[3] In the chapter, he avers both that mind is not mixed with the body and it is separate from the body. Aristotle states, (CLAIM 1) "[mind] must be unmixed (ἀνάγκη ... ἀμιγῆ εἶναι)" (DA.III.4.429a18). He adds, (CLAIM 2) "it is reasonable to consider [mind] not to be mixed with the body (διὸ οὐδὲ μεμῖχθαι εὔλογον αὐτὸν τῷ σώματι)" (*ibid.* 429a24–25). Finally, he states, (CLAIM 3) "for perception is not without the body, while mind is separate [from the body] (τὸ μὲν γὰρ αἰσθητικὸν οὐκ ἄνευ σώματος, ὁ δὲ χωριστός)" (*ibid.* 429b4–5). These statements appear to be linked with supporting claims. So, it seems that, in DA.III.4, Aristotle argues that mind is metaphysically disparate from other psychological abilities and capacities.[4] Yet, according to some scholars, all is not as it might seem: interpreters are at odds when it comes to the import and meaning of Aristotle's claims.

On one prominent view (A), Aristotle argues that intellect lacks its own dedicated organ, while he also infers that intellect is a non-localized bodily capacity: a capacity of the entire human body (see Caston 2001). On this first approach, intellect is *with the body* and Aristotle supposes that changes between positive mental states are accompanied by bodily changes.[5] On a second approach (B), Aristotle's key claims concerning mind being 'unmixed' (ἀμιγῆ) and 'separate' (χωριστός) are taken, either individually or jointly, not to be part of a reasoned thesis concerning the nature of mind. On one variation of this second approach (Bi), Aristotle is said not to argue for any thesis whatsoever concerning the metaphysical status of mind.[6] An offshoot of this variation brings us back to the puzzle of whether Aristotle even has a theory of mind. A second variation of the second approach (Bii) begins with the observation that CLAIM 3 is a premise in an argument and not a conclusion.[7] This is taken to suggest that, in DA.III.4, Aristotle advances just one extended argument concerning the metaphysical status of mind (i.e., the argument for CLAIM 1 and CLAIM 2). So, on this variation, Aristotle does not argue that the mind is separate from the body. Instead, he argues only for the thesis mind is unmixed. Further, it is suggested that this thesis (in context) requires that, while mind lack a dedicated organ, it, nevertheless, stands as a capacity of the entire body. So, this second variation (Bii) coheres with the first approach (A).

In light of scholarly opposition to the view that Aristotle argues for the thesis that mind is *separate from the body*, we must give close consideration to the details of the discussion in DA.III.4. Yet, Aristotle's progress in the chapter is fueled by a series of comparisons that he draws between perception and thought. So, before we turn to DA.III.4, we need to consider Aristotle's theory of perception. As it happens, a study of Aristotle's theory of perception will prepare us to assess, not only Aristotle's views on mind's distance from the body, but also his views on mind's dependence on the body; for, Aristotle cashes out this dependence in terms of mind's reliance on certain states and changes within the body's perceptual system.

2. Perception and the body

2.1 The causal story

For Aristotle, perception has four causes. Its final cause is self-preservation: equipped with an ability to discern food and predators or other dangers, animals are geared for survival (see *Sens*.1.236b20–437a1). The formal cause of perception is a state of awareness. Aristotle claims, "it is not possible to perceive and see without being aware of it" (*Sens*.2.437a27–28). According to Aristotle, when we become aware of an object, we are assimilated to the object: we become like the object (see DA.II.5.415a22–417b28). This assimilation to the object is a non-destructive alteration of our sensory power. The alteration is non-destructive (except in certain non-standard cases) because the subject, in perceiving, does not suffer a loss of what is essential to having the ability to perceive (see Lorenz 2007 and Sisko 1996, pp. 141–143).

Special sensibles and common sensibles are the efficient causes of perception. A special sensible is one that is accessible through just one sense modality. The color red, for example, is a special sensible. A common sensible is one that is directly accessible through more than one sense modality. Movement and shape are among the common sensibles. When acted upon by the special and common sensibles, a subject can also become aware of incidental sensibles. These sensibles, like 'an apple' or 'that man there' are objects in which special and common sensibles inhere. Incidental sensibles are not efficient causes of perception: they do not act on us directly as such (see DA.II.6.418a20–24). Finally, for Aristotle, perception is always of particulars (again, 'that man there'): he affirms that universals (i.e., 'humanity') cannot be perceived (see Posterior Analytics (APo) 1.31.87b29–33).

When accounting for the various sense modalities, Aristotle focuses on the causal impact of the special sensibles. He defines each special sensible by a ratio of fundamental qualities within a specific range (see Caston 2005, pp. 312–314). As examples, each color is defined as a ratio of light/dark and each flavor is defined as a ratio of sweet/bitter (see *Sens*.3.440b18–25). So, the immediate objects of sight are qualities within the light/dark range and the immediate objects of taste are qualities within the sweet/bitter range. Aristotle holds that perceptible qualities within different ranges can be analogues of one another. Analogues are defined by same proportion or ratio of constituent qualities (see *Gen. et Corr.* II.6.333a28–30). As examples, Aristotle posits that the colors red, purple, green, and blue are, respectively, analogues of the flavors harsh, pungent, astringent, and acid (*Sens*.4.442a12–29).

Perceptual assimilation, as Aristotle understands it, requires material conditions of receptivity. These are standing conditions. Color, for example, acts upon the transparent. So, in order for a subject to see a color, there must be a transparent medium (say, air or water) between the object and the subject's eyes and the eyes themselves must be composed of transparent material (see DA.II.7).[8] Loss of transparency within the eyes entails loss of vision. Similarly, if a subject is to hear or smell, its ears must be soundless and its organ of smell must be scentless. (In this context, the organ of touch is an outlier. In virtue of the organ's bodily constitution, characteristic qualities within the ranges of hard/soft, wet/dry, and hot/cold already inhere in the organ.)

On the issue of whether, for Aristotle, bodily processes somehow underwrite perception, there are three prominent interpretations: Spiritualism, Literalism, and Proportionalism.[9] A signal claim, in DA.II.12, serves as a touchstone for delimiting these views: Aristotle states,

> in perceiving we are receptive of the sensible form of the object without the matter, just as the wax receives the impression of the signet-ring

without the iron or gold, and receives the impression of the gold or bronze, but not as gold or bronze.

(424a18–22)

Aristotle claims that perception is a reception of form without matter. The statement has been understood in three ways. Under Literalism, reception of form without matter is a taking on of perceptible qualities without absorbing the matter of the object in which those qualities in here. So, just as the wax takes on and displays the shape of the signet's surface, without taking on its matter (gold or bronze), so too when we see, say, the red of an apple, our eyes take on and display redness, without absorbing any material bits of the apple. If Aristotle embraces Literalism, he thinks that when we see red our eyes go red.

Under Spiritualism, reception of form without matter is a change in awareness that does not involve material change in the organ. It is argued that, just as a wax block 'registers' the circularity of the signet, without the block itself becoming circular, we 'register' – we become aware of – the red of the apple, without suffering a bodily change. On this account, Aristotle thinks that the eyes are "pregnant with consciousness" (Burnyeat 1995, p. 19): when requisite standing conditions are met and we turn to the object, we see the object without suffering any change that serves as the material cause of our newly acquired state of perceptual awareness. If Aristotle is a Spiritualist, he thinks that when we see red there is no change of material state within our eyes.

Under Proportionalism, reception of form without matter is a kind of transduction (see Caston 2005, pp. 302–305). The signet holds information in one form but transmits it in another. The ring is a vehicle through which the prerogatives and obligations of its owner are expressed. But with the act of sealing, the owner's claims and commitments are conveyed in patterned wax, not in a copy of the ring itself. On this view, perception involves bodily change (*contra* Spiritualism), but this change is not that of taking on the perceptible qualities of the object (*contra* Literalism). Under Proportionalism, perceptual information is conveyed when the proportion or ratio that defines a special sensible within one qualitative range comes to be instantiated in the organ within a different qualitative range (see Caston 2005, pp. 305–307 and 310–314). If Aristotle embraces Proportionalism, he thinks that when we see red our eyes suffer a material change to an analogue of red. So, perhaps, in seeing red, the interior of the eye acquires a new state of viscosity, where the ratio of hard/soft that defines the acquired state of viscosity is equal to the ratio of light/dark that defines red.

The textual evidence favors Literalism and Proportionalism over Spiritualism. When Aristotle seeks to account for specific limits and constraints that are evident in our perceptual lives, certain of his claims are amenable to Literalism and Proportionalism, but not to Spiritualism. Consider two examples: blind spots for touch and the causal efficacy of intense sensibles.[10] Regarding blind spots, Aristotle states, "we do not perceive what is just as hot or cold, hard or soft, as we are, but only the excesses of these qualities" (DA.II.11.424a2–4). This claim suggests that we cannot come to be aware of a tactile sensible, when that sensible already inheres in the body. This is easily explained under Literalism: taking temperature as an example, one might say that the organ cannot be altered within the hot/cold range towards the proportion of hot/cold that it already instantiates and, accordingly, we cannot come to be aware of a temperature that we already possess. Tactile blind spots can also be explained under Proportionalism: one might claim that, since a specific temperature already inheres in the body (which is an extension of the medium of perception), the appropriate analogue of this temperature, expressed by a proportion within a range other than hot/cold, must already inhere in the internal organ of touch. Thus, since the body cannot be altered within the hot/cold range towards the proportion that it already instantiates, so too the organ of touch cannot be altered within its native range towards a proportion that it already instantiates and, accordingly, we cannot come to be aware of a temperature that we already possess.

Spiritualism is not equipped to explain tactile blind spots. The best that can be done is to insist that Aristotle's focus, in the passage, is on formal causes and not material ones (see Burnyeat 1995, p. 24). On this approach, Aristotle's claim amounts to no more than the assertion that we cannot *become* aware of that of which we are *already* aware. Problematically, for Spiritualism, however, this is a general truth about states of awareness as such. So, the interpretation advanced under Spiritualism fails to show why, in discussing blind spots, Aristotle's main focus is on the modality of touch and not on perception taken generally.

Regarding the causal efficacy of intense sensibles, Aristotle states, "men become deafened by loud noises and they have their sense of smell damaged by strong odors, and so on [i.e., each sense can be damaged by intense sensibles]" and "excess in any sensible quality destroys the organ" (*De Insomniis (Insomn.)* 2.459b1–23 and DA.III.13.435b15). Aristotle acknowledges that exposure to intense sensibles can damage, or even destroy, the organ of perception. This phenomenon is easily explained under both Literalism and Proportionalism. Reception of an intense sensibles involves intense material change within the organ (either in the range of the sensible object, under Literalism, or in some other range, under Proportionalism) and this intense change robs the organ of the material standing conditions that are required for reception of perceptible form.

Aristotle also holds that the physical constitution of perceptual organs varies (sometimes quite broadly) among species and (less broadly) among individuals within a species. These differences explain why species and individuals vary in respect to the upper and lower limits (intensity and faintness) of the sensibles of which they can become aware (see *Generation of Animals* (GA) V.2.781b2–13). Since upper and lower limits vary, the perceptibles that test these limits will also vary. Both Literalism and Proportionalism account for relative intensity by identifying the material conditions that limit the possible dimensions of perception-related material change within the organ. So, for example, Aristotle states, "the eye which is intermediate between too much and too little liquid is the best, for it has neither too little so as to be agitated and impede the movement of the colors (τὸ ταράττεσθαι ἐμποδίζει τὴν τῶν χρωμάτων κίνησιν), nor too much so as to cause difficulty of movement (παρέχει δυσκινησίαν)" (GA.V.1.780a21–24). Here Aristotle suggest that, when the eye-jelly is too viscous, weak colors have little impact on the organ, and when the jelly is too fluidic, strong colors can agitate the organ and impede perception. Under Proportionalism, the explanation is especially straightforward: since the material cause of vision may well be a change of viscosity in the eye-jelly, the standing level of viscosity in the jelly may make changes of viscosity either difficult or disruptive. Under Literalism, the explanation is that some materials are better suited to taking on color than others (for example, Aristotle claims it is easier to dye a clean garment than a dirty one: see GA.V.1.780b29–31) and, when it comes to fluids, the level of viscosity is a factor that contributes to color-absorption suitability.

Spiritualism is not equipped to explain how organs might be damaged or destroyed by intense sensibles. The best that can be done is to insist that it is some concurrent cause, not the sensible as such, which brings about change in the organ. It might be argued that, when exposure to bright light results in damage to a subject's eyes, it is some concurrent cause (perhaps, an accompanying rush of air) and not the light itself that causes the damage. Problematically, for Spiritualism, however, Aristotle identifies cases in which intense sensibles damage or destroy organs, without the presence of a concurrent cause. For example, after noting that tangibles can destroy, not only the organ of touch, but the animal as well, Aristotle states, "other sensibles – I mean color, sound, and scent – do not by their excess destroy the animal, but only the corresponding organ: except incidentally, as when concurrently with the sound some thrust or blow is given" (DA.III.13.435b7–11). Aristotle holds that intense color, sound, and scent can destroy the organs of sight, hearing, and smell (respectively) in the absence of any relevant concurrent cause. Spiritualism, then, not only fails to account for blind spots and range limits in perceptual acuity, it also fails to account for the efficacy of intense sensibles. Spiritualism is a non-starter.

Literalism and Proportionalism appear to be on equal footing.[11] First, as we have shown, each interpretation accounts for blind spots, the destructive power of intense sensibles, and range limits; and each accounts for such phenomena in largely the same way. Second, while certain of Aristotle's claims favor Proportionalism, others favor Literalism. First, certain of Aristotle's claims may be taken to suggest that the material cause of vision involves a change of viscosity in the eye-jelly. For example, explaining why subjects with blue eyes are not keen-sighted by day, he states, "blue eyes are changed, *in respect to liquidity* (ἢ ὑγρὸν) and in respect to transparency, more easily by the light and the sense-object, because there is little liquid in them" (GAV.1.779b36–780a1, my emphasis). Passages of this sort look to favor Proportionalism.[12] Second, while arguing for the *thesis of causal reciprocity*, according to which the organs of perception act on objects in the same way that objects act on organs, Aristotle states, "when women look into clean mirrors, during menstruation, the mirrors take on a blood-red stain ... [a stain] that is not easy to wipe away" (*Insomn*.2.459b23–460a26).[13] In this curious discussion, Aristotle argues that literal redness in the eyes (caused by menstruation) brings about a literal reddening in the surface of mirrors. Since he also affirms that objects act on organs in the same way as organs act on objects, the claim favors Literalism.

The debate over Literalism and Proportionalism is likely to continue for some time. Yet, for our purposes, we need not decide between Literalism and Proportionalism.[14] The very phenomena that both Literalism and Proportionalism (similarly) explain – blind spots, range limits, and destructive power of intense sensibles – are at the heart of the comparisons which Aristotle draws between perception and thought in DA.III.4. So, to whatever extent these comparisons fuel and shape Aristotle's inferences concerning mind, they do so in roughly the same way, whether Aristotle is a Literalist or a Proportionalist.

We now see that perception, for Aristotle, has a concurrent material cause: on Aristotle's account, in order to move from seeing red to seeing green, from tasting bitter to tasting sweet, or from feeling cold to feeling warm, a subject must suffer bodily change. Yet, just as boiling blood is not sufficient for anger, so too material change in the organ of perception is not sufficient for awareness of the object. Aristotle, states "the greater change nullifies the lesser, which is why we do not see things presented to our eyes, if we happen to be engrossed in thought, or in a state of fear, or listening to a loud noise" (*Sens.*7.447a14–17). Here we see that a change in the eye, which might otherwise underwrite awareness of some color, may occur without the subject becoming aware of that color: when the subject is distracted (or diseased or fatigued), an appropriate change in bodily state may fail to trigger awareness of the object.

At this stage, one might be inclined to think that perception, just like anger, is *with the body*. However, Aristotle never indicates that perception is *with the body*. Instead, he insists that perception is *not without the body* (see DA.I.1.403a5–7 and III.4.439b4–5). In marking this distinction, Aristotle may be signifying that change in the organ of perception is less determinative of psychological content, than is, say, the boiling of blood in the case of anger. For Aristotle, ferment of blood about the heart is the material cause of just one positive psychological state: anger. Yet, when it comes to perception, Aristotle allows that change in the organ can bring about awareness of special, common, and incidental sensibles. He states, "in perceiving the beacon that is fire, and seeing it moving you recognize . . . that it signals the approach of the enemy" (DA.III.7.431b4–6). Here Aristotle avers that the same causal input generated by color (the fire) can bring a subject to awareness of the color as such (a special sensible), but it can also trigger awareness of motion (a common sensible) and the beacon (an incidental sensible). Owing to a subject's attention and experience, the same basic material change may come to trigger different states of perceptual awareness. So, Aristotle may hold that perception has a more sophisticated relation to the body than does emotion or desire: he may hold that a single bodily state can underwrite more than one positive state of perceptual awareness.[15] Yet, even if he denies that causal input determines all the bodily changes that underwrite perception, Aristotle, nevertheless firmly maintains that positive states of perceptual awareness require accompanying bodily states and changes. In addition, he maintains that a change of bodily state can be sufficient for a change in state of perceptual awareness (when the subject is not diseased, fatigued, or distracted).

Αἰσθήματα, Φαντάσματα, and Νοήματα

Aristotle calls the states and changes that serve as the material causes of perceptual awareness αἰσθήματα (perceptual happenings). These changes, he insists, may persist when the efficient cause of awareness is no longer present. Aristotle claims, "the affection persists in the sense organs, both deep down and on the surface, not only while we are perceiving, but also when we have ceased to do so" (*Insomn*.2.459a7–8). Residual αἰσθήματα are φαντάσματα (representational happenings) and just as αἰσθήματα are bodily states, so too are φαντάσματα. Active φαντάσματα deep within the perceptual system manifest themselves as kinetic disturbances in the blood, while φαντάσματα stored in memory are physical marks impressed into the central locus of the perceptual system (see *Insomn*.3.461b1–21 and *Mem*.1.450b16–20). Aristotle posits that φαντάσματα serve as material causes of all non-standard states of perceptual awareness (states for which no external efficient causes is present): these include hallucinations, dreams, and remembrances (see *Insomn*.I.459a21–22 and *Mem*.1.450b12–17). Further, he claims, "the imaginative is the same as the perceptual faculty, although imagination and perception are different in being" (*Insomn*.I.459a17–19). To differ in being is to differ in account. So, for Aristotle, the account of imagination (φαντασία) will differ from the account of perception and, yet, imagination is not a faculty in its own right. Imagination is an aspect of the perceptual faculty and both φαντάσματα and αἰσθήματα are bodily happenings within the perceptual system.

It is evident that, for Aristotle, mind (νοῦς), in its functioning, is dependent on φαντάσματα. Aristotle states, "it is not possible even to think without φαντάσματος" and he adds, "whenever we think, it is necessary at the same time to think some φάντασμά" (*Mem*.1.449b31–32 and *DA*.III.8.432a8–9). So, for Aristotle, all episodes of thought, all νοήματα (noetic happenings), require the use of φαντάσματα: φαντάσματα are necessary material conditions for thought. Mind, then, for Aristotle, depends on the body insofar as thought relies on bodily states and changes within the perceptual system.[16]

A problem stands on the horizon: the thesis that νοήματα require φαντάσματα could be taken to suggest that mind's reliance on the body is no more sophisticated than what we see with perception: perhaps, mind, like perception, is *not without the body*. Nevertheless, as we shall see, Aristotle's considered view is that mind, unlike perception, is *separate from the body*. So, after examining DA.III.4, we will need to show how the role played by φαντάσματα in thought differs from the role played by αἰσθήματα in perception.

3. Mind and body (1): realizing distance

In the opening section of DA.III.4, Aristotle both sets out a framework for discussion and advances a pair of arguments concerning νοῦς.[17] He states,

> **(FRAMEWORK)** Concerning the part of the soul by which the soul knows and thinks, whether it is separate or not separate in respect to extension or only in respect to account (εἴτε χωριστοῦ ὄντος εἴτε μὴ χωριστοῦ κατὰ μέγεθος ἀλλὰ κατὰ λόγον), we must consider what differentia is has and how thinking ever comes about.
>
> (429a10–13)

> **(ARGUMENT 1)** If understanding is like perception, then it will be a sort of being acted on by the object of thought or something else of that sort. Thus (ἄρα) it must be unaffected and receptive of form, and it will be potentially such as this sort of thing: as perception is related to the objects of perception so will intellect be similarly related to the objects of thought. Thus (ἄρα), since it thinks all things, **(CLAIM 1) [mind] must be unmixed**, just as Anaxagoras says, in order for it to rule, that is in order for it to know, for if it is present alongside, it hinders and occludes what is extraneous (παρεμφαινόμενον γὰρ κωλύει τὸ ἀλλότριον καὶ ἀντιφράττει).... So (διὸ), **(CLAIM 2) it is reasonable (εὔλογον) to consider [mind] not to be mixed with the body**; for (γὰρ) if it were it would come to have some quality, like cold or hot, and it would even have an organ, as the perceptual faculty does; but, as it is, there is none.
>
> (429a13–27)

> **(ARGUMENT 2)** That the unaffectedness of the perceptual faculty differs from that of intellect is made manifest by a consideration of the organs of perception and perception (itself). For (γὰρ) the perceptual faculty loses its ability to perceive after (being affected by) an intense perceptible, as with sound after loud noises, and after strong colors and odors it is neither able to see or to smell; but whenever intellect thinks some intense intelligible, it is not less able to think inferior ones, rather it is better able to do so; **(CLAIM 3) for (γὰρ) perception is not without the body, while mind is separate [from the body]**.
>
> (429a31–b5)[18]

By announcing, in the FRAMEWORK, that he aims to identify the distinguishing characteristics of mind, Aristotle signals that his investigation will be a scientific one. He will proceed from what is more knowable to us (i.e., what is evident from experience) to what is more knowable by nature (i.e., underlying causes, definitions, and principles) (see *Physics* I.1). He will identify properties of mind and approach knowledge of mind's definition by securing a hypothesis (a candidate definition (or partial definition) of mind). Further, he will confirm the hypothesis against the data of experience (see APo.I.10.76b11–23 and II.8).

One prominent scholar contends that the FRAMEWORK significantly constrains the range of possible outcomes in DA.III.4. Caston (2001) argues that, by asking whether mind is separate in respect to extension or in respect to account, Aristotle limits discussion that follows to just two alternatives: either (1) mind is localized in a distinct part of the body, having its own dedicated organ, or (2) mind, not being localized, is "a capacity of the entire human body" (*ibid.*, p. 137). So, on Caston's interpretation, the possibility that νοῦς is an immaterial faculty is not a live issue in DA.III.4. However, this view is too narrow. An earlier discussion frames the FRAMEWORK. In DA.II.2, Aristotle, considering nutrition, perception, and thought, states, "whether each is separate only in account or also in place (χωριστὸν λόγῳ μόνον ἢ καὶ τόπῳ), this is easy to answer in some cases, but others involve difficulties" (413b13–16). Here, as in DA.III.4, Aristotle advances the question as to whether mind is separate in extension (i.e., place) or separate in account. But, in DA.II.2, Aristotle goes on to contemplate two types of separation relating to extension. The first is *separation within extension*. Items are *separate within extension*, if they occupy different, non-overlapping, places (see *Physics* VI.1.231b4–6 and Miller 2012, p. 309). Dedicated organs are *separate within extension*. The second type of separation is *separation from extension*. Aristotle states, "mind alone might be separate, as the immortal is from the perishable" (413b26–27). Here Aristotle considers a type of separation that he elsewhere attributes to the prime mover. The mover, being immortal and imperishable, is *separate from extension*: as Aristotle states, the mover is "separate from sensible things (κεχωρισμένη τῶν αἰσθητῶν)" and "without any magnitude (μέγεθος οὐδὲν ἔχειν)" (*Met.*XII.7.1073a4–6). The prime mover is not in any place whatsoever. So, in DA.II.2, Aristotle suggests that mind, like the prime mover, could be *separate from extension*. This shows that the FRAMEWORK does not bar Aristotle from exploring the specific category of *separate from extension*. As we shall see, Aristotle's chief aim in DA.III.4 is to show that νοῦς is *separate from extension*.

3.1 Argument 1: securing the hypothesis[19]

Aristotle's first argument may be represented as follows:

I   Thought and perception are akin insofar as each is a cognitive assimilation: a reception of form.
II <If a faculty is mixed with the body, then it suffers constraints and limitations.>
III <Perception is mixed with the body.>

IV <Perception suffers constraints and limitations.> (from II & III)
V <If a faculty does not suffer constraints or limitations, it is not mixed with the body.>
VI Mind thinks all things: mind suffers neither constraints nor limitations.
VII So, mind is not mixed with the body. (Claim 1: from V & VI)
VIII Further, mind, in fact, lacks an organ.
IX So, mind is not mixed with the body. (Claim 2: from VII & VIII)

Considerations of specific differences between perception and thought drive the argument. For Aristotle, whether he is understood as a Literalists or a Proportionalist, positive states of perceptual awareness require accompanying material states and changes. These changes involve the instantiation of determinate proportions or ratios within bodily structures. Whenever the appropriate organ is unable to take on a specific proportion, the subject is unable to perceive the relevant object. These limitations are a product of the material composition of the relevant organs. On the one hand, the constitution of the organ may hinder (κωλύει: DA.III.4.429a20) or impede reception of form. For example, since the viscosity of eye-jelly is a determining factor in demarcating visual range limits, whenever a subject is exposed to an object with a level of intensity nearing the upper limit of receptivity, the state of the jelly impedes (ἐμποδίζει: GA.V.1.780a23) or hinders reception. On the other hand, standing conditions within the organ of touch engender blind spots. The organ cannot be altered to a proportion within its native qualitative range, when the body already possesses the same proportion in the hot/cold range (or in any other tangible range). So, conditions within the organ occlude (ἀντιφράττει: DA.III.4.429a20) or obstruct reception.

Aristotle insists that mind, unlike perception, suffers neither hindrance nor obstruction. He states, "mind thinks all things" (DA.III.4.429a18).[20] The statement is echoed in *Parts of Animals* (PA) I.1. There, in what has come to be called the *correlatives argument*, Aristotle supposes that any science must study its correlative objects and he infers that natural science should not study mind. Aristotle's concern is that, were mind to fall within the purview of natural science, this would have the unwanted consequence of collapsing the three theoretical domains – natural science, mathematics, and metaphysics – into one: metaphysics and mathematics would become natural science. Emphasizing this point, Aristotle states, "natural science would be knowledge about all things (πάντων ἡ φυσικὴ γνῶσις ἂν εἴη)" (*ibid*. 641b1). So, to think all things (to know all things) is to have the ability to cognize the objects of natural science, metaphysics and mathematics. Accordingly, for Aristotle, mind is able to cognize principles, causes, definitions, and essences (all of which are universals): as examples, mind cognizes 'humanity,' 'unity,' and 'being' (see *Meta*.I.2 and 2013, pp. 366–367). Further, Aristotle contends that it is through knowledge of principles that we are able to gain a firm grasp on particulars (see APo.I.2.72a26–28). So, mind is able to grasp both universals and particulars. Thus, in its breadth of reach, mind greatly outshines perception. Perception has no access to universals and it is blind to natural science, metaphysics and mathematics. It grasps only some of the particulars that fall within the realm of nature. So, Aristotle infers that, since mind is free from the sorts of limitations and constraints suffered by perception (limitations which are a product of material composition), thought is not realized in the body. Mind, he infers, is unmixed (CLAIM 1).

'Unmixed' (ἀμιγῆ) is potentially ambiguous. So, Aristotle clarifies his meaning by affirming that, as regards the specific thesis that mind is unmixed, he is allied with Anaxagoras. A key thesis within Anaxagoras' physics is the principle of *universal mixture*. On this principle, every kind of matter is thoroughly mixed in every place (no matter how small) within the universe.[21] Anaxagoras contends that, unlike matter, "mind is unmixed" (DK59B12): mind does not participate in *universal mixture*. Thus, for Anaxagoras, mind is not in any place whatsoever: mind is *separate from extension*. Aristotle allies himself with Anaxagoras on this specific point. Further, since a faculty is *separate from extension* only if it is *separate from the body*, Aristotle's assertion that mind is unmixed (CLAIM 1) entails the proposition that mind is *separate from the body* (CLAIM 3).

Having argued that mind is unmixed (CLAIM 1), Aristotle offers empirical verification for the thesis (see Polansky 2007, p. 441). He states, "as it is, there is none" (429a27): Aristotle asserts that, as a matter of fact, there is no organ of thought. Why he should think this is a bit of a mystery. I suggest that, since Aristotle holds that the brain is a cooling system for the body (see PA.II.10.656a14–36), while the heart is the seat of perceptual awareness, he infers that no major organ remains as a candidate seat of intellectual awareness. The empirical evidence, as Aristotle understands it, suggests that mind lacks a bodily organ. In light of this buttressing consideration, Aristotle reaffirms CLAIM 1 and states, "it is reasonable (εὔλογον) to consider mind not to be mixed with the body" (CLAIM 2). Importantly, Aristotle takes the thesis that mind is unmixed to be merely reasonable or plausible. For him, ARGUMENT 1 is not conclusive.[22]

That Aristotle does not take ARGUMENT 1 to be decisive is entirely in keeping with his scientific method. In the argument, Aristotle reasons to the proposition that mind is unmixed: he *argues towards the definition* (or part of the definition) of mind. However, for Aristotle, definitions are first principles: definitions are posits that cannot be demonstrated (see APo.I.2). He maintains that in order to secure a principle or definition we must *argue from the definition*. Since definitions are fundamental, we can prove the truth of a definition only when we take it as a basic premise and go on to demonstrate, from the premise, other non-fundamental truths.[23] Aristotle states that in such an argument, "no deduction and no demonstration of the essence comes about, but the essence is made clear through demonstration" (Apo.II.8.93b16–17). So, in ARGUMENT 1, Aristotle, *arguing towards the definition*, establishes the hypothesis that mind is unmixed. The argument, however, is inconclusive and the hypothesis stands as merely reasonable or probable until Aristotle is able to confirm the thesis by *arguing from the definition*.

3.2 Argument 2: making the definition clear through demonstration

Aristotle's argument may be represented as follows:

I Perception is *not without the body*.
II Mind is *separate from the body*.
III <Faculties that are *not without the body* suffer damage or destruction when exposed to intense objects.>
IV <Faculties that are *separate from body* do not suffer damage or destruction when exposed to intense objects.>
V So, perception suffers damage or destruction when exposed to intense objects. (from I & III)
VI So, mind does not suffer damage or destruction when exposed to intense objects. (from II & IV)

In the argument, the thesis that mind is *separate from the body (i.e., separate from extension)* serves as a premise and Aristotle argues from the thesis – he *argues from the definition* – to a relevant and determinative empirical truth. Thus, Aristotle confirms the thesis that he had first marked as merely reasonable in ARGUMENT 1. In ARGUMENT 2, Aristotle, again, compares thought and perception. He affirms that thought and perception relate differently to intense objects. As we have seen, Aristotle acknowledges that intense sensibles can damage, or even destroy, organs of perception. According to Aristotle, whether he is understood as a Literalists or a Proportionalist, when a subject is exposed to an intense sensible, the intense change in proportion or ratio within the relevant organ that would be required to underwrite perceptual awareness of the object exceeds the limits of the organ's capacity for change: the extreme material change that transpires robs the organ (either temporarily or permanently) of its standing conditions for reception of form. One limitation that follows exposure to damaging (but not destructive) intense sensibles is a temporary inability come to awareness of weaker objects. As Aristotle states, "on changing from strong, brilliant colors [to inferior ones] . . . people cannot see: for the movement which is already present in the eyes is so strong that it precludes (κωλύει) the movement which comes from without" (GA V.1.780a10–13).

Thought, Aristotle insists, is unlike perception: intense objects of thought neither impede nor destroy our ability to think. Further, Aristotle asserts that, we are actually better able (not less able) to think inferior intelligibles, after thinking intense ones. The difference between thought and perception, when it comes to the impact of intense objects of cognition, follows from the thesis that νοῦς is *separate from the body* (while perception is *not without the body*). So, in ARGUMENT 2, Aristotle *argues from the definition* and confirms the thesis that mind is *separate from the body*. Thus, in DA.III.4, Aristotle secures the thesis that mind is distant from the body insofar as it is a non-bodily faculty.[24]

4. Mind and body (2): addressing dependence[25]

We have learned that Aristotle thinks νοῦς is *separate from the body*: its activity somehow takes place in isolation from the body. Yet, we have also learned that, for Aristotle, thought requires the use of φαντάσματα and φαντάσματα are bodily states and changes. The problem that had once been on the horizon is now upon us. Interestingly, though, Aristotle's claims about mind and φαντάσματα do not appear to be inconsistent.[26] Φαντάσματα are necessary conditions for thought (see Cohoe 2013, p. 371). For both emotion and perception (except in certain non-standard cases) specific bodily changes are sufficient for changes in awareness. When an apple is put before me in a lighted room, I see it; and when my blood boils, owing to an insult, I am angered. So, for Aristotle, both perception and emotion are occasioned by bodily change. Yet, the activation of φαντάσματα need not occasion thought. Φαντάσματα are perceptual processes, not intellectual ones (see *Mem*.1.450a22–25). When feeling peckish, I might imagine or dream about an apple. In the experience certain φαντάσματα will be activated, but thought need not transpire. For Aristotle, thought is something in addition to, both over and above, imagination. Thus, the role played by φαντάσματα in thought differs from the role played by αἰσθήματα in perception. Φαντάσματα serve as necessary, but not sufficient, conditions for states of mental awareness. Further, the act of mind, whereby a subject, employing φαντάσματα, comes to thinks, remains, according to Aristotle, a non-bodily happening. For Aristotle, were an ideal scientist to examine my perceptual system, she could determine both whether I am perceiving and whether I am imagining. Further, she could (to some extent) assess the content of my perceptual experiences. But, this scientist would be unable to determine whether I am thinking: evidence from the perceptual system is not sufficient to show that the mind is active.

In addition, the relation between νοήματα and φαντάσματα is more attenuated than the relation between states of perceptual awareness and αἰσθήματα. When exposed to the light of a beacon, I might become aware of the colored light, the motion, or even the beacon itself. However, these objects constitute a limited set of particulars. By contrast, φαντάσματα may be employed in thought of particulars and in thought of universals. Aristotle states,

> the same effect is involved in thinking as in drawing a diagram; For in this case we make no use of the fact that the triangle is determinate, yet we draw it as having a determinate size. In the same way someone who is thinking, even if he is not thinking of something with size, still puts something with size before his eyes, but does not think of it as such. If the nature of the object is to have size, but not a determinate one, he puts before himself something with a determinate size, but thinks of it simply as having size.
>
> (*Mem*.1.450a1–6)

Here Aristotle affirms that the same φάντασμα might be employed in thought of (1) an object with determinate size, (2) an object with size, but an indeterminate one, and (3) an object lacking size altogether. So, on Aristotle's account, the same φάντασμα might be employed in thought of, say, (1) a triangular component within a carpentry project, (2) a triangle in a Euclidean proof, or (3) 'triangularity' itself. Φαντάσματα support thought of both particulars and universals. Further, it appears that any universal under which an item represented by a given φάντασμα might be subsumed is a potential object of thought, in an act of mind with which the given φάντασμα is employed. So, our sample φάντασμα might be used in thought, not only of 'trangularity,' but also of, say, 'shape,' 'extension,' 'unity,' and 'plurality.' The link between mental content and φαντάσματα is, for Aristotle, highly attenuated. Accordingly, Aristotle thinks that mental content neither covaries with nor supervenes upon bodily states. To return to our ideal scientist: in studying my perceptual system, she would not only be unable to determine whether I am thinking, but, even if I were thinking, she would be unable assess the content of my thoughts. In order to move from thought of 'this triangle' to thought of 'shape,' from thought of 'shape' to thought of 'extension,' or from thought of 'extension' to thought of 'unity,' I need not suffer a bodily change.

5. Conclusion

I have shown that Aristotle has a theory of mind; plus, on his theory, mind is distant from the body insofar as it is *separate from the body*. For Aristotle, the mind is an immaterial faculty. Further, I have shown that, according to Aristotle, mind is dependent on the body insofar as every episode of thought relies on bodily states and changes within the perceptual system. Finally, I have suggested that Aristotle provides a consistent explanation of dependence-compatible distance in his treatment of the mind-body relation.

Notes

1 The formulation is borrowed from Broadie, who describes the larger issue to be that of explaining "dependence-compatible distance" in Aristotle's account of the mind-body relation (Broadie 1996, p. 167).
2 For more on the role of the four causes within Aristotle's account of anger see Bolton 2005, pp. 213–217.
3 In this chapter, I examine Aristotle's core arguments concerning mind's distance from the body. These arguments are found in DA.III.4: the only chapter in the corpus that unequivocally deals with the issue of the metaphysical status of human mind. I do not offer an interpretation of DA.III.5. While the chapter, with its compressed presentation and loose metaphors, has given rise to a broad variety of candidate interpretations, I find that the textual evidence therein does not provide sufficient evidence for determining which, if any, candidate interpretation captures Aristotle's intended meaning. I agree with Shields when he writes, "it is tempting to regard *De Anima* III.5 as a sort of Rorschach Test for Aristotelians: it is hard to avoid the conclusion that readers discover in this chapter the Aristotle they hope to admire" (Shields 2011). Miller (2012, pp. 320–326) and Cohoe (2014, pp. 597–600) provide useful synopses of recent

approaches to DA.III.5. For the outcome of my own 'Rorschach Test,' see Sisko 2001, pp. 189–197.
4 The thesis that, for Aristotle, mind is a non-bodily faculty is defended in Sisko 1999a and 2001; Gerson 2004; Polansky 2007, pp. 434–457; and Cohoe 2013.
5 Caston claims that, for Aristotle, "there is a certain covariation between understanding and the total state of the body" (Caston 2001, p. 171). In addition, Caston gestures towards the possibility of supervenience, when he states that, on his own interpretation, Aristotle's theory is "compatible with the supervenience of acts of understanding on certain bodily states" (*ibid.*, p. 172).
6 For example, Pakaluk states, "As I see it, Aristotle brings to his treatise on psychology, as somewhat settled in his own mind, his view of the essential kinship of human and divine intelligence. He leaves room for this view throughout the treatise . . . [b]ut I do not see that he ever argues for it" (Pakaluk 2001, p. 205).
7 See Caston 2001, p. 136, n. 5. Caston rightly notes that, in Sisko 1999a, I erroneously take the claim to function as a conclusion and not a premise. In this chapter, I show that Aristotle situates the claim as a premise in the argument in order to confirm the thesis that mind is separate from the body.
8 Strictly, for Aristotle, there is one organ of perception: the common sense. This is an interconnected system of special sub-organs – like eyes and ears – and a central locus, found in the region about the heart (see DA.III.2.426b17–25 and *Sens*.7.449a5–10).
9 Spiritualism is advanced in Burnyeat 1995 and Johansen 1998. I critique the interpretation in Sisko 1996 and 1999b. Literalism, first suggested in Sorabji 1974, is defended in Everson 1997, Woolf 1999, and Sorabji 2001. I assess Everson's chief arguments in Sisko 1998. The magisterial and definitive essay on Proportionalism is Caston 2005. A key precursor to Caston is Bradshaw 1997.
10 Here I elaborate on an account that I have argued for elsewhere (Sisko 1996, pp. 144–147).
11 Caston (2005, pp. 293–295) attempts to rule out Literalism. He argues: (1) under Literalism, perception results in the replication of objects; (2) Aristotle, insofar as he rejects Empedocles' theory of perception, denied that perception results in the replication of objects; thus, (3) Aristotle cannot be a Literalist. Ducharme (2014, pp. 306–308) rightly notes that on Empedocles' theory there is no replication. Rather, Empedocles holds that perception involves the activation of objects that preexist within the body. Now Aristotle does think it absurd to suppose that perception of incidental perceptible relies on the presence of such objects in the body. He states, "it is not the stone which is in the soul, but the form of the stone" (DA.III.8.431b30–432a1). But he makes no such claim regarding either special or common sensibles. Since Literalism points to replication of only special (and common) sensibles, the interpretation survives this specific attack.
12 Also, for Aristotle, perception of flavor involves a moistening of the tongue (see DA.II.10.422a17–19). But, as Bolton (2005, pp. 226–228) argues, it is unlikely that Aristotle believes the tongue takes on the actual flavor of the object of taste (except under certain abnormal conditions (see DA.II.10.423b27–434a10)). On the moistening of the tongue in the perception of flavor also see Lorenz 2007, pp. 191–192.
13 For a thorough assessment of the passage, see Woolf 1999.
14 In Sisko 2001, I evaluate Aristotle's discussion of mind in DA.III.4, while presuming that Aristotle is a Literalist. In this chapter, I show that, while Aristotle may be a Literalist or a Proportionalist, the difference between these two theoretical frames does not engender a difference in the way his views on perception impact interpretation of the main arguments in DA.III.4
15 We cannot be certain that Aristotle thinks that one bodily state can support a multiplicity of states of awareness. It remains possible that, on his account, states of perceptual awareness supervene on bodily states. Awareness of incidental sensibles, as opposed to awareness of special sensibles or common sensibles, could be linked to additional bodily states and changes within the perceptual system and these conditions might

constitute a supervenience base for, say, awareness of a beacon as opposed to awareness of fiery light. Bolton (2005, pp. 231–238) contends that, for Aristotle, material causes fully determine states of perceptual awareness.

16 Some scholars contend that, for Aristotle, thought of immaterial objects does not require the use of φαντάσματα. For example, Johansen (2012, p. 24) states, "when we think about god . . . our thinking will not be dependent on *phantasmata*." This view, however, runs counter to Aristotle's own claims.
17 Aristotle offers ancillary and supporting arguments in later parts of DA.III.4. Useful assessments of these arguments may be found in Sisko 2001, pp. 185–189; Lewis 2003; and Polansky 2007, pp. 445–457.
18 The prevalence of inferential connectives (γὰρ 429a20, 429a25, 429a31, and 429b5; ἄρα 429a15 and 429a18; and διὸ 429a24) shows that Aristotle is advancing arguments in this section of DA.III.4. Thus, we must reject interpretation (Bi), according to which Aristotle does not offer a reasoned thesis in DA.III.4 (see p. 197).
19 In both this and the following sub-section, I expand upon an account that I have argued for elsewhere (Sisko 1999a, pp. 256–263).
20 Here Aristotle has been interpreted in a number of ways. Minimally, he has been taken to indicate that that if anything can be understood, it can be understood by mind (see Sisko 1999a, pp. 257–258). Maximally, he has been taken to indicate that no thing exists that cannot be understood by mind (see Cohoe 2013, pp. 365–366).
21 I present an overview of the principles of Anaxagoras' physics in Sisko 2010.
22 Caston (2001, p. 136, n. 5) disagrees.
23 For example, Aristotle notes that we might surmise that a lunar eclipse could be a rotation of the moon, an extinguishing of fire on the moon, or a screening of the sun's light by the Earth, but only one of these hypotheses provides a basis from which to demonstrate why changes in patterns of light and dark on the moon, witnessed during an eclipse, occur just as they do (see APo.II.8.9b3b4–7).
24 ARGUMENT 2 has its weaknesses. One difficulty is that Aristotle does not show that objects of thought and objects of perception are 'intense' or 'weak/inferior' in similar ways (see Sisko 1999a, pp. 265–266). Of course, neither ARGUMENT 1 nor ARGUMENT 2 will convince us that mind is non-bodily, if we do not already accept either Literalism or Proportionalism for perception (and contemporary philosophers of mind accept neither of these theories).
25 In this section I develop an account that I have argued for elsewhere (Sisko 1996, pp. 152–157).
26 To be more precise, these claims are consistent, when considered in broad outline. If we were to press Aristotle and ask him how the immaterial mind goes about employing material φαντάσματα, his answer would most likely prove to be inadequate. A quasi-Cartesian mind-body problem lurks in the shadows of Aristotle's *De Anima*.

Bibliography

Bolton, R. (2005) Perception naturalized in Aristotle's De Anima. In Salles, R. (ed.) *Metaphysics, Soul, and Ethics in Ancient Thought: Themes from the Work of Richard Sorabji.* Oxford: Clarendon Press, pp. 209–244.
Bradshaw, D. (1997) Aristotle on perception: The dual-logos theory. *Apeiron* 30: 143–161.
Broadie, S. (1996) Nous and nature in Aristotle's De Anima III. *Proceedings of the Boston Area Colloquium in Ancient Philosophy* 12: 163–176.
Burnyeat, M. F. (1995) Is aristotle's philosophy of mind still credible? A draft. In Nussbaum, M. C., and Rorty, A. (eds.) *Essays on Aristotle's De Anima.* Oxford: Oxford University Press, pp. 15–26.

Caston, V. (2001) Aristotle on understanding and the body. *Proceedings of the Boston Area Colloquium in Ancient Philosophy* 16: 135–175.

———. (2005) The spirit and the letter: Aristotle on perception. In Salles, R. (ed.) *Metaphysics, Soul, and Ethics in Ancient Thought: Themes from the Work of Richard Sorabji.* Oxford: Clarendon Press, pp. 245–320.

Cohoe, C. (2013) Why the intellect cannot have a bodily organ: De Anima 3.4. *Phronesis* 58: 347–377.

———. (2014) Nous in Aristotle's De Anima. *Philosophy Compass* 9 (9): 594–604.

Ducharme, A. (2014) Aristotle's mark of sentience. *Apeiron* 47 (3): 293–309.

Everson, S. (1997) *Aristotle on Perception.* Oxford: Oxford University Press.

Gerson, L. (2004) The unity of intellect in Aristotle's 'De Anima'. *Phronesis* 49: 348–373.

Hett, W. S. (1936) *Aristotle: On the Soul, Parva Naturalia, on Breath.* Cambridge, MA: Harvard University Press.

Hicks, R. D. (1907) *Aristotle De Anima: With Translation, Introduction, and Notes.* Cambridge, MA: Cambridge University Press.

Johansen, T. K. (1998) *Aristotle on the Sense-Organs.* Cambridge, MA: Cambridge University Press.

———. (2012) *The Powers of Aristotle's Soul.* Oxford: Oxford University Press.

Lewis, F. (2003) Is there room for Anaxagoras in Aristotle's Theory of Mind. *Oxford Studies in Ancient Philosophy* 25: 89–129.

Lorenz, H. (2007) The assimilation of sense to sense object in Aristotle. *Oxford Studies in Ancient Philosophy* 33: 179–220.

Miller, F. (2012) Aristotle on the separability of mind. In Shields, C. (ed.) *The Oxford Handbook of Aristotle.* Oxford: Oxford University Press.

Pakaluk, M. (2001) Commentary on Sisko. *Proceedings of the Boston Area Colloquium in Ancient Philosophy* 16: 199–206.

Polansky, R. (2007) *Aristotle's De Anima.* Cambridge, MA: Cambridge University Press.

Shields, C. (2011) The active mind of De Anima iii 5: supplement to Aristotle's Psychology. In Zalta, E. (ed.) *The Stanford Encyclopedia of Philosophy.* http://plato.stanford.edu/entries/aristotle-psychology/active-mind.html

Sisko, J. (1996) Material alteration and cognitive activity in Aristotle's De Anima. *Phronesis* 41: 138–157.

———. (1998) Alteration and quasi-alteration. *Oxford Studies in Ancient Philosophy* 16: 131–152.

———. (1999a) On separating the intellect from the body: Aristotle's De Anima III.4, 429a10-b5. *Archiv fur Geschichte der Philosophie* 81: 249–267.

———. (1999b) Review of Johansen, Aristotle on the Sense-Organs. *Classical Review* 49 (1) ns: 122–123. Cambridge, MA: Cambridge University Press, 1998.

———. (2001) Aristotle's Nous and the modern mind. *Proceedings of the Boston Area Colloquium in Ancient Philosophy* 16: 177–198.

———. (2010) Anaxagoras on matter, motion, and multiple worlds. *Philosophy Compass* 5 (6): 443–454.

Sorabji, R. (1974) Body and soul in Aristotle. *Philosophy* 70: 470–484.

———. (2001) Aristotle on sensory processes and intentionality: A reply to Myles Burnyeat. In Perler, D. (ed.) *Ancient and Medieval Theories of Intentionality.* Leiden: Brill Publishing, pp. 49–61.

Woolf, R. (1999) The coloration of Aristotelian eye-jelly: A note on on dreams 459b9–460a. *Journal of the History of Philosophy* 37 (3): 385–391.

11

RATIONAL IMPRESSIONS AND THE STOIC PHILOSOPHY OF MIND

Vanessa de Harven

At the heart of Stoic philosophy of mind is the rational impression (*logikē phantasia*). As it happens, the Stoics think that the mind resides in the heart, but this is not what makes the Stoic account interesting; seating the mind in the heart is a commonplace for the time. What sets the Stoics apart is their focus on mental phenomena of soul (*psychē*) over Aristotle's physiological mechanisms, and on semantic content over Plato's desiderative psychology – all of which begins with the rational impression. Much scholarly attention has been directed to the cataleptic impression central to Stoic epistemology, and to the downstream functions of assent and impulse at the heart of Stoic moral psychology. The rational impression itself, however, and thus the Stoic philosophy of mind proper, has been relatively neglected.[1] This chapter seeks to elucidate the distinctive nature of the rational impression on its own terms, asking precisely what it means for the Stoics to define *logikē phantasia* as an impression whose content is expressible in language.[2]

First some brief background on Stoic theory. The Stoics are well known for their robust corporealism: they say that only bodies exist, or are, and they cast a large swath of reality as corporeal. For example, all qualities or properties encompassed by Plato's Forms, including even the virtues, and the soul itself are considered bodies. They reason that insofar as the soul and body interact, and all interaction must be corporeal, the soul must itself be a body.[3] Virtue is also a body, namely the corporeal soul disposed a certain way, or in some state, like a well-worn leather glove with its own patina, shape, and suppleness.[4] The Stoics are also well known for saying that, while only bodies exist, not everything that is Something (*ti*, the Stoics' highest ontological genus) exists. Alongside their innovatively robust category of corporeals (*sōmata*) that *exist* or *are* (*einai, on*), the Stoics recognize a class of incorporeal entities that *subsist* (*huphistanai*, have *hupostasis*); these include, canonically, place, void, time, and the *lekta*, or sayables, roughly the meanings of our words.[5] Thus the Stoics are not brute corporealists, but sophisticated physicalists grappling with Plato's beard.[6]

Indeed, in order to approach the Stoics on their own terms, one must recognize how they cut across their predecessors' ways of thought. In this case, the differences between Plato, Aristotle and the Stoics on the philosophy of mind must be couched as a debate over the scope of physics – namely, whether there is a place for soul in physics. They each give different answers to the question, *How much can you say about the soul independent of body?* For Plato (and Descartes), the answer is (*almost*) *everything*, for Aristotle the answer is *some*, and for the Stoics it's *none*. Insofar as the Stoic soul is itself a body, there is no sense in which one can speak of soul without thereby speaking about body; and the topic of soul is squarely in the domain of physics, in stark contrast to Plato. On the other hand, insofar as the Stoics also see soul as a psychic entity entirely mixed with and yet separable from a distinct corporeal entity (the body), the Stoics are more like Plato than Aristotle. On this dualist understanding, the Stoic answer to how much can be said about soul without body is Plato's, (*almost*) *everything*; in contrast to Aristotle, Stoic soul is not what unifies an animal's body, but rather what gives it sensation and desire.[7]

1. Soul

I will begin by saying more about the soul considered as a body. Soul is *pneuma*, a portion of fiery breath in a certain tension (*tonikēn kinēsin*) "moving simultaneously inwards and outwards, the outward movement producing quantities and qualities, and the inward one unity and substance".[8] The cosmos is pervaded by *pneuma* as the immanent divine guiding principle, and each body is what it is in virtue of the particular state of rarity and tension of the portion of that *pneuma* that constitutes it. The Stoic *scala naturae* is a function of increasing complexity and unity due to the state of a body's *pneuma*.[9] A stone, for example, is a solid object that holds together in virtue of the tenor (*hexis*) of its *pneuma* acting on its matter. Plants are alive and are said to have physique (*phusis*) because their *pneuma* is more rarefied and in a greater state of tension than mere *hexis*; plants are therefore more complex entities than stones in that the tension of their *pneuma* is an internal principle of motion and rest rather than of mere unity. Finally, the *pneuma* in animals is yet more rarefied and complex, and is called *psychē* because the internal principle of motion and rest includes the capacity for impression and impulse. Thus, from the standpoint of Stoic physics, soul is a body insofar as it is *pneuma* in a certain state of tension.[10]

The soul's corporeality can also be considered from a metaphysical standpoint, in terms of the so-called Stoic categories: substrate (*hupokeimenon*), qualified individual (*poion*), disposed individual (*pōs echon*), and relatively disposed individual (*pros ti pōs echon*).[11] According to the Stoics, a complete analysis of any body makes reference to all four of these metaphysical aspects. Applying this fourfold analysis to soul, we can see that (1) soul *qua* substrate is *pneuma*; (2) each particular soul is a *poion* because its *pneuma* is in a state of tension such as to constitute an individual soul with certain qualities, characteristics, and abilities;

(3) the *pōs echon* is that individual soul in a certain state, literally *being in a certain way* – this is how the Stoics corporealize the virtues that flummoxed their materialist predecessors, and how they corporealize our thoughts. Virtue for the Stoics is a stable state of character by which you see the world aright; it is a *pōs echon* because it is a habituated state of the *poion*. Impressions, though they are temporary and fleeting, fall into this category as well because an impression just is the soul undergoing a *pathos* (i.e., being affected in some way and thus in a certain state). (4) Finally, every soul also lies in a determinate relation to its immediate surroundings and, ultimately, to the cosmos as a whole, so it is relatively disposed.

Now, the Stoics recognized two senses of the term *soul*, or *psuchē*: (a) the corporeal entity as a whole that is mixed through and through with body, sustaining the composite animal, and (b) the commanding faculty (*hēgemonikon*, and sometimes *kurieuon*), which is the highest part of soul.[12] We have been considering soul in the first sense; the second sense refers to the *hēgemonikon*, the part by which an animal is aware of and engaged with itself and its surroundings – the locus of impressions. We turn now to this second sense of soul and thus to Stoic psychology and the philosophy of mind proper. The Stoics famously liken the soul to an octopus, with the commanding faculty located in the region of the heart, and seven other parts growing out from it and stretching into the body. Five of these parts are the senses; for example, sight is *pneuma* that extends from the commanding faculty to the eyes. The other two are the reproductive faculty, or seed (*sperma*), extending from the commanding faculty to the genitals; and, in a deeply innovative move whose implications are at the heart of this chapter, voice (*phonē*), extending from the commanding faculty of soul to the windpipe and tongue.[13] Again, what is characteristic of soul, in contrast to the mere *phusis* of plants, is that it has impression (*phantasia*) and impulse (*hormē*); these psychic functions make an animal aware of the world, and able to interact with it. *Phantasia* and *hormē* are in effect the input and output faculties of the *hēgemonikon*, a stimulus-response mechanism presupposing a single subject or self that thinks and acts.[14]

2. *Phantasia*, generically

We turn now to the Stoic account of *phantasia* considered generically, as the animal's input function.[15] Starting from Aëtius' testimony about Chrysippus, in the following passage, I will argue that *phantasiai* are states of direct, reflexive awareness of the world.

> **A. (1) (a)** On the one hand, impression (*phantasia*) is an affection (*pathos*) coming about in the soul, revealing (*endeiknumenon*) itself and what has made it (*to pepoiēkos*); for example, whenever through sight (*dia opseōs*) we observe (*theōrōmen*) what is white (*to leukon*), an affection is what has been engendered in the soul through seeing (*dia horaseōs*). **(b)** And it is according to this impression (<*kata*>

touto to pathos) that we are able to say that something white stands behind the motion in us (*hupokeitai kinoun hēmas*); and likewise, too, through touch and smell. **(c)** The impression is so-called from light; for just as light reveals (*deiknusi*) itself and the other things in its compass (*periechomena*), also impression reveals itself and what has made it. **(2)** On the other hand, an impressor (*phantaston*) is what produces an impression; for example, what is white, and what is cold, and everything able to move (*ho ti an dunētai kinein*) the soul, this is an impressor.

(Aëtius, 4.12.1–5 (39B))[16]

The faculty of *phantasia* is defined in A1a as affection revealing itself and what has made it, then illustrated by the paradigm case of seeing. Speaking generally, the work of *phantasia* is to receive information from the world, be impressed by it and produce particular impressions, or states of awareness in reaction to impressors that move the soul. Speaking more technically, *phantasia* is a state of awareness, in contrast to the raw sensory data before it reaches the mind. The language of *observing something white through sight* reflects this distinction, between the senses considered as arms of the octopus (*through sight*), and the awareness that takes place only at the *hēgemonikon* (*observing*).[17] I will make use of this distinction in my analysis with the terms *sensing* and *sensation* to refer to what takes place in the arms of the octopus and the sense organs (what is *through sight* and *through seeing*), *perceiving* and *perception* to refer to the impression that takes place in the *hēgemonikon* (*when we observe*), and *sense-perception* for sensory impressions specifically, as opposed to non-sensory impressions "obtained through thought (*dianoia*), like those of the incorporeals and of other things acquired by reason" (DL 7.51 (39A4).[18] The difference between sensation and perception lies in the animal's awareness of the impressor's information: the motion that carries raw sensory data from the organ to the *hēgemonikon* is not something the animal is aware of; the imprint it makes on the *hēgemonikon*, however, must be a case of awareness – given the psychic nature of the *hēgemonikon*, its affections can't fail to be cases of awareness. This is the force of defining *phantasia* in A1a as *pathos* revealing itself and what has made it; revealing is awareness. A1b then confirms that *phantasia* gives us cognitive access to the impressor that moved it, enabling us to say things about it. And A1c elucidates the reflexive dimension. I will take each in turn.

We can get a little clearer on our cognitive access to the impressor by looking at the mechanics of perception. The importance of impression understood as a corporeal *pathos* must not be underestimated; herein lies the transfer of information from impressor to soul.

B. They [the Stoics] say there are eight parts of soul: the five senses, the principles of procreation, the vocal faculty (*phonētikon*), and the reasoning faculty (*logistikon*) [i.e., the *hēgemonikon*]. Seeing is when the light between sight and what stands behind it (*tou hupokeimenou*) [the visual impressor, cf. A2] is stretched in the form of a cone.... The conical portion of air comes to be at the point of the eye, while the base is at what is seen; thus the thing seen is reported through the stretched air, like a walking stick.

(DL 7.157 (53N+))

The comparison to a walking stick illustrates that air is no less direct and corporeal a conduit to the *hēgemonikon* than a walking stick; both are conveying their information by touching. So even though the object of sight does not itself touch the eye, seeing remains direct in that the object moves the eyes via the medium of air, and the eyes convey that very motion to the *hēgemonikon*. The air and the walking stick are conduits but not intermediaries; and so too the portions of *pneuma* extending between *hēgemonikon* and sense organs are conduits, but not intermediaries. Crucially, neither is any particular *phantasia* an intermediary between the world and the person perceiving it, because the *phantasia* is nothing but a temporary state of the commanding faculty receiving it.

So, when an impressor strikes the senses it makes an impact that imparts information about itself to the sense organs, and when that motion reaches the *hēgemonikon*, the animal is aware of the impressor. The details of impact and transfer of information are hazy at best. However, we do know the Stoics embrace an analogy with wax being stamped and impressed to capture all the idiosyncrasies of a signet ring.[19] Crucially, the Stoics are not comparing the *hēgemonikon* itself with wax, but rather comparing the wax's taking on of all the ring's idiosyncrasies with the *hēgemonikon*'s taking on all of *its* impressors' idiosyncrasies.[20] Thus the mechanism by which the wax and soul take on their impressors' qualities is not the explicit point of comparison, and their being similarly sensitive to their impressors does not entail that the *hēgemonikon* is itself like wax in any further respect, nor that impressions are pictorial or imagistic in any literal way. Although the details of the mechanism elude us, it is clear that there is a direct transfer of information when the impressor strikes the sense organs, creating a motion in the soul that carries the information imprinted on it to the *hēgemonikon*, where it becomes a *pathos* revealing what has made it.[21]

Now we will turn to the reflexive dimension of *phantasia* revealing itself as well its impressor, illustrated in A1c in analogy with light revealing itself and what is in its compass. What is salient in the analogy is that light and *phantasia* both serve to *reveal* things, themselves and their objects. In the case of light, revealing is obviously to be understood as illumination, making things visible, so at face value the Stoics have said that light makes itself visible alongside the objects it illuminates. In the case of impression, revealing is to be understood as making aware, giving cognitive access to; so the analogy taken on its own terms dictates just that *phantasia* makes an animal aware of itself alongside its impressor.[22] Sextus Empiricus even makes it explicit that there are two things being grasped in *phantasia*: "one is the alteration itself, this is the *phantasia*; and the second is what made the alteration, and this is what is visible".[23] What sense can we make of this self-awareness? To begin with, we can say with A. A. Long that having an impression involves awareness of oneself as the locus of that impression.[24] This reflexive dimension of *phantasia* is a natural extension of an animal's self-perception present from birth.[25] Hierocles' *Elements of Ethics* is an important source of information about self-perception in the Stoic school, and here is how he puts it:

> C. (1) Since an animal is a composite (*suntheton*) of body and soul, and (2) both of these are tangible (*thikta*) and impressible (*prosblēta*) and of course subject to resistance (*prosereisei*), and also (3) blended through and through (*di' holōn kekratai*), and (4) one of them is a sensory faculty (*dunamis aisthētikon*) which itself undergoes movement in the way we have indicated, it is evident that an animal perceives itself continuously. For (5) by stretching out and relaxing, the soul strikes against (*prosballei*) all the body's parts, since it is blended with them all, and (6) in striking against the body it receives a striking in response. For the body, just like the soul, offers resistance (*antibatikon*); and the affection (*pathos*) that results (*apoteleitai*) is a joint pressure (*sunereistikon*) and resistance (*antereistikon*) in common (*homou*). (7) From the outermost parts, inclining in, it [sc. the *pathos*] travels . . . to the commanding faculty (*hēgemonikon*), with the result that there is an apprehension (*antilēpsin*) of all the body's parts as well as the soul's. This is equivalent to the animal perceiving (*aisthanesthai*) itself.
>
> (Hierocles, 4.38–53 (53B5–9))

Self-perception is defined as an affection in the soul, an inherently psychic *pathos* of the *hēgemonikon*, resulting from the reciprocal pressure of body and soul. The reciprocal nature of this *pathos* is what makes the impression reveal both itself and the impressor, two things. As Hierocles explains, (1) the body and soul are in contact; and (2) being corporeal, they can touch as agents, be impressed as patients, and in so doing offer resistance to each other. Thus (6) the soul strikes the body and thereby receives a blow in response, and the result is a single but joint event or activity shared by agent and patient. This much follows just from body and soul being in contact, as described in (1) and (2). The conclusion (7), that self-perception is *apprehension* of *all* the parts of body and soul, requires additional premises. Premises (3) and (5) establish blending as the kind of contact in question, which yields the *all* the conclusion; if soul and body were not in contact by total blending, there would be awareness of only the parts that make contact (as in an ordinary case of perception, where the impressor is an external object of perception). And Hierocles confirms this reading (at 4.4–11) when he tells us that blending is responsible for the joint affect (*sumpatheia*) being *total* for both body and soul (but not for its being joint). Premise (4) then secures that the joint *pathos* is a case of *apprehension* (i.e., awareness); because the patient is a sensory faculty (psychic by nature), its *pathos* is *eo ipso* a case of awareness.[26] More from Hierocles:

> **D.** For in general the apprehension (*antilēpsis*) of something external is not completed (*sunteleitai*) apart from perception of itself; for in common with (*meta*) perception of what is white, it bears saying that we also perceive ourselves being whitened (*leukainomenōn*) . . . with the result that since in all cases straight from birth the animal perceives something, and perception of something else is naturally conjoined (*sumpephuken*) with perception of itself, it is clear that from the start animals perceive themselves.
>
> (Hierocles, 6.3–10; cf. 6.17–22)

This passage makes clear that an impression requires for its completion a perception of the animal itself as undergoing something – it is not an impression without a reflexive component. And because self-perception in the sense of continuous self-awareness is itself a state of the rational soul (i.e., the patient of the striking), that self-perception is conjoined with the incoming information from the impressor. Just as the psychic nature of the *hēgemonikon* means its affections are cases of awareness, so too the *hēgemonikon*'s state of continuous self-perception makes its impressions reflexive. The preposition *meta* indicates the closeness of this relationship, echoing the force of *sumpephuken*, literally *grown together*, and *sunereistikon* in C6. So, while the impression is itself a second object of awareness alongside its impressor, the reflexive story is rather more nuanced than this. In the logical analysis of impression, there is only one impressor; but in the physical and psychological analysis, the *hēgemonikon* is aware of two things jointly: the impressor in relation to the self that is perceiving it. The impressor is the agent and hence the proper impressor, but the *pathos* is a joint product (*sumpatheia*) of agent and patient: impressor and soul together. The reflexive role of impression revealing itself is thus not to be confused with the role of direct impressor.

Nevertheless, the self (i.e., the animal's constitution or articulation) *can* serve as an impressor in its own right; in that case, the reflexive element remains in play and the story is no different. The animal perceives itself as impressor, such as by flapping its wings and focusing on how its wings or legs work, and in so doing has an impression that is a joint product of impressor (self) and impression (also self).[27] It is aware of the self in relation to itself: this is *my* constitution, these are *my* parts and their functions . . . this is *my* impression. Thus there are two senses of self-perception in play for the Stoics. First, the continuous joint *pathos* that is a contributing cause to every impression; this is the reflexive element of *phantasia*. Second, self-perception with the self (the animal's present constitution and articulation) in the role of impressor, conjoined with the reflexive element. Note that neither sense of self-perception entails that the world is revealed through *phantasia* as an intermediate entity. The animal is directly aware of two things in relation to each other, not one via the other. Thus *phantasia* is best characterized as direct, reflexive awareness of the world.

3. *Phantasia logikē*, the rational impression

Thus far I have avoided using the term *content*, usually speaking in terms of *information* that is conveyed, but it should be clear from my analysis that I take impressions to be quite content-*ful*. Indeed, insofar as an impression is a state of awareness, it is characterized precisely by its content – what is impressed. As we turn to the nature of the rational impression specifically, content will be front and center. The question now will be: in what does the content of the uniquely human rational impression consist? The short answer is that rational impressions have content expressible in words or language. What makes our utterances language, as opposed to mere vocal sound, is that they are significant (*sēmantikē*), and what is signified by the speaker and grasped by the rational hearer is a *lekton*.[28] As we will see, *lekta* are inextricable from rational impressions. The question then will be: what is the relation between rational impressions and *lekta*? We will begin with some passages describing the rational impression unique to humans.

> E. Further, among impressions, there are those that are rational (*logikai*) and those that are irrational (*alogoi*); and rational are those of the rational animals, while irrational are those of the irrational. Thus rational impressions are called thoughts (*noēseis*), while the irrational ones don't happen to have a name. And there are those that are expert and those that are inexpert; at any rate (*goun*), a statue (*eikōn*) is viewed one way by an expert and another way by a non-expert.
> (DL 7.51 (39A6–7); cf. Galen, *Def. med* (SVF 2.89))

> F. For the impression arises first (*proēgeitai*), and then thought, which has the power of speaking out (*eith' hē dianoia eklalētikē huparchousa*), expresses (*ekphereî*) in language (*logo(i)*) what it undergoes by (*ho paschei hupo*) the impression.
> (DL 7.49 (39A2/33D))

> G. They [sc. the Stoics] say that the *lekton* is what subsists (*to huphistamenon*) according to (*kata*) a rational impression (*logikē phantasia*), and a rational impression is one in which the content of the impression (*to phantasthen*) is expressible (*esti parastēsai*) in language (*logo(i)*).
> (SE, *M.* 8.70 (33C); cf. DL 7.63 (33F))

This sequence of passages shows that what is characteristic of humans is the rationality of their impressions, and that impressions are rational when they are thoughts whose contents can be expressed in words or language. One might even frame these passages as a syllogism: rational impressions are thoughts (E); thought is linguistic and semantic (F); therefore *lekta* (the Stoics' linguistic and semantic entities) subsist according to thought, the rational impression (G). Now, this much is uncontroversial, but only because it does not yet take a stand on what it means for the *lekton* to subsist according to, or *kata*, the rational impression (cf. A1b). Everyone agrees that *lekta* are the expressible content of rational impressions, but there is an important disagreement as to whether the *lekta* give otherwise semantically empty impressions their propositional content, or whether *lekta* owe their propositional content to the rational impressions according to which they subsist. We can sloganize the debate by asking whether rational impressions are conduits or causes of *lekta*.[29]

I avoided operating in terms of content because the term is laden with interpretive baggage, which it is now time to lay bare. The most basic presupposition about mental content is that it is propositional. This by itself says little, since everything hangs on what it means to be propositional; so let's accept it and see what comes out with different senses of *propositional*. One sense is practically axiomatic in the literature: to be propositional is to have content that is all and only from *lekta* construed as mind-independent entities (i.e., propositional content comes from thought grasping propositions).[30] It is a corollary of this view that sense-perception reports only bare sensory qualities (e.g., colors, shapes and sounds), which are not part of the propositional content, on the model of the wooden horse in Plato's *Theaetetus* (184–186). If all content comes from *lekta*, whatever else there is (including the sensory information from the wooden horse), it doesn't count as content. It is also a corollary of the view, that sense-perceptions are objects or inputs for reason construed as something distinct; the mind that thinks is aware of *phantasiai* as its objects. Since reason is what distinguishes humans from animals, it must be some part of soul in addition to the faculty of impression they have in common.

This picture first took hold with William and Martha Kneale, Jan Łukasiewicz, and Benson Mates who brought much insight and attention to Stoic logic in the mid-20th century. The philosophical currency of propositions is established there by reference to Frege, Carnap, Quine, Church, and others.[31] The *lekton* is thereby taken to be an independent semantic entity that gives our subjective and private thoughts their objective semantic content. Call this the de-psychologizing orthodoxy. Michael Frede, who did much to establish this picture as the orthodoxy, takes the view that impressions are the *way* that a *lekton* is perceived, but of themselves have no propositional content.[32] This assumption that all semantic content is from *lekta*, plays out in an ongoing debate over the status of non-rational impressions in animals and children. This debate is thought to be instructive on an Aristotelian-style assumption that since animals and humans have impression in common, their impressions must be the same (on the wooden horse model, corollary one) and reason must be something further receiving those impressions (corollary two). So if we can get clear on what goes in animals and children, we'll know about the added ingredient of reason as well.[33] The problem facing the orthodox view is that if all mental content is propositional and conceptual, then it looks like animals and children (since they are classified as irrational) cannot have mental contents, only the bare sensory qualities of the wooden horse; but these are not sufficient to explain complex animal behavior. Thus one solution is to say that content can be propositional without being conceptual, in which case children and animals can have articulable mental contents sufficient to explain behavior without having to grasp that content.[34] This is an unfortunate choice: either animals and children have mental content without being able to grasp it, or they have no mental content at all. My suggestion is that this is a false dichotomy resting on the mistaken axiom and corollaries of the de-psychologizing orthodoxy. So, I propose to suspend the axiom that semantic content only comes from *lekta* and see where it leads when we take our inquiry to the texts and read the Stoics on their own terms. We will begin with Sextus.

> **H.** They say that the human does not differ from irrational animals in respect of uttered speech (*prophoriko(i) logo(i)*) (for crows and parrots and jays utter articulate sounds), but in respect of internal speech (*endiatheto(i)*), nor merely by the simple impression (for these too have impressions) but by the transitive (*metabatikē(i)*) and synthetic (*sunthetikē(i)*) impression. Wherefore (*dioper*), having the conception of implication (*akolouthias ennoian echōn*), straightaway one also grasps the thought of a sign, through implication; for, that is, the sign itself is such: "if this, then that." Therefore the fact that there are signs also (*to kai sēmeion huparchein*) follows from (*hepetai*) the nature and constitution (*kataskeuē(i)*) of the human being.
> (SE, *M*. 8.275–6 (53T); cf. *M*. 8.285, *PH* 1.65)

Sextus reports that humans differ from animals in two ways: internal speech and rational impressions. First, it is not the actual proffering of speech that makes us different from animals, but *endiathetos logos*, which we can think of as the ability to make statements to oneself.[35] This gap between impression and utterance where internal discourse takes place is what gives us the uniquely human control over assent and impulse, in contrast to blue jays that utter articulate cries as an automatic response to their impressions.[36] Origen confirms this picture when he reports that the rational animal "has reason that passes judgment on impressions (*logon . . . ton krinonta tas phantasias*), rejecting some of these and accepting others, in order that the animal may be guided according to them [sc. those they accept]".[37] Passing judgment on impressions does not signal that the mind takes impressions as its objects on a wooden horse model, but rather that there is a gap between perception and assent where reflection and deliberation take place. This is self-perception in the second sense described previously, not merely reflexive but with the self in the role of impressor. Indeed, examination of our impressions is the most important kind of self-perception because it is for the sake of evaluating the way we see the world, analyzing our seeings before owning them with our assent. In this gap we have the opportunity to evaluate and examine our impressions before passing judgment, choosing the *lekton* we assent to and becoming responsible for the resulting impulse and action. Epictetus calls it *parakolouthia* and even personifies the process for rhetorical effect: "Wait for me a bit, *phantasia*; let me see who you are and what are about, let me test you".[38] Given this gap between impression and assent, there must be something about the rational impression that makes it available for this kind of examination prior to assenting to a *lekton*.

And this is precisely the other thing differentiating us from animals: because impressions are rational they can be examined and evaluated. Sextus explains that our impressions are transitive, literally moving from one place to another (*metabatikē*), and constructive or compositional (*synthetikē*). We can capture this point by saying they are discursive: being *metabatikē* signals that rational impressions are inferential, and being *synthetikē* signals that they are compositional – they are *seeings as* (as I will put it).[39] And this is to say that rational impressions are conceptual and thus propositional. To see something as F is to predicate a concept of it; and since Stoic concepts are analyzed as conditionals, seeing as is inherently inferential.[40] The rational impression, being discursive, thus looks quite content-*ful*, with precisely the kind of content whose implications can be evaluated and selected for assent or rejection. Here we see how the rational impression is at the heart of Stoic moral psychology, as the foundation of *oikeiosis* and *prohairesis*, and the lynchpin of their compatibilist ethics, as the one thing in the cosmos over which we have control. So, to summarize, the content of the rational impression is inherently inferential, conceptual, semantic, and linguistic – that is, propositional.[41] Thus, with the benefit of passage H, we see an alternative sense of *propositional* emerging, which does not make reference to propositions grasped as independent objects of thought.[42] We see an alternative axiom emerging as well: the content of the rational impression is in the impression. That is why they are called thoughts (E).

With the help of Cicero's *Acad.* 2.21, we can also see an alternative to the first corollary, the wooden horse model of perception. This passage has been of interest in the animal minds debate, as a sort of loophole to ascribe enough content to animals to account for their behavior without giving them full-fledged rationality. But with the axiom that mental content comes all and only from *lekta* suspended, there is no reason to seek this loophole. Denying *lekta* to animals need not deny them any mental content whatsoever, nor does it give any reason to think that sense-impressions merely provide raw sensory data.

> I. Those characteristics that belong to those things we say are perceived (*percipi*) by the senses (*sensibus*) are equally characteristic of that further set of things said to be perceived not by the senses themselves (*ipsis*) but by them in a certain respect (*quodam modo*), e.g. "That is white," "This is sweet," "That is melodious," "This is fragrant," "This is bitter." We have comprehension (*tenemus conprehensa*) of these by the mind now

(*animo iam*), not the senses. Next (*deinceps*), "That is a horse," "That is a dog." The rest of the series follows next, connecting greater things that are as if to encompass a complete comprehension of things: "If it is a human, it is a mortal, rational animal." From this class [sc. of things perceived by the mind] conceptions (*notitiae*) of things are imprinted (*imprimuntur*) on us, without which there can be no understanding (*intellegi*) nor discussion (*disputari*) of anything (*quicquam*).
(Cicero, *Acad.* 2.21 (39C))

Those things perceived by the senses themselves are colors, tastes, and sounds et al. that get communicated to the soul by the sense organs; this is the raw sensory data. These colors, tastes, and sounds are *equally characteristic of* (i.e., still present when those things are registered by the senses *in a certain respect*, such as predicatively, *as* white, sweet, or melodious). The idea here is that the sensory content delivered by the arms of the octopus persists and in that respect is equally characteristic of the content of the impression when it strikes the *hēgemonikon* and is seen as F. The force of saying these are comprehended by the mind *now* is to signal the awareness that takes place once the sensory impact reaches the *hēgemonikon* from the arms of the octopus – the mind, but not the walking stick will be aware of the impressor as F. So much is confirmed by Sextus:

For what grasps the truth in those things underlying (*hupokeimenois*) [sc. the impressors, A1b] must not only be moved in a white manner (*leukantikōs*) or a sweet manner (*glukantikōs*), but also be led (*achthēnai*) to an impression of such a thing that "This is white" and "This is sweet."
(*M.* 7.344, cf. 7.293)

Sextus goes on to confirm that this is no longer the job of sense because sense grasps only color, flavor and sound, but cannot grasp "This is white." Thus I take the idea that the mind grasps what the senses offer *in a certain respect* to indicate that rational impressions are inherently conceptual, echoing Sextus' description of them as synthetic and inferential. I do not find the wooden horse model in this passage, taking impressions to report only bare sensory qualities to thought as something distinct. Rather, taking the testimony that rational impressions are thoughts (E) at face value, I find the alternative corollary that impressions are inherently conceptual states of mind, which I have sloganized as: *all seeing is seeing as*.

An alternative to the second corollary that mind, or thought is something distinct that takes impressions as its inputs, is also discernible in Cicero's testimony. This passage is in fact describing the Stoics' developmental account of rationality, according to which reason is constituted by the concepts we acquire through experience.[43] For the Stoics, humans have *logos*, or reason, from birth; it is the faculty or capacity for rationality, which develops gradually through our interactions with the world. The Stoics are akin to modern empiricists in this regard, starting us with a tabula rasa "fit for writing upon," and equating our rationality with the concepts we write on it.[44] The initial development of rationality consists in our basic concept acquisition, first of preconceptions that arise naturally from the world, and then conceptions, which are a function of study, art and convention.[45] Thus, in passage I, we begin to get rationalized with basic sensory concepts like white, sweet, melodious, fragrant, and bitter; next we move to kinds like horse and dog. Then we move from basic predication to connecting our concepts together and appreciating their inferential import, as in: *If something is a human, then it is a mortal, rational animal*. The human soul is considered rational once it has acquired a complete stock of concepts from experience, and a proper grasp of their inferential import. Only then is a person considered to have voice; that is, to be a reliable language user who understands the meanings of her words and is responsible for her actions. Only then do our impressions become thoughts.

It is important to appreciate the full force of this point, that impression *are* thoughts. I said earlier that the psychic nature of the *hēgemonikon* (the kind of *poion* that it is) makes the impressor's imprint result in a case of awareness, a *pathos* that reveals itself and its cause. Further, that the state of continuous self-perception (the *poion pōs echon*) makes every impression reflexive. Now, by that same token, we can appreciate that the rationalized state of the human *hēgemonikon* makes the *pathos* propositional in addition. The habituated state of the *hēgemonikon* (*pōs echon*) determines how the incoming information is conceived (i.e., how the patient is affected). And the way the patient is affected is what is impressed (*to phantasthen*), that is, the content of the rational impression that is expressible in words. So, in answer to the first question posed in this section, in what does the content of the rational impression consist, the answer is this: incoming information from the impressor, as it is conceived. This is not two steps or two components, but one. Another way to put my point is to say that I reject the distinction between *character* and *content*; the content of an impression just is the incoming information, the way it is conceived.

This idea that the state or disposition of a person's soul determines the content of the rational impression is confirmed by the Stoic account of expertise. Earlier, in passage E, rational impressions were subdivided into expert and inexpert. Let's take this at face value and ask what it means for a rational impression to be expert. We know that the Stoics explicitly categorize expertise (e.g., having the art of medicine or, ideally, the art of life) as a tenor (*hexis*) of soul, and so a *pōs echon*. Further, that "expertise is a system [developed] out of (*ek*) cognitions (*katalēpseōn*) in joint training (*sunggegumnasmenōn*) relative to some goal useful in life".[46] To be an expert, then, is to have developed one's rationality with care and attention to some goal. Just as basic human rationality is constituted by the development of our preconceptions and conceptions from our interactions with the world, so expertise is just a further habituation or training of the *hēgemonikon* with a certain end in mind, say carpentry, medicine, or virtue (the art of life). As the preposition *ek* signals, expertise is not a new ingredient or part of soul, but soul itself disposed in a certain way – *pneuma* that is maximally sensitive to the world's maximal intelligibility and detail, just as the comparison with wax dictates.

Julia Annas finds it puzzling that the impression itself is characterized as expert or inexpert and suggests an interpretive dilemma.[47] On the first model, the expert and the non-expert have the same *phantasiai* with the same content at step one, but assent to different *lekta* at step two because they only take in or accept part of the information contained in the impression. On this picture, the information contained in the *phantasia* is raw sensory data (on the wooden horse model) and step two marks the introduction of conceptual or propositional content. On the second model, the expert and inexpert have different *phantasiai* with different content, but there is no distinction to be made between perception and assent, only a distinction between the striking of the sense organ (step zero) and what happens at the *hēgemonikon* (step one = step two). Annas, stumped, finds no reason to prefer either horn of the dilemma. But notice that the dichotomy rests on the orthodox assumption that the *lekton* assented to contains the content of the *phantasia*. If *phantasiai* only have content derivatively in virtue of grasping an external, independent *lekton*, experts and inexperts can only differ in these two ways: either they have the same raw, non-conceptual data (same *phantasiai*) and assent subsequently to different *lekta*, or they have different *phantasiai* with different conceptual content and *eo ipso* assent to different *lekta*. With the orthodoxy suspended, however, there is no reason to accept Annas' dichotomy.

Rather, a natural alternative emerges that takes the expert and inexpert to have different *phantasiai* with different content at step one and sees assent (step two) as a distinct phase of cognition on the other side of internal discourse. The world in all its specificity makes a causal impact (*tupōsis*) on our sensory apparatus (step zero); this much is the same in everyone, expert and inexpert alike (assuming comparable eyesight, e.g., neither needs glasses). Then, in analogy with the walking stick, the *tupōsis* imprinted with the impressor's information travels up the arms of the octopus to the *hēgemonikon*, where it becomes a *phantasia*. This is step one, and it is not the same in the expert and inexpert, because their souls are differently habituated and so they receive the information differently. An expert soul is sensitive to more of the incoming information, capable of seeing more than the novice. When an arborist looks at a certain tree, she sees a silver birch at a particular stage of its life, in some determinate state of health, etc. I see a tree. When an artist looks at a painting, she sees scale, composition, brush strokes, media, and technique, reading the creative process off the canvas. I see a painting. We see the same painting, and we have the same incoming sensory data, but we do not see it the same way. As Cicero puts it just before telling us that things are perceived by the senses *in a certain respect* (*Acad.* 2.20): "How many things painters see in shadows and in the foreground which we do not see!" The content of an expert's impression (the expert's seeing as) is different from the non-expert's because the expert soul is habituated by experience and art, a collection of inferential conceptions and maximal sensitivity to detail. There is thus a wealth of content in the expert's rational impression, which cannot be captured by any one simple *lekton*.

This is why impressions are neither objects of thought for a separate mind (corollary 2) nor reporters of mere sensory data on a wooden horse model (corollary 1), but thoughts about their impressor – thick with conceptual and inferential content resulting from the impressor making an impact on the *hēgemonikon*.[48]

4. *Phantasia logikē*, source of *lekta*

We now turn to the second question raised earlier in the chapter, what is the relation between the rational impression and the *lekton*? What does the preposition *kata* convey when we are told that the *lekton* subsists *according to* the rational impression (A1b, F)? The order of explanation in passages F and G already suggests that *lekta* depend on the rational impression: F says, first we have an impression, then we express its content (by uttering *lekta*);[49] G says, *lekta* subsist according to the rational impression, because the rational impression has the content to give them their subsistence.[50] More concretely, in passage H after telling us that humans have internal discourse and rational impressions, Sextus goes on to infer (and reiterate at 8.285) that the existence of conditionals follows from the human nature and constitution. Given that conditionals are composed of *lekta*, this conclusion amounts to an explicit claim that *lekta* depend on rational impressions as prior semantically (since they have conceptual content of themselves) and ontologically (the fact that there are conditionals follows from the rational impression).

We can add to this now the explicit testimony that *lekta* arise out of (*ek*),[51] that is, from and in consequence (*parhuphistamenon*)[52] of the rational impression. Further, Sextus tells us at *M.* 8.80 that for the Stoics speaking (*legein*) is uttering voice that signifies the subject matter in mind (*to tēn tou nooumenou pragmatos semantikē propheresthai phōnēn*). Likewise, Diogenes reports that "language is semantic voice (*phōnē sēmantikē*) sent forth from thought (*ekpempomenē apo dianoias*)".[53] Galen also lays bare the Stoic commitment to the dependence of *lekta* on thought, quoting Zeno, Diogenes of Babylon, and Chrysippus on this point: mind is the source of language. Following is the quote he attributes to Chrysippus, telling us explicitly, that words receive their meaning from thought.

> **J.** [16] It is reasonable (*eulogon*) that that in which (*eis ho*) the meanings at that point (*hai en touto(i) sēmasiai*) come to be and out of which discourse (*logos*) comes to be, is the ruling (*kurieuon*) part of soul. For the source (*pēgē*) of [internal] discourse (*logos*) is none other than thought (*dianoias*), and the source of voice (*phōnēs*) none other than [internal] discourse, and [i.e.,] (*kai*) on the whole, simply, the source of voice is none other than the ruling part of soul. . . . [18] For on the whole, whence (*hothen*) discourse (*logos*) issues must be where (*ekeise*) reasoning (*dialogismos*), thinkings (*dinanoeseis*) and preparations (*meletas*) of linguistic expressions (*rēseiōn*) come to be, just as I said. [19] And these things

228

clearly come to be around the heart, both voice and [public] discourse issuing from the heart through the windpipe.

(Galen, *PHP* 2.5.16–20)[54]

Here is a breakdown of the passage: (16) the commanding faculty is where meanings and discourse (*logos*) come to be. Why? First, because internal discourse has its source in thought, and voice has its source in internal discourse; therefore (simply put) voice comes from the *hēgemonikon* (where thought takes place).[55] (18) Second, because the source of discourse *must be* (i.e., on principle) the place of reasoning and thinking, and where words are imbued with meaning. Diogenes of Babylon confirms: "discourse is sent forth having been imprinted (*ensesēmasmenon*) and in a way stamped (*hoion ektetupōmenon*) by conceptions in the mind" (Galen, *PHP* 2.5.12). Thus we see that the mind-dependence of *lekta* is attested by a wide variety of sources: a hostile skeptic, neutral doxographer, fussy Platonizing physician, and now in a grammatical context by Ammonius, head of the neoplatonist school in Alexandria:

K. The Stoics reply [to the peripatetic] that the nominative case itself has fallen (*peptōken*) from thought (*apo noēmatos*), which is in the soul. For when we wish to reveal (*dēlōsai*) the thought of Socrates that we have in ourselves, we utter (*propherometha*) the name Socrates [i.e., Socrates in the nominative case]. Therefore, just as a pen is said both to have fallen and to have its fall upright if it is released from above and sticks upright, so we claim that the nominative case [literally 'the direct case'] falls from thought (*apo tēs ennoias*), but is upright because it is the archetype of meaningful utterance (*tēs kata tēn ekphonēsin prophoras*).

(Ammonius, *In Ar. De int.* 43,9–15 (33K))[56]

Jonathan Barnes has objected to taking this (and a plethora of other texts connecting *lekta* with thoughts) as evidence of Stoic semantic theory. He urges that passage K expresses no more than the commonplace that producing someone's name is a good way of telling someone who you are thinking about, and cautions that

[e]ven if Ammonius in this passage is referring to the Old Stoa (which is not clear), and even if he is reporting Stoic views with fidelity (which cannot be taken for granted), nevertheless his report has nothing to do with any theory of meaning. In general, we should not read philosophical theories into platitudes.

(Barnes 1993, p.54)

As a founder of the de-psychologizing orthodoxy, Barnes' dogma should be taken with a grain of salt. It is doubtful that Ammonius spends his time rehearsing platitudes rather than theory. Further, his caution about platitudes cuts both ways, since it is equally important that we not allow philosophical theories to upend platitudes, in this case to upend the wealth of clear textual evidence attesting to the mind-dependence of *lekta*.

For example, Barnes writes off Galen's testimony as a physiological comment about the windpipe, which says nothing about words receiving their meaning from thought; then he adds, even if we do have to read this evidence as establishing that thinking causes speaking, it is obviously false that speech is caused by thought because we sometimes speak unreflectively (i.e., without thinking). But the fact that we sometimes speak unreflectively is hardly a counterexample to the general claim that human voice is made semantic by thought. And Barnes' dismissal of Sextus' testimony at 8.80 as telling us that voice is significant because the *pragma* it has in mind is just a *lekton* is circular: presupposing that rational impressions have semantic content only because they grasp independent *lekta*. The scarcity of our textual evidence makes every passage precious, so Barnes' summary dismissal of a dozen different passages connecting *lekta* with thoughts is not to be taken lightly. Tossing so much evidence aside is a steep price to pay for any interpretation.[57] However, my point is not just that the cost is too high, but that the expense is artificial. With the axiom suspended, there is no need to dismiss all this textual evidence, or to fall on the horns of false dichotomies.

5. Conclusion

Taken on its own terms, the Stoic rational impression reveals a rich philosophy of mind driven by content. The rational impression is a state of the rational mind, the human *hēgemonikon* rationalized by experience. It gives us direct cognitive access to the world (as the image of the walking stick suggests), conjoined with self-perception. Being an affection of rational soul, it is inherently propositional and thick with content for internal discourse. We can now see how many ways rational impressions are at the heart of Stoic philosophy of mind. First, to have a mind just is to have rational impressions; Stoic psychology is entirely monistic and cognitive through and through, paving the way to an austere Socratic intellectualism. Second, to be subject to internal discourse is to be able to engage in the most important kind of self-perception, *parakolouthēsis*: the ability to put the impressor in the role of impression to see what it tells us about ourselves. Third, for rational impressions to be subject to internal discourse is also to have control over our assents, actions and state of character, and thus to have both moral responsibility and hope for moral improvement; here we find the famous doctrine of *oikeiosis*. Further, the fact that rational impressions are direct and reflexive states of awareness has implications for Stoic epistemology; it will be clear already to the initiated that my account of rational impressions will psychologize the cataleptic impression, in contrast to externalist readings that are part and parcel of the orthodoxy I have been describing. Finally, because rational impressions are thick with propositional content, they are the source of *lekta*: causes not conduits. Thus we can see how the Stoic philosophy of mind reaches across ethics, epistemology and into logic. To define *logikē phantasia* as an impression whose content can be expressed in words is to get to the very heart of the human mind: we are above all the language animal, and *lekta* are the currency of agency, knowledge and rationality.[58]

Notes

1 With the exception of Barnouw (2002)
2 Sextus Empiricus (SE), *M.* 8.70 (33C), passage G later; parenthetical citations like 33C refer to Long & Sedley (1987) by chapter (33) and order therein (C).
3 Nemesius 78,7–79,2 (45C), 81,6–10 (45D).
4 SE, *M.* 11.22–26 (60G); Stobaeus 2.70,21–71,4 (60L), 2.73,1–13 (60J); Simplicius, *In Ar. Cat.* 212,12–213,1 (28N).
5 Alexander, *In Ar. Top.* 301,19–25 (27B); SE, *M.* 1.17 (27C); Galen, *Meth. med.* 10.155,1–8 (27G). I will often transliterate Greek terms to avoid awkward English, here *lekton* (singular) and *lekta* (plural); alternate translations of *lekton* include *what is said, what is meant, thing said, articulable, meaning*.
6 As Quine (1948) terms the problem of non-being; cf. de Harven (2015) and Vogt (2009).
7 Annas (1992, pp. 50–56) and Long (1999, p. 564, 1982, pp. 34–36 & 44, contra Bonhoffer and Pohlenz).
8 Nemesius 70,6–71,4 (47J).
9 Annas (1992, pp. 51, 50–56).
10 Nemesius 291,1–6 (53O); Philo, *Leg. alleg.* 1.30 (53P), 2.22–3 (47P); Hierocles 1.5–33, 4.38–53 (53B); Galen, *Intr.* 14.726,7–11 (47N).
11 I follow Long & Sedley in describing these as metaphysical *aspects* under which an object can be considered, although I am not entirely satisfied with the term; cf. Menn (1999), Rist (1971), Sedley (1982), and Sorabji (1988).
12 SE, *M.* 7.232, 7.234 (53F); Calcidius 220 (53G); Annas (1992, p. 63); Long (1982, p. 239).
13 Aëtius 4.21.1–4 (53H); Calcidius 220 (53G); DL 7.157 (passage B); Long (1982, p. 51); Sedley (1993, pp. 330–331).
14 For the relevant notion of self see Annas (1992, pp. 58–59, & 64), Inwood (1984, pp. 162–164), and Long (1991, p. 107 & 1999), all of which I take to be compatible with cautions from Gill (2006).
15 This vexed term has been translated many different ways, as *appearance, image, representation, presentation, impression*, and others. Although I will often transliterate *phantasia* (singular) and *phantasiai* (plural), I have chosen *impression* as the most phenomenologically neutral translation, which also captures the literalness of the impact of the world on soul and aptly conjures the empiricism of the modern era.
16 This is part of a fourfold analysis comparing *phantasia* and its objects, impressors, with imagination and its objects, apparitions.
17 Galen, *PHP* 2.5.35–36 (de Lacy); Aëtius 4.23.1 (53M); Hierocles 4.38–53 (53B5–9); cf. Long (1982, pp. 47–48 & 95–97) and Annas (1992, pp. 62–63 & 85) for comparison to the brain and central nervous system.
18 The account I give will proceed in terms of sensory impressions and often just in terms of vision, which are the paradigm cases of impression, but everything I say is meant to be applicable to non-sensory impressions as well, with the soul acting as corporeal agent to generate the *pathos* by being impressed in relation to (*epi*) things with a nature like the incorporeals (what is intelligible, vs. sensible), as reported in SE, *M.* 8.409 (27E).
19 SE, *M.* 7.251 (40E3).
20 As Chrysippus' resistance to overextending the analogy confirms, DL 7.50 (39A3).
21 Cf. Inwood (1984, pp. 161–164) and Sedley (1993, pp. 330–331) for confirmation that no gap is possible between body and soul.

22 Note that the causal direction is reversed in these two cases: light makes itself and the things it illuminates visible, but *phantasia* does not make the world intelligible; this difference does not undermine, but rather reinforces what is salient in the analogy.
23 SE, *M.* 7.162.
24 Long (1982, p. 47).
25 Seneca, *Ep.* 121.6–15 (57B), Hierocles 1.34–9, 51–7, 2.1–9 (57C); cf. Long (1982 & 1991, p. 107) on self-perception, and (1993, p. 96) for a comparison of self-perception to proprioception.
26 Thus Reed (2002) cannot be right in relegating the impression to a bodily precondition for awareness and thought, something we are aware of only indirectly via the impressor.
27 Hierocles 6.50–7.9, where the self is even described as an *aisthēton*, an object of sense-perception.
28 SE, *M.* 8.11–12 (33B); DL 7.57 (33A).
29 I do not intend the word *cause* in the technical Stoic sense, which requires all causes to be capable of action and passion; by cause I mean source, or grounding body.
30 Cf. Brittain (2002) as the notable exception to Annas (1992), Barnes (1993, 1999), Caston (1999, unpublished), Frede (1987), Inwood (1985), Lesses (1998), Mates (1961), Sedley (1993), and Sorabji (1990).
31 See especially Mates (1961, pp. 19–26).
32 Cf. Frede (1987, p. 156).
33 Cf. Brittain (2002, pp. 256–257) and Lesses (1998, pp. 1–3) for perspicuous summaries of the issues.
34 As Caston (unpublished) and Sorabji (1990) suggest; note here the seeds of epistemic externalism, which is a related orthodoxy established by Annas (1990), Frede (1987), Striker (1974); cf. Nawar (2014) and Perin (2005) for recent defenses of internalism.
35 As Long (1971, p. 88) puts it; cf. Gourinat (2013) for additional texts and valuable cautions against assimilating Stoic *endiathetos logos* to the Platonic notion more akin to internal dialogue than declamation (*diexodos*).
36 This point may be put either in terms of denying assent to animals and introducing it only with humans, or granting animals assent but calling it voluntary only with humans; cf. Brittain (2002, p. 257, n. 10).
37 Origen, Princ. 3.1.3 (53A5); cf. Calcidius 220 (53G).
38 Epictetus, Diss. 2.18.24–26.
39 As Bury (1935) translates, they are *transitive* and *constructive*; cf. also Long (1971, p. 87 and n. 54). For synthesis as combination, see DL 7.53; SE, *M.* 8.60; Cicero, *Fin.* 3.33–34 (60D).
40 SE, *M.* 11.8–11 (30I); this paraphrasing move is how the Stoics eliminate concepts from the ontology (cf. Caston (1999)).
41 I will now use these terms interchangeably – with the axiom suspended, priority among them is not material.
42 I take this sense to be akin to Brittain (2002) and Lesses (1998).
43 Galen, *PHP* 5.2.49, 5.3.1 (53V).
44 Aëtius 4.11.1–4 (39E); cf. Long (1982, p. 51) for whom *logos* is not one faculty among others, but the *mode* of the whole soul's operation.
45 I am in agreement with Sandbach (1930, contra Bonhoffer), that *prolēpseis* are not innate ideas; cf. Henry Dyson for a more recent defense of such Platonizing.
46 Olympiodorus, *In Plat. Gorg.* 12.1 (42A). Cf. also Stobaeus 2.73,1–13 (60J); Cicero, *Acad.* 2.22 (42B); Plutarch, *Virt. mor.* 440E–441D (61B).
47 Annas 1992, pp. 82–83.
48 Cf. Long (1991, pp. 109–110) who speaks of rational impressions as thick with content and potential judgments; Caston (unpublished) has recently called into question the thin notion of content and passive model of mind, but he remains committed to

the orthodox axiom and thus differs only in requiring more propositions to imbue the impression with its full content
49 This priority is not merely temporal; immediate context (not quoted) shows that this order explains the priority of rational impression to assent, knowledge and reasoning.
50 Others in the current minority that favors mind-dependence include Imbert (1978), Long (1971, 1991, 1999, 2006), and Nuchelmans (1973).
51 DL 7.43; Barnes (1993, p. 56) does cop to the "lameness" of dismissing this piece of testimony as generally confused in order to work around the obvious language of dependence.
52 SE, *M.* 8.11–12 (33B); Sryianus *In Ar. meta.* 105,25–30; Lloyd (1985) has argued nicely that *parhuphistamenon*, which is also used to describe the relation of the incorporeal, place, to its occupying body, signals strong dependence, a parasitic relation between the *lekton* and rational impression.
53 DL 7.56; cf. 7.55 (33H+).
54 Reading en *touto(i)* adverbially in the sense of *at that point in time/place* (LSJ IV), corresponding to *ensēmainesthai* in 20, confirmed by *ekeithen* (thence) in 20, and *hothen* in 18; attributive position signals that they become semantic at that very point; I am grateful to David Crane for discussion of this passage.
55 I disambiguate *logos* as *internal* or *external* (i.e., *public*) discourse based on context: the salient contrast is between discourse arising in thought, on the one hand, and voice on the other; since voice, which is clearly public, has its source in discourse – it must be some other kind, namely internal discourse; therefore, on the assumption that being a source is transitive, the source of voice is the commanding faculty, where thoughts happen and meanings come to be.
56 Translation Long & Sedley with modifications; for argument that *ptōseis* should be considered elements of *lekta*, alongside predicates, see M. Frede (1987); cf. Long (1971) for the opposite position.
57 And the nonchalance of Barnes' approach hardly makes the cost easier to bear; after summarily dismissing five different texts unfriendly to his view, he offers no more defense than the following imaginary exchange in a footnote: " 'So we should discard most of the texts which inform us about Stoic sayables?' -Yes. – 'Surely that is not methodologically defensible?' -Yes; it is."
58 I am indebted to Victor Caston, Jean-Baptiste Gourinat, and A. A. Long for helpful conversations about this material, as well as to Verity Harte and my fellow participants in the *JHP* 2014 Master Class.

Bibliography

Annas, J. (1990) Stoic epistemology. In Everson, S. (ed.) *Epistemology, Companions to Ancient Thought*, 1. Cambridge, MA: Cambridge University Press.

———. (1992) *Hellenistic Philosophy of Mind*. Berkeley: University of California Press.

Barnes, J. (1978) Principles of stoic grammar. In Rist, J. M. (ed.) *The Stoics*. Berkeley: University of California Press, pp. 27–75.

———. (1993) Meaning, saying and thinking. In Döring, K., and Ebert, T. (eds.) *Dialektiker und Stoiker: Zur Logik der Stoa und ihrer Vorläufer, Philosophie der Antike*. 1. Stuttgart: F. Steiner.

———. (1999) Meaning. In Algra, K., Barnes, J., Mansfeld, J., and Schofield, M. (eds.) *Hellenistic Philosophy*. Cambridge, MA: Cambridge University Press.

Barnouw, J. (2002) *Propositional Perception: Phantasia, Predication, and Sign in Plato, Aristotle, and the Stoics*. Lanham, MD: University Press of America.

Brittain, C. (2002) Non-rational perception in the Stoics and Augustine. *Oxford Studies in Ancient Philosophy* 22: 253–308.

Bury, R. G. (1967) *Sextus Empiricus: Against the logicians*. Vol. 2. Cambridge, MA: Loeb Classical Library, Harvard University Press.

Caston, V. (Unpublished) *The Metaphysics of Stoic Representation*. Presented at The Metaphysics of the Stoics: Causes, Principles, and Mereology. Corpus Christi College, Oxford, June 23, 2015.

———. (1999) Nothing and something: The stoics on concepts and universals. *Oxford Studies in Ancient Philosophy* 17: 145–213.

de Harven, V. (2015) How nothing can be something: The stoic theory of void. *Ancient Philosophy* 35 (2): 1–25.

Dyson, H. (2009) *Prolepsis and Ennoia in the Early Stoa*. Berlin: Walter de Gruyter.

Frede, M. (1987) Stoics and skeptics on clear and distinct impressions. In *Essays in Ancient Philosophy*. Minneapolis: University of Minnesota Press.

———. (1994) The stoic notion of a 'lekton'. In Everson, S. (ed.) *Language, Companions to Ancient Thought: 3*. Cambridge, MA: Cambridge University Press.

Gill, C. (2006) Epictetus: A new subjective-individualist self? In *The Structured Self in Hellenistic and Roman Thought*. Oxford: Oxford University Press.

Gourinat, J. B. (2000) *La dialectique des stoïciens*. Paris: Vrin.

———. (2013) Le discours intérieur de l'âme dans la philosophie stoïcienne. *Chôra: Revue d'études anciennes et médiévales* 11: 11–22.

Graeser, A. (1978) *The stoic theory of meaning*. In Rist, J. M. (ed.) *The Stoics*. Berkeley: University of California Press.

Hicks, R. D. (1925) *Diogenes Laertius: Lives of Eminent Philosophers*. Cambridge, MA: Loeb Classical Library, Harvard University Press.

Imbert, C. (1978) Théorie de la représentation et doctrine logique dans le stoïcisme ancien. In Brunschwig, J. (ed.) *Les Stoïciens et leur logique*. Paris: Vrin.

Inwood, B. (1984) Hierocles: Theory and argument in the second century AD. *Oxford Studies in Ancient Philosophy*: 151–184.

———. (1985) *Ethics and Human Action in Early Stoicism*. Oxford: Oxford University Press.

Kneale, W., and Kneale, M. (1962) *The Development of Logic*. Oxford: Oxford University Press.

Lesses, G. (1998) Content, cause and stoic impressions. *Phronesis* 43 (1): 1–25.

Lloyd, A. C. (1985) Parhypostasis in Proclus. In Boss, G., and Seel, G. (eds.) *Proclus et son influence, actes du colloque de Neuchâtel*. Zürich: GMB Editions du Grand Midi.

Long, A. A. (1971) Language and thought in stoicism. In Long, A. A. (ed.) *Problems in Stoicism*. London: The Athlone Press.

———. (1982) Soul and body in stoicism. *Phronesis* 27: 34–57.

———. (1991) Representation and the self in stoicism. In Everson, S. (ed.) *Psychology, Companions to Ancient Thought: 2*. Cambridge, MA: Cambridge University Press.

———. (1993) Hierocles on 'oikeiosis' and self-perception. In Boudouris, K. (ed.) *Hellenistic Philosophy*. Athens.

———. (1999) Stoic psychology. In Algra, K., Barnes, J., Mansfeld, J., and Schofield, M. (eds.) *Hellenistic Philosophy*. Cambridge, MA: Cambridge University Press.

———. (2006) Stoic psychology and the elucidation of language. In *From Epicurus to Epictetus: Studies in Hellenistic and Roman Philosophy*. Oxford: Oxford University Press.

Long, A. A., and Sedley, D. N. (1987) *The Hellenistic Philosophers*. Cambridge, MA: Cambridge University Press.

Łukasiewicz, J. (1951) *Aristotle's Syllogistic from the Standpoint of Modern Logic*. Oxford: Clarendon Press.
Mates, B. (1961) *Stoic Logic*. Berkeley: University of California Press.
Menn, S. (1999) The stoic theory of categories. *Oxford Studies in Ancient Philosophy* 17: 215–247.
Nawar, T. (2014) The stoic account of apprehension. *Philosopher's Imprint* 14 (29): 1–21.
Nuchelmans, G. (1973) *Theories of the Proposition*. Amsterdam: North-Holland Publishing Co.
Perin, C. (2005) Stoic epistemology and the limits of externalism. *Ancient Philosophy* 25 (2): 383–401.
Quine, W. V. O. (1948) On what there is. *The Review of Metaphysics* 2: 21–38.
Rackham, H. (1967) *Cicero: De Natura Deorum, Academica*. Cambridge, MA: Loeb Classical Library, Harvard University Press.
Ramelli, I., and Constan, D. (2009) *Hierocles the Stoic: Elements of Ethics, Fragments and Excerpts*. Atlanta, GA, USA: Society of Biblical Literature.
Reed, B. (2002) The stoics' account of the cognitive impression. *Oxford Studies in Ancient Philosophy* 23: 147–180.
Rist, J. M. (1971) Categories and their uses. In Long, A. A. (ed.) *Problems in Stoicism*. London: The Athlone Press.
Sandbach, F. H. (1930) Ennoia and Prolepsis in the stoic theory of knowledge. *Classical Quarterly* 24: 44–51.
Schaffer, J. (2010) Monism: The priority of the whole. *Philosophical Review* 119 (1): 31–76.
Sedley, D. (1982) The stoic criterion of identity. *Phronesis* 27: 255–275.
———. (1993) Chrysippus on pscyhophysical causation. In Brunschwig, J., and Nussbaum, M. (eds.) *Passions and Perceptions*. Cambridge, MA: Cambridge University Press.
Sorabji, R. (1988) *Matter, Space and Motion*. Ithaca: Cornell University Press.
———. (1990) Perceptual content in the stoics. *Phronesis* 35 (3): 307–314.
Striker, G. (1974) κριτήριον τῆς ἀληθείας. *Nachrichten der Akademie der Wissenshaften su Göttingen, I. Phil-hist: Klasse* 2: 48–100.
Vogt, K. (2009) Sons of the earth: Are the stoics metaphysical brutes? *Phronesis* 54 (2): 136–154.
von Arnim, H. (1905) *Stoicorum Veterum Fragmenta*. Stuttgart: BG Teubner.

12

MIND IN AN ATOMISTIC WORLD

Epicurus and the Epicurean tradition

Francesca Masi and Francesco Verde[1]

One of the main aims of contemporary philosophy of mind is to explain the nature and functioning of the mind in the physical world. The problem which this discipline seeks to address, commonly referred to as the mind-body problem, concerns the general question of the relation between mental states and the states of matter which constitute the human organism. Directly connected to the solution of this problem is not only the possibility to account for the causal efficacy and epistemic relevance of mental states (beliefs, emotions, memories, thoughts, etc.) but also, more generally, the possibility to attribute wholeness and personal identity to human beings, to think of them as autonomous agents.

Epicurus addresses two questions that link back to the mind-body problem. The first concerns the composition of the soul and its functioning with respect to the body. The second question concerns the nature and function of mental states, such as memories, in relation to the atomic constitution of the human organism. Epicurus addresses the first question in his *Letter to Herodotus*; the second one in Book 25 of *On Nature*, a text preserved by some Herculaneum papyri (*PHerc.* 419/1634/697; *PHerc.* 454/1420/1056; *PHerc.* 1191, critical edition: Laursen 1995 and 1997).

This chapter is devoted to an investigation of these two questions. In particular, it seeks to establish whether and in what way, within Epicurean psychology, the mind is distinguished from the rest of the soul; what it consists in and where it is located; how it operates in relation to the rest of the human organism; and, finally, whether and in what way it develops.

1. The soul-body relation

The starting point for any attempt to understand the main features of Epicurean psychology is the *Letter to Herodotus*. Here Epicurus explicitly addresses two topics: the nature of the soul; its location and functioning within the body. The aim of this exposition is to emphasise the markedly unitary nature of each living being, the mutual dependence – both structural and functional – between soul and body.

1.1 The corporeal soul

Concerning the nature of the soul, Epicurus writes:

> After these things, referring to our perceptions and affections – for thus we will have the surest grounds for belief – we must consider that the soul is a body composed of fine parts (*leptomeres*), dispersed throughout the atomic complex, most nearly resembling wind (*pneumati*) with a certain admixture (*krasin*) of heat, in some respects similar to the former, in others to the latter. This part (*to meros*) is also very different from these (i.e. wind and heat) on account of its fineness, and hence more similar to the rest of the atomic complex. And this is shown by the mental faculties, the affections, the correct movements of the mind, thoughts and those things the loss of which causes death.
> (Epicur., *Ep. Hrd.*, 63. See Verde 2010, 187–197)[2]

The first indication we get from the text, then, is that the soul is a body. Lucretius adduces two proofs of the corporeality of the soul that revolve around its capacity to act and to suffer, an aspect which Epicurus too mentions in the *Letter to Herodotus* (67). Both these arguments rest on the assumption that movement and change are only possible by virtue of the mutual contact of corporeal entities, and therefore that they can only fully be explained within the framework of an explicitly materialist theory. According to the first argument, the soul is corporeal insofar as it has the power to move the body, something which is only possible through physical contact (Lucr. III.162–167). According to the second argument, the soul partakes in the suffering of the body, and *vice versa*: when the soul suffers, so does the body. Given that pain can only pass from one body to another, the soul too must be corporeal (Lucr. III.152–162, 170–176).

The reference to "those who behave like fools" (*Ep. Hrd.*, 67) may help better define the context of the Epicurean discussion of the soul. Epicurus calls "fools" those who claim that the soul is incorporeal: it is fairly obvious, therefore, that this criticism must refer to those who explicitly uphold such a theory. The fact that the whole polemic revolves around the notion of incorporeality, however, also enables us to take a different approach to the issue of just who might be Epicurus' target. The word *asomaton* could recall a passage of the *De anima* in which, after stating that according to Democritus the soul is made up of atoms of fire, Aristotle argues that fire is "regarded as the element composed of the finest particles (*leptomerestaton*) and the most incorporeal one (*malista asomaton*)" (Aristot., *DA*.I.2.405a 5 = DK.68.A.101). The philosopher thus infers that all his predecessors "define the soul according to three characteristics: movement, perception and incorporeality". The fact that Epicurus was keen to note the most appropriate way to understand the term *asomaton* and to criticise those who associate this notion with the soul, suggests that he is targeting not just those who regarded the soul as incorporeal – the immediate reference being Plato, of course – but also those who, by referring to Democritus' use of this notion, had drawn from Democritean psychology conclusions incompatible with atomism. Epicurus' observations on the corporeal nature of the soul may therefore be viewed not only in opposition to Platonic doctrine, but also as an attempt to perfect Democritean doctrine in the light of Aristotle's *De anima*, a text which Epicurus probably knew well – although there is no clear evidence of this (see Verde 2016).

In order to understand in what terms Epicurus conceives of the corporeal nature of the soul, it is necessary to focus first on the meaning of the term *leptomeres*. In employing this term, Epicurus would appear to be embracing Democritus' corpuscular conception of the soul. This word, formed from the adjective *leptos*, fine or of a small size, and the noun *meros*, part, means composed of fine particles (see Lucr. III.179–180). Moreover, as may be inferred from the aforementioned passage from *De anima*, Aristotle maintains that for Democritus the soul is made up of atoms of fire and explains that fire is believed to consists of the finest elements (*leptomerestaton*).

On the other hand, through his particular description of the soul Epicurus also shows himself keen to somehow distance himself from the psychology of his predecessor. Epicurus clearly intends to treat the psychic complex as a unitary system: it is the corporeal soul as a whole that is like wind and like heat, in some respects similar to the former, in others to the latter. Moreover, in referring to *pneuma*, an element foreign to Democritean psychology, Epicurus may be pointing to the inadequacy of Democritus' explanation which, by invoking only the element of fire, fails to account for the variety of psychological phenomena (see Bailey 1929, p. 388, and Annas 1992, p. 138).

Two further questions emerge from these considerations. The first is how Epicurus can uphold a conception of the soul as something both corpuscular and whole. The second is what the function of *pneuma* might be within Epicurean psychology. In order to answer the first question, it may be useful to focus on Epicurus' use of the term *krasis*. In a passage of the *De mixtione*, Alexander of Aphrodisias explains that according to Epicurus *krasis* describes a mixture of different substances, deriving from their breakdown into their constitutive elements and their recombination into a new, homogeneous synthesis, operating as a single whole (Alex. Aphr., *De mixt.*, 140 = 290 Us. see Kerferd 1971, and Masi 2006, p. 64). In the light of all this, one may be led to conclude that the soul stems from the aggregation of constitutive elements that stem from different substances but come together into a single whole which, in turn, shares some of the features of heat and *pneuma*. This solution allows us to compare what Epicurus argues in his *Letter* with the doctrine of the composition of the soul recorded in Book 3 of Lucretius' *DRN*, as well as in other secondary sources. Several scholars have suggested that we interpret the paragraphs of the *Letter to Herodotus* dealing with psychology in the light of Lucretius' exposition (for example, Repici 2008). However, in the particular case at hand, the characterisation of the soul as a body consisting of fine parts and the reference to the admixture of wind and heat undeniably suggest that Epicurus envisages the soul as having not a simple nature but one composed of different parts. The fact that he does not further investigate the issue of the composition of the soul in his letter – as Lucretius instead does in his work – might mean either that Epicurus had not yet fully developed his psychological doctrine at the time (Bignone 1940, p. 175; Verde 2015) or that, when focusing on the problem of the mutual interaction of soul and body in a doctrinal compendium such as the *Letter to Herodotus* (Spinelli 2012), he simply did not feel the need to examine the theory of the constituent elements of the soul. On the other hand, Epicurus' reference to this doctrine helps us better understand the reason why he felt compelled to mention *pneuma*. It is therefore worth examining it in greater detail.

In Book 3 of *DRN* (231–234), Lucretius takes up the idea of the admixture (*mixta*) of wind and heat outlined by Epicurus in the *Letter to Herodotus*. Lucretius explicitly refers to a third element, air, and introduces a fourth nature, which he defines *nominis expers*. The four components of the soul listed by Lucretius are also recorded by other sources (see Aet. IV.3.11, *Dox*. 388 = 315 Us.). What is more interesting, however, is to investigate the reasons for this quadripartite division. Secondary sources inform us that the first three elements (fire, wind and air) were brought into play to account for different psycho-physical phenomena, namely: breathing (Lucr. III.231–234), movement, rest and bodily temperature; "the direction and magnitude of emotions" (Diano 1974, p. 131); the temperament and character of animals (Lucr. III.288–307). Much has been said about the defining features of the fourth, unnamed component of the soul, which is introduced to account for the faculty of perception and the main psychic faculties. First, Epicurus is believed to have based the anonymity of this nature on one of the exoteric writings of Aristotle, possibly the *Peri philosophias* (Bignone 1973, II p. 202–251) or the *Eudemus* (Mariotti 1940, p. 179–189). In a controversial passage of the *Tusculanae Disputationes*, Cicero appears to be quoting some passages of the *Peri philosophias* in which, with reference to the soul, Aristotle theorises a *quintum genus vacans nomine* in addition to the four Empedoclean elements. Ever since antiquity, interpreters have argued that the anonymity of the fourth nature reflects Epicurus' difficulty in justifying the qualitative difference of the fourth substance compared to the rest within the framework of atomism (Plut., *Adv. Col.*, 1118D = 314 Us.). Among modern scholars, for example, Annas (1992, p. 139) has suggested that the anonymity of the fourth nature derives from the linguistic empiricism of the philosopher, which – at any rate in the *Letter to Herodotus* (Epicur., *Ep. Hrd.*, 38) – prevents him from coining technical terms to describe anything that cannot be confirmed through sense data. Bailey (1929, p. 392), by contrast, while acknowledging that Epicurus here is really pushing the limits of atomism, believes that the philosopher is nonetheless still operating within them, as the element in question has a strictly physical character. Indeed, the fourth nature is a particularly tenuous and mobile *sygkrisis* which, by virtue of its peculiar constitution, "has the privilege of commencing sensory motion, as that [nature] which immediately reacts to the slightest stimulus" (Diano 1974, p. 134), transmitting it to the rest of the soul and body through the kinetic gradation of the other three elements.

Then, we can now embark on some considerations regarding the question we have left open, namely why in his letter Epicurus feels the need to refer not just to heat but also to *pneuma* in order to explain the corporeal nature of the soul.

Interpreters have suggested different possible solutions to this problem. A first explanation – which is arguably even too economical – is that the soul is compared to *pneuma* as a way of indicating the almost gaseous composition of the *psyche*, in order – as we will see in greater detail later on – to explain its close dependence upon the body (Repici 2008). Other commentators maintain that the reference to *pneuma* and therefore to an articulate composition of the soul is meant to highlight the inadequacy of Democritus' doctrine and account for the wide range of psychological phenomena (Bailey 1929, p. 388). Other interpreters (Englert 1987) still believe that the philosopher reached this conclusion after engaging with Aristotle's biological treatises, where the *pneuma* that spreads throughout the living organism from the heart through dilation and contraction (*MA*.10.703a14ff.) is described as the most suitable physical means to set the body in motion (*GA*.V.8.789b9 and *MA*.10.703a4ff.); to connect peripheral sensory organs to the central organ (*GA*.II.6.744a1ff.); to ensure breathing and the generation of living beings (*GA*.II.6.741b37ff.); and to account for their thermal variations and the expression of emotions (*MA*.7.701b28ff.). According to this view, then, by mixing heat and *pneuma*, Epicurus sought to combine the Democritean concept of *psyche-pyr* and the Aristotelian one of *pneuma* (Silvestre 1985, p. 90).

The main problem with the second solution is that the components of the soul are unquestionably invoked in place of Democritean fire to account for many of the functions exercised by the Aristotelian *pneuma*: it thus seems unlikely that we should rule out Aristotle's influence on Epicurus with respect to this aspect of his psychology. The main problem with the third solution instead lies in the fact that the Epicurean notion of *pneuma* is radically different from the Aristotelian one: not only because Aristotle's *pneuma* refers to a breath of cold air (*GA*. II.3.736b35ff. See Annas 1992, p. 138.), whereas Epicurus' *pneuma* suggests a breath of warm air, but also because the Epicurean *pneuma* only partly accounts for those phenomena which the Aristotelian *pneuma* is instead meant to fully explain. One way to overcome these difficulties would be to argue, with Diano (1974, p. 135ff.), that Epicurus' *pneuma* is not an exact conceptual counterpart to Aristotle's *pneuma*, but rather that the Epicurean theory of the four components of the soul as a whole constitutes an atomistic transposition of the Aristotelian doctrine of *pneuma*. As already noted, in his letter Epicurus claims that it is the whole psychic body which shares some of the characteristics of wind/*pneuma*. Epicurus' mention of *pneuma* in this work, then, may be an implicit acknowledgement of his philosophical indebtedness to Aristotle.

The hypothesis that Epicurus adopted a more complex articulation of the soul in order to alter Democritus' doctrine in the light of Aristotle's criticism is further confirmed by another piece of evidence. According to Aëtius, Epicurus resorted to the doctrine of the four elements in order to explain not just the movement of the body but also its rest. To understand the reason for this, it is necessary to consider one specific criticism that Aristotle had brought forward against the Democritean conception of the soul. Aristotle criticises Democritus on the grounds that fire can at most be regarded as being responsible for the movement of the body – although only in a paradoxical way, as quicksilver is said to have been used by Daedalus to set the wooden statue of Aphrodite in motion – but cannot in itself account for rest (*DA*.I.3.406b15ff. = DK.68.A.104).

1.2 The soul within the body

By defining the corporeality of the soul in terms of its fineness and comparing its consistency to a gaseous state, Epicurus also provides some useful clues for understanding its distribution within the organism as a whole. For although the rather bold juxtaposition of *psyche* and *soma* might lead to the absurd idea of having a body within a body, the different degree of fineness of the matter constituting the *psyche* compared to that of the matter composing the rest of the organism helps clarify the localisation of the soul within the body, as well as the close interaction between the two. The comparison drawn between the soul and wind and the reference to heat, the finest of all elements (Aristot., *DC*.III.5.303b19–21), are used to justify its diffused distribution within the body. The soul requires a solider and firmer framework, capable of preserving it against dispersion. In the *Letter to Herodotus*, Epicurus makes two allusions to such a condition: first he claims that the *psyche* is somehow contained within or sheltered by the rest of the organism (Epicur., *Ep. Hrd.*, 64.); then he argues that the soul would disperse if the body containing it were destroyed (*ibid.* 65). The same idea is stressed by Lucretius (III.434–444) through the metaphor of the vase, which is used to prove the mortality of the soul.

As regards the exact nature of the soul's connection to the body, by invoking the idea of dissemination Epicurus would appear to be suggesting that the soul is arranged in the body as seeds are in the ploughed soil (Repici 2008). By contrast, Lucretius provides no clear indications on this point. The explanation he gives is developed in opposition to the Democritean theory according to which the atoms of the soul are arranged in the living organism in alternation with those of the body, one after another. The poet notes that, with a similar distribution of the constitutive elements of the human organism, each movement made by the corporeal atoms would automatically be transmitted to those of the soul which, being smooth, fine and round, are especially mobile and respond to the slightest impulse. But in fact – Lucretius notes – we cannot always perceive the impact of objects touching our body. In the light of all this, the poet hypothesises that the atoms constituting the soul are separated by intervals larger than those posited by Democritus, and which may be measured according to the number of particles constituting the smallest perceivable object (Lucr. III.370–390). Lucretius' argument, however, is not enough to elucidate the nature of the connection between soul and body. In order to explain how the *psyche* adheres to the rest of the organism Bailey suggests we focus on the composition of the latter. Lucretius (*ibid.*

566–568; 691–695; 788) describes the human body as a complex whole consisting of different parts, such as the blood, veins, organs, nerves and bones, that vary in terms of compactness and solidity: bones are formed by tight-knit atoms, whereas blood, veins, organs and nerves are constituted by finer and smoother atoms, which are therefore bound together in a looser way. In all parts, however, pores are to be found between one set of atoms and the next (*ibid.* 255; 702; 707). According to Bailey (1929, p. 397), it is through these passages that the atoms of the soul penetrate "into every part, yet constantly shifting with their own atomic motion and the changes of the surrounding structure caused by the movement of the body of atoms". In this case too, Lucretius' polemical reference to Democritus suggests that the discussion of the distribution of the soul within the rest of the human organism constituted as attempt made by the Epicureans to overcome their predecessors' limits.

The Epicurean discussion of the distribution of the soul in relation to the living organism may fruitfully be connected to certain questions raised by Aristotle in the *De anima*, namely: (1) whether the soul may be regarded as the only subject of certain affections and hence whether it may be considered separately from the body (*DA*.I.1.403a1ff.); (2) what effects the union of soul and body, and how the latter's condition is to be understood (*DA*.I.3.407b). The first problem, for Aristotle, stemmed from the fact that some of his predecessors had assumed that the *psyche* and its functions could exist independently of the body; the second problem instead stemmed from the fact that previous thinkers had conjoined soul and body, and located the former within the latter, while only explaining the nature of the soul and never bothering to define the support destined to house it. Now, in relation to these questions we have reason to believe that Epicurus considered the Democritean explanation inadequate. As regards the first question, in particular, Democritus' doctrine presented two problems. The first was that the philosopher of Abdera posited the existence of *psychic atoms* (i.e. qualified ones) even in the air outside the body, hence the connection between breathing and the persistence of the soul within the body (*DA*.I.2.404a1ff.). The second problem was that although according to Democritus the soul decays with the body, the philosopher also maintained that part of the soul can endure in corpses, and that the latter preserve a degree of sensibility and heat by virtue of this enlivening power (Aet., IV.4.7, *Dox.* 390 = DK.68.A.117; Cic., *Tusc.*, I.34.82 = DK.68.A.160 = 17 Us.). As concerns the second question, we have learned from Lucretius that Epicurus did not share the notion of an alternation of soul atoms and body atoms suggested by Democritus. It is likely, therefore, that the theory of the relation between soul and body formulated by the philosopher in his letter is to be understood as an attempt to overcome the difficulties posed by Democritus' psychology.

First, it is worth noting that by virtue of its close adherence to the rest of the organism, the soul develops as the organism matures. Lucretius explains the way in which this process take place, from a physical point of view, as an initial thickening of the psychic substance due to the hardening of the surrounding corporeal framework and the progressive rarefaction of this substance with the weakening of the organism; from a psychological perspective, he instead describes it as the progressive consolidation and later weakening of the psychic faculties (Lucr. III.445–454). Lucretius' explanation finds a close counterpart in what Epicurus states in Book 25 of *On Nature*, where he mentions the fact that the atomic constitution of the human organism has different degrees of fluidity depending on its stage of development, and that it grows harder as it matures (Epicur., *Nat.* XXV, Laursen 1997, p. 25 = [34.23] Arr. [Arrighetti]; Laursen 1997, p. 46ff. = [34.32] Arr).

Second, as further confirmation of the fact that Epicurus makes use of the spatial interrelation of soul and body in a functional way for his own polemical ends, it will be useful to briefly consider the dynamics of sense perception.

Epicurus devotes several paragraphs of the *Letter to Herodotus* (63–65) to the issue of sense perception linked to the existence of the soul.

The basic idea is that the soul derives most of its capacity/causal power to perceive from its particular disposition within the human organism and from the activity which it performs by virtue of this disposition. Briefly put, sense perception stems from the convergence and coexistence of soul and body. In one respect, the soul is more responsible for perception, since what accounts for this is the soul's composition and movement; in another respect, however, the soul is not the only cause of sense perception, since without the participation of the body, the living organism would not perceive anything at all. Epicurus, therefore, speaks of *symptoma aisthetikon*, of the accident of sense perception, since perception is not something that intrinsically belongs to either soul or body, but is rather the result of their union (see Lucr. III.892–896). The capacity to perceive, then, comes about through direct interaction with elements from the environment or through changes undergone by the body (see Lucr. III.246–251 and 566–572). This mechanism – as Epicurus later explains in greater detail – lies at the basis of all the other psychic functions and constitutes a prerequisite for their exercise. According to Epicurus, the perceptual, intellectual and emotional life of a living being depends first on the reception and assimilation of elements (such as smells, sounds and images) from the surrounding environment. Before investigating this aspect of his theory, however, it is necessary to address a preliminary question, namely whether Epicurus conceived the soul as a single subject in relation to its functions or whether he distinguished between different functional parts of the soul (see Kerferd 1971, Gill 2009, Verde 2013, pp. 113–122).

2. From psychological monism to the functional bipartition of the soul

According to our secondary sources – especially the exposition of Epicurean psychology in Book 3 of *DRN* but also other testimonies by later authors – Epicurean philosophy inherited from the earlier philosophical tradition the distinction between an *alogon* component of the *psyche* and a *logikon* one, which is to say between the soul as the vital and sentient principle, on the one hand, and, on the other, the soul as the source of emotions and thought. Actually, the psychological perspective adopted in the *Letter to Herodotus* appears to differ in several respects from that of Lucretius. Whereas Lucretius clearly distinguishes between two parts of the soul, a rational one called *animus* and a non-rational one called *anima*; see Verde 2017b, Epicurus' position is more nuanced. In the *Letter to Herodotus* he does not set out to establish a bipartition of the soul: on the contrary, he appears to endorse a monist conception of the soul. In Book 25 of *On Nature*, the discussion is centred on *dianoia* rather than the soul in general and one ambiguous fragment, whose text is difficult to reconstruct, mentions a mental aggregate probably located in a specific part of the atomic constitution of the human being and clearly removed from peripheral sense organs (Epicur., *Nat.* XXV, Laursen 1995, p. 91 = [35.10] Arr.).

Let us more specifically examine the passages that shed light on this point. Lucretius states,

> Next, I say that mind and spirit (*animum atque animam . . . coniuncta*) are held in conjunction together and compound one nature in common (*unam naturam*), but that the head so to speak and lord over the whole body is the understanding (*consilium*) which we call mind and intelligence (*animum mentemque*). And this has its abiding-place in the middle region of the breast (*media regione in pectoris*). For in this place throbs terror and fear (*pavor ac metus*), hereabouts is melting joy (*laetitiae mulcent*): here therefore is the intelligence and the mind. The rest of the spirit (*cetera pars animae*), dispersed (*dissita*) abroad through the whole body, obeys and is moved according to the will (*numen*) and working (*momenque*) of the intelligence.
> (Lucr. III.136–14 [transl. Rouse-Smith])

Alongside this passage from Lucretius, we can quote the *scholium* to § 66 of the *Letter to Herodotus*:

> In other works it is said that it (*scil.* the soul) is composed of smooth and spherical atoms, very different from those of fire; and that there is an irrational part of it (*to men ti alogon autes*) which is disseminated throughout the rest of the body, whereas the rational part (*to de logikon*) resides in the thorax (*thoraki*), as is evident from fear and joy (*hos delon ek te ton phobon kai tes charas*).

These are two interesting passages, particularly because they present some common features: both in Lucretius and in the scholium a clear distinction is drawn between the two parts of the soul. Some interpreters believe that this distinction is already assumed in the *Letter to Herodotus* (leaving the scholium aside): for they read § 63 of the letter according to a conjecture proposed by Jan Woltjer (see Verde 2010, p. 189; see Verde 2017a, pp. 39–47). If, however, we do not wish to accept Woltjer's suggestion, § 63 may be taken as evidence of the fact that when Epicurus wrote the *Letter to Herodotus* – apparently a rather early work – he probably had not yet developed the idea of the bipartition of the soul reported and confirmed by the Epicurean Demetrius Laco (col. XIII.6–9 Puglia), Lucretius, and Diogenes of Oenoanda (fr. 37.I.5–7 Smith; see Verde, forthcoming). In other words, we might conclude that what we find in Epicurus is not a single (and static) doctrine of the soul, but rather an 'evolving' psychology, in which (at least) two phases may be detected. The first phase, witnessed by the *Letter to Herodotus*, would be marked by an absolute psychological monism, with no distinction between different functions and locations; the chief function of the soul in this case would be to make sense perception possible. The second phase would instead feature a bipartition of the soul into a rational part and a non-rational one, which would essentially turn the Epicurean position into a sort of psychic dualism, not all that different from the Platonic and Aristotelian perspectives (Giussani 1896, p. 19, on Lucr. III.136–160).

The phase of transition from a monist view of the soul to a bipartite one might be illustrated precisely by Book 25 of *On Nature*. Epicurus is very keen to emphasise the role played by rationality in human psychological development. The need to mark out *dianoia* from the rest of the soul-body complex is thus more evident in this text.

In light of this view – the supposition of diachronic development – there is nothing surprising in the lack of any partition of the soul in the *Letter to Herodotus* (as is instead suggested by Annas 1992, p. 144). The diachronic development in question might easily be justified on the basis of the progressive emergence of certain theoretical requirements. We might posit, in other words, that seeking to clarify the corporeal nature of the soul in his letter, so as to account for its capacity for sense perception, Epicurus chose to focus on the problem of the relation between soul and body, without addressing the question of the distinction of the psychic functions and endorsing a monistic psychology instead; and that, by contrast, in later works where he needed to address the question of the difference between those states of the soul exclusively deriving from its capacity to receive and accurately record environmental data and those states stemming from an autonomous reprocessing and reinterpreting of sense data, the philosopher opted for a bipartite conception of the soul.

Further significant evidence of the lack of any such bipartition in the *Letter to Herodotus* comes from § 66, according to which in other works Epicurus upheld the idea of the existence of a non-rational part of the soul and a rational one. Clearly, if the scholiast had detected any traces of the notion of bipartition in the letter, he would have not reported this information.

The text of the *scholium* and the passage from Lucretius also present some interesting parallels. Lucretius stresses the idea that, while distinct from one another, *animus* and *anima* are conjoined (see Lucr. III.398–401 where the soul is described as the "companion" of the *animus*) and constitute a single nature, that of the soul, distinct from the aggregate of the body (yet just as material). The *animus*, or rational part of the soul – which Lucretius conceives of as 'the understanding' (*consilium*), in turn defined as *mens*/mind (*dianoia* in Epicurus' Greek) – not only governs the body, but also operates at a higher level than the soul. The latter obeys the *animus/mens* and moves in accordance to its orders. The *scholium* and Lucretius' verses agree with regard to the location of the two parts of the soul and the reason for it: the *animus* resides in the thorax, at the centre of the chest, and hence in the heart, whereas the *anima* is dispersed throughout the rest of the body, since it is responsible for sense perception. The bipartition traced in the *scholium* and more clearly outlined by Lucretius must therefore be understood in functional spatial terms rather than ontological terms. In other words, by residing in a specific part of the body and having a certain arrangement, the *animus*, which has the same composition as the rest of the soul, exercises specific functions that the *anima*, distributed as it is throughout the organism and conditioned by its movements, cannot exercise (Bailey 1929, pp. 402–403; Diano 1974, p. 145). As has already been noted, the two sources under scrutiny also agree on the reason for the specific location of the *animus*: Lucretius reports that it is located in the heart because that is where anxiety, fear and joy come from. Based on the evidence from the *scholium*, it seems as though Epicurus also referred to fear and joy when locating the *animus/mens* in the cardiac region. For the philosopher, fear and joy are emotions involving the rational part of the soul, i.e. they are not mere affections (*pathe*). Affections, which is to say pleasure and pain, constitute the third criterion within Epicurus' system and are strictly connected to sense perception (*aisthesis*, Epicur., *Ep. Men.*, 124), which is 'non-rational' (*alogos*, DL X.31), even if the *pathe* (pleasure and pain) are rational, since by means of them we judge what to choose and what to avoid (DL X.34). Strictly speaking, fear and joy are not affections (like pleasure and pain); therefore, they concern the rational part of the soul, since they are states requiring a degree of rational processing that the *anima* – responsible for *aisthesis*, which is *alogos* – cannot provide (Konstan 2007, pp. 5–48, and, now, 2015). The fact that fear and joy have their abiding-place in the chest and that they result not just from sense perception but also from rational processing might be the reason why Epicurus and his followers identified the thorax as the specific seat of *dianoia* or the *animus/mens*.

From the evidence gathered so far two facts can be inferred that may help us further investigate the question addressed in Book 25 of *On Nature*. The first fact is that Epicurus conceives the soul as a homogeneous atomic structure which is closely connected to the body and which, by virtue of this relation, is constantly evolving and interacting with its environment. The second fact is that the soul-body explanatory model provided in Epicurus' letter is the outcome of an anti-Aristotelian development of Democritean psychology. In light of all this we may now set out to uncover the reasons why Epicurus felt compelled to better define the relation between mental states and the condition of the soul-body complex as a whole. As we will see, this question can only partly be associated with the contemporary problem of the relation between mental and physical states in the human organism.

3. The mind-nature problem

The enquiry conducted in Book 25 concerns the study of the affections of the soul-body complex and their causes (Laursen 1997, p. 48 = [34.33] Arr.). In particular, this study reflects Epicurus' need to take account of human beings' capacity to govern the course of their own psycho-physical and moral development through the exercise of rationality, so as to avoid some of the deterministic implications of Epicurean psychology. The philosopher's aim is to prove that the causal power of those mental faculties, dispositions and activities – such as memories, thoughts, beliefs and desires – through which individual agents exercise their capacity to determine their own attitudes and actions, are not the result of the causal inheritance of factors falling beyond the agents' control, but rather constitute a means of self-determination for them.

The surviving texts from Book 25 of *On Nature* reveal that – within the context of a polemic possibly engendered by disagreements within the Epicurean school and then extended to other unnamed opponents – Epicurus found himself facing the following difficulties:

1   the fact that the states, dispositions and activities which the mind develops over time may be regarded as the inevitable outcome of a causal chain extending *ex infinito* (Epicur., *Nat.* XXV, Laursen 1995, p. 92 = [35.11] Arr., Masi 2006, pp. 73–76);
2   the fact that the causal power and overall condition of the mind at each stage of its development may depend on the causal power and condition of its individual atomic components (*ibid.*, p. 93 = [35.12] Arr.; p. 101 = [34.10] Arr.; p. 102 = [34.11], Masi 2006, pp. 76–82);
3   the fact that the sum of states, dispositions and activities which the mind develops over time may result from the preordained growth of the original nature or atomic make-up of the individual (*ibid.*, pp. 18–29 = [34.4–25] Arr., Masi 2006, pp. 82–94);
4   the fact that mental development may be determined by the mechanical interaction between one's nature and one's environment (*ibid.*, pp. 32–40 = [34.26–30] Arr. = Long-Sedley 20C).

The investigation conducted in Book 25 of *On Nature*, therefore, revolves around the relation between 'original products' or 'developing products' or 'developed products' (*apogennethenta, apogennomena, apogegennemena*) on the one hand – terms which recall the mental level – and, on the other, 'the atoms' (*ai atomoi*)/ 'nature' (*physis*) /'constitution' (*systasis*) of the living organism – terms which instead recall the physical level. In particular, the philosopher is concerned with disproving the ideas:

(1) that mental properties (what he calls "products") may depend on the action of individual atoms and that the causal power of the former may coincide with that of the latter;
(2) that mental properties which have developed over time ("developed products") may amount to the same thing as the original constitution of the organism – in other words, that nature may be the ultimate cause of the development of mental states.

We may therefore conclude that the mind-body problem investigated by Epicurus in Book 25 is to be understood more specifically as the problem, on the one hand, of the reducibility of the properties of the mind to those of its individual components and, on the other, of the reducibility of the outcomes of the character, intellectual and moral development of the mind to the biological and psychological characteristics of the organism as a whole at the time of its conception. Having thus outlined the problem, let us now examine the solution which Epicurus suggests in the book.

Epicurus' solution is developed according to two directions. On the one hand, in order to reverse the causal relations between atoms and products, as well as to show how the causal power of the former depends on that of the latter – rather than the other way round – the author highlights the systematic character and structuring capacity of products with respect to the constitutive elements of the organism which has generated them. On the other hand, in order to show that developed products cannot be reduced to the nature or original constitution of the human organism, Epicurus makes two apparently conflicting suggestions. The first is that once it has *necessarily* reached a certain stage of development – that is, according to a deterministic process of formation – a product is capable of *self-determination* by virtue of its intrinsic causal activity. The second suggestion is that a developed product causally depends not on the original constitution of the organism but on its grown atomic constitution. We must enquire, then, as to how Epicurus succeeds in combining these two explanations. With regard to the former, in particular, we must clarify how the philosopher conceives of this intrinsic power of self-determination of each product. With regard to the latter, we must instead investigate how Epicurus conceives of the causal dependence of the mental level upon the physical one.

4. Epicurus' philosophy of mind

In order to clarify how the formation, development and self-determination of mental states come about according to Epicurus, it is necessary to address the following questions: how mental states arise; how they develop; in what way the human being is capable of self-determining the course of this development; and why psychological development does not always coincide with moral development.

The soul and the mind come about through a specific aggregation of suitable atoms and immediately acquire a range of properties, called *apogennethenta* (Epicur., *Nat.* XXV, Laursen 1997, p. 18 = [34.4] Arr.). As soon as it is generated, just like any other unitary and stable atomic interrelation, which by virtue of its structuring and systematic character is capable of causally acting upon its components for the benefit of the whole, the mind acquires a causal power independent from its constitutive principles and in turn becomes capable of conditioning their mode of operating (*ibid.*, pp. 19–20 = [34.20] Arr. = Long-Sedley 20B).

The mind, moreover, and the range of its inborn properties are capable of evolving and fully developing along with the atomic constitution of the organism. According to Epicurus, three basic patterns of human mental development are to be found, reflecting the original constitutive conditions and growth potential of individuals: a tendency towards intellectual, ethical and practical inclinations of a certain kind, for instance ones suitable for the attainment of *ataraxia*; a tendency towards thoughts, habits and behaviours of the opposite sort, meaning ones utterly unsuitable for the attainment of the *telos*; and, finally, a tendency to acquire both sorts of traits, which is to say mixed ones which are neither utterly favourable nor utterly unfavourable to the ethical ideal (*ibid.*, Laursen 1997, p. 32s. = [34.26] Arr. = Long-Sedley 20C1; see too Sen., *Ep.*, 52). Given these initial tendencies, determined by nature (Epicur., *Nat.* XXV, Laursen 1997, p. 28 = [34. 24] Arr.), every individual can mentally and ethically progress according to two different directions: either towards the attainment of the intellectual and practical characteristics already embedded in his/her original constitution, or towards the attainment of characteristics in keeping with the ethical ideal.

Regardless of whether a person's mind develops in the direction of his/her original constitution or whether it follows a different course, Epicurus believes that the mind is the only, or at any rate the main, factor responsible for the development of an individual. For although other factors – such as one's age, nature and environment – are bound to influence the development of the mind, the latter has the power to determine itself and acquire dispositions of one kind or another. To be more precise, this occurs when the mind starts interpreting things independently, which is to say when it starts to form beliefs of its own, and through this work becomes capable of conditioning the impact of environmental stimuli on the developing constitution (*ibid.*, p. 28 [34.24] Arr.; p. 29 = [34.24–25] and p. 32ff. = [34.26] Arr. = Long-Sedley 20C1. See too Bobzien 2000, p. 318; O'Keefe 2005, p. 84ff.).

It is important to note that Epicurus envisages this stage as marking a break not only between individual components and the mental aggregate, but also between the process of development of the constitution and that of the mind. This clearly emerges from a series of clues strewn throughout the text. First, Epicurus treats individual agents as independent causal factors with respect to their nature and environment. Furthermore, the philosopher draws a contrast between the causal power of individual agents and that of the original constitution and environmental stimuli. He then draws a contrast between "the natural cause of growth and decrease of fluidity" and "the cause that comes to be out of ourselves". Likewise, Epicurus contrasts the nature of atoms with the causality of the "developed products". Finally, he warns us not to conflate the "developed product" and the "original constitution" and argues that "For that which is exempted from a necessary causality must be released from the original constitution, since it does not fulfil the same causality as that" (Epicur., *Nat.* XXV, Laursen 1997, pp. 29–30). Second, according to Epicurus, both the causal responsibility of individual agents and the causal power of the product are *autonomous*, meaning they do not stem from any causal heritage, but are rather something intrinsic.

Third, Epicurus assigns a *different mode of operating* to the causal power of the individual agent or product compared to that distinguishing all other factors. The philosopher attributes a *necessary* causality to the original constitution and the environment but a causal capacity to the product, where the latter implies a break with the necessary causal processes stemming from the original constitution and its interaction with environmental stimuli.

Now, these three elements may all be viewed within the framework of a conception that nowadays would be described as the agent causation theory (see De Caro 2004, p. 49ff.).

Although Epicurus makes no reference to will or any decision-making faculty, he nonetheless assigns each product a causal power of self-determination which is not itself determined by other causal factors but is rather capable of breaking all deterministic causal chains. Epicurus, in other words, outlines a theory of mind according to which the *dianoia/mens*, once it has reached a certain degree of development and acquired certain properties (such as the capacity to form beliefs, judge according to criteria of truth, and deliberate), attains autonomous causal power. By virtue of such power, the mind is capable of affecting the development of the atomic constitution and hence of engendering a new process of causation with respect to mental development compared to the one determined by the interaction between the nature of the organism and its environment.

Although the mind has an intrinsic power of self-determination enabling it to orient its psychological development and moral progress, in certain cases this does not occur. Epicurus explicitly addresses this problem. In some passages of Book 25, the philosopher examines the condition of a mind that has developed according to the original inclinations of its constitutive principles and has reached a stage of development where it is no longer capable of acquiring dispositions – or performing actions – contrary to the tendencies originally embedded within its nature and by now fully realised. Epicurus' aim, then, is twofold. On the one hand, he seeks to show why, even in a situation of this sort, the mind cannot be freed from the responsibility which its condition implies and why the outcome of its development must not be attributed to its original constitution, as in the case of animals and especially wild beasts – whose development is bound to stem from the mechanical interaction between the nature of the organism and the environment. On the other hand, the philosopher wishes to explain that the case of a product that has developed according to its nature, far from demonstrating the determinism governing the human mind and the futility of any attempt to improve it, actually confirms the need to adopt adequate and rigorous methods of education.

With respect to the first question, Epicurus explicitly states that the mind was not forced to develop the characteristics intrinsic to its original structure, but rather spontaneously followed the direction suggested by its nature. It should be clear by now that the philosopher is referring to the capacity of the mind to develop, by exercising its power to interpret reality, in a direction other than the one suggested by its nature.

With regard to the second question, Epicurus instead argues:

> And if it [*scil.* the developed product] precisely because of the cause out of itself, goes in the direction of what is similar to the original constitution and this is a bad one, then at time we censure it even more – in a more admonitory way, and not, as we do indeed [purify] the wildest animals, we purify in the same way these very same developed products and the original constitution, waving the developed products themselves and the constitution into one thing, and not because of this we do not use either the admonitory and correct method . . . forgive.
>
> (Epic., *Nat.* XXV, Laursen 1997, p. 31)

The meaning of these words, abruptly broken off by a lacuna, may be grasped in the light of a testimony from Seneca. In *Epistle 52*, we read that according to Epicurus many men are not strong enough to follow the path of truth but require some external support to guide them – or, in the most difficult cases, compel them.

This evidence suggests that after considering the case of the mind which has reached an irreversible stage of its development, Epicurus may have wished to recall the need for prompt intervention by applying an admonitory and corrective method to the product which, while exercising its power of self-determination, struggles to progress on its own and risks falling under the influence of its evil nature for good.

The philosopher thereby achieves a twofold aim. On the one hand, he can affirm the legitimacy and usefulness of those methods which individual agents adopt to condition other people's conduct and change deviant behaviour. On the other hand, Epicurus can, more specifically, justify certain methods which he had personally adopted within the Garden in order to steer the moral progress of his pupils.

Having clarified the way in which according to Epicurus mental states develop starting from their formation, it is now necessary to examine in what terms he conceives of the relation between these properties and the atomic constitution of the human organism.

4.1 Mental states and the atomic constitution: the case of memory

It worth focusing on a pair of passages in which Epicurus discusses the aetiology of memory as a notable example of those mental states essential for full moral development. The philosopher provides an outline of the relations between mental states and the atomic constitution that is quite comprehensive yet presents certain ambiguities and difficulties.

(a) At some point [the mind] remembered or got an affect analogous to the remembering and stayed in a state where with calm as well as in the investigation of the things that would have produced the . . . and greatest fear according to the circumstances ... mainly fears of physical pain, researches for the truth, on the basis of what is defined, regarding both human beings and the things above human beings (Epicur., *Nat.* XXV, Laursen 1997, p. 14 = [34.19] Arr.).

(b) The memory, or the affect analogous to the memory of the more necessary things came in, reference being made to the well-defined and all refuting and not to things that cannot be defined but need judgment. This memory, then, of that, or the movement analogous to memory, was in some cases in the state of having been immediately co-generated, in other cases it was in the state of having grown, being the beginning and the cause for, in the one case, the first constitution of both the atoms and the original product, in other, the grown (constitution) by means of which we perform all our actions, of both the atoms and the developed product itself, that in some cases is necessarily something opposite to what produced (*ibid.*, p. 16ff.= [34.20] Arr.).

In these passages Epicurus first explains that memory stems from a series of suitable mental operations. Then, after drawing a distinction between the inborn aspect of memory, which is to say the faculty of retaining traces of previous experiences and recalling them when need be, and the developed aspect of memory, which is to say the actual recalling of such traces, the philosopher states that the former is causally dependent upon the "first constitution of both the atoms and the original product", the latter upon the "the grown constitution ... and the developed product itself". Epicurus' reference to these two constitutions has somewhat baffled interpreters: for is not clear how the same *systasis* may belong to both the atoms and the product. Moreover, it seems strange that the notions of constitution and product should be associated, since they are usually kept separate. The explanation which Epicurus offers in this passage has understandably been dubbed "mysterious" (Annas 1993, p. 61). Nevertheless the passage may be interpreted as follows. The phenomenon of recollection is the outcome of the full functioning of memory, which is to say the capacity to retain traces of past experiences and recall them, if need be, through a series of appropriate operations. The fact that every individual has the power to receive and retain given imprints from birth is explained by his/her first atomic constitution, which is to say the particular composition of his/her mind and the disposition it has acquired within the organism as a whole. The fact that a person will exercise such faculty in relation to certain *typoi* rather than others instead depends on his/her grown constitution, which is to say the way in which the composition and disposition of his/her mind have changed over time.[3] If this interpretation is correct, we may therefore conclude that Epicurus is here providing a twofold description of memory. On the psychological level, active memory is described in relation to its functionalism, which is to say in relation to its causal links with other mental states. On the physical level, memory is described in relation to the specific state of the organism that is implementing it.

It is now a matter of understanding how Epicurus succeeds in reconciling this explanation with the previously expressed notion that the product is capable of self-determination. In other words, we must examine how the developed product can be both the outcome of a process of self-determination and of a process of vertical causation on the part of the overall grown constitution of the organism. The only solution is to assume that, according to Epicurus, the grown constitution results not just from the action of the original constitution, which is to say the biological development of the organism, but also from the action of the product upon the organism, which is to say of the mind's rational processing of environmental information.

The explanatory model for mental states suggested by the Epicurean study of memory is therefore reminiscent of the modern notion of *supervenience*. While always operating within a physicalist framework, Epicurus acknowledges the stratified nature of reality, where higher levels depend on lower ones, while preserving a degree of autonomy. Memory certainly derives from a particular atomic arrangement, yet it is also the outcome of the intellectual and rational activity of the soul. In turn, rationality is interpreted as the subject's causal power of self-determination, which is not itself determined by any other causal factor and is capable of breaking all deterministic causal chains. Rationality enables the soul to act upon the atomic constitution and to engender a new process of causation of mental development in addition to the one determined by the mechanical interaction between one's nature and one's environment. This interpretation, however, poses two difficulties which find no solution in Book 25 of *On Nature* and which may well be the reason why the doctrine of the *clinamen* (see Lucr. II.216–293) was introduced into Epicurean psychology. The first question concerns the tension between the horizontal and the vertical level of the explanation provided for the phenomenon of recollection. For it is clear that the explanatory model described entails a risk of causal over-determination. A recollection or developed product will appear to be the outcome both of its mental antecedent (i.e. of the capacity to retain traces of a past experience, which is to say of the original product, and of the capacity to recall this through the appropriate intellectual and rational operations) and of its physical counterpart, i.e. the grown constitution. In this regard, however, it may be observed that at the mental level a different causality is at work, one that is independent – so to speak – from the one operating at the level of the atomic constitution of the organism, insofar as the mind is capable of self-determination from a given stage of its development onwards, by virtue of its interpretative rational activity.

Acknowledging the mind's causal power of self-determination and identifying it with its rational activity is enough, from a diachronic perspective, to disprove the idea that the dispositions and actions of a subject depend upon his/her genetic heritage and the environmental context which he/she interacts with. From a synchronic perspective, however, this is not enough to explain why the causal power in question differs from – and cannot be reduced to – the combined action of the atoms that underlay its exercise. The solution presented, in other words, raises the problem of understanding how this causal anomaly at the mental level may be accounted for from a physical perspective. What remains open is the question of the compatibility between a principle of self-determination in the individual agent and a physical doctrine according to which everything derives its causal efficacy from its atomic constitution, i.e. from the combined motion of the atoms composing it.

Actually, although Book 25 provides no indications that might help solve the aforementioned difficulties, it is likely that during a subsequent drafting of the treatise Epicurus realised the implicit problems of his explanatory model for the development of mental states and sought to make up for them by introducing the famous doctrine of the *clinamen* into his psychology – a doctrine intended to reconcile the ethical-psychological agenda with the physical-cosmological one.[4]

It may be argued, then, that Epicurus resorted to an element of physical indeterminateness in order to justify an anomalous notions of mental causality. More in particular, it may be suggested that Epicurus included the *clinamen* within his physics with a chiefly negative aim in view: to ensure that the power of self-determination of a subject would not be reduced to the combined action of his/her atoms and thus ultimately be determined by matter (see Masi 2006, pp. 254–255).

5. Conclusion

In the *Letter to Herodotus* Epicurus develops a complex and overall theory of the composition of the soul, its distribution and its functioning in relation to the body, a physicalist psychology which appears to stem from a redefinition of Democritus' materialistic doctrine of the soul in the light of the criticism and suggestions to be found in the *De anima* and Aristotle's biological treatises. In Book 25, Epicurus attempts to reconcile this systematic, unitary and integrated model for the soul-body atomic complex with the key principle of his ethics – again, probably drawn from Aristotelian philosophy – according to which there are certain things, such as human dispositions and actions, that depend on us.

By associating the soul-body question with that of the origins of human dispositions and actions, Epicurus came to define – possibly for the first time – one of the most widely debated aspects of the mind-body problem in the contemporary philosophy of mind, namely the problem of affirming and accounting for the causal efficacy of mental states within the framework of a doctrine that conceives the world in purely physical terms (see Kim 2005, p. 7.ff.).

With regard to the solution presented by Epicurus in Book 25, moreover, some commentators nowadays tend to interpret Epicurean philosophy of mind in the light of categories drawn from contemporary philosophical debate, such as *emergentism* (Sedley 1983) and *reductionism* (O'Keefe 2005). These categories, however, do not provide a clear idea of the terms in which Epicurus investigates the mind-body relation. We are thus left with two ways of interpreting the Epicurean solution. If we wish to continue interpreting Epicurus' model in the light of contemporary notions, it is more plausible to believe that the most useful one to portray the solution in question in all of its ambiguity is that of *supervenience*. Aside from grasping the essential aspects of the Epicurean theory of the mind-body relation, the category of supervenience is subject to the same theoretical difficulties.

It is useful to resort to the modern notion of supervenience in order to explain the Epicurean conception of the mind insofar as this operation – its historiographical limits notwithstanding – enables us to credit Epicurus not so much with having solved a problem as with having identified one (see Kim 1998). What Epicurus realised was, on the one hand, the need to preserve a relation of mutual dependence between mental states and the atomic constitution, in order to safeguard the inner consistency of his system; and, on the other, the need to grant mental states a degree of autonomy with respect to the atomic constitution, so as to justify the moral autonomy of the individual agent.

It is also possible to develop an alternative interpretation of Epicurus' solution, however, by integrating the evidence from Book 25 with the information gleaned from the *Letter to Herotodus* concerning the functioning of the soul-body complex, so as to conclude that Epicurus sought to strike a balance between Democritean atomistic psychology and Aristotelian functionalism. The theory of mind-body relations delineated by Epicurus recalls Aristotelian functionalism insofar as it explains mental states, on the one hand, in terms of their structuring function – which is to say on the basis of the causal links between them, as well as between these states and the environment – and, on the other hand, as functions implemented by a whole living organism. Epicurus' theory instead differs from Aristotelian functionalism for two basic reasons: because what enables the organism to realise its functions, by lending it an appropriate form, is the body and not the soul, whereas what provides the matter that may be shaped so as to instantiate the psychic functions is soul and not the body; because within Epicurus' framework Democritean anti-teleologism still holds: applied to the study of the mind, it entails that while the states of the organism are not in function of mental states, mental states are in function of the states of the organism.

To conclude, the analysis conducted in the present contribution confirms the significant role played by Epicurus ever since antiquity with regard to the problem of the relation between mind and body. It may furthermore be argued that Epicurus' position has a considerable *Wirkungsgeschichte*, given that – at any rate *in nuce* and taking all due differences into account – the contemporary debate on the mind-body problem is both historically and theoretically indebted to the Samian philosopher and his attempt to lend indeterminateness to matter as the constitutive element of the mind.

Notes

1 The introduction and conclusion, just like the final revision of this contribution, are the joint work of the two authors. The subsection *The corporeal soul* and section *Epicurus' philosophy of mind* were written by Francesca Masi. The section *The soul-body relation* (but for the subsection *The corporeal soul*), and the sections *From psychological monism to the functional bipartition of the soul* and *The mind-nature problem* were written by Francesco Verde. Since the authors submitted this chapter in 2015, unfortunately they could not take into account the volume by A. Németh (*Epicurus on the Self*, London and New York, Routledge) published in 2017.
2 Unless explicitly noted, translations are by the authors.

3 On memory in Epicurean psychology, see Masi 2014, and Spinelli forthcoming.
4 For a first overview of the function of the *clinamen* within Epicurus' psychology, see Masi 2006, pp. 218–255, Spinelli and Verde 2014, pp. 61–71, and Mitsis 2014, pp. 179–227.

Bibliography

Annas, J. (1992) *Hellenistic Philosophy of Mind*. Berkeley and Los Angeles: University of California Press.

———. (1993) Epicurus on agency. In Brunschwig, J., and Nussbaum, M. C. (eds.) *Passions and Perceptions: Studies on Hellenistic Philosophy of Mind*. Proceedings of the fifth Hellenistic Symposium. Cambridge, MA: Cambridge University Press, pp. 53–71.

Bailey, C. (1929) *The Greek Atomists and Epicurus*. Oxford: Oxford University Press.

Bignone, E. (1940) La dottrina epicurea del *clinamen*. *Atene e Roma* 42: 159–198.

———. (1973) *L'Aristotele perduto e la formazione filosofica di Epicuro*. 2 vols. Florence [I ed. 1936]: La Nuova Italia.

Bobzien, S. (2000) Did Epicurus discover the free will problem? *Oxford Studies in Ancient Philosophy* 19: 287–337.

De Caro, M. (2004) *Il libero arbitrio: Una introduzione*. Rome and Bari: Laterza.

Diano, C. (1974) *Scritti epicurei*. Florence: Olschki.

Englert, W. (1987) *Epicurus on the Swerve and Voluntary Action*. Atlanta: Scholars Press.

Gill, C. (2009) Psychology. In Warren, J. (ed.) *The Cambridge Companion to Epicureanism*. Cambridge, MA: Cambridge University Press, pp. 125–141.

Giussani, C. (1896) *Studi lucreziani*. Torino: Loescher.

Kerferd, G, B. (1971) Epicurus' doctrine of the soul. *Phronesis* 16. 80–96.

Kim, J. (1998) *Mind in a Physical World*. Cambridge, MA: MIT Press.

———. (2005) *Physicalism, or Something near Enough*. Princeton and Oxford: Princeton University Press.

Konstan, D. (2007) *Lucrezio e la psicologia epicurea*. Milan: Vita e Pensiero.

———. (2015) Where in the psyche are mental pleasures experienced? In De Sanctis, D., Spinelli, E., Tulli, M., and Verde, F. (eds.) *Questioni epicuree*. Sankt Augustin: Academia Verlag, pp. 151–158.

Laursen, S. (1995) The early parts of Epicurus, *On Nature*, 25th book. *Cronache Ercolanesi* 25: 5–109.

———. (1997) The later parts of Epicurus, *On Nature*, 25th book. *Cronache Ercolanesi* 27: 5–82.

Mariotti, S. (1940) La 'quinta essentia' nell'Aristotele perduto e nell'Accademia. *Rivista di Filologia e d'Istruzione classica* 18: 179–189.

Masi, F. G. (2006) *Epicuro e la filosofia della mente*: *Il XXV libro dell'opera Sulla natura*. Sankt Augustin: Academia Verlag.

———. (2014) Gli atomi ricordano? Fisicalismo e memoria nella psicologia di Epicuro. *Antiquorum Philosophia* 8: 121–141.

Mitsis, P. (2014) *L'Éthique d'Épicure: Les plaisirs de l'invulnérabilité*. French translated by A. Gigandet. Paris: Garnier.

O'Keeke, T. (2005) *Epicurus on Freedom*. Cambridge, MA: Cambridge University Press.

Repici, L. (2008) Il pensiero dell'anima in Epicuro e Lucrezio. In Alesse, F., Aronadio, F., Dalfino, M. C., Simeoni, L., and Spinelli, E. (eds.) *'Anthropine Sophia': Studi di filologia e storiografia filosofica in memoria di Gabriele Giannantoni*. Naples: Bibliopolis, pp. 379–406.

Sedley, D. (1983) Epicurus' refutation of determinism. In *ΣΥΖΗΤΗΣΙΣ: Studi sull' Epicureismo greco e romano offerti a Marcello Gigante*. Naples: Gaetano Macchiaroli Editore, pp. 11–51.

Silvestre, M. L. (1985) *Democrito ed Epicuro: Il senso di una polemica*. Naples: Loffredo.

Spinelli, E. (2012) Physics as philosophy of happiness: The transmission of scientific tenets in Epicurus. In Sgarbi, M. (ed.) *Translatio Studiorum: Ancient, Medieval, and Modern Bearers of Intellectual History*. Leiden and Boston: Brill, pp. 25–36.

———. (forthcoming) Physics, memory, ethics: The Epicurean road to happiness (or better, as Miles would play it: 'Seven Steps to Heaven' . . .). In Castagnoli, L., and Ceccarelli, P. (eds.) *Greek Memories: Theory and Practice*. Cambridge, MA: Cambridge University Press.

Spinelli, E., and Verde, F. (2014) Alle radici del libero arbitrio? Aporie e soluzioni nelle filosofie ellenistiche. In De Caro, M., Mori, M., and Spinelli, E. (eds.) *Libero arbitrio: Storia di una controversia filosofica*. Rome: Carocci, pp. 59–98.

Verde, F. (ed.) (2010) *Epicuro: Epistola a Erodoto*. Intro by E. Spinelli. Rome: Carocci.

———. (2013) *Epicuro*. Rome: Carocci.

———. (2015) Monismo psicologico e dottrina dell'anima in Epicuro e Lucrezio. In Canone, E. (a cura di) (ed.) *Anima-corpo alla luce dell'etica: Antichi e moderni*. Florence: Olschki, pp. 49–64.

———. (2016) Aristotle and the garden. In Falcon, A. (ed.) *Brill's Companion to the Reception of Aristotle in Antiquity*. Leiden: Brill, pp. 35–55.

———. (2017a) Gli Epicurei e la psicologia di Epicuro, in Alesse, F., Fermani, A., Maso, S. (eds.) *Studi su ellenismo e filosofia romana*, Rome: Edizioni di Storia e Letteratura, pp. 33–64.

———. (2017b) Accio, Lucrezio e la psicologia di Epicuro: *Osservazioni su Trag.* 296 R.3 (589 Dangel), *Museum Helveticum* 74: 158–171.

———. (forthcoming) The partition of the soul: Epicurus, Demetrius Lacon, and Diogenes of Oinoanda, *Proceedings of XIV Symposium Hellenisticum "The Metaphysics of the Soul"* ed. by B. Inwood and J. Warren).

13

GALEN'S PHILOSOPHY OF MIND

R.J. Hankinson

Just as health of the body is the proper balancing (συμμετρία) of its simplest parts, which we call the elements – I mean hot and cold and dry and wet – in the same way I think that health of the soul should be some proper balancing of its simple parts. You need to lay out what these are, how many they are, and what are their mutual interrelations.... Moreover, disease of the soul will be an equivalent unbalancing of and mutual dissension (στάσις) between those very same parts for which the proper balancing constitutes health of the soul. And these parts are, as Plato said, the spirited, and the rational, and a third in addition to these, the appetitive, so that this likeness between health and disease of body and soul is preserved in every respect. For when the three parts are in harmony with one another and do not conflict in any way, they produce health of the soul, but when they are discordant and in conflict, they produce disease.

(**1**: Galen, *The Doctrines of Hippocrates and Plato* [*PHP*] V 440–441 Kühn, = 302,2–16 De Lacy, 1978)[1]

Galen was principally known as a medical man (as indeed he still is); but he wrote voluminously on philosophical topics (little of which survives), and aspired to a philosophical reputation as well, and, for all his rhodomontade, not unreasonably so. His surviving *oeuvre*, largely medical in general orientation, is shot through with philosophical argument. Indeed he believed, as the title and contents of a short surviving treatise attest, that *The Best Doctor is also a Philosopher*,[2] and in a non-trivial sense. The physician needs logic to construct and assess demonstrations (and refute sophistry), ethics (not merely of a professional kind) to remain honest and hard-working, and physics in order to understand the basic structure of the world, of which human physiology is an integral part. The passage just quoted gives one version of his general structural account of disease, as applied to mental illness (and health), which (as a medical man) he has of course more than a merely avocational interest in.

Indeed, his interest in questions that we would regard as falling within the purview of the philosophy of mind (what is the nature of the soul and its relation to the body? Does it survive physical death? Etc.) is largely determined by his medical concerns. Issues regarding the mind (broadly construed) and its functioning matter only insofar as they contribute to the preservation of mental health and the therapy of psychological illness. Indeed questions such as that of its possible immortality, being by nature incapable of being settled, are to be relegated to the useless cul-de-sacs of speculative philosophy, where they can be worried at inconclusively by inconsequential theorists. What matters is what we can understand, and what we can affect. In pursuit of such practical understanding, we need not even settle the vexed question of what the soul really is:

> As for the soul, I see that it exists, and I know about it that we have a soul, just as everyone does; for I see that all men call the cause of voluntary motion and sensation the soul. But I do not claim to know the soul's substance, and *a fortiori* I should not claim to know whether it is mortal. I have written a book *On the Doctrines of Hippocrates and Plato*. But I make no claim anywhere in it as to whether the soul is mortal or immortal, corporeal or incorporeal.
> (**2**: *My Own Opinions* [*Prop.Plac.*][3] 3.1–2, 58,22–60,11 Nutton)

That text encapsulates Galen's general attitude (and not just in regard to questions of psychology). Some things are just obvious, such as that animals have certain distinctive capacities, primarily those of sensation and movement (with the addition of intellectual faculties in humans). We can ascribe these abilities to their particular souls, since (following a hallowed Greek orthodoxy) to have a soul (of a particular type) just is to exhibit certain distinctive psychic capacities. But as to what souls actually are, Galen has never been able to come to any even plausible, much less demonstrable, conclusion; and without such knowledge, he can have no well-founded opinions as to its mortality or corporeality. Such is the view he expounded in *Doctrines of Hippocrates and Plato* [*PHP*],[4] as part of his general rejection of speculative philosophy:

> It is not surprising that the majority of disagreements in philosophy have not been resolved, since these issues are not susceptible of clear adjudication on the basis of empirical tests. Thus some assert that the universe is ungenerated, others that it had a beginning, just as some say there is nothing outside it enclosing it, while others say that there is, and of the latter some hold it to be void containing no substance in it while others say there are other universes uncountable in number, a multitude stretching to infinity. It is impossible to adjudicate such a disagreement on the basis clear perception.
> (**3**: *PHP* V 766, = 576,27–578,2 De Lacy)[5]

Still there are things about the way the psychological powers operate which can be known, and which do matter from the point of view of medical intervention. Most important, in Galen's view, is the truth of the Platonic account of the soul's structure. A passage at the end of *PHP* sums up his view. Having quoted from *Timaeus* in support of the contention that Plato held his views about the soul's immortality to be at best plausible and not demonstratively established (*PHP* V 791–793, = 598,5–25 De Lacy; he quotes from *Tim.*29c–d, and 72d), Galen goes on to say:

> On the other hand, I claim to have demonstrations that the forms of the soul are multiple and located in three different places, and that the one with which we reason is divine, while the others are affective (we are emotionally motivated by one, while with the other, which plants have too, we desire bodily pleasures), and moreover the first is located in the brain, the others in the heart and the liver. There are scientific demonstrations of these things. But I said nothing about the substance of the soul's three parts, nor about their immortality. The knowledge that the forms of the soul are situated in three places, and of what their capacities are and how many they have, is useful for medical science and for that part of philosophy called moral and political . . . but the further inquiry whether the spirited and appetitive parts happen to be immortal . . . is of no use either to medicine or to moral and political philosophy; and doctors as well as many philosophers have passed over it, reasonably enough; it belongs to the theoretical [sc. speculative] rather than the practical branch of philosophy.
> (**4**: *PHP* V 793–794, = 598,28–600,19 De Lacy)

Much of the first six books of *PHP* is devoted to the demonstrations of the locations and separate functioning of the different parts.[6] What is striking (apart from the claim that he follows Plato in not supposing that the immortality of even the rational part of the soul is *provable*)[7] is his contention that he has *scientific* proof for tripartition and trilocation. In the earlier books, he does indeed say that the location of the rational soul in the brain is demonstrable, by anatomical observation and experiment; the association of the spirited part with the heart is rather less firmly grounded (although Galen does not admit this), relying as it does on the fact that arteries ramify from the heart, and the observation that ligation of the arteries suppresses the pulse downstream of the ligation. But the location of the desiderative part in the liver, is, as Galen admits, even less securely established:

> The proof is not from such clear evidence as those before, and its premises . . . will not be taken directly from the very nature of the thing investigated, but from its particular properties.
> (**5**: *PHP* V 519, = 372,19–22 De Lacy)

Particularly vulnerable to objection is his attribution of desire to the liver on the grounds that it attracts nourishment to itself.[8] As text **1** showed, Galen is keen to assimilate the Platonic desiderative part to the Aristotelian nutritive soul (an identification made explicit at 521, = 374–13–19, even though the Stoics prefer to call this faculty 'nature', a practice Galen himself elsewhere endorses: *Natural Faculties* II 1–2),[9] which we share with plants; thus plants too must, in the appropriate sense, have desires.

Galen seeks to buttress this rather flimsy contention by offering an account of the blood-producing function of the liver, and in terms of his complex theory of digestion and the assimilation of food. The liver attracts to itself the processed food from the stomach, and transforms it into venous blood, which then is distributed by the veins throughout the body to nourish its tissues. In order to get the processed food, obviously food needs to be ingested and then preliminarily worked up in the digestive system into *chyle*, before being attracted into the liver for further elaboration.[10] How this involves desire as such is another question. Galen begins by establishing that the liver is the source of the venous system, just as the heart and brain are the sources of the arterial and nervous systems respectively (*PHP* V521–532, = 374,20–82,33 De Lacy), making extended use of the analogy with plant structure derived from Aristotle: the roots are like mouths, drawing raw nutriment into the centre, the trunk or stalk. The burden of his argument is expressed at 533, = 384,7–9: "So if blood-production is for the sake of nourishing the animal, and blood is produced in the liver, then this organ rather than the heart will be the source of the nutritive power".

But however that may be, what about its also being the seat of desire? Galen does little more than gesture towards *Timaeus* 70d–e, quoting its claim that "the part of the soul that desires food and drink . . . they placed in the region between the diaphragm and the boundary of the navel . . . and there they fixed the desiderative part of the soul," which he assimilates, un-Platonically in spite of what he says, to the liver (cf. *PHP* V 580, = 422,2–7 De Lacy). He concludes by saying that "the liver has been demonstrated to be the source of the veins, of the blood, and of the desiderative soul" (582–583, 424,9–11). The basic idea is that the liver attracts to itself the partially worked *chyle*, which it then transforms into properly nutritious material; and since it does so, it must in some sense desire it. But this could be applied to any 'natural power' for attraction, such as that of the magnet for iron, where Galen does not want to draw any such conclusion. The nearest he gets to a plausible argument is to be found in *Function of the Parts* (*UP*) i 226–8 Helmreich,[11] where he notes that the liver is innervated by a small nerve, which would not be required for purely vegetative functions; on the other hand, it is too small to have a motor function, but,

> as Plato says (*Tim*.69c–71d), the liver is like a wild animal . . . the reasoning part of us, which is the real man, is situated in the brain, and has as its handmaiden and servant the irascible soul to protect it against this wild animal. For this reason, the demiurge connected these parts with

offshoots [sc. veins, arteries and nerves], and so contrived for them to heed one another.

(**6**: *UP* i 228 Helmreich)

This is obviously very sketchy; but the general idea must be that the nerve from the liver alerts the brain to the need for a supply of raw nutriment; in this sense the liver is the source of desire. But at the very least such hepatic 'desires' cannot be conscious ones, since consciousness for Galen resides in the brain, as he has established (rather more convincingly) earlier in *PHP* and elsewhere.

He does this on the basis of anatomical (and indeed vivisectional) investigation, the details of which are to be found in his *Anatomical Procedures*,[12] relying on general methodological principles to be found in *PHP* (V 219–221) and *Therapeutic Method* (*MM* X 30–50).[13] I (and others) have dealt with these arguments at length elsewhere,[14] and shall not rehearse them in detail here. But fundamental to them (and to his attack on the cardiocentric and monistic thesis of the Stoics) is his insistence that scientific arguments must take their premises from the very essence of the subject under discussion (see text **5** quoted previously). In order to do this, Galen says, we need to take account of the relevant 'common conception', which in his usage means what people generally, reflectively take to be the core meaning of a crucial term – thus, he says, everyone really agrees that what is meant by 'disease' is 'damage to a natural function', or the disposition which causes such damage (*Difference of Symptoms* VII 50; cf. *Art of Medicine* I 379;[15] *MM* X 78–81);[16] the job of the physician is to distinguish between such functions and specific types of damage to them, in order to isolate their causes (since it is a self-evident axiom that nothing happens without a cause: *MM* X 36, 50), and hence (as a result of reflecting on the aim of medicine as being the restoration and preservation of health), by removing or counteracting them, to treat the disease.

In the case of the rational soul, or its ruling part (as Galen, indifferently adopting Stoic terminology, will sometimes call it), its specific properties include sensation and the production of motion, as well as more purely mental functions such as rational calculation, memory, imagination, and so on. That much is a commonplace, a conceptual truth even; but what is not so obvious is how it does it. For Galen, the key to answering this question, and by extension that of the ruling part's location, was provided by the isolation of the nervous system (begun by Praxagoras in the 4th century BC), and refined by the anatomical discrimination between the sensory and motor neural systems owed to the great 3rd-century Alexandrian Herophilus.[17] In a brilliant series of experiments on live animal subjects, often in bravura public demonstrations, Galen showed that ligating and sectioning nerves produced paralysis, either temporary or permanent, downstream of the cut (summarized at *PHP* V 644–647, = 476,3–478,8 De Lacy).[18] These interventions worked, he thought, by interrupting the transmission of motion and sensation through the nerves by way of the *pneuma*:

I also showed in the 7th book of my work *The Doctrines of Hippocrates and Plato*,[19] and in other books, that psychic *pneuma* exists in the ventricles of the brain and that it is chief among the instruments of the rational soul, which inhabits the body of the brain and not the ventricles.

(**7**: *My Own Opinions* 7.5, 80,10–13
Nutton, 1999; trans. after Nutton)

The existence of *pneuma* of various kinds is central to Galen's psychology (and physiology) and places him in a tradition that stretches back, by way of the pneumatist doctors such as Athenaeus (with whom Galen disagrees, but about the function of the stuff, not its existence), through the Stoics to Aristotle and (more distantly) the Hippocratics.[20] For Galen, *pneuma* is worked-up air:

From the outside air, *pneuma* is drawn in by the rough artery [i.e. the trachea] and receives its first elaboration in the flesh of the lungs, its second in the heart and the arteries, especially those of the retiform plexus, and then a final elaboration in the ventricles of the brain, which completes its transformation into psychic *pneuma*.

(**8**: *UP* III 541–542, = i 393,23–394,6 Helmreich)[21]

Pneuma, whatever it is and however it works, is clearly vital to the functioning of the soul. But Galen rejects the Stoic view that the *pneuma* actually constitutes the soul:

On the basis of these facts[22] one might think that one of the following two possibilities concerning the *pneuma* in the ventricles of the brain obtained: if the soul is incorporeal, it [sc. the *pneuma*] is as one might say its primary dwelling-place;[23] but if it is a body, this very *pneuma* is the soul.[24] But when it occurs that, shortly after the ventricles have been closed up, the animal perceives and moves again, one can maintain that neither of these alternatives concerning *pneuma* is true. It is thus better to suppose that the soul dwells in the actual body of the brain, whatever it might turn out to be as regards its essence . . . and that its primary instrument in regard to all the animal's sensations, and its voluntary movements as well, is this *pneuma*, and for this reason when it is emptied out the animal does not lose its life, but is rendered incapable of sensation and motion, until it is re-assembled, whereas if it really were the substance of the soul, the animal would die immediately upon its being emptied out.

(**9**: *PHP* V 605–606, = '442,36–444,11 De Lacy; cf. 280–4,
287–9, 609 = 164,8–166,23, 170,6–27, 446,11–15
De Lacy; *The Composition of Simple Drugs* XI 731;
The Function of Breathing IV 501–502)

Pneuma cannot itself be the substance of the soul, since although psychic functions are interrupted when it is evacuated, they are not thereby irrevocably destroyed. As noted previously, Galen is committed to tripartition, not just in functional terms (a position which he attributes to Aristotle too), but also in terms of the un-Aristotelian distribution of the faculties into three separate organs. Aristotle is better than the Stoics, who (with the exception of Posidonius, whom Galen presents, somewhat tendentiously, as a crypto-Platonist)[25] make the soul unitary, denying even the existence of separable spirited and desiderative powers, and thus being unable adequately to explain the phenomena of psychic conflict.[26] But he still makes the crucial mistake of making the heart the seat of all psychic functions, including the rational, at least insofar as it requires the physical mechanism of φαντασία (*DA*.3.7.431a14–18, 431b2–5).[27]

Aristotle, Praxagoras,[28] and the Stoics could make this cardinal error only because they were ignorant of the crucial fact that the nerves have their origin (in the sense of the central source from which they ramify) in the brain (*PHP* V 187, = 80,21–26 De Lacy). Aristotle "twice spoke confusedly and imprecisely about the origin of the nerves" (200, = 90,28–29 De Lacy); but could not show "how the nerves ramified from it [sc. the heart] to every part of the body, as we have just now done in the case of the arteries" (200, = 90,30–32 De Lacy). Indeed, the falsity of Aristotle's claims can be demonstrated according to his own principles (*PHP* V 202, = 92,21–23 De Lacy), not least the famous slogan that nature does nothing in vain. For, on his account, the brain's sole function is to cool the body, but it is far too large and structured an organ just to do that, and in any case as Aristotle himself rightly allows, the respiratory system serves the cooling function. Moreover, he is quite wrong to hold that the sense-organs have no direct connections with the brain (*Parts of Animals* 2.7.652b3–5). This argument is rehearsed at *UP* i 449–453 Helmreich.[29] The superiority of the Platonic account is elaborated in detail at *PHP* V 505–519, = 360,4–372,15; it is encapsulated as follows:

> Since Plato holds that these forms are both separated by their location in the body and that they differ very greatly in essence, he has good reason to call them both forms and parts. But Aristotle and Posidonius do not speak of forms or parts of the soul, but say that there are powers of a single substance which stems from the heart.
> (**10**: *PHP* V 516, = 368,20–24 De Lacy)

Galen wrote a lost treatise *The Parts and Powers of the Soul* (*Lib.Prop.* XIX 46) in support of the basic Platonic position regarding powers and their locations. His major departure from the Platonist position is, as we saw (in texts **2** and **4**), his refusal to commit himself on its substance and possible immortality. Indeed, he leans strongly towards a sort of materialism (with an associated coolness to the idea of the immortality even of the rational soul) in one of his latest texts, *The Powers of the Soul Follow the Mixtures of the Body* (*QAM*).[30] That 'title' (in fact, as frequently, the first sentence of the text) is a good summation of the text's basic *probandum*. The verb 'follow' is deliberately vague, reflecting a vagueness in the Greek (ἀκολουθεῖν); at the very least, it points to a correlation between physical states and psychological tendencies and dispositions. But in fact Galen clearly takes the view that the relation is causal – physical alterations produce psychological effects.[31]

The mixtures in question (κράσεις) are for Galen fundamentally ratios between the basic four qualities, hot, cold, wet and dry, his understanding of which is fundamentally Aristotelian, with the partial departure that he considers the wet and the dry also to be fundamentally active, which is more than Aristotle (and certainly the Stoics) were prepared to admit.[32] He wrote a general treatise entitled *Mixtures*,[33] which he recommends serious beginning medical students to read, on the importance of understanding this aspect of basic physics in order to come to a proper understanding of animal physiology. In particular, the degree to which animals are, for example, hot and dry, correlates with their courage and pugnacity (lions are especially, and dogs relatively so: *Mixtures* I 537–8, 548), even though individuals in the species vary in the extent to which they exhibit the particularly species-specific tendencies; and there is in the case of each species, a natural mean state which represents 'good condition' (ευεξία)[34] for that species (542–50). For Galen, fundamental quality theory is related first to the theory of the elements (which is also, in his version, basically Aristotelian), and ultimately to his humoural doctrine of the fundamental constitution of animals' bodies. All of this is beyond the remit of this study;[35] but excesses of these humours correlates in the first instance with general character types (indeed the typology survives in our language of the sanguine, phlegmatic, choleric and melancholic),[36] and ultimately (if of an extreme and prolonged nature) into actual disorder and disease, psychological as well as physical.

QAM begins with the claim that "we derive good bodily mixture from our food and drink and other daily activities, and that this mixture is the basis upon which we build the virtue of the soul", a view he ascribes to "the followers of Pythagoras and Plato" (IV 767–8). "The starting-point for this whole inquiry" is, he continues, the evident fact that very young children differ significantly in their innate characters; some are cowardly, some greedy, some "quite the opposite"; some are shameless, others modest. The upshot is that "there are innate differences in the powers of in the powers of the three forms or parts of the soul" (768). And this in turn entails that their particular souls differ in their actual structure or substance, since if they didn't, "the activities and affections [of their souls] would be identical, given the same causal circumstances" (769). Galen's main target here is the (orthodox; not Posidonian) Stoic view that every individual starts out with the same basic equipment, and whether or not they turn out well or badly is entirely dependent upon their upbringing (821).[37] A substance has as many powers (δυνάμεις) as it has determinable (observable) activities (ἐνεργείαι); this is itself a conceptual truth. Powers as such should not by hypostasized:

> On this point, many philosophers seem to be in some confusion, lacking a clearly articulated notion of 'power'; they seem to think of powers as

things which inhabit substances, much as we inhabit our houses, not realizing that the effective cause of each event is conceived of in relational terms; there is a way of talking of this cause as of a specific thing, but the power arises in relation to the event caused. Hence we attribute as many powers to a substance as it has activities.

(**11**: *QAM* IV 769)

Thus aloe (the cause or agent) has the power to 'cleanse and tone' the throat, the power to stanch bleeding and promote cicatrization, and to dry the eyes; these are separate powers but are owed to the substance itself, what it really is, its intrinsic properties (770). And equally, to say that "the rational soul seated in the brain is able to perceive through the organs of perception, and through . . . [them] to remember, and by itself to discern conflict and consistency between facts" is precisely equivalent to saying that the rational soul has several powers, including perception, memory and understanding (770–771). Perception itself involves the individual sensory powers, sight, hearing, etc.; and "Plato also attributes to it the power of desire", desire in the broad sense, "since he says that the rational soul has a number of desires, the spirited part even more, and the third part even more still", which is why the third part, the hepatically-located appetitive, is labeled 'desiderative' since it has desires in spades (771–772).

Thus the account of *QAM* is firmly founded on Galen's physical tripartitional account of the soul, which is, as he says, "demonstrated elsewhere" (772). So far, so conventional:

> There is however a further belief that of these forms or parts of the soul as a whole the rational is immortal, and of this Plato seems convinced. For my part, I am unable to make a confident assertion one way or the other.
>
> (**12**: *QAM* IV 772–773)

In fact, as it will turn out later, Galen finds it very hard to understand how it might be immortal, just as elsewhere he finds the Platonic view that the World Soul is somehow directly responsible for the development of all embryos difficult to swallow for more than one reason (*Formation of the Foetus*[38] IV 687–702, esp. 700–702): "the skill and power involved would be worthy of that entity, but I could not tolerate the conclusion that scorpions and venomous spiders . . . were constructed by it, for such a doctrine seemed to me to verge on blasphemy". But in *QAM*, for strategic reasons, he chooses to begin with the lower parts,

> Which both Plato and I agree[39] cease to exist at death. Each of these organs has its particular substance, but we should not immediately demand an accurate definition of these substances, but first recall the nature of the common substance of all bodies . . . [which] is comprised of

two principles (*archai*), matter and form. Matter is conceptually lacking in quality, but contains within it a mixture of four qualities, heat, cold, dryness and wetness; and these qualities give rise to bronze, iron gold, and also to flesh, sinew, fat, gristle and all such entities – those which Plato calls 'first-born'[40] and Aristotle 'uniform'.

(**13**: *QAM* IV 773)

The assimilation of Plato to Aristotle in the last clause (and indeed elsewhere) is as tendentious as it is characteristic; but that can be left on one side. What matters is Galen's evident queasiness with any kind of substance-dualism. He notes Aristotle's definition of the soul as the form of the body, emphasizing (correctly) that 'form' in this context is obviously not a matter of mere physical morphology, but rather "the other principle which constructs the very body of physical bodies, which is of the uniform and simple kind and devoid of any organic composition" (773–774). But he infers from this that if bodies are matter-form composites, and physical bodies fundamentally consist in mixtures of the four qualities in matter, "then we must take Aristotle's form as meaning the mixture of those qualities; thus the substance of the soul too must be some mixture of these four qualities" (774). From which it follows that if the rational faculty has such a physical basis, "it too will be a mixture, namely one within the brain" (774–775). Galen thus adopts a strikingly physicalist interpretation of Aristotle's hylomorphism, a view to which he himself is evidently strongly drawn.

Next he contrasts this 'Aristotelian' view of the soul as a whole, including the rational faculty, with the Plato's insistence on its incorporeality and immortality, a view which Galen will not absolutely rule out, but which he finds deeply problematic, since if it is correct, how is one to account for its evident susceptibility to physiologically induced alteration, even destruction? It would be nice, Galen says puckishly, if Plato were around to explain how this was possible – but of course, unfortunately, he's dead (775). He allows that his own view that "not every form of body is fitted to receive the rational soul" (at *UP* i 54, he remarks that monkeys' ridiculous bodies suit their absurd souls) is consistent with Plato's position, but even so he finds it deeply problematic; he finds it hard to see how such a non-physical substance could exhibit suitable differentiations in order to produce the innate variations in behaviour whose evident existence provides the starting point for the treatise,

> Nor can I see how, if this substance is no part of the body, it can extend throughout the whole body. I have been unable even to form a vague conception of this. . . . What I can observe clearly, though, is that blood-loss and the drinking of hemlock cools the body, while a powerful fever causes excessive heat. So I ask – why does the soul definitively abandon the body which is excessively cooled or heated? Intensive research has not revealed to me why an accumulation of yellow bile in the brain leads to delirium, or why one of black bile produces melancholy, or why

phlegm and other refrigerants cause lethargy, which in turn produces impairment of memory and cognition.

(**14**: QAM IV 776–777)

This passage is important, since it emphasizes Galen's caution about causal explanation – he can *see* the effect of heating and refrigeration, but he cannot really account for them, nor does he know why it is that certain substances have the powers they have. But for all that, the materialist position is in better shape than its substance-dualist competitor, which leaves everything mysterious. Equally, we might not know precisely why wine produces the various effects that it does (promoting digestion when taken in moderation, and "rendering the soul both gentler and more confident": 777–778), but that it does so is incontrovertible; "and this effect is clearly brought about through the medium of bodily mixture, which in turn is brought about through the medium of the humours" (779); so, he writes,

> Even those who think that the soul has a particular substance must accept that it is a slave to the temperaments of the body, at any rate if the latter have the power to separate it, to cause it to become delirious, to destroy memory and intelligence, and to make it sadder and more timid and more despondent, as occurs to melancholics, while the man who drinks wine in certain quantities experiences the opposite of these things.
>
> (**15**: *QAM* IV 779; cf. 782, 787–788)

Plato himself acknowledges these facts in the *Timaeus* (from which Galen goes on to quote, albeit selectively and self-servingly: 780–781 [43a–b, 44a–b], 789–91 [86c–87a]).[41] Galen has, effectively, hit upon the interaction problem for substance dualism; which is why he leans heavily in the direction of what he takes to be an Aristotelian materialism: "if the reasoning faculty is a form of the body,[42] it must be mortal; for it too will be a mixture, namely one in the brain (774–775). This is the closest Galen gets to committing himself on the substance of the rational soul. At 782–783, he praises "Andronicus the Peripatetic," who "dared to state . . . that the substance of the soul was a mixture or power of the body; I have great respect for this man and I follow his line." Even so he castigates him for saying that soul is "either a mixture or a power dependent on that mixture," since the soul itself, being a substance, consistently with the contentions of 769–771, will *have* powers, and thus cannot be identified with them. Indeed, he says,

> This was correctly stated by Aristotle, who clearly distinguished an ambiguity here. For, as he pointed out, substance is used to mean both matter and form, and the composite of both, and soul is substance in the sense of form; so it is illegitimate to define it as anything other than the mixture, as was shown earlier.
>
> (**16**: *QAM* IV 783)

Elsewhere, he is slightly less emphatic ("the soul is either a mixture of the active qualities, or is altered as a result of their mixture": *Affected Parts* VIII 181; see further later in this chapter); but the tendency of his thinking here is unmistakable. To have the abilities associated with the rational soul is to have physical tissues (and perhaps organs) structured in particular ways. Galen is, in a sense, a *harmonia* theorist – the reference to Pythagoreans at the outset is not a random one.[43]

In the context of anti-dualism, but also in opposition to the Stoic unitary account of the soul, according to which emotions are to be identified with mistaken judgements, and weakness of the will analyzed not as a conflict between opposing sources of internal motivation, but rather as a rapid vacillation of the unitary soul between opposing points of view, the following is worth quoting:

> Loss of memory, intelligence, or the ability to move, or of sensation, resulting from the stated causes, can be regarded as impairments of the soul's ability to perform its natural functions. But cases of people seeing things which are not there, or hearing things that no-one said, or making obscene or blasphemous or utterly meaningless utterances, seem to indicate not just a loss of faculties which the soul possesses intrinsically, but the presence of some opposite power.
> (**17**: *QAM* IV 787–788)

As I said at the outset, Galen's basic motivation in investigating the nature of psychological powers is medical. For him, what we might classify as disorders are definitely mental illnesses, at least insofar as they interfere with the ability of the sufferer to perform normal human functions. *Akrasia* (weakness of will) then, can be a genuine mental illness, as can a tendency to extreme irascibility, or indeed any other condition where one's better judgement (in the objective sense of one's correct judgement of what is in fact in one's interest as an exemplar of humanity) is overcome or derailed by other motivations. Galen wrote two separate treatises on the diagnosis and treatment of these issues, *Affections of the Soul* (V 1–57) and *Errors of the Soul* (V 58–103),[44] and while they are usually printed consecutively, and often treated as two chapters of a single text, they are importantly distinct. The treatment for the former is in large part a precursor of contemporary cognitive behavioural therapy;[45] in order to avoid errors, on the other hand, which are intellectual mistakes, one needs training in logic in order to construct valid arguments and detect sophisms. The fact that the different sorts of condition require quite different sorts of treatment is in itself an argument in favour of their radical distinction. But even more interestingly, the passage in *QAM* continues:

> This fact may cast doubt on the entire account of the nature of the soul as non-physical. For if it were not some quality, form, condition, or power of the body, how could it come to acquire a nature opposite to its normal state just as a result of its association with the body? . . . Indeed, the overwhelming effect on the soul of the ills of the body is clearly demonstrated by the

case of people suffering from melancholy, phrenitis and mania.... All of this creates a strong presumption with regard to the whole of the soul that it is not incorporeal; for how could the soul be driven into an unnatural state as a result of its association with the body, unless it were some quality of the body, or some form, or affection, or power of the body?

(**18**: *QAM* IV 788)

For a Stoic unitarian, all failures of the soul must simply be due to weakness; but, Galen argues, that cannot account for radical departures from normal behaviour, which demand explanation in terms of opposing, and hence quite distinct, forces; and that in turn also tells against psychic immaterialism.

Finally, I want to look a little more closely at Galen's therapeutic approach, in particular in his treatise *Affected Parts* (VIII 1–452). In the third book, he turns to psychological disorders; and he notes that even cardiocentrists still apply remedies to the head, thus giving the lie to their theory by their practice, or so at least he maintains. Galen's own theory is complex and relies on a fundamental differentiation between the part primarily affected by the responsible imbalance, and other parts affected sympathetically, as he puts it. This distinction applies to all types of condition, including the purely physiological; but it is of particular importance in his humoural psychology, as the following lengthy extract shows:

> The melancholic humour also clearly exhibits different kinds of composition. One kind is like the sediment of blood and clearly shows itself as being quite thick, like wine lees. I call this 'melancholic humour' or 'melancholic blood', for I think one should not yet call it black bile....
> This thick melancholic humour, just like the phlegmatic one, sometimes causes cases of epilepsy when it is trapped where the cavities of the brain, either the central or the posterior, have their outlets. But when it is present in excessive quantities in the very body of the brain, it causes melancholy, just as the other kind of black bile, the one produced by the burning of yellow bile, results in bestial delirium and hallucinations, both with and without fever, when it clogs the body of the brain. This is also why one kind of phrenitis, namely that arising from pale bile, is more moderate, whereas the other one which arises from yellow bile is more severe. There is still another kind of delirium, both bestial and melancholic, that arises from the burning of yellow bile. In those cases of delirium that arise at the peaks of fever, the brain is suffering through *sumpatheia*, not as a proprietary affection in its own right. This is why these people lose their wits, are delirious, and are beside themselves. These are not cases of phrenitis, since cases of phrenetic delirium do not subside after the fever peaks. So just as in the case of phrenitics, fever is a symptom of the condition of the brain, likewise delirium is a symptom of burning fever, when a large quantity of hot vapour rises into the brain.

(**19**: Galen, *Affected Parts* VIII 176–178)

We need not here go deeply into how the conditions mentioned are differentiated; what matters is that, in the case of mental impairment, one way or another, either directly or indirectly, the brain is affected, sometimes intrinsically, and sometimes merely as a symptom, or consequent effect, of something else. But however the impediment occurs, it is fundamentally physical in nature. This is emphasized a couple of pages later:

> Since the soul is either a mixture of the active qualities, or is altered as a result of their mixture . . . the bile that damages the brain considered as an organic part tends to affect the body of the brain, by way of obstructions, while the bile that affects it as a uniform part tends to affect the mind.
>
> (**20**: *Affected Parts* VIII 181)

Once again, Galen maintains a careful façade of agnosticism as to whether the soul is really to be identified with a qualitative mixture; but the distinction between affections of the brain as an organic, structured part (by way of blockages and so on), and its being affected simply in virtue of changes to its constitutive tissue (this is the force of the Aristotelian language of uniform parts) is highly suggestive: it is the brain tissue itself that is conceived of as the seat of the intelligence, and changes in its temperament induce mental disorder and disease. How? In *QAM*, as we saw (quoted previously, text **14**), he confesses ignorance. But in this text, at least in the case of the depressive effects of black bile, he suggests an account that goes beyond (or perhaps beside) that humour's supposed cold and dry qualities:

> For just as external darkness induces fear in just about everyone, apart from the naturally brave and those who have been educated, so too the black bile, which is similar in colour to the dark, induces fears by casting a shadow over the reasoning part.
>
> (**21**: *Affected Parts* VIII 190–191)

I do not know how seriously Galen intended this – perhaps he didn't either. Later in the same treatise, he is notably cautious about explaining the various modalities of causal transmission, citing the striking example of a fisherman receiving an electric shock through a bronze trident in contact with an electric fish (420–421); again, what matters for him is the evident *fact* of the causal effect and transmission, apparently through a solid object (albeit by contact). Whether or not, and if so how, it can be accounted for is another matter, and one which may well be of no practical relevance.

Which brings me finally to the issue of psycho-physical interaction. We have seen how, in *QAM*, Galen emphasizes the importance of the evident fact that the physical can have psychological effects. He is also sensitive to the impact of these facts on crucial questions in moral psychology regarding freedom and responsibility.[46] Galen takes seriously the Platonic idea that bad people are bad "because of two kinds of condition both of which are completely outside their control" (*Tim.* 87b), namely their intrinsic nature and their upbringing (86d–e). This follows another long disquisition, replete with quotes from the *Laws*, on the effects, and proper usage, of wine (806–812), and on the impact of environmental factors on the powers of the soul. At 814, he turns to the questions of human nature and moral responsibility, claiming first that "our argument is not destructive of the fine teachings of philosophy", and that both those (pre-eminently the Stoics) who think that people are by nature good, and those who think the exact opposite,

> Are mistaken in presenting human nature from a one-sided perspective – not all are born enemies of justice, nor are all its friends, but each kind comes about through bodily mixture. But how, then, they say, can one be justly praised, blamed, love or hated for good or evil qualities which are not due to oneself, but to a mixture, which obviously derives from other sources?
>
> (**22**: *QAM* IV 814–815)

Galen's response is strikingly Humean – it is a "human universal to show affection, inclination, and love for the good, and to reject, despise, and flee the bad" (815). We don't bother to ask whether vipers and scorpions are somehow responsible for their own nastiness before we kill them; we kill them because of what they are, not why they are that way, and the same should apply to the irremediably reprobate among human beings. In fact "we do so for three good reasons": public security, deterrence, and because it is actually better for them to die, as their lives are intrinsically not worth living if they are incapable of rehabilitation (815–816).

The upshot is that the Stoic view that evil comes into us from the outside is wrong; bad men derive the majority of their badness from within. Indeed, "there is in fact a seed of evil within us"; and "the part due to external influences is much smaller", accounting for the formation of certain sorts of habits, both good and bad, both in the irrational soul and in the rational (820–821). But, Galen adds,

> Such phenomena in the rational part as shrewdness, or various degrees of foolishness, are dependent on mixture; and mixture itself is due to birth and to good-humoured regimen. And these conditions give rise to vicious or virtuous circles; the sharp-spirited become so because of the hot mixture, but then by the sharpness of their spirit inflame their innate heat; similarly, people with a well-proportioned mixture enjoy well-proportioned motions of the soul and are thus assisted towards good spirits.
>
> (**23**: *QAM* IV 821)

So nature outweighs nurture; but at least equally importantly, the last sentence gestures towards a genuine psycho-physical interactionism, for all that *QAM* has emphasized the role of the bodily in conditioning mental attitudes. Characteristically, this is merely a hint; and he essays no attempt at a causal explanation of how it is supposed to work. But I think it is clear that whatever else this amounts to, it is no mere epiphenomenalism. It is not simply that the effects of heat, for instance, can be self-reinforcing, with the associated mental conditions (irascibility, let's say) being mere Searleian froth on the wave. That might of course be simply because Galen did not see any issue here. But this is not an isolated claim. In the *Art of Medicine*, after talking of the importance of diet and exercise to the maintenance of the proper bodily balance, Galen writes,

> Obviously one must refrain from excess of all affections of the soul: anger, grief, pride, fear, envy and distress, since these will change the natural composition of the body.
>
> (**24**: *Art of Medicine* I 371)

It is the affective qualities themselves, the experienced emotions, which are being given causal responsibility for physical effects (cf. 373: "all mental affections dry the body"). It is tempting to think that here Galen's Platonic leanings are influential – the rational soul is an agent, after all, and agents do things. Even if the having of such a soul is a matter of having certain physical structures in certain conditions, the powers of that soul directly involve and rely upon conscious experience. And that, one can imagine him saying, is just a matter of obvious experience, however one might try to analyze its deep causal structure. It is also of a piece with his commitment to cognitive behavioural therapy; we can reduce our tendency to irascibility, for instance, by reflecting on its hideous and shameful manifestations; thinking, that is, that it's not a good idea to indulge one's anger. But that in the long run (it can take five years, apparently) will re-condition our fundamental humoural structure in virtue of which we are prone to such regrettable and unbecoming outbursts in the first place. This is, in large part, the burden of *Affections of the Soul* (see especially V 20–29); it is also a theme dealt with in the recently recovered *Freedom from Distress*.[47] If your causal theory can't make sense of that evident fact, so much the worse for your theory. That is a typically Galenic stance; and it is reflected in the concluding words of *QAM*, which may equally serve as mine:

> Thus, our argument agrees with observed fact. It explains the causes of the effects we experience from wine and from medicines, as well as from good and bad regimen. It explains, further, why we experience beneficial and harmful effects from certain kinds of training and education; and last but not least it provides an account of the natural differences between children. Those who do not agree that the soul derives benefit and harm from the mixture of the body have no explanation whatsoever to give of the differences in children, or of the benefits derived from regimen or of

those differences in character which make people spirited or otherwise or intelligent or otherwise.

(**25**: *QAM* IV 821)

Notes

1. Texts of Galen are referenced where possible by of the edition of Kühn (Leipzig 1821–1833; repr. 1965, Hildesheim) which, for all its faults, is still the most complete. Where later and better editions exist I mention them at least at the first reference, and sometimes more generally; but as most of them print the Kühn pagination in their margins, Kühn remains a convenient way to focus on texts.
2. I 53–63 Kühn; most recently edited in Boudon-Millot 2007; English translation in Singer 1997.
3. *Prop.Plac.* is probably Galen's last work; until the discovery and edition of the hitherto unknown complete Greek text (Boudon-Millot and Pietroelli 2005), the work survived only as a macaroni of fragments of Greek, Latin, Arabic and Hebrew, which was collated, edited, translated and commented upon by Vivian Nutton in *CMG* V 3,2 (1999). Although we now have a complete Greek text, I refer to Nutton for ease of reference.
4. V 181–805 Kühn; it is edited, with English translation and commentary, by P.H. De Lacy as *CMG* V 4,1,1 (1978–1984).
5. For this fundamental claim. See e.g. *Prop. Plac.* 2, 56,12–24, 3,58,22–60,6 Nutton (cf. 14–15, 110,4–18,10 Nutton); *Errors of the Soul* V 67; the text (V 58–103) is edited in Marquardt 1884, and De Boer 1937, and translated in Singer, 1997, along with its companion piece *Affections of the Soul* (V 1–57).
6. On the arguments here, see Hankinson 1991a; and Tieleman 1996, 2003.
7. In order to play down his disagreements with the master, he characteristically chooses to ignore the evidence of *Phaedo*.
8. On this (as on much else), see Donini 2008, esp. pp. 193–194; see also De Lacy 1988.
9. Edited in Helmreich 1893; and, with translation, in Brock 1916.
10. On the functioning of digestion, and its associated powers, see *Natural Faculties* II 152–7.
11. *UP* appears in Kühn, III 1-IV 366; I cite the edition of Helmreich (1907–1909) since the English translation of May 1968 is keyed to it.
12. This survives partly in Greek and partly in an Arabic translation; see Garofalo 1984, 2000; English translations in Singer 1956; and Duckworth et al. 1962.
13. Books 1 and 2 of *MM* are translated with commentary in Hankinson 1991b.
14. See Hankinson 1991a, 1993, 2006, 2014a; see also Tieleman 1996, 2003.
15. *Art of Medicine* (I 305–412, is edited in Boudon 2000; translated in Singer 1997.
16. See Hankinson 1991b, ad loc.
17. For Praxagoras, see Steckerl 1958; for Herophilus, von Staden 1989.
18. For details, see Hankinson 1993, 1994; Rocca 2003, 2008. Gleason (2009) offers a classicist's perspective. Salas (2014) provides an interesting analysis of what Galen claimed to have seen, and could not have, and why.
19. See *PHP* V 605–6, = 442,36–444,11 De Lacy, quoted in text 9.
20. Galen's views on *pneuma* derive from a long tradition, both philosophical and medical. For Aristotle, *pneuma* furnished the medium for the soul's power (*GA*.2.3.736b30–37a8; cf. *PA*.2.7.652b8–15). It was central to the Stoic account of the structural coherence of the material world, as well as being the vehicle of consciousness (47C-J, L-Q; 53B, G-H, K-L LS). Post-Aristotelian physicians such as Herophilus first began to differentiate 'psychic' from 'vital' *pneuma*.

21 See also *The Function of Breathing* (IV 470–511) and *The Function of the Pulse* (V 149–180), both edited with translation and commentary in Furley and Wilkie 1984.
22 Namely that animals undergoing brain surgery do not lose sensation or the power of motion until the ventricles themselves are damaged: *PHP* V 604–5, = 442,19–35 De Lacy. On Galen's investigations of cerebral anatomy, see Rocca 2003.
23 This would be the Platonizing view.
24 The view to which Galen says the Stoics and Aristotle are drawn in spite of themselves: *PHP* V 643, = 474,22–29 De Lacy; it is unclear why he thinks the Stoics in particular would be reluctant to adopt the view.
25 For Galen's Platonizing interpretation of Posidonius' psychology, see Cooper 1998. For Galen's presentation of Posidonius's anti-Chrysippean views, see *PHP* V 397–399, 416–426, 463, 472, = 264,17–266,21, 280,27–290,9, 320,23–28, 330,2–31, = Frs. 161–162, 164–165, 169 Edelstein and Kidd. Posidonius certainly does think that Chrysippus's strong unitary account is empirically inadequate and emphasizes irrational sources of motivation; but he this is a far cry from actually adopting Platonic (functional: see 10) tripartition.
26 See Hankinson 1991a, 1993, and particularly Tieleman 1996; for general discussion, see Hankinson 2006.
27 As Galen puts it: "the sense organ is altered, and the discernment of its alteration arises through a single power common to each sense organ which flows to them from the ruling part; and it makes no difference whether you choose to designate the ruling part itself as common perception, or as that which first perceives" (*PHP* V 644, = 474,30–476,3 De Lacy).
28 Galen attacks Praxagoras's view that nerves are the thinned-out extremities of the arteries, and hence originate in the heart, at V 188–200, = 80,33–90,25 De Lacy.
29 Galen quotes from *Parts of Animals* (3.4.666b14–16): "it is reasonable that the heart has a large number of nerves, since movements originate from it, and are accomplished by their tension and relaxation"; and he points out the argument's inadequacy: mere numbers of a particular structure in a certain organ doesn't establish that that organ is the source of the structures; but in any case the heart is not particularly well-endowed with nerves (*PHP* V 201–202, = 92,2–21 De Lacy): rather "it contains certain nerve-like outgrowths; but these are in no way actually nerves".
30 Edited in Müller 1891; translated (as 'The Soul's Dependence on the Body') in Singer 1997.
31 Although the dependence is not necessarily one-way only: see 271–3.
32 On these issues, see Hankinson 2008b, esp. pp. 214–215. For Aristotle's view, see *Generation and Corruption* 2.2.329b24–6; *Meteorology* 4.1.378b12–26.
33 I 509–694; it is edited in Helmreich 1904, and translated in Singer 1997.
34 This is an important Galenic concept, essentially equivalent to that of health – he wrote a treatise of that name (IV 750–756), and a related text on *The Best Constitution of the Body* (IV 737–749); both are translated in Singer 1997.
35 But see Hankinson 2008a, pp. 215–223.
36 This too Galen attributes to Aristotle; he is particularly impressed by Aristotle's physiognomical doctrines (*QAM* IV 791–798; he quotes *Parts of Animals* (2.2.648a2–13; 2.4.650b14–651a12) to show that the differences between different animals' characters is to be explained in terms of their differing physical constitutions, and then *History of Animals* 1 (1.8.491b11–14; 1.9.491b14–34; 1.10.491b34–492a13; 1.11.492a33–b3) in support of general physiognomical correlations (for example, that those with large protruding ears tend to stupidity and talkativeness). All of this exemplifies Aristotle's view "that the construction of the whole body is, in each kind of animal, especially fitted to the characteristics and faculties of that animal's soul" (*QAM* V 795).

37 See also *PHP* V 459–62, 466–8, 500–1, = 316,22–318,34, 324,3–326,8, 356,6–11 De Lacy.
38 Edited in Nickel 2001; translated in Singer 1997.
39 Plato is never in fact explicit on this point.
40 *Prôtogenes*: *Pol.* 288e, 289a; cf. Galen, *On Hippocrates' 'Nature of Man'* XV 8, = 6,20 Mewaldt.
41 Galen has often been accused of an extreme tendentiousness in his appeals to his predecessors (see e.g. Lloyd 1988; Singer 1991); of course, he quotes in order to support his own position (who does not?), and he is prone, as I have noted, to eliding important differences. But he is less disreputable on this score, in my view, than he is often made out to be.
42 This requires an emendation of the text – the manuscript reads, and editors print, "the reasoning faculty is a form of the soul"; but that is an uncontroversial truth and will not serve Galen's argument here. I defend the emendation in Hankinson 2006, 247 n 44.
43 The Pythagorean theory that the soul is a *harmonia*, an attunement, is attacked by Plato in *Phd.*91c–95a; Aristotle too is dismissive: *DA*.1.4.407b27–498a29.
44 See endnote 5.
45 See Hankinson 2014a and 2014b.
46 I discuss these issues at length in Hankinson 1993.
47 Discovered in a Greek monastery a decade ago; edited with French translation in Boudon-Millot et al. 2010; English translation in Singer 2014. On Galen's psychotherapy, see Hankinson 2014a.

Bibliography

Barnes, J., and Jouanna, J. (eds.) (2003) *Galien et la Philosophie Entretiens sur l'antiquité classique*. XLIX. Vandoeuvres-Genève. Fondation Hardt.
Boudon, V. (2000) *Galien, Exhortation à la Médecine: Art medical* (ed. and tr. [French]). Paris: Les Belles Lettres.
Boudon-Millot, V., and Pietrobelli, A. (2005) Galien résussicité: editio princeps du texte grec du De propriis placitis. *Revue des Études grecques* 118: 168–213.
———. (2010) *Galien, Ne pas se chagriner*. Paris: Les Belles Lettres.
Brock, A. J. (1916) *Galen on the Natural Faculties*. London: Loeb Classical Library.
Cooper, J. (1998) Posidonius on the emotions. In Sihvola, J., and Engberg-Pedersen, T. (eds.) *The Emotions in Hellenistic Philosophy*. Dordrecht: Kluwer Academic Publishers, pp. 71–112.
De Boer, W. (1937) *Galeni de Animi Affectuum et Peccatorum Dignotione et Curatione; de Atra Bile*. CMG V 4,1,1. Leipzig: Teubner.
De Lacy, P. H. (1988) The third part of the soul. In Manuli and Vegetti (1988), pp. 43–64.
———. (ed., tr. and comm.) (1978–1994) *Galen: On the Doctrines of Hippocrates and Plato (PHP)*. 3 vols. CMG V 4,1,2. Berlin: Akademie Verlag.
Donini, P. L. (2008) Psychology. In Hankinson (2008b), pp. 184–209.
Duckworth, W. L. H., Lyons, M. C., and Towers, B. (1962) *Galen on Anatomical Procedures: The Later Books*. AA IX.6-XV, from Arabic. Cambridge, MA: Cambridge University Press.
Edelstein, L., and Kidd, I. (eds.) (1972) *Posidonius: The Fragments*. I. Cambridge, MA: Cambridge University Press.
Furley, D. N., and Wilkie, J. S. (1984) *Galen on Respiration and the Arteries*. Princeton: Princeton University Press.

Garofalo, I. (1986) *Anatomicorum administrationum libri qui supersunt novem: Earundem interpretatio arabica Hunaino Isaaci filio ascripta*. Vol. 1, libri I-IV (AA). Naples: Bibliopolis.

———. (2000) *Galenus – Anatomicarum Administrationum Libri qui supersunt novem, Earundem interpretatio arabica Hunaino Isaaci filio ascripta*. Vol. II. Libri V-IX. Naples: Bibliopolis.

———. (1986) *Anatomicorum administrationum libri qui supersunt novem: Earundem interpretatio arabica Hunaino Isaaci filio ascripta*. Vol. 1, libri I-IV (AA). Naples: Bibliopolis.

Gleason, M. (2009) Shock and awe: The performance dimension of Galen's anatomy demonstrations. In Gill, C., Whitmarsh, T., and Wilkins, J. (eds.) *Galen and the World of Knowledge*. Cambridge, MA: Cambridge University Press, pp. 85–114.

Hankinson, R. J. (1991a) Galen's anatomy of the soul. *Phronesis* 36 (3): 197–233.

———. (1991b) *Galen: On the Therapeutic Method, Books I and II*. Oxford: Oxford University Press.

———. (1993) Actions and passions: Affection, emotion, and moral self-management in Galen's philosophical psychology. In Brunschwig, J., and Nussbaum, M. (eds.) *Passions & Perceptions: Studies in Hellenistic Philosophy of Mind*. Cambridge, MA: Cambridge University Press, pp. 184–222.

———. (2006) Body and soul in Galen. In King, R. A. H. (ed.) *Common to Body and Soul*. Berlin: De Gruyter, pp. 231–257.

———. (2008a) Philosophy of nature. In Hankinson (2008b), pp. 210–241.

———. (ed.) (2008b) *The Cambridge Companion to Galen*. Cambridge, MA: Cambridge University Press.

———. (2014a) Partitioning the soul: Galen on the anatomy of the psychic functions and mental illness. In Corcilius, K., and Perler, D. (eds.) *Partitioning the Soul: Debates from Plato to Leibniz*. Berlin: De Gruyter, pp. 85–106.

———. (2014b) Galen and the ontology of powers. In Marmodoro, A. (ed.) *Causing Health and Disease in Classical and Late Antiquity: British Journal of the History of Philosophy* Special Issue, 22 (5): 951–973.

Helmreich, G. (1893) *Galeni Scripta Minora III*. Leipzig: Teubner.

———. (1904) *Galeni de Temperamentis*. Leipzig: Teubner.

———. (1907–1909) *Galeni de Usu Partium*. 2 vols. Leipzig: Teubner.

Lloyd, G. E. R. (1988) Scholarship, authority and argument in Galen's *Quod animi mores*. In Manuli and Vegetti (1988), pp. 11–22.

Manuli, P., and Vegetti, M. (eds.) (1988) *Le Opere Psicologiche di Galeno*. Naples: Bibliopolis.

Marquardt, J. (1884) *Galeni Pergameni Scripta Minora*. 1. Leipzig: Teubner.

May, M. T. (1968) *Galen on the Usefulness of the Parts of the Body*. 2 vols. Baltimore: Jsohns Hopkins.

Müller, I. (1891) *Galeni Scripta Minora II*. Leipzig: Teubner.

Nickel, D. (ed., tr. and comm. [German]) (2001) *Galeni de Foetuum Formatione*. CMG V 3, 3. Berlin: Akademie Verlag.

Nutton, V. (ed., tr. and comm.) (1999) *Galen: On My Own Opinions: Corpus Medicorum Graecorum* V 3.2. Berlin: Akademie Verlag.

Rocca, J (2003) Galen on the Brain: Anatomical Knowledge and Physiological Speculation in the Second Century A.D. *Studies in Ancient Medicine*, no. 26. Leiden: Brill.

Salas, L. A. (2014) Fighting with the heart of a beast; Galen's use of the elephant's cardiac anatomy against cardiocentrists. *Greek, Roman, and Byzantine Studies* 54: 697–726.

Singer, C. (1956) *Galen on Anatomical Procedures*. Books I-IX.6. London: Oxford University Press.
Singer, P. (1991) Aspects of Galen's Platonism. In Férez, L. (ed.) *Galeno: Obra, Pensamiento y Influencia*. Madrid: UNED, pp. 41–55.
———. (1997) *Galen: Selected Works*. Oxford: Oxford University Press.
———. (2014) *Galen: Psychological Writings*. Cambridge, MA: Cambridge University Press.
Steckerl, F. (1958) *The Fragments of Praxagoras and His School*. Leiden: E.J. Brill.
Tieleman, T. (1996) *Galen and Chrysippus on the Soul*. Argument and Refutation in the *De Placitis* Books II-III. Leiden: E.J. Brill.
———. (2003) Galen's psychology. In J. Barnes and J. Jouanna (eds.), *Galien et la Philosophie Entretiens sur l'antiquité classique XLIX*. Vandoeuvres-Genève: Fondation Hardt.
Von Staden, H. (1989) *Herophilus: The Art of Medicine in Early Alexandria*. Cambridge, MA: Cambridge University Press.

14

PLOTINUS' THEORY OF AFFECTION

Ana Laura Edelhoff

Plotinus' psychology is an important part of his philosophy that has had a great impact on later philosophers in the Western tradition, most notably on the Neo-Platonists, Augustine, Pseudo-Dionysius the Areopagite, as well as the 'Cambridge Platonists'. For Plotinus, psychology is the study of the soul (ψυχή), its ontological status and its attributes. Plotinus conceives of the soul as an immortal and immaterial substance that can exist independently from the body and that is that in virtue of which living beings perceive, feel, think, and act. Like many ancient thinkers, most importantly Plato and Aristotle, Plotinus thinks that the soul is not only responsible for cognition but is also the principle of life. This means that living things are alive in virtue of having a soul, i.e. they grow, digest, reproduce and breathe in virtue of their soul.[1]

This chapter analyses Plotinus' theory of the soul-body relation, which is a central concern of his psychological theory. In particular, it focuses on Plotinus' theory of affection (πάθος). This focus offers an important insight into his own thinking, since it connects and brings together Plotinus' account of the nature of soul and body and their interaction, as well as his engagement with the earlier philosophical tradition, most notably Plato, Aristotle and the Stoics.

Plotinus' theory of affection is primarily a discussion of whether the subject of affections is the soul or the body. He investigates this topic in the three treatises: *What Is The Living Being?* (*Enn.*I.1.1–7), *On the Impassibility of Things Without Body* (*Enn.*III.6.1–5) and *On Difficulties About The Soul II* (*Enn.*IV.4.18–21 and 28).[2] Although Plotinus develops and defends his theory across three treatises, what emerges is nonetheless a unified theory without any major tensions or inconsistencies. Each treatise contributes to the understanding of the discussions in the other two works, by remaining in the same theoretical framework, yet illuminating different aspects of it. Whereas Plotinus argues primarily for the non-affectedness of the soul in *Enn.*III.6, he gives an account of the origin of affective and desiderative states, such as pain, desire and anger in *Enn.*IV.4. In *Enn.*I.1 he investigates the nature of the human self, focusing on whether a human being should be identified with the compound of body and soul or only with its highest intellectual capacities.

1. Soul-body dualism in Plotinus

Plotinus' theory of affection can best be understood with reference to the central aspects of his view on the soul-body relationship. His theory of affection builds on a soul-body dualism and he assigns some roles in generating affections to the soul, and others to the body, according to their different natures.

According to Plotinus, an organism can be analysed into a soul and a body. He is a dualist in the sense that in his view the soul is a different kind of entity from the body. The soul has both a different essence from the body, and different existence conditions, whereby the difference in essence explains why they differ in terms of their existence conditions. In holding this view, Plotinus considers himself to be following Plato, who also thinks that the soul is not a kind of body.[3] By contrast, many of Plotinus' predecessors – for example, the Stoics – think that there is no difference in kind between soul and body.[4] Plotinus rejects both the strong view that the body is identical to the soul, and the weak view that body and soul are the same kind of thing, since he believes that there are differences in their essential and necessary properties. Plotinus' beliefs about these differences can be summarised as follows:

(1) Whereas a body is necessarily extended, a soul is necessarily unextended.[5]
(2) Whereas souls are causally efficacious, bodies lack causal efficacy in their own right.[6]
(3) Whereas souls cannot be altered, bodies can be.[7]

Plotinus' theory of the body-soul relation is complicated by the fact that Plotinus believes that there are at least four different kinds of soul: (1) there is a transcendent soul that is not engaged with anything bodily and is ontologically prior to every being apart from the first principle, called 'One', and the second principle, called 'Intellect';[8] (2) there is a 'world soul' which accounts for the life of the whole cosmos.[9] Plotinus thinks that every organism there is in the world, including earth and rocks, is dependent on the world soul. In some cases Plotinus further subdivides the world soul into (2a) a higher being that structures the cosmos without being in it (*Enn*.IV.3.4.21–23; IV.8.2; IV.8.4.4–6) and (2b) a lower being that is generated by this higher being, often called 'nature' ($\varphi\acute{v}\sigma\iota\varsigma$) or 'vegetative soul' (*Enn*.II.9.7.15–18; IV.3.4.27); finally, (3) there are individual human souls.[10] Again, Plotinus often subdivides the individual human soul into (3a) a higher being, which is the rational soul and (3b) a lower being, the non-rational soul,[11] which is generated by the rational human soul (*Enn*.VI.7.4.10–18). Plotinus often calls this lower soul as well 'nature' or 'vegetative soul', i.e. with the same name with which he labels the lower kind of the world soul. As a consequence, there is a dispute in the literature about whether he means to refer to the numerically same entity in both cases.[12] In my view, the two vegetative souls are not identical, because they ontologically depend on different entities, i.e. in the one case on the higher world soul and in the other case on the rational human soul.

As we have seen, Plotinus thinks that there are many differences between souls and bodies and that there are various kinds of soul. In order to understand Plotinus' theory of affection, we need to clarify how the soul is related to the body in a human being.

2. The relation of the soul to the body in a human being

Plotinus thinks – a thought he takes to be Plato's – that in the case of a human being only the non-rational soul connects with the body.[13] He calls the product of this connection 'the compound' (τὸ συναμφότερον or τὸ σύνθετον) or 'the living being' (τὸ ζῷον).[14] This compound is essentially dependent on the non-rational soul – insofar as the soul is its essence – and is existentially dependent both on the body and on the non-rational soul.

Whereas the rational part of soul is only responsible for the highest cognitive capacities of this living being (*Enn*.IV.9.3.26, see Emilsson 1988, p. 31), the non-rational soul is responsible for its living and affective capacities.[15] To be more precise, some faculties of the non-rational soul are responsible for the living functions of the living being, such as nutrition, growth and reproduction. This set of faculties is the 'generating soul' (γεννητικόν), 'vegetative soul' (φυτικόν) or 'nature' (φύσις) (*Enn*.I.1.8.21; IV.4.27.1; IV.4.28.16). Another set of faculties of the non-rational soul, namely the affective soul (παθητικόν), accounts for the affective capacities of the living being (*Enn*.III.6.4). Its faculties are the passionate power (θυμοειδές) and the desiderative power (ἐπιθυμητικόν).[16]

Because the rational part of the soul does not involve the body for any of its functions, and is not present throughout the body, its activities do not have as their subject the compound (*Enn*.I.1.9.16–20). By contrast, the non-rational soul uses the body in its activities and is as a whole present in every part of the living body (*Enn*.I.1.9.16–20; IV.1.1.10–12; IV.9.3.10–16; III.4.6.34–38). Although the non-rational soul is present in the whole body, changes that involve its passionate or desiderative power take place only in specific regions of the body. For example, the bodily affections connected with the passionate power are centred about the heart. Likewise, the bodily affections connected with the desiderative power take place in and around the liver, with the exception of sexual desire, which is located in the sexual organs (*Enn*.IV.4.28.10–19).[17]

Plotinus thinks not only that the *rational* soul can exist independently from the body, but also that the *non-rational* soul can likewise exist independently from the body (*Enn*.I.1.3–4). In addition, he thinks that the non-rational soul, being a soul, is incorruptible and cannot be affected. The view that the soul that accounts for the living activities of a body is existentially independent from the body and unaffected is, however, problematic, since it is difficult to see how such a soul could be causally efficacious and be able to know about and react in response to bodily conditions.[18]

In trying to explain how it is possible for the non-rational soul and the body to interact, such as in the case of sense-perception or affection, Plotinus considers Aristotle's hylomorphism to have certain advantages over the Platonic soul-body dualism (despite criticising the hylomorphic account of the soul-body relation extensively (*Enn*.IV.7.8[5])). For he implicitly acknowledges that it is easier to account for the interaction between the non-rational soul and the body in a hylomorphic framework than in a setting in which the non-rational soul is not in the body, since in the hylomorphic framework the soul is said to be affected by the bodily condition by being a part of the living being itself.

In particular, Plotinus integrates a hylomorphic element into his theory of the soul-body relationship by arguing that there is a so-called soul-trace (ἴχνος) that functions, analogously to an Aristotelian soul, as the enmattered form of a living organism. What distinguishes Plotinus' account from Aristotle's hylomorphism is that the soul-trace is not itself a soul, but a subsidiary entity generated by the non-rational soul.[19] This intermediate entity is supposed to explain the interaction between the body and the non-rational soul.[20]

By taking over an important aspect of Aristotle's account of the soul-body relation, in particular by arguing that soul-traces can play the role of enmattered forms, Plotinus distances himself from the Platonic theory. While agreeing with Plato that the soul is not a part or aspect of the body, he nevertheless defends the view that it is not the soul that accounts directly for the vitality of the body, but rather the soul-traces.[21]

The introduction of soul-traces into his ontology has consequences for his view on the body of a human being. This, as he claims, gets a life of its own:

> As regards the question whether the body has something of its own (ἐφ᾽ ἑαυτοῦ τι) and lives when the soul (ψυχή) is present by then having something of its own (τι ἴδιον), or whether what it has is nature (φύσις), and this is what is in association with the body, viz. nature: Isn't it the case that also the body itself, in which there is both soul and nature (ψυχὴ καὶ φύσις), must not be like what is soulless (οἷον τὸ ἄψυχον) and like air that has been illuminated, but like air that has been warmed, and the body of an animal or a plant has a shadow of soul as it were (οἷον σκιὰν ψυχῆς) and suffering pain and having bodily pleasures pertain to a body qualified in this way (τὸ τοιόνδε σῶμα)?
>
> (*Enn*.IV.4.18.1–9; transl. Noble)

In this passage Plotinus says that the non-rational soul is only connected with a specific kind of body, namely a *living* body (he says that this kind of body is not ἄψυχον). He explains that the body is living in virtue of the soul-traces, which are implanted in it by the non-rational soul. Following Aristotle, Plotinus uses the expression 'such a body' (τοιόνδε σῶμα), in order to express the distinction between a living body and a non-living body.[22] Plotinus distinguishes between living and non-living bodies in the following way: In contrast to a non-living body, a living body can be in an emotional state as a result of an external or internal cause. Although non-living bodies can be subjects of change, for instance a table can be broken and a coat can wear out, neither table nor coat will sense that it is being taken apart nor can they feel sad about this.[23]

Plotinus thinks that the body becomes capable of being in an emotional or desiderative state in virtue of the soul-traces: "The body 'acquired a trace of soul, not a part [of the soul], but a sort of heating or illumination that came from the soul, and the coming-to-be of appetites and pleasures and pains grew up in it" (VI.4.15.13–17; transl. Noble). Although he does not say explicitly that the soul-traces are causally relevant for the possession of such states, the fact that he mentions the acquisition of soul-traces and the generation of emotional and desiderative states together strongly suggests that there is a closer connection than mere temporal succession. Rather, Plotinus explains the possibility of these states in the body by means of the acquisition of soul-traces (cf. *Enn*.IV.4.18.8–9).

It is a striking aspect of Plotinus' theory of affection that the body is a subject of psychological states, such as desires and emotions. Since he makes the body the subject of psychological states, the question arises what role he assigns to the soul in his theory of affection.

3. The soul: a subject of affections?

As we have just seen, Plotinus thinks that the living body is a subject of affections. In fact, he holds that it is *in a strict sense* the *only* subject of affections. This is because he thinks that only bodies but not souls can be altered.[24] Plotinus thinks, following Aristotle, that only compounds can undergo an alteration, since three distinct entities are required in a process of alteration: a form that is lost, a form that is gained, and a substrate that underlies the change.[25] It is for this reason that souls, which are simple, cannot be affected, yet bodies, being matter-form compounds, can be.

Plotinus' motivation for the view that the soul is unaffected is his desire to establish that the soul is immortal. Taking up Plato's arguments for the immortality of the soul in the *Phaedo*, he argues for the soul's immortality extensively in "On the Immortality of the Soul" (*Enn*.IV.7), criticising several philosophical positions according to which the soul is mortal, such as the Stoic view and the Aristotelian view. According to Plotinus, the soul cannot both be immortal and capable of being affected. For he thinks that, if something can change and be affected, it is a bodily compound, and that if something is a compound, it is corruptible (*Enn*.III.6.1.24–31).[26]

While denying that the soul can be affected, Plotinus does acknowledge that there are many ways in which a soul seems to change and be a subject of affections:[27]

> [H]ow [. . .] can the part which comes before that subject to affections [sc. the affective soul], and the part before sense-perception [sc. the perceptive soul], and in general any part of the soul, be unchangeable when

vice and false opinions and stupidity occur in the soul? And the soul accepts things as its own or rejects them as alien when it feels pleasure and pain, anger, envy, jealousy, lust, and in general is never quiet but always moved and changed by every casual contact.

(*Enn*.III.6.1.18–24; transl. Armstrong; my additions)

In this passage, Plotinus lists several kinds of change in the soul: change due to perception, change due to belief and change due to affections. Take the following example: Socrates thinks that he sees a snake and is, therefore, afraid. Later, he perceives that the object of his original fear is just a green stick and he stops being fearful. Socrates' perceptions, beliefs and emotions change in this scene. His soul is, hence, undergoing changes and affections.

Yet Plotinus claims that to say that in these cases the soul changes *in the strict sense* is analogous to saying that the soul blushes or turns pale and alleges that someone who says this ends up ascribing changes that can only take place in the body to the soul:[28]

> But what about the soul's accepting things as its own or rejecting them as alien? And, surely, feelings of grief and anger, pleasures, desires and fears, are changes and affections present in the soul and moving there. About these, too, one must certainly make a distinction, in this way. To deny that alterations in the soul, and intense perceptions of them, do occur is to contradict the obvious facts. But when we accept this we ought to enquire what it is that is changed. For we run the risk, when we say this of the soul, of understanding it in the same sort of way as if we say that the soul blushes or turns pale again, not taking into account that these affections are brought about by the soul but occur in the other structure [sc. the body].
>
> (*Enn*.III.6.3.1–12; transl. Armstrong)

In this passage, Plotinus claims that it is an obvious fact that the soul changes in certain ways.[29] The soul engages in strong emotions and desires, for example, when the soul feels grief or anger. Denying that there are any such changes in the soul would be contradicting everyday experience. However, following Aristotle, he raises the worry that it might not be the soul itself that is the subject of changes, even if the soul *seems* to be the subject of changes in such cases. He suggests that, as in the case of blushing and turning pale, it is the body, and not the soul, that is the subject of changes. So, in the case of emotions and desires it is the body, and not the soul, that is undergoing changes.

Plotinus acknowledges that the soul changes in some manner in these cases. But he claims that all such changes in the soul are not changes *in the strict sense*. Following Aristotle, he distinguishes between two kinds of changes: (i) there are transitions from a mere potentiality to its exercise where that exercise is not a change in the subject. For example, Aristotle takes it as intuitive that the exercise of the potentiality of a housebuilder, i.e. when the housebuilder is building a house, is not a change in the housebuilder (*DA*.II.5.417a30–b9); (ii) there are changes where there is a change in the subject. For example, when water gets boiled, an intrinsic change takes place, since there is a replacement of intrinsic bodily opposites (e.g. hot and cold). Plotinus thinks that the former changes are changes *in a loose sense*, whereas the latter, which are intrinsic alterations, are changes *in the strict sense* (*DA*.II.5.417b2–16).

While the soul only changes *in the loose sense*, all changes that take place in the body are changes *in the strict sense*. By introducing the distinction between changes *in the strict sense*, in which the subject of change is intrinsically altered, and changes *in a looser sense*, in which the subject of change is not intrinsically altered, Plotinus aims to make the two previously inconsistent beliefs, namely that the soul changes and that the soul is unaffected, consistent. He describes his view as follows:

> Well, then, is not the soul different before it remembers in this way, and afterwards, when it remembers? Would you like to call it different? Very well, then, as long as you do not say that it is intrinsically altered, unless one is to call the passage from potentiality to actuality alteration, but nothing is added to it but it simply does what it is by nature. For in general the actualisations of immaterial things take place without any accompanying alteration, otherwise they would perish; it is much truer to say that they remain unaltered when they become actual, and that being affected in actualisation belongs to things which have matter. But if a thing which is immaterial is going to be affected, it has no ground of permanence; just as in the case of sight, when the seeing faculty is active it is the eye which is affected, and opinions are like acts of seeing.
> (*Enn*.III.6.2.45–54; transl. Armstrong)

In this passage, Plotinus uses the case of remembering as a typical activity of the soul in order to illustrate his view that the soul is not changed or altered while engaging in its own activities. Plotinus thinks that the soul does not change *in the strict sense* when engaged in the process of remembering something: memory is a power of the soul which can be actualised, in order to apprehend objects that are not present (*Enn*.IV.6.3.1–63; IV.7.6.37–46). Thus, according to Plotinus, in the case of remembering, an exercise of the soul's power to remember takes place without an alteration in the subject. Hence, it is correct to say that the soul changes in some way, for example, when it remembers something that it had previously forgotten. Yet one always ought to clarify that this is a change *in the loose sense*, in that the soul is not intrinsically altered when it undergoes this change.[30]

After giving his account of the nature of changes in the soul in the case of memory, Plotinus makes a more general claim about all changes that occur in immaterial entities, thereby including all changes in the soul, because, as we have already seen, the soul is an immaterial entity. He claims that all changes that take place in immaterial entities are changes *in the looser sense*, i.e. exercises of potentialities that do not entail any alterations. He argues that if there were any changes *in the strict sense* taking place in immaterial entities, the immaterial entities would go out of existence. The implicit premise is that immaterial entities are identical to their essences. Any change they were to undergo would, thus, be an essential change and so would lead to their going out of existence.[31] Finally, Plotinus claims that, in the case of perception, the soul does not undergo any alteration. Rather, the soul actualises its own 'power of perception' and becomes aware of the (material) alterations in the sense organs without itself being affected.[32]

For the same reason that the soul does not undergo an alteration in the case of memory and perception, neither the soul, or its parts undergo alterations when they change from virtuous to vicious states and conversely:

> But when false opinions are there in the soul (and this is what most of all produces vice), how will one be able to assert that they have not come in and that this part of the soul has not in this way become different? And is not the spirited part in one state when it is cowardly and in another when it is brave? And is not the desiring part when it is unrestrainedly lustful in one state, and in another when it is under control? Well, then, it has been affected.
>
> (*Enn*.III.6.2.24–29; transl. Armstrong)

In this passage, Plotinus lists several examples of vicious and virtuous states of the different soul parts. According to Plotinus, each part of the soul can act either virtuously or viciously. For example, the passionate power can act bravely (being virtuous) or act cowardly (being vicious); and the desiderative power can desire bodily pleasures to excess (being vicious), or in moderation and appropriately (being virtuous).

Plotinus denies that changes to virtuous or vicious states are the result of an external stimulus.[33] In his view, the being-in-a-vicious-state of the soul part is the product of the non- or only limited actualisation of the soul's nature, rather than the result of an external stimulus. He thinks that a part of the soul actualises its own nature whenever it listens to reason.[34] In other words, the actualisation of its own nature is nothing but its acting according to reason.[35] Hence, the soul is in a vicious state when it does not listen to reason, but rather directs its attention towards the body, thereby considering the body as a part of itself.[36] By contrast, it is in a virtuous state whenever it listens to reason, thereby actualising its own nature to a high or even the highest degree.[37] Listening to reason and accepting reason's advice does not involve the parts of the soul being affected.[38] The soul, thus, does not undergo an alteration due to an external stimulus when it becomes vicious or virtuous. Rather, it actualises its own essence to a higher or lower degree.

Plotinus thinks that *all* changes in the soul are only exercises of the soul's powers without any intrinsic alterations that take place in the soul:

> In fact, when we say that the soul moves itself in lusts or reasonings or opinions, we are not saying that it does this because it is being shaken about by them, but that the movements originate from itself. For when we say that its life is movement, we do not mean that it is movement of something different, but the activity of each part is its natural life which does not go outside it. The sufficient conclusion is: if we agree that activities and lives and impulses are not alterations, and that memories are not stamps imprinted on the soul or mental pictures like impressions on wax, we must agree that everywhere, in all affections and movements, as they are called, the soul remains the same in substrate and essence, and that virtue and vice do not come into being like black and white or hot and cold in the body, but in the way which has been described, in both directions and in all respects, what happens in the soul is the opposite of what happens in the body.
>
> (III.6.3.22–35; transl. Armstrong)

In this passage Plotinus summarises his view, repeating that all changes that are in the soul, such as, for example, desires and cognitions (motions in lusts or reasonings or opinions) are not changes *in the strict sense*, but merely changes *in the loose sense*, originated by the soul itself. The changes in the soul are categorically different from the changes in the body, since the latter are alterations and the former are not.[39] The soul is not altered by the actualisations that take place in it. As we have seen, it is even impossible that the soul changes without thereby going out of existence. Vicious and virtuous states in the soul are not brought about by an external stimulus, but by different degrees of actualisations of the soul's powers.

So far, we have seen why Plotinus thinks that the soul does not undergo an affection or change *in the strict sense* when it is in an emotional or desiderative state. We have not yet seen how Plotinus explains the alterations in the body that occur whenever a human being is in an emotional or desiderative state nor how he accounts for the interaction between the living body and the soul in such cases. He dedicates separate discussions to the origin of bodily pain and pleasure, desiderative states, and passionate states, in each of which he explains how the respective state arises, analysing the alterations that take place in the body and the actualisations that happen in the soul. His discussions of desiderative states and passionate states presuppose the discussion of bodily pain and pleasure. So I start with the latter.

4. Bodily pain and pleasure

Plotinus discusses the subject of bodily pain (ἀλγηδών) and pleasure (ἡδονή) primarily in *Enn.* IV.4.19. He focuses on the origin of pain in cases such as inflammations and wounds in the body. According to Plotinus, the feeling of pain is produced by the separation of the soul-trace from the living body, due to an external or internal cause (for example, the cutting in a surgical operation) (*Enn.*

IV.4.19.1–3), and the feeling of pleasure is produced by the union of the living body with the soul-trace (*Enn*.IV.4.19.4–5). The subject of these affections is the living body:

> And it was the body which felt the pain – I mean by "felt the pain" that the body was affected; as in a surgical operation when the body is cut the division is in its material mass, but the distress is felt in the mass because it is not only a mass, but a mass qualified in a particular way; it is there too that inflammation occurs. But the soul perceives it, taking it over because it is, so to speak, situated next to it.
> (*Enn*.IV.4.19.7–13; transl. Armstrong)

In contrast to many of his predecessors, Plotinus claims that the living body, and not the soul, is the subject of all strict changes that take place during an affection.[40] The soul merely perceives the bodily affection and has an 'unaffected knowledge' of these bodily changes (*Enn*.IV.4.18.6–11). His primary objective is to explain how the soul can be informed about these bodily changes without being affected by them.[41] He does so in the following way:

> Nature knows the explicit desire which is the final stage of that which begins in the body, and sense-perception knows the image, and the soul starts from the image, and either provides what is desired – it is its function to do so – or resists and holds out and pays no attention either to what started the desire or to that which desired afterwards.
> (*Enn*.IV.4.20.16–20; transl. Armstrong)

Plotinus thus explains the way in which the soul is informed about bodily states as follows:[42] (1) The body is in a specific state, for example, in a state of pain. (2) The non-rational soul (called 'nature' in this passage but more precisely conceived of as the 'affective soul') becomes aware of this state and forms a mental image (φαντασία) of it.[43] (3) The rational soul perceives this mental image.

Both the rational and the non-rational soul are unaffected in this process. He explicitly states that when the non-rational soul recognises bodily states it remains unaffected:

> The whole soul perceives the affection in the body without being affected itself. For *it perceives as a whole* and says that *the affection is there where the wound and the pain* are. But if it was affected itself, being wholly present in every part of the body, it would not have said or indicated that the affection was there [in that particular place] but would all have been affected by the pain, and in pain as a whole, and would not have said or made clear that the pain was there [in that particular place] but would have said that it was there where the soul is; *but the soul is everywhere*.
> (*Enn*.IV.4.19.13–19; transl. Armstrong [my italics])

In this passage, Plotinus supports his claim that the non-rational soul perceives pain and pleasure without itself being affected, by arguing that if the soul, rather than the body, were affected, pain would be felt wherever the soul is, i.e. in the whole body, because the soul is as a whole present in each of the parts of the body. In his view, the fact that human beings often feel pain in only a part of the body indicates that pain affects the body, and not the soul (*Enn*.IV.4.19.19–20).

According to Plotinus, the non-rational soul perceives the pain and pleasure in the body, but these perceptions are not affections, but rather knowledge or awareness of these bodily states (*Enn*.IV.4.19.26–27). In his view, one can be in pain without being aware of it, for example, because of medications or because one intensively concentrates on something else (*Enn*.IV.4.19.23–24). Awareness is not a necessary condition of being in pain. Yet normally pain is noticed (*Enn*.IV.4.19.24–27).

Plotinus thus assigns two quite separate and distinct roles to the living body and to the affective soul in the case of an affection. Whereas the body is altered by the removal or reunion of soul-traces and suffers or rejoices, respectively, because of them, the soul merely becomes aware of the bodily states without being affected itself.

According to Plotinus, people act differently with respect to bodily pains and pleasures according to their moral disposition. Although the non-rational soul is in all cases unaffected, only wise people can remain unaffected when they suffer physical pain or other affections. They do so, because they distinguish between the life of the body and their own – non-bodily – life. They take care of the body, while not thinking that in doing so, they take care of their own lives, because they do not consider the body to be a part of themselves (*Enn*.I.4.4; see Caluori 2008, p. 134).

5. Desires

Plotinus discusses bodily desires in *Enn*.I.1.5, *Enn*.III.6.4–4 and *Enn*.IV.4.20–21. Examples of bodily desires are hunger, thirst and the desire for warmth (*Enn*. IV.4.21.19–22). As in the case of bodily pain and pleasure, Plotinus thinks that the subject of bodily desires is the living body, whereas the soul merely perceives the desiderative states of the living body.

Plotinus thinks that, as in the case of pleasure and pain, the soul can be the subject of desires as well. However, when the soul forms a desire, the soul is not altered. Thus, the soul is not affected when it desires. It merely actualises its potentiality to desire something. In some cases, such a desire of the soul is triggered by a bodily desire. When the soul perceives a bodily desire, it either acts on the desire or refuses to act on it. If the soul agrees to act on the bodily desire, then it comes to form its own distinct desire for the object of the body's desire. Plotinus says that there are, thus, two distinct kinds of desires, namely a bodily desire and a desire in the soul whenever a bodily desire triggers a desire in the soul. He explains the origin of these two kinds of desire as follows:

> But why are there two appetites (ἐπιθυμίαι), and why is it not the case that the qualified body alone desires? Isn't it that, if nature (φύσις) is one

thing and the qualified body (τὸ σῶμα τὸ τοιόνδε) is something that comes to be so-qualified from nature – for nature is prior to the generation of the so-qualified body, given that it shapes and moulds the so-qualified body – it is necessary that nature not be the starting point of appetite, but rather that the body be what suffers these things and when in pain, yearns for 'the opposite of what it suffers' viz. pleasure instead of pain and fullness instead of emptiness. But nature, like a mother, aiming at the wishes of what has been affected, attempts to set it right and lead it back to itself, and in conducting a search for what will cure the body, it attaches itself in this pursuit to the desire of what has been affected and the fulfilment of the desire passes from the body to nature. The result is that the body has an appetite from itself – someone might perhaps call this a proto-appetite (προεπιθυμία) or preliminary urge (προθυμία) – whereas nature has an appetite from another and through another, while the soul that provides [what is desired] or does not is yet another.

(*Enn.*IV.4.20.21–36; transl. Noble)

In this passage Plotinus says that the difference between the two kinds of desire is the following: the first kind of desire has as its subject the living body. The living body is affected by something and feels, for example, pain, and desires to be in a different state of its current condition, i.e. to be in a neutral state or in a state of pleasure. The soul does not necessarily perceive these desiderative states of the body. Some of these 'unconscious desires' that are not necessarily accompanied by an awareness of the soul are presumably goal-directed physiological processes in the living body.[44] The second kind of desire, by contrast, has φύσις as its subject, or, to be more precise, the desiderative power of the affective soul. After perceiving the bodily desires, the affective soul either starts itself to desire to provide a remedy for the body or it rejects the bodily desire. If the soul acts on behalf of the bodily desire, it "desires from and through something else", namely the living body.

Plotinus calls the bodily desires 'proto-desires' or 'preliminary desires' (προεπιθυμία). He presumably calls them 'preliminary' because they normally precede a soul's desire for something that concerns the body. However, they are neither necessary nor sufficient conditions for a soul to desire something that concerns the body. They are not necessary, because a patient might eat something in order to get better, even though she has no bodily desire for it. They are not sufficient for the desire in the soul because, as Plotinus says, the soul might not form a desire itself. For example, a temperate person might not form a desire in the soul for a further piece of cake, although the body desires it (*Enn.* IV.4.21.7–8).

Plotinus supports his view that the body is the subject of bodily desires with the following biological observation: We can observe that people do not desire the same things that concern the body when they are young as when they are old, when they are healthy as when they are sick. The desiring faculty is the same in the young and old, and in the healthy and sick. These groups only differ in their bodily conditions. This suggests that it is the living body that is the subject of our bodily desires and not the affective soul (*Enn* IV.4.21).

As I have already mentioned, Plotinus thinks that bodily states are not enough to originate a desire in the affective soul. In his view, the soul, after becoming aware of the desires in the body, judges whether it should desire the object of the bodily desire itself or whether it should reject the bodily desire and refuse to form a desire on its behalf. Its judgement depends on its own moral disposition:

> And the desiring part when it acts by itself produces what is called unrestrained lust, for it does everything by itself and the other parts of the soul are not present to it, whose function it would be, if they were present, to master and direct it. If it saw the other parts it would be different, and would not do everything but might perhaps take a rest by looking, as far as it could, at the other parts.
> (*Enn*.III.6.2.60–65; transl. Armstrong)

If the desiderative faculty is virtuous, the soul will only agree to desires that are in accordance with nature, but never to desires that are against nature.[45] By contrast, if the desiderative faculty is vicious, the soul will agree to all bodily desires. As we have seen earlier, its virtue consists in following the advice of the rational part of the soul, its vice consists in not listening to it.

As regards the successful implementation of the various goals, the desiderative faculty depends on the rational soul. For in order to get advantages and avoid disadvantages one needs to calculate and reason well.[46] After having discussed bodily pain and pleasure and desires, let us turn to the most difficult affective state: the passions.

6. Passions

Plotinus' most important analysis of the passions occurs in *Enn*.III.6.3–4 and *Enn*. IV.4.28. Examples of passions are anger, fear and grief. As in the case of his discussions of bodily pain, pleasure, and desire, Plotinus aims to show that the soul remains unaffected throughout the occurrence of a passionate affection. He argues that, as with desires, there are two kinds of passion: one whose subject is the living body, and another whose subject is the passionate faculty of the non-rational soul. Whereas the living body is altered when it is subject to a passion, the soul is not.

Plotinus uses the example of anger to illustrate his views on passionate states. The first kind of anger has the body as its subject and is essentially characterised by the boiling of the blood and bile.[47] Plotinus locates this kind of anger in the region of the heart, because the boiling of the blood, which is an essential part of bodily anger, starts there (*Enn*.IV.4.28.73–77). The intentional object of bodily anger is bodily pain (*Enn*.IV.4.28.39–43; see Emilsson 1998, p. 349). Plotinus points out that people whose blood boils due to any kind of bodily suffering more easily are more ready to feel this kind of anger (*Enn*.IV.4.28.30–36). He claims that usually when the body of such a person feels anger, the soul gets angry, too. He explains this reaction as follows:

> And when the same people are more prone to anger when they are ill than when they are healthy, and when they have not tasted food than when they have eaten, they indicate that fits of anger, or the origins of anger, belong to the qualified body, and that the bile or the blood, as a kind of animating principle, produce these movements of such a kind that, when the qualified body suffers, the blood or the bile are immediately set in motion, and a perception occurs, and the mental image puts the soul in touch with the state of the qualified body, and the soul launches itself against what has caused the pain.
> (*Enn*.IV.4.28.36–43; transl. Armstrong)

In this passage, Plotinus explains the relation between bodily anger and anger in the soul as follows: First, the living body suffers (and this suffering is the intentional object of bodily anger). Then, blood and bile are immediately set in motion, and the body gets angry. Then, the soul perceives that the body is angry and gets angry itself.

As in the case of desire, the passion in the body can originate a passion in the soul. The soul can choose whether it responds to the passion in the body or not. How the soul reacts depends on how it evaluates the cause of the bodily anger and on its own moral disposition. In this passage, Plotinus describes how choleric people usually react to bodily pain: their souls get angry as well. For example, when a choleric person is hungry, his body becomes angry and, as a result, his soul gets angry as well. By contrast, a person who is not choleric but virtuous does not get angry in her soul when the body is hungry and, thus, angry. The soul judges that it would be inadequate to get angry because one feels hungry.

The second kind of anger has as its subject the passionate power of the non-rational soul. It is caused by a judgement that (1) somebody closely connected with us is suffering or that (2) someone is behaving improperly:

> It is obvious, I think, that we are angry not only over whatever our bodies suffer, but over the sufferings of anyone closely connected with us, and in general over anyone's improper behaviour. So there is need of perception and some kind of understanding in being angry. For this reason anyone looking at these facts would not think that passion arose from the power of growth, but would try to find that it had its source in some other power of soul.
> (*Enn*.IV.4.28.23–29; transl. Armstrong)

According to Plotinus, anger in the soul involves in most cases (1) a slighting or down ranking; (2) of oneself or people closely connected with us; (3) that is improperly done; (4) accompanied by suffering or pain; (5) linked to a desire for retribution

(*Enn*.IV.4.28.55–56).⁴⁸ This kind of anger requires that the subject of anger understands the situation and uses its rational powers in doing so (*Enn*.IV.4.28.22–29). Then, the soul animates the body and sets the living body in motion, by making the blood boil (*Enn*.IV.4.28.44–48; cf. *Enn*.III.6.4, see Caluori 2008, p. 132).

As we have seen, Plotinus distinguishes anger whose subject is the living body from anger whose subject is the soul. Furthermore, he distinguishes angers in the soul that arise because of anger in the body from angers in the soul that arise because of a judgement in the soul. In a similar way, he distinguishes angers in the body that arise because the body suffers from angers in the body that arise because the soul is angry.

The account of anger is supposed to be paradigmatic for all passions. In his view, all passions have as their subject either the living body or the soul. In addition, he classifies passions on the basis of their origin: bodily passions either arise due to a bodily stimulus or because of a passion in the soul. Passions in the soul either arise because of a bodily passion or because of a judgement of the soul.

7. Conclusion

Plotinus thinks that a human organism's soul, which he analyses into both a rational and a non-rational part, is categorically different from that organism's body. Whereas the non-rational soul is responsible for the living and affective capacities of the body, the rational soul accounts for the highest cognitive capacities. In order to explain how the body and the non-rational soul interact, he introduces intermediate entities into his ontology, namely the *living* body and the soul-trace. According to Plotinus, the living body can be the subject of psychological states: it can feel pain and pleasure, and can have desires and passions, whereby it has these capacities in virtue of the soul-trace. While both the living body and the non-rational soul can be the subject of affective states, the only subject of affection *in the strict sense*, however, is the living body. This is because it is the only thing that is intrinsically altered when it undergoes an affection, while the soul, though changing as well, is not intrinsically altered but undergoes a mere transition from a potentiality to its exercise.

Notes

1 See, for example, Plato's *Phaedo* (esp. 105b–c) and Aristotle's *De Anima* (DA), esp. I.5.410b16–411a2; II.2.413a21–b8; II.3.414a31. For further references see: Caston (2006, p. 317).

2 According to Porphyry, the treatise *On the Impassibility of Things Without Body* chronologically directly precedes the treatise-series *On the Soul*. The treatise *What Is The Living Being?*, however, is, according to Porphyry's testimony, written considerably later, at the end of Plotinus life and, thus, a mature work. See Porphyry's *On the Life of Plotinus and the Order of His Books*. See Kalligas (2014, pp. 3–18).

3 There are several passages in Plato that suggest that the soul is not a kind of body: To begin with, in the *Phaedo*, Plato argues that the nature of the soul must be like the essence of the forms: everlasting and immaterial. By contrast, the nature of the body

is not eternal, but is changing (*Phd*.78c–79e). Thus, because the soul has different essential properties, the soul is not a body. Secondly, in the *Timaeus* Plato argues that the soul belongs to the realm of 'being', whereas the body belongs to the realm of 'becoming' (*Tim*.27d–28c). Thirdly, in the *Timaeus*, Plato argues that the soul comes into being at a different time than the body and that the *demiurge* constructs it independently from the body (*Tim*.35a–36d; 69c–70b). Fourthly, Plato suggests in several myths in his dialogues that the soul can exist disincarnated (*Gorg*.524b–524c; *Phd*.64c; *Phaedr*.250b–250c; *Apol*.40b–40e). See Noble (2013, pp. 252–253). Plotinus believes, as Plato does, that body and soul belong to different realms: whereas the body has no *being* in the real sense and merely belongs to the realm of *becoming*, the soul, which belongs to the realm of forms, has real being (*Enn*.IV.2.1.8–9; IV.3.2.9; Nikulin (2005, p. 278).

4   See Plotinus' criticism of the Stoic view that the soul is a body in *Enn*.IV.7.1–8 and his discussion of the differences of bodies and souls in *Enn*.IV.1.1.
5   *Enn*.III.6.1.28; IV.1.1.12–17; IV.6.3.70; VI.2.4.22. Plotinus says that the soul cannot be extended, since the unity of sense-perception could otherwise not be accounted for. See Emilsson (1991). By contrast, Plato thinks that the soul is extended (*Tim*.34b; 36e; 37b–c; 44d; 73d–74a; 90c–d; 91e–92a).
6   Most Platonists agree that only immaterial entities, such as souls and intellects, are ultimately causally efficacious. Such entities are the principles of motion that govern the universe in most philosophical theories of the Platonic tradition. Kalligas (2014, p. 535). By contrast, the Stoics think that only bodies can be causes (Long 1974, p. 153).
7   See sec. 4: The Soul: A Subject of Affection? p. 8.
8   Emilsson (1988, p. 23) and Blumenthal (1974).
9   Emilsson (1988, pp. 23–24).
10 Emilsson (1988, p. 24).
11 Plotinus is influenced both by Plato and Aristotle in dividing the soul into rational and non-rational elements (see Plato's tripartition of the soul in *Republic* IV and Aristotle's *DA.II.2–3* and *EN*.I.13.1102a26–1102a32).
12 See Emilsson 1988, pp. 26–27 for a more detailed discussion and an outline for a solution of the inconsistencies.
13 Here and in what follows I speak about the *human* soul, unless noted otherwise.
14 See the distinction between soul, body and the compound in Pseudo-Plato's *Alcibiades* (129a–130e). Plotinus takes the dialogue to be authentic. Emilsson (1988, p. 31).
15 The view that the soul is responsible for the cognitive capacities and activities of the living being as well as for its living capacities and activities can be traced back to Plato, who in several dialogues argues that a soul is the principle of life of a living body, which means that a body is alive in virtue of its soul. He expresses this view explicitly in *Phae*. 105c. In the *Timaeus* Plato says that the soul animates the body (*Tim*.35a–36a; 69c–70b), Noble (2013, pp. 252–253). Many ancient philosophers think that the soul not only accounts for the cognitive functions of a living being, but also for its living functions. It remains, however, unclear whether Plotinus thinks that the functions of the vegetative soul are restricted to these living functions: In *Enn*.IV.9.3.24–27 he says that the vegetative soul only accounts for the vegetative functions of the living being, whereas he says in *Enn*.IV.3.27–31 that the world soul is responsible as well for perceptions and memories.
16 In agreement with Aristotle, Plotinus is committed to the view that the irascible (θυμοειδές) and the desiderative power (ἐπιθυμητικόν) are not independent parts, but rather faculties of the non-rational part. By contrast, in the *Republic* Plato separates the soul into a rational part, the λογιστικόν (442c) and two non-rational parts, namely the irascible element (440e–f; 442a–b; 581a) and the desiderative element (439d,

580e–581a). Before Plotinus, Alcinous already integrated the Platonic θυμοειδές and ἐπιθυμητικόν into a single part of soul (*Didask.* 24). Caluori (2008, p. 129).
17 He adopts these localisations from Plato: *Tim.*69c–72d. See Caluori (2008, p. 129).
18 Aristotle already criticised Plato on this point. While he agrees with Plato that the body is alive in virtue of a soul, he disagrees with him as to how the non-rational soul functions as the principle of life of an organism and, in particular, how it accounts for its affective states. Whereas Plato is committed to the view that the soul can function as the principle of life despite not being in a body, Aristotle thinks that the soul can only function as the principle of life because it is in the body, insofar as it is an enmattered form (*DA*.II.2.414a17–22; see Caston (2006, pp. 317–320)). According to Aristotle's hylomorphism, the soul is the fulfilment or actualisation (ἐντελέχεια) of the potentialities of a body (*DA*.II.1.412b5–6), which implies that the soul cannot exist independently from the body (*DA*.II.2.414a19–28).

The only part of soul regarding which Aristotle seriously considers whether it can exist independently from the living being or not is the intellect (νοῦς). He says that it is unmixed and separate (*DA*.III.4.429a10–b6). However, it is still a disputed question in the literature on Aristotle's psychology how to interpret these claims (see Miller (2012)).

According to Aristotle, body and soul are two aspects of one and the same entity, the living being, body being its matter and soul its form (*DA*.II.1.412a15–b6). In the case of humans, this means that flesh and bones and so on constitute the matter, whereas the soul is the structure that accounts for the appropriate functioning of all the parts and that integrates them into a whole (Caston 2006, p. 318). All the activities of a living being will be activities of both body and soul, or, to be more precise, they will be activities of the compound that is constituted by body and soul (*DA*.I.1.403a3–19, b17–19; Caston (2006, p. 318)).
19 A soul-trace is not itself a soul, but it is similar to soul in its nature (Noble 2013, p. 256). This is because the body is living in virtue of its soul-trace, which means that the soul-trace plays a role that is analogous to that of a soul, which is the principle of life (Noble 2013, p. 252]). Because of its similarity to the soul, Plotinus sometimes calls the soul-trace an 'image of soul' (*Enn.*IV.4.20.15–16).
20 As such, it plays a role analogous to that of the pineal gland in Descartes' theory of how an unextended mind can interact with an extended body. See Emilsson 1988, pp. 145–148; and 1991, pp. 161–165.
21 Noble (2013, p. 251).
22 Aristotle uses this notion to refer to a body that has organic functions, such as nutrition and growth: DA.403a26; 412a11ff; 414a22; Caluori 2008, p. 128.
23 While it is clear what role Plotinus assigns to the soul-traces, his theory of soul-trace is problematic in several respects: Unfortunately, Plotinus does not give any account of how the soul-trace is supposed to come into existence. Plotinus scholars have pointed out that the soul-trace is generated by a so-called double activity of the soul (Noble 2013, pp. 268–277, Emilsson 1998, pp. 341–342); for a general study of Plotinus' account of 'double activity' see Emilsson (2008, ch. 1). As pointed out earlier, Plotinus believes that entities that are on higher ontological levels 'generate' entities that are on lower ontological levels. By 'generation' he most plausibly means that the higher entities are the formal and material causes of the lower entities. Most likely, Plotinus believes that soul-trace is generated in this way by the soul. However, it is not clear how an immaterial being, such as the soul, could be the formal and material cause of the soul-trace which itself is supposed to be an intermediate entity between material and immaterial entities. Relatedly, the original problem that Plotinus tries to address by means of the soul-trace simply seems to arise again. In particular, Plotinus introduces the soul-trace, in order to give an account how a soul that can exist independently from

a body can engage in an interaction with a body. The problem now is that the soul-trace just postpones this difficulty to another level, since we seem to be faced with the original problem again when we try to explain how the soul-trace interacts with the soul, on the one hand, and with the body, on the other.

If the soul-trace is sufficiently like body that it can genuinely interact with it, which it does on Plotinus' view insofar as it is an enmattered forms, it is not clear how such an enmattered form can interact with independently existing souls. On the other hand, if the soul-trace is sufficiently soul-like, for it to genuinely interact with the soul, it will be unclear how the soul-trace can interact with the body.

By introducing a new entity into his ontology, Plotinus only seems to be creating further difficulties without solving any problems, making his theory even less plausible than the Platonic theory from which he departed. In addition, by bringing in elements that cannot be found in any of Plato's writings, he calls into question the correctness of his theory as an interpretation of Plato.

24 Plotinus argues for the non-affectedness of the soul in *Enn*.III.6.1–5. Plotinus' discussion is strongly influenced by Aristotle, who holds that the soul can cause motion, yet that it is not itself moved by this act (*DA*.406a1–3; 408b1–31; *GC*.323a25–324b24. Emilsson 1988, p. 35). In *Enn*.III.6 Plotinus also argues for the non-affectedness of matter. His view on matter is influenced by Plato's description of matter in the *Timaeus* (Kalligas 2014, p. 538). By contrast, the Stoics, not drawing a difference between body and matter, think that matter is the subject of affection (*SVF* 1:85,493, 2:301–5; Kalligas 2014, pp. 537–538]) as do the Middle Platonists (Alcinous *Didask*. 11, 166.33; and Atticus fr.5.69–73; Kalligas 2014, p. 538).
25 Arist. *Gen. Corr*. I.4.319b8–14 and I.7.324a34-b9.
26 The view that the alterability of the soul implies its being corruptible can be found as well in the Stoic tradition. Carneades argues that all entities that can perceive are corruptible, because the capacity for perception implies the capacity for alteration (Cic. *Nat. D*. III.29–34; Sext. Emp. *Math*. IX.139–147; Kalligas 2014, p. 541). Panaitios thinks that the human soul is corruptible because of its being capable of alteration (Cic. *Tusc*. I 79). Many Middle Platonists have the same motivation for arguing in favour of the non-affectedness of the soul (Severus apud Eus. *PE* XIII.17; Kalligas 2014, p. 541).
27 The way in which Plotinus sets up the discussion about whether the soul is in motion is strongly influenced by Aristotle's discussion of the same topic in *DA* I.3-4. In this treatise Aristotle also discusses whether the soul is in motion and can be subject to affections (*DA* I.4.408a34–408b4). Cf. *Enn*.I.1.4–5, where Plotinus actually cites *DA*.1.4 as his starting point.
28 Aristotle influences Plotinus' reasoning (*DA*.I.4.408b4–18). Aristotle's solution is that it is not the soul, but the human being in virtue of the soul, that is the subject of these affections. As we are going to see, Plotinus develops a different solution.
29 Stoic thought and terminology influence Plotinus' discussion (see Plut. *De Libidine et Aegritudine* 6, pp. 5, 14–23; Armstrong 1967, p. 220, n. 1).
30 His discussion can be construed as an implicit criticism of the Stoic materialistic theory of memory, which often uses the example of the 'stamping of the wax' as an illustration of the material process that the soul undergoes when engaged in acquiring memories. Plato discusses this materialistic model in *Theaet*.191c8–e1; cf. Arist. *Mem*.1.450a27–32. In contrast to this materialistic model of memory, Plotinus thinks that the soul does not receive any impression in the case of acquiring memories.
31 Kalligas 2014, p. 545. This idea has a precedent in Aristotle, at *DA*.1.3.406b11–15.
32 See Emilsson 1988, esp. pp. 67–69.
33 Plotinus presumably is concerned with the worry that some of his discussions in other treatises might have misled his readers to think that the origin of vice is such an external stimulus. In particular his discussion in *Enn*.I.6.5.25–58 might suggest that vice arises

because it is something external added to the soul and thereby renders it impure. However, this account of the origin of vice is not adequate for the kinds of virtues of the soul that he discusses in this passage, the so-called civic virtues (Kalligas (2014, p. 543)).
34 *Enn*.III.2.22–32; III.8.6.12–27. Kalligas (2014, p. 544).
35 This idea is influenced both by Stoic thought (*SVF* 1:179) and by Plato (*Tim*.70a2–7).
36 Kalligas (2014, p. 543).
37 Plotinus explains the virtuous and vicious activity and its relation to reason of the passionate part in *Enn*.III.6.2.54–60 and of the desiderative part in *Enn*.III.6.2.60–66. Unfortunately, he does not explain why the soul in some cases actualises its own nature to a high degree and in some other cases to a lesser degree.
38 Kalligas (2014, pp. 544–545).
39 Since Plotinus talks about soul change as the 'opposite' of material change, he may be referring to Aristotle's idea in *DA*.II.5, that a change *in the strict sense* involves the '*destruction*' of a property, and a change *in the loose sense* (such as actual perception and actual thinking) involves the '*preserving*' of a property, which would make it the 'opposite' process.
40 Plato ascribes these affections to the soul and not the body (*Phd*.83c–d; *Tim*.42a–b; 69c). Aristotle also ascribes these affections to soul (*DA*.II.5.1105b20) as do the Stoics (Stob II.88.8–9; Sen. *De Ira*).
41 Cf. *Enn*.I.1.1.6; III.6.1.2; IV.3.26.8. See Emilsson (1988, ch. IV and VII) and Kalligas 2014, p. 542.
42 For further discussions see Blumenthal (1971, pp. 38–39), Emilsson (1998, p. 346) and Caluori (2008, pp. 132–135).
43 It is very difficult to understand what the mental images that the nutritive soul produces are supposed to be. In another passage Plotinus describes the images that the nutritive soul produces as 'unjudged' (*Enn*.III.6.4.19–23). For a detailed discussion of the nature and role of the mental images see Emilsson (1998, p. 348).
44 Emilsson (1998, p. 347).
45 Kalligas (2014, pp. 544–545).
46 Caluori (2008, p. 131).
47 In his discussion of bodily anger Plotinus is influenced by Aristotle: According to Aristotle we are in certain emotional states whenever certain material states are given, even if an external stimulus that requires judgement is absent (*DA*.I.1.403a19–25; Caston (2006, p. 323)).
48 Both Plato and Aristotle influence his conception of this kind of anger. (*R*.440b–441c; *Tim*.70b; *Rhet*.II.2.1378a30–2). According to Aristotle, anger is "a desire accompanied by pain for an imagined retribution on account of an imagined slighting inflicted by people who have no legitimate reason to slight oneself or one's own" (*Rhet*. II.2.1378a30–2; transl. Nussbaum). As Nussbaum points out, anger is, thus, characterised by (1) slighting or down ranking (ὀλιγωρία); (2) of the self or people close to the self; (3) wrongfully or inappropriately done (μὴ προσῆκον); (4) accompanied by pain; and (5) linked to a desire for retribution (Nussbaum 2015, p. 42). However, in *De Anima* Aristotle criticises such 'dialectical' definitions of anger (that cite only the form). He takes anger to have a hylomorphic essence (*DA*.I.1.403a30–b2).

Bibliography

Armstrong, A. H. (1966–1988) *Plotinus*. 7 vols. Cambridge, MA: Harvard University Press and London: Heinemann.

Blumenthal, H. J. (1974) Nous and soul in Plotinus: Some problems of demarcation. In *Atti del Convegno internazionale sul tema Plotino e il neoplatonismo in Oriente e in Occidente*. Roma: Accademia nazionale dei Lincei, pp. 203–219.

———. (1976) *Plotinus' Psychology: His Doctrine of the Embodied Soul*. The Hague: Martinus Nijhoff.

Caluori, D. (2008) Plotin: Was fühlt der Leib? Was empfindet die Seele? In Landweer, H., and Renz, U. (eds.) *Klassische Emotionstheorien: Von Platon bis Wittgenstein*. Berlin: De Gruyter, pp. 121–140.

Caston, V. (2006) Aristotle's psychology. In Gill, M. L., and Pellegrin, P. (eds.) *The Blackwell Companion to Ancient Philosophy*. Oxford: Blackwell Publishing, pp. 316–346.

Emilsson, E. K. (1988) *Plotinus on Sense-Perception*. Cambridge, MA: Cambridge University Press.

———. (1991) Plotinus and soul-body dualism. In Everson, S. (ed.) *Psychology: Companions to Ancient Thought 2*. Cambridge, MA: Cambridge University Press, pp. 148–165.

———. (1998) Plotinus on emotions. In Sihvola, J., and Engberg-Pedersen, T. (eds.) *The Emotions in Hellenistic Philosophy*. The New Synthese Historical Library 46. Dordrecht: Kluwer Academic Publisher, pp. 339–363.

———. (2008) *Plotinus on Intellect*. Oxford: Oxford University Press.

Kalligas, P. (2014) *The Enneads of Plotinus: A Commentary*. Princeton and Oxford: Princeton University Press.

Long, A. A. (1974) *Hellenistic Philosophy*. London: Duckworth (2nd edn. 1986, Berkeley and Los Angeles: University of California Press).

Miller, F. D. (2012) Aristotle on the separability of mind. In Shields, C. (ed.) *The Oxford Handbook of Aristotle*. Oxford: Oxford University Press, pp. 306–339.

Nikulin, D. (2005) Unity and individuation of the soul in Plotinus. In Chiaradonna, R. (ed.) *Studi sull'anima in Plotino*. Napoli: Bibliopolis, pp. 275–304.

Noble, C. I. (2013) How Plotinus' soul animates his body: The argument for soul-trace at Ennead 4 4 18 1–9. *Phronesis* 58: 249–279.

Nussbaum, M. (2015) Transitional anger. *Journal of the American Philosophical Association* 1: 41–56.

O'Meara, D. J. (1995) *Plotinus: An Introduction to the 'Enneads'*. Oxford: Clarendon Press.

Rehm, D. (1997) The structure of emotions in Plotinus. *American Catholic Philosophical Quarterly* 71: 469–488.

15

INTELLECT IN ALEXANDER OF APHRODISIAS AND JOHN PHILOPONUS

Divine, human or both?

Frans A.J. de Haas

By his philosophy of mind, soul and body Aristotle bequeathed to his heirs an intellectual challenge, rather than a lucid theory of intellect. The challenge is highlighted by the fact that a crucial text in the dossier, *De anima* III.5, has been transmitted to us in a more or less corrupt state. Why? The question whether our soul is divine, or entirely human, or perhaps part divine and part human, touches an open nerve that has produced intriguing philosophy of mind, and a long-standing and wide-ranging academic discussion parts of which have been recorded in other chapters in this volume. Since each ancient commentator on *De anima* III.5 takes his own pick from the tradition, and serves his own aims, an ancient commentary is best read as an attempt to align Aristotle with concerns contemporary to the commentator. I shall here compare the interpretation of Aristotle's theory of intellect by Alexander of Aphrodisias (fl. 200 AD) with that by John Philoponus (c. 490–570 AD). In this chapter I shall merely touch upon the problems of interpreting *De anima* III.5 and its Aristotelian context in so far as a proper understanding of Alexander and Philoponus requires.[1]

The tradition has provided us with two different accounts of intellect for each of these philosophers. For Alexander we have his *De anima*, including a section devoted to intellect,[2] alongside a part of the so-called *Mantissa* that had an independent history of transmission.[3] The relationship between these two texts is an issue of scholarly debate. Since I believe that the *De anima* is not contradicted by the *Mantissa*, I shall focus on the *De anima* account as the more elaborate version.

For Philoponus we have a commentary on Aristotle's *De anima* that was handed down under his name. Unlike the commentary on *De anima* I–II, the commentary on *De anima* III is not authentic, although it is now generally believed to have been written in the same century.[4] On the other hand we have an independent commentary on *De anima* III.4–8 that goes under the title *De intellectu*. It is lost in Greek, and only survives in the Latin translation of William of Moerbeke.[5] There is consensus among scholars that the Greek commentary on *De anima* III and *De intellectu* cannot be of the same author. Therefore I shall focus on Philoponus' *De intellectu* instead, which shows agreement with the Greek commentary on *De anima* I–II. Since *De intellectu* is highly critical of Alexander's interpretation of *De anima* III.4–8, it constitutes an interesting witness to the history of the reception of Alexander's theory of mind and his interpretation of relevant passages from Aristotle's *De anima*.

In this chapter I shall first present two important Aristotelian texts that play a role in each commentator since Theophrastus. Then I proceed to outline Alexander's theory of intellect, followed by Philoponus' theory. In a final section I shall show how the fact that each of them tried to get maximum support for his own view from the text of Aristotle's *De anima* led to a strong disagreement of Philoponus with Alexander.

1. Intellect in Aristotle beyond *De anima*

Both Alexander and Philoponus include in their discussions of *De anima* III.4–8 references to two important Aristotelian texts in the intellect dossier:

(1) In *Generation of Animals* II.3, 736b27–29 Aristotle claims that the intellect (*nous*) enters the human embryo 'from outside' (*thurathen*), i.e. from outside the body of the female by means of the male semen.[6] Aristotle here seems to call intellect 'divine' because it does not share its actuality with any corporeal actuality (*sômatikê energeia*).[7] The vegetative, sensitive and intellectual powers of the soul are first present in potentiality in the embryo and develop over time.

(2) Aristotle also refers to the active intellect as divine in *De anima* III.5 430a23.[8] Aristotle's choice of vocabulary in *DA* III.5 has been taken as a clear reference to the nature and characteristics of the divine act of intellection of *Metaphysics* XII. The so-called active, or productive, intellect (*poiêtikos nous*) is called separable or separate (*chôristos*) and separated (*chôristheis*), impassible (*apathês*), unmixed (*amigês*), essentially an actuality (*têi ousiai energeia*), immortal (*athanaton*) and eternal (*aidion*), and (by implication) it thinks always. This description of intellect, which indeed has strong echoes in *Metaph.* XII.7–9,[9] may suggest that Aristotle means to *identify* the active intellect with the divine Intellect. Alternatively, the text may indicate the correspondences between the divine act of intellection of *Metaph.* XII and the state of a human soul that desires to make itself as similar to it as possible.[10]

2. Alexander on intellect

Alexander of Aphrodisias was the main teacher of Peripatetic philosophy in the Athens of his day. He held the chair of Aristotelianism, one of the four chairs established by Marcus Aurelius in Athens in 176 AD.[11] Alexander's *De fato* is dedicated to the emperors Septimius Severus and Caracalla, which fixes the only available date for his professional activity between 198–209 AD. The other Athenian chairs were given to Stoic, Platonic, and Epicurean philosophers.[12] In this context polemics are bound to be strong. Indeed, in Alexander's works we find many explicit and implicit instances of criticism of rival schools – also in his theory of intellect. At the same time Alexander addresses a diverse Peripatetic tradition, which started with Theophrastus, and was revived in the 1st century AD after Andronicus newly brought Aristotle's works into circulation.[13] Just like Middle Platonists tended to rewrite Plato's philosophy in dogmatic and systematic terms after what they considered the outrage of the skeptical Academy, so Alexander aimed at presenting Peripatetic thought as a coherent whole that was a match for the Stoics and Platonists in all philosophical issues of his time. Fate, determinism and human responsibility get special treatment in *De fato*; in *De mixtione* the Aristotelian doctrine of mixture is pitted against the Stoic theory of the complete fusion of bodies (*krasis*) that supported the pervasive influence of the Stoic god on matter; *De providentia* (transmitted in Arabic) deals with the issue of divine providence. All of these issues were hotly debated in Hellenistic and post-Hellenistic philosophy, but had not yet been dealt with by Aristotle at any great length. Hence Alexander had to update his Aristotelianism by collecting relevant texts from the Aristotelian corpus, and sometimes by extrapolating from scraps of Aristotelian doctrine. Some of his predecessors in the Peripatetic tradition interpreted Aristotle in ways that gave Platonists or Stoics grounds for critique of Aristotelian philosophy – at least according to Alexander. Hence we also find him attacking older Peripatetic views as part of his philosophical enterprise.

Alexander's *De anima*, which is not a commentary but a reworking of Aristotelian psychology in Alexander's own voice (though closely modeled on Aristotle's work of the same name), shows how Peripatetic psychology is nothing but a special application of Peripatetic physics, and culminates in describing the role of a divine Intellect that resides beyond the physical realm, and was treated by Aristotle in *Metaphysics* XII.

What follows is my paraphrase of Alexander's discussion of Aristotle's *DA* III.5 as described in *DA* 80.16–91.6, which stays close to Alexander's text in order and wording. In this way I hope to bring out what I take to be crucial aspects of Alexander's argument some of which have not always received the attention they deserve in existing scholarship.[14]

1   Alexander explains that the rational soul is a power (*dunamis*) that is more perfect than, and comprises, the powers of the irrational soul to which it constitutes a kind of addition. That this power is twofold follows from the difference among its objects: one rational power deals with the practical, which is subject to generation and capable of coming to be in different ways, and is called opiniative and deliberative; the other rational power deals with what is eternal and necessary, and is called scientific and theoretical. A human being does not immediately (at birth) have either of these *in actuality*, she possesses

only a potentiality (*dunamis*) and fitness (*epitêdeiotês*) for receiving these actualities through instruction and habituation. The practical disposition, which deals with more useful and familiar objects, is acquired first, the theoretical follows later. (80.16–81.22)

2 This twofold potential intellect is called material or natural intellect (*hulikos, phusikos nous*), and is present in all non-impaired human beings, albeit in different degrees: some have more talent than others. The intellect-in-actuality that comes to be later is the form (*eidos*), disposition (*hexis*), fulfillment (*entelecheia*) or perfection (*teleiôsis*) of the material intellect. It is present only in those people who have been sufficiently trained and instructed, who are called noble (*spoudaios*). Of course all human beings naturally develop the actuality of intellect up to a certain point, since all human beings naturally acquire universal concepts (e.g. 'the colour white') by the familiar process of concept formation from particular perceptions, via imagination and memory, to experience and the grasp of the universal.[15] This is properly called the common intellect (*koinos nous*). Putting similar things together (*tôn homoiôn sunthesis*), as in the grasp of the universal through the similarity of particulars, viz. intellection (*noêsis*), is the work of intellect. (81.22–83.13)

3 Intellect does not receive the forms in the way matter receives affective qualities, i.e. in a merely passive way. Even in perception, which occurs by means of qualitative bodily affections, the activity of perceiving as such (*to aisthanesthai*) is not ordinary passion (*paschein*), but discrimination (*krinein*). Intellect, also a discriminative power though one which (unlike perception) does not need the help of a bodily organ to grasp its objects, separates and grasps only forms, apart from their material circumstances. (83.13–84.14)

4 Since intellect can grasp everything that way and separates objects of sense from their concomitant material attributes, it cannot be any of the things it can think. It merely is the potentiality or fitness to receive all forms, like a writing tablet without writing on it, or rather like the lack of writing on such a tablet. In this analogy the writing tablet is the soul, whereas the lack of writing in it, or the fitness to be inscribed, is the material intellect. While the soul can be said to 'suffer' when written upon, the fitness does not suffer anything – precisely because it is nothing in actuality. In this way the description 'place of forms' for the soul turns out to be quite apt if people were to take their cue from the potentiality of intellect, and use it *pars pro toto* for the entire soul. (84.14–85.10)

5 The dispositional intellect (*nous hôs hexis*) is the form and perfection of the material intellect. The disposition comes to be in the material intellect through (*ek*) the grasp of the universal, or – what is in a way the same thing – through separating the forms from matter. Seeing the common feature in particulars, intellect grasps the form apart from the matter that differentiates the particulars. The disposition comes to be in intellect at the point of the transition (*metabasis*) away from the continuous actuality concerning sensibles, when it obtains from them a kind of theoretical view of the universal, which is

called object of thought (*noêma kai ennoia*) right from the start. When this[16] has become fuller (*pleonasan*), varied (*poikilon*) and versatile (*polutropon*) to the extent that it can do this [i.e. obtain a theoretical view of the universal] also without the perceptible substrate, *then* it is intellect. From that moment onwards intellect-in-disposition can be active through itself (*di' autou*), no longer through an actuality concerning sensibles. At this point the intellect is like a knower who is in the middle state between being a potential knower, and a knower who exercises his knowledge. He is the thoughts stored away together and resting. When active, this disposition becomes intellect in actuality (*ho kat'energeian nous*). (85.10–86.6)

6   Because intellect does not need the service of the body, it remains impassive when confronted with perceptibles, and because in a sense it has practised this attitude with respect to sensibles, it is better prepared to deal with its own actualities. Hence it is not at all affected by more or less thinkable objects, in the way that perception is affected by e.g. the lingering effects of strong sense impressions. (86.6–14)

7   In virtue of the fact that dispositional intellect primarily becomes what it thinks, it can think itself because it becomes that which it thinks. Before actual thinking that which thinks and that which is thought are opposed to each other as relatives, but this opposition ceases to be when they are in actuality and become one. Such identity is not possible in perception because it discerns (*kritikê*) sensibles as composites of form in matter, even though perception does not receive the form as matter does. The difference in sensible objects between e.g. bronze and the essence of bronze requires different modes of cognition: perception for the composite particular, intellect for the universal such-and-such, or *logos*, according to which the particulars are the same. (86.14–87.23)

8   If there are forms that exist by nature without any matter, these are intelligible in the proper sense of the word and are such in actuality without the help of something that thinks them. Given the identity of intellect and object, such a matterless form will be intellect in the proper sense of the word; it will never need to *become* intellect as enmattered forms do, and it will *not* be fully identical to forms which it thinks when dealing with forms and essences that exist as enmattered, which are therefore not themselves intellects outside of thinking.[17] On the same principle *our* intellect will become matterless forms when it thinks them, even though these will be the same whether our intellect thinks them or not. (87.24–88.16)

9   If we return now to the wording of *DA* III.5 it is clear that in the realm of composite nature something is matter in that chosen domain (*genos*), viz. that which is in potentiality everything in that domain. There is also something that is productive of the generation in matter of those things it is receptive of, in the same way as art (*technê*) possesses the explanation (*aitia*) of the form coming to be in the matter. Since in all instances that which is something most of all (*malista*) and in the proper sense of the word (*kuriôs*) is also

responsible for others being such, this will also apply in the case of intellect. That which is productive is the form that is intelligible properly and most of all. This is plausible from an analogy with light, which is itself the most sensible object, as well as responsible for the sensibility of all other sensibles; and with the primary good, which is responsible for the goodness of all other good things.[18] Hence that which is by nature intelligible is the productive intellect (*poiêtikos nous*) without which nothing else would become an intelligible. (88.17–89.8)

10 In addition, if this intellect would be the first cause and principle of being for everything, it would be productive also in the sense of being responsible for the existence (*einai*) of all things known.[19] Such intellect is separate, impassible, unmixed, by itself: all because it exists apart from matter. As actuality and form without potentiality, it is immortal. Such Aristotle has shown the first cause to be.[20] Therefore this intellect is more valuable than the material intellect in us, as the active is more valuable than the passive, and that which is without matter is more valuable than that which comprises matter. When our intellect thinks it, it somehow becomes it and makes itself like it. We may recall that enmattered forms, as well as mathematical objects gained by abstraction, obtain their existence *qua* objects of thought and intellects only while they are being thought by our intellect; these intellects perish as such when they are separated from the intellect that thinks them. Not so the incorruptible intellect that comes to be in an intellect that thinks it as a true 'intellect from outside': whereas all objects of thought come from outside and *become* intellects only when thought, only this intellect comes to be in us from outside *as already an intellect* and remains incorruptible even when removed from our thinking. What is more, the intellect in activity that thinks it, becomes like it. The 'intellect from outside' is neither our material intellect which is the power of the soul in us [and therefore not 'from outside'], nor the disposition in accordance with which the intellect in potentiality thinks both that intellect from outside along with everything else [for this disposition is perishable], nor is the thought (*noêma*) of it imperishable *qua* thought because it is thought by us mortals at a given point in time. So if anyone cares to have something divine in themselves, they should set out to be able to think something like this too. (89.9–91.6)

Through this dense and intricate argument Alexander has conceived a single continuous account that combines all keywords from *De anima* III.4–8 and incorporates the intellect from outside and the divine intellect in creative ways.

The *material* intellect is part of our natural make-up as a potentiality or rather fitness of our souls to receive forms.[21] As such this natural ability is not nothing. It develops naturally into the *common* intellect in all people. Its potentiality for *all* things is required because our intellect can think literally everything by becoming the forms it thinks. The potential intellect *becomes the object of thought* by the familiar process of concept formation, which relies on its *discriminative* power.

By means of this power it *separates forms* from all matter, also from the matter that still clings to forms as they are perceived in sense perception.[22] By continuous activity concerning perceptions the potential intellect develops itself to the point of *completion*, or *perfection*, such that it cannot only separate a universal from sensible particulars repeatedly, or even continuously, but can also think of this universal without having recourse to perceptions any longer. At this point it has become *dispositional intellect*, is capable of thinking at will, and of thinking itself as having become the dematerialized form it is thinking. Since the intellect can think at will only *after* it has reached the state of perfection that is dispositional intellect, this cannot be the efficient cause of the development.[23] We are to understand that the discriminating power of the material intellect, by which it separates forms from matter, amounts to the same thing as its receptivity for forms (which thereby gains significance). The productive intellect is not naturally cognate, nor is it involved in any kind of mixture. Alexander employs a long and at times repetitive argument to stress that in intellection the intellect *is* its objects, and its objects *are* thereby intellects. Most objects of our intellection are enmattered forms (perceptible or otherwise) which our intellect has separated from matter.[24] Our intellect only becomes identical with *part* of what these themselves are (viz. it leaves out their being enmattered), and they perish as objects and intellects when our intellection ceases.

Interestingly, Alexander then contrasts enmattered forms with matterless forms (in the plural) which are by nature intelligible objects and (thereby) intellects. These must be unaffected by our thinking them, and for this reason they are worthy of all attributes that Aristotle ascribed to the first cause, the primary Intellect of *Metaph*. XII. If in every domain the most prominent representative of the type is somehow responsible for the lesser representatives belonging to the type, this first intellect, which is at the same time the first object of intellection (first for itself *qua* intellect), should be responsible for the fact that all other objects of thought and intellects are such. In addition, since, according to Alexander, we are dealing here with the Intellect of *Metaph*. XII, which is the first cause of the universe, one might add that it is also responsible for the *existence* of all objects of thought as such. From this one may infer, with *Mantissa* 111,27–112,5, that the productive intellect cooperates with our own intellect, in the sense that it is responsible even for the potential objects of intellect.

The general physics expounded in the first pages of Alexander's *De anima* (2,10–11,13) helps to provide a general framework for the terminology employed in the context of intellect. According to Alexander, all physical forms come to be 'over and above' (*epi*) suitable mixtures of corporeal elements. This does not mean they are identical with the ratio of the mixture (as in the much denounced *harmonia* theory of soul); they are rather like health, which is not a characteristic of any of the bodily constituents, but the result of their mixture. It would be wrong to suppose that such additional characteristics were somehow the subject of the changes that lead to their appearance, nor are they present from the start to determine these changes. It is rather that, once they have appeared, they exist as long as the required mixture, or fitness, is sustained. Alexander is emphatic that at higher levels than mixtures of the elements a 'mixture' is in fact a form-matter composite. A new form comes to be over and above a given form-matter composite when the latter has reached its perfection, or culmination (*teleiôtes*). In the development of an embryo to a full-fledged adult member of the species leading a full life, the succession of powers of the soul from vegetative and reproductive, via perceptive, to rational is to be regarded as a series of ever more complex *culminations* of underlying form-matter composites which have reached a suitable state. It will now be clear that the succession of intellects is to be regarded as a similar series: from material intellect, through disposition and (first) actuality to the (second) actuality of our thinking the forms we know, culminating in the thought of the divine productive intellect as object of thought in our soul in the (second) actuality of our thinking it. Therefore Alexander emphasizes that while material intellect is with us from birth, it needs a process of concept formation (present in all humans), and further training and instruction (which not everyone will have access to), to reach a state of perfection in dealing with perceptions that gives rise to a new form: intellect-in-disposition, which has capabilities the previous state did not have. It can think about universals apart from perceptions, at will, and it can think itself. Alexander ends our section with the paradoxical exhortation that if someone wants to have the divine within him, he should try, in this life, to think the first principle. This can only imply that we do *not* need to think this principle in order to think universal forms in everyday life, or even as first object of thought to reach the dispositional stage or acquire the power of abstraction. Its significance is indirect: just like light, itself supremely visible, also renders colours visible just by being there; so the first principle, itself supremely intelligible and intelligized by itself *qua* intellect, renders all objects of intellection intelligible, just by being there, even if it happens not to be thought by our intellect at every point in time.

3. John Philoponus on intellect

John Philoponus has left us, in the Latin of William van Moerbeke, a commentary on *De anima* 3.4–8, here referred to as *De Intellectu* (*DI*). Since this is a running commentary in the style of the Alexandrian school, it does not provide the kind of carefully crafted continuous argument we found in Alexander's *De anima*. However, from over a dozen critical references to Alexander's *De anima* it is clear that Philoponus has written this part of his commentary with Alexander as his main opponent in mind. In his *De anima* commentary on books I and II preserved in Greek, Philoponus' attitude to Alexander is more relaxed. He often refers to Alexander approvingly, and in one case he even advises the reader to look for Alexander's comments for more details.[25] There is, however, one issue on which he takes a stand against Alexander both in *In De anima* and in *De Intellectu*: the immortality of the human intellect. We shall turn to his attack on Alexander in a moment.[26] Let us first sketch Philoponus' own philosophy of intellect.

As a pupil of Ammonius, Philoponus has a thoroughly Neoplatonic outlook on human psychology. He concedes that the human intellect is a part of the human soul. There is no other way to explain Aristotle's careful comparison between sensation and intellect *in the same living being* (*DI* 2,23). However, he mitigates the meaning of 'part': it only makes sense to speak of parts in the sense of falling under the extension of the same term, 'soul', since he believes that intellect is in fact a separate kind of soul, a substance of its own (*DI* 2,33–3,53). As such, our intellect exists in three modes of being: (i) in potentiality (in children), (ii) in disposition (possessing but not using knowledge, as in a sleeping geometer, or in someone not displaying his knowledge) and (iii) in actuality, having its operations already on display so that it can become active by its own agency – this is the ratiocinative intellect, which does not know everything at once, and so still exhibits a movement from one argument to the next, which implies that it has its own type of potentiality.[27] At *In DA* 2.12–15 Philoponus adds that only a fully purified human intellect, which can operate without sense-perception and imagination and has reached the most perfect disposition, 'gets to know the intelligible objects by straightforward apprehension in a way that is superior to demonstration'.

There is another, contemplative intellect, different from these modes of intellect, which lacks potentiality altogether. From this intellect, which all people call immortal, the potential intellect derives the principles of the sciences. Some people recognize this intellect in Aristotle's text where he speaks of an intellect that is separate, impassible and unmixed (*DI* 3,55–4,69). Philoponus does not, as will be clear from the sequel. Philoponus is convinced that Aristotle also knew of the universal and creative intellect, 'but it perfects our intellect as the sun is said to generate men: it is a cause at a higher level, not an embedded cause'.[28]

However, according to Philoponus everyone – including Aristotle – believes that the human intellect is an immortal, rational substance, separable, unaffected and not mixed with the body.[29] Hence, the soul does not need to develop its rational powers by means of a process of growth and development. As an immortal substance that becomes lodged in a human body the intellect need only go through various stages of so-called learning, which has become necessary as the result of the delirium, or alienation, that the soul experienced when descending into the body. For Philoponus holds that our rational soul already possesses – as joined with its own substance – the *logoi* of everything, the 'shadows of the Forms'.[30] After all, the human soul is an image of the Demiurgic Intellect. Learning is therefore recollection: teachers do not put knowledge into us, but remove the obstacles, the ashes that hide the spark, so that we may become aware of its presence. Perception provides the imagination with images that trigger our intellect. We instantly recognize which opponent in a debate is right because their discussions arouse our innate knowledge (*in DA* 4,32–5,14).

In this context, the first potentiality of knowledge turns out to be a 'reduced actuality' of formal principles already actually present from birth.[31] When Aristotle calls the soul a writing tablet without writing on it, Philoponus explains, he does so because of 'the holding down of cognition by the passions which makes it *seem* as if it did not have forms at all' (*DI* 39,16–18, my emphasis). Aristotle already recognized the latitude in potentiality in terms of distance from it actualization proper: a sleeping geometer, or a drunk geometer, indeed, the ingredients in a mixture, are all further or nearer to actualization proper.[32]

Philoponus also acknowledges a distinction between the solid (perceptible) body and the pneumatic body. He believes that the rational part of the soul can exist apart from both, and is therefore immortal, whereas the non-rational part of the soul can be separated from the solid body but is inseparable from the pneumatic body and perishes along with it. He interprets Aristotle's discussion of the separation of soul from body in these terms (*In DA* 9,3–12,9).

Philoponus' Neoplatonic background thus demands that the human rational soul is immortal. Hence he regards it as a grave mistake on the part of Alexander to have claimed that the human intellect, and thereby the entire human soul, is mortal.

It is a striking feature of Philoponus' polemics that he uses (his interpretation of) Aristotle's text in *De anima* III.4–8 to refute Alexander, thus showing over and over again that the famous commentator got his Aristotle wrong. Philoponus is right to point out that Alexander could only consider the human soul mortal after disconnecting the active intellect, which Aristotle called immortal, from the human soul altogether – by identifying it with the divine intellect. Thus the connection between *DA* III.5 and *Metaph.* XII becomes the centre of Philoponus' attack. And yet, for Philoponus, too, there is no doubt that a higher divine Intellect has an important role in the explanation of the creation of the sensible world, the descent of human souls and the *logoi* they possess in their intellects. The point is not that human rationality depends on a divine intellect one way or another, but that Alexander's construal of this dependence leads him to calling the human intellect mortal. Nor is it the issue that the intellect in potentiality is perfected by another intellect which is in actuality. But according to Philoponus this is the intellect that is *in the teacher*, which is *external to* and *other than* the intellect which is perfected.[33]

Three passages in *DI* are particularly helpful to understand the substance of Philoponus' attack.

1   Right at the start of *De intellectu*, commenting on the first lines of *DA* III.4, 429a10–11, Philoponus notes[34] that Alexander 'wishes to drag Aristotle over to his opinion' by claiming that Aristotle's phrase 'the part of the soul by which the soul gets to know things and is prudent' refers to the creative intellect (*de conditore intellectu*), or the First Cause. For Philoponus this is 'not an intelligent suggestion', because (i) there is no need to *argue* that the creative intellect is immortal, separate etc.; (ii) in *DA* 408b18–20 Aristotle stated that the intellect comes to be in us and is not destroyed, and if it would be, only by old age – which makes no sense regarding the creative intellect; (iii) it would be irrational to say that the intellect in actuality, which is the culmination of our potential intellect, is not our own; and (iv) in *DA* 411b18–19 Aristotle

wonders what part of the body intellect might hold together, which again shows he cannot be thinking of the creative intellect.

2   In his comments on *DA* 431a16–17 'therefore the soul never thinks without an image' Philoponus notes[35] that Alexander 'tries very hard to prove' from this phrase that our intellect is mortal. For if intellection never happens without an image, which is based on sense perception, which is not immortal, then neither is intellect.[36] This would mean that the entire soul is mortal, which is why Aristotle is saying here that *the soul* never thinks without an image.

Philoponus opposes this argument in two ways: (i) this passage is about the deliberating soul (431a14 *dianoêtikê psuchê*) which Aristotle suggested earlier (408b13–15) to be a capacity of the whole animal rather than the intellect alone. Elsewhere[37] Philoponus explains at more length that, indeed, deliberation is imperfect intellect, viz. intellect in so far as it is impeded by the body. Hence it may involve the use of images. (ii) Since the context speaks of seeking or avoiding good and bad (431a15–16), the topic is clearly practical deliberation; but it should not be surprising that intellect has to be involved with images in practical deliberation which deals with particulars. Surely, images are not necessary when the intellect is thinking about mathematics, logical conversions or intelligibles. Hence, Alexander's argument to prove the mortality of the soul fails.

3   The most elaborate discussion of the status of intellect in actuality is found in the *theoria* to *De anima* III.5, *In DA* 42,91–54,84.[38] Philoponus notes that all interpreters agree that the intellect in potentiality is ours. However, there is a dispute about the intellect in actuality, in which four different positions can be discerned. Since this survey conveniently maps the larger part of the ancient discussion, as well as significant parts of the modern discussion about *DA* III.5, it is worthwhile to set out the arguments for comparison.

   (i) The intellect in actuality is the divine and creative intellect, because our intellect is not in essence actuality (430a18), nor does it make everything (430a12), nor does it understand always (430a22). Our intellect in potentiality is perfected by an intellect in actuality which is universal and external. This corresponds to Alexander's position.

   Philoponus offers his full array of arguments against Alexander, including the ones rehearsed in the context of *DA* III.4 (see section 1 above):

   - why raise the question of separability at all if the creative intellect is at stake?
   - how will the creative intellect ever enter our soul from outside?
   - how can the creative intellect be included in the definition of soul as actuality of an instrumental body (412b5–6)?
   - in Aristotle's phrases 'knowledge in actuality is identical with the thing known; knowledge in potentiality is temporally prior in the individual' (430a19–21) the term 'knowledge' must refer to intellect in actuality, which is identical with intelligibles. But it would

be unreasonable to imply that the creative intellect is temporally posterior or comes to be in individuals at all.
- it would be unreasonable to announce a discussion about soul (430a13), and then switch to the divine and transcendent intellect which is the business of a theologian.

(ii) The intellect in actuality is not the creative intellect but an angelic or demonic intellect placed directly above ours in the hierarchy, which irradiates our human souls. Hence, the reference to light (430a15–16), which is also intermediate between its source, the sun (the creative intellect) and the illuminated objects (our souls). This position is attributed to Marinus, the pupil of Proclus (Pseudo-Philop. 535,5).

Philoponus rejects this interpretation because it does not match all of Aristotle's descriptions either; for instance, it would be odd to ask about this intellect whether it is separate. Interestingly, Philoponus also rejects the possibility that our intellect would transcend its own substance to become identical with such a higher intellect: 'For every substance has [only] a certain perfection attaining to it.[39] Just as a non-rational soul would never come to be of the same dignity as a rational one, so our intellect would never be the equal of those kinds which are above it. Hence Aristotle will not be speaking of any other intellect superior to us'.[40] Aristotle is made to adhere to the rules of Neoplatonic metaphysics.

(iii) The intellect in actuality does not transcend us, but we have two different intellects in us, one in potentiality, which is always in us, and another one in actuality, which enters from the outside (*qui actu de foris ingredi*, a reference to *GA* II.3 *thurathen* discussed previously). This view is attributed to 'some ostensible Platonists' (Plotinus in Pseudo-Philop. 535,8), who inferred as much from Plato's use of the term 'change' in cognition.[41] Against this position Philoponus argues that it would be odd that we would not notice the presence of an intellect in actuality in us, and that our intellect falls back into potentiality e.g. when asleep or in a stupor.

(iv) The intellect in actuality is the human intellect which is identical with the intellect in potentiality when it has reached perfection. Philoponus subscribes to this interpretation, which Pseudo-Philop. 535,13 attributes to Plutarch (of Athens).

Philoponus' own argument rests on an analogy with all natural cases of potentiality that are led to actuality by another instance of the same species previously in potentiality, but now in actuality: a man, or a vine in potentiality becomes a man, or a vine in actuality by another man, or vine in actuality (which in their turn were in potentiality before). The latter clause rules out that 'the maker' is something that was never in potentiality before, such as the creative intellect. The intellect in actuality that leads our intellect in potentiality to actuality is . . . the intellect of a teacher, viz. another intellect that is in another soul, but the same in *species*.[42] At *In DA* 306,24–307,5 Philoponus argues that once the state of disposition has been reached, for instance due to the agency of a teacher, the pupil's intellect in actuality can activate itself without needing anything from outside (*exôthen*), contrary to sense perception that relies on external perceptibles. Although this is an Aristotelian commonplace, for Philoponus such statements seem to take on the force of a denial of the need for an intellect in actuality that enters from outside (*thurathen*) to bring the intellect in potentiality to perfection: 'therefore the intellect does not need something that perfects it from the outside'.[43] In addition, Philoponus adduces a whole series of quotes from Aristotle to corroborate his conviction that Aristotle intends *our* intellect to be unmixed, pure, separate and immortal.[44]

The more difficult passages that figured in Alexander's argument are also confronted head-on.[45]

Our intellect 'makes all things' (430a12) not because it produces the substance of all things, but because it makes our intellect in potentiality come to be receptive of all things, just as the intellect in potentiality becomes all things, not literally, but by receiving the forms of all things. Philoponus rightly claims that Alexander will agree that our intellect does not really make *all* things in this sense: intellects that are by nature intelligible need not be made actually intelligible by us at all, only material forms.

Our intellects are 'always understanding' from a cosmic point of view: in the universe as a whole (430a21 *holôs*) there are always intellects in actuality next to intellects in potentiality. The words 'it understands always' are applied to all and to the pool of souls in the whole universe, not because each person on his own understands always.[46]

Our intellect is 'in essence actuality' in the sense that essence is always defined by referring to something's actuality, and by what is most honourable in it (430a17–19). In the case of intellect, its essence lies in its actuality. This is precisely what Plato taught us when he indicated that we should free the immortal soul from the incrustations of the passions to see its splendour, just as we should remove the incrustations from the sea-god Glaucus (*Rep.* 10, 611C–D). Since our soul attains things that are wholly separate, it must be separate from all body. And 'It is a direct consequence of this that it is immortal' (*DI* 54,77). Harmonization is near: 'Therefore Plato taught that the soul's substance is characterised according to its highest operations, and Aristotle now brings out the consequences in saying that the intellect is in substance actuality' (*DI* 54,81–84).

It will be clear that Philoponus' reading of Aristotle is heavily influenced by Neoplatonic metaphysics and tends to be equally creative as Alexander's reading in making individual phrases in Aristotle's text support his overall view. They both impress by the sheer knowledge of the Aristotelian corpus at their disposal. But there is much at stake here: if our rational soul is inseparable from the body it must be perishable. If not only Plato but also Aristotle tell us that our rational soul is a separate substance associated with the body, its immortality is confirmed.

In the preceding pages I have opposed Alexander's ingenious reading of Aristotle's theory of intellect to Philoponus' theory of intellect. In structure they have much in common: both accept that our rational powers somehow depend on a higher intellect, and both accept a development through various stages of potentiality to actuality. Alexander, however, concluded from Aristotle's texts that the productive intellect in *DA* III.5 could only be the divine creative intellect he found in *Metaph.* XII, thereby robbing our individual intellects from their culmination. What remains for us is intellect in disposition, that has gained its knowledge through sense perception, and by that dependence shows its irreparable connection to our mortal body. Philoponus, who takes his starting-point from the Platonic immortality of our rational soul, reinterprets the notions of separation, potentiality, actuality, and essence involved in Aristotle's psychology so as to preserve our personal intellect's immortality. After the long tradition of anti-Alexandrian and anti-Averroist polemics in the line of Philoponus, by all defenders of the immortality of the soul, Platonists, Muslims, Jews and Christians alike, we have somewhat lost sight of the fact that Alexander was not interested in the (im)mortality of our souls at all. He aimed at bringing Aristotle's *De anima* in line with the principles of Aristotle's general physics and biology, as well as came up with an intriguing evolution of powers of the soul and their respective potentialities and actualities. For what it is worth, it seems to me that our age feels more comfortable again with the project of Alexander.

Notes

1 See John Sisko's chapter in this volume for a survey of the problems involved.
2 Alex. *DA* 80.16–91.6 (Bruns 1887). For translations and commentaries see Fotinis (1979), Accattino and Donini (1996), Bergeron and Dufour (2008). A new English translation by Victor Caston, who has already published a translation of Alex. *DA* 1.1–46.19 (2012), is in preparation.
3 Alex. *Mant.* § 2, 106,18–113.24 (Bruns 1887). For translations and commentaries see Fotinis (1979) 137–153, Schroeder and Todd (1990), Accattino (2005), Sharples (2004a), (2008). See Sharples (2004b) for the meaning and modern origin of the title *Mantissa*. *Mantissa* § 2 reports various views that helped shape Alexander's own, with Alexander's more considered responses to them.
4 See Lautner (1992), who proposes a younger member of Philoponus' school as the author, and Charlton (1999), pp. 1–10, who opts for Stephanus.
5 The Latin text was edited in Verbeke (1966), translation in Charlton (1999) with emendations to the Latin by Bossier.
6 For discussion of this difficult passage, see e.g. Charlton (1987), pp. 411–416, Caston (1999), pp. 215–216.
7 Aristotle famously hints that intellect may be independent from the body in *DA* I.4 408b18–19, 29; II.1 413a3–7; II.2 413b24–27 and III.7 431b17–19, but also concludes in *DA* III.7 431a14–14 and 431b2–4 that discursive human thinking (*dianoêtikê*) cannot do without *phantasmata* that result from sense perception – for which human intellect would need the body for its actualization after all.
8 Cf *DA* II.3 415a11–12.
9 See Caston (1999) 211–212 for a full comparison (from which Caston concludes that the active intellect in Aristotle is identical with Aristotle's God).

10 Cf Arist. *EN* 1177b31–34.
11 See Chaniotis (2004) for epigraphic evidence that locates Alexander in Athens, with Sharples (2005) on its implications.
12 It is not clear who were Alexander's contemporaries in the other chairs during his period of office. Taurus and Atticus may have held the Platonic chair in the decades before Alexander was appointed.
13 See Barnes (1997) for a critical assessment of fact and fiction surrounding the editorial work of Andronicus.
14 I wish to acknowledge my debt to the detailed and perceptive studies listed in the bibliography. This is not the place, however, to record each and every detail of agreement and disagreement with previous scholarship, so I shall simply present my own reading here. Nor is this the place to defend any particular interpretation of Aristotle's seminal texts. The informed reader will recognize that I find much of value in the work of Charlton, Sharples, Caston, Wedin and Diamond.
15 Here Alexander closely follows Arist. *Anal.Post.* II.19.
16 I.e. the *noêma*. The Greek is tortuous, but seems to turn on the identification, already at this stage, of the thought and the intellect, as will come out further on, 86.14ff.
17 Thus the relation of an intellect by nature to the enmattered intelligible forms it thinks, is analogous to the relation of actual perception to enmattered sensible forms it perceives.
18 Given Alexander's propensity to argue against Platonism, we should not ascribe a kind of participation theory to Alexander here. Rather, he draws on Aristotle's famous theory of 'focal meaning' which holds that things that are identified as 'good' or 'healthy' in various senses of these words are all united by reference to a single item like goodness or health. This is not just a linguistic issue since the teleological structure of the universe can be held responsible for this type of coherence.
19 One is reminded of Plato's analogy of the Good and the sun in *Rep.* VI: the Good is responsible for both the existence and the intelligibility of intelligibles (both Forms and mathematical objects), as the sun is responsible for both the existence and the perceptibility of perceptibles. I believe these echoes are not a source of inspiration for Alexander, but part of an anti-Platonic refutation, since he will be offering a different explanation of the significance of the productive intellect in the universe.
20 Here the transition from *DA* III.5 to *Metaph.* XII is complete, and no longer phrased as a conditional as in 89.9.
21 Cf. Arist. *Anal.Post.* II.19, 100a13–14: 'soul is such that it can undergo this'.
22 Note that the soul does not need the divine intellect to acquire the power of abstraction: for Alexander the discriminative power, viz. its receptive power under a different description, is responsible for the separation of forms from matter.
23 One might think that the intelligible objects are the efficient cause of intellection, but they are only actually intelligible in the act of thought, and powerless when still in potentiality.
24 *Mantissa* 107.21–24 elaborates on this aspect by emphasizing that in this sense our intellects are themselves productive and like artisans, in imitation of the primary productive intellect. See further De Haas (forthcoming 2018).
25 See e.g. *In DA* 35,10; 43,10; 151,32; 160,8; 182,11; 216,9; 237,17; 361,5; he refers the reader to Alexander's comments at 118,25–28.
26 See *In DA* 10,1–3; 21,21–23; 159,1–29; 194,12; 200,3; 261,11–262,4; for *DI* see below.
27 So Arist. *DA* III.4, 429b8.
28 *DI* 51,6–10; cf. Arist. *Phys.* 194b13. Here for once I modify Charlton's translation 'not part of the causal chain' for *incoordinatam causam*. I suspect this phrase reflects something like *akatatetagmenon aition*, a cause that is not embedded in the horizontal causal nexus of the sublunary realm.

29 Philop. *In DA* 10,10–11,29 quotes, in support for the fact that Aristotle holds this position, a series of Aristotelian texts: *PA* 641a17ff, 641a33ff, *GA* 736b27ff (wrongly quoted by Philoponus as also deriving from *PA*), *DA* 403a27, 413b24, 429a13, 430a22, 429a22, 429a31–b5, 430a17, 408b18, 411b18, 413b24.
30 See Tempelis (1997).
31 *DI* 39,1–18; 39,27–40,43; see De Haas (2000) for further discussion of these passages. At *DI* 16,82–96 Philoponus argues that first potentiality sits ill with Aristotle's claim that the world is eternal, and with a limited number of immortal souls – this would only work on the assumption of multiple rebirths of the same souls which makes a persistent first potentiality implausible. So either the soul is mortal and continuously generated anew (*quod non*) or the soul has the forms potentially in the second sense of potentiality listed ('as Plato said').
32 See e.g. Arist. *GA* II.1 735a8–11, *Phys.* VII.3 247b13–248a6. For its application to mixture see De Haas (1999).
33 See *In DA* 10,33–37 and p. 310–311.
34 What follows paraphrases *DI* 4,70–5,98.
35 Philop. *DI* 97,8–98,43.
36 Cf. Arist. *DA* 412b25–413a7: a part of the soul that is not the actuality of any bodily part may be separable. Although Philoponus does not invoke this text here, in his commentary *ad loc*, *In DA* 223,37–224,4, he is ready to infer that Aristotle wants the rational soul to be separate.
37 Cf Philop. *In DA* 155,4–35.
38 This passage is closely paralleled in the larger discussion in Pseudo-Philop. *In DA* 535,1–539,12. There the four positions Philoponus outlines in *DI* are attributed to Alexander, Marinus, Plotinus and Plutarch of Athens respectively. Philoponus follows Plutarch.
39 Following the conjecture *assectibilem* (translating *parakolouthêtiko*n) for *affectibilem* (Bossier), see Charlton (1991) p. 65, n. 17.
40 *DI* 47,9–16.
41 The statement is puzzling. Charlton (1991) 63n6 refers to *Phaedr.* 245C, *Leg.* 10, 894–896B, but notes these texts concern life rather than cognition. The reference is rather to Plotinus' application the category of motion to thought and Intellect in e.g. *Enn.* V.1.4, 36–37; V.8.4, 11–13; VI.2.4–8 (in conscious opposition to Aristotle), and VI.7.13. See Charrue (1987) 93–95 on Plotinus' reception of the second hypothesis of the Parmenides and 206–223 on *Sophist* 254D4–255C7.
42 See above p. 308.
43 *In DA* 307,4–5: *dio ou deetai ho nous exôthen tinos teleiountos*.
44 *DI* 49,55–50,81 lists *DA* 430a22; 430a19–20; 429a25–26; 411b18–19; 408b19–20; 429a15; 429a29–30; 429b4–5; *Metaph.* XII 1070a24–26 (taken to support pre-existing, simple and everlasting forms, some of which might be human intellects; cf. 1069a30–36).
45 *DI* 50,82–54,84.
46 See also *In DA* 216,28–217,7 which includes the same cosmic perspective: 'But in the whole universe the perfect might be put before the imperfect; for as I said, the introducing causes which are in perfect activity precede, and in general the creation of the whole universe ought to begin from what is perfect not from what is imperfect'. In this way, Neoplatonic causal theory is in line with Aristotle's priorities.

Bibliography

Editions, translations and commentaries

Accattino, P., and Cobetto Ghiggia, P. (2005) *Alessandro di Afrodisia: De anima II (Mantissa): Premessa, testo rivisto, traduzione et note*. Alessandria: Edizioni dell'Orso.

Accattino, P., and Donini, P. (1996) *Alessandro di Afrodisia: L'anima: Traduzione, introduzione e commento*. Roma and Bari: Editori Laterza.

Bergeron, M., and Dufour, R. (2008) *Alexander Aphrodisiensis: De l'âme: Texte grec introduit, traduit et annoté*. Paris: Vrin.

Bruns, I. (1887) *Alexandri Aphrodisiensis praeter commentaria scripta minora. De anima liber cum mantissa*. Supplementum Aristotelicum volumen II pars I. Academia Litterarum Regiae Borussica. Berlin: Georg Reimer.

Caston, V. (2012) *Alexander of Aphrodisias on the Soul: Part 1: Soul as Form of the Body, Parts of the Soul, Nourishment, and Perception*. Ancient Commentators on Aristotle. Bristol: Bristol Classical Press.

Charlton, W. (1991) *Philoponus: On Aristotle on the Intellect (De Anima 3.4–8)*. Ancient Commentators on Aristotle. London: Duckworth.

———. (1999) *'Philoponus' on Aristotle on the Soul 3.1–8*. Ancient Commentators on Aristotle. London: Duckworth.

———. (2000) *'Philoponus' on Aristotle on the Soul 3.9–13 with Stephanus on Aristotle on Interpretation*. Ancient Commentators on Aristotle. London: Duckworth.

———. (2005a) *Philoponus on Aristotle on the Soul 2.7–12*. Ancient Commentators on Aristotle. London: Duckworth.

———. (2005b) *Philoponus on Aristotle on the Soul 2.1–6*. Ancient Commentators on Aristotle. London: Duckworth.

Dufour, R. (2013) *Alexandre d'Aphrodise: De l'âme II (Mantissa)*. Collection Zêtêsis, Textes et essais. Québec: Presses de l'Université Laval.

Fortenbaugh, W. e.a. (1992) *Theophrastus of Eresus: Sources for His Life, Writings, Thought and Influence Philosophia Antiqua* 54. 2 vols. Leiden, New York and Köln: Brill.

Fotinis, A. P. (1979) *The De anima of Alexander of Aphrodisias: A Translation and Commentary*. Washington, DC: University Press of America, dissertation.

Gutas, D. (2010) *Theophrastus on First Principles (known as his Metaphysics)*. Philosophia Antiqua. Leiden and Boston: Brill.

Huby, P., and Gutas, D. (1999) *Theophrastus of Eresus: Sources for His Life, Writings, Thought and Influence: Commentary vol. 4: Psychology*. Philosophia Antiqua 81. Leiden and Boston: Brill.

Schroeder, F., and Todd, R. (1990) *Two Greek Aristotelian Commentators on the Intellect: The 'De intellectu' Attributed to Alexander of Aphrodisias and Themistius' Paraphrase of Aristotle 'De anima', 3.4–8*. Medieval sources in translation. Toronto: Pontifical Institute of Medieval Studies.

Sharples, R. W. (2004) *Alexander of Aphrodisias: Supplement to on the Soul*. Ancient commentators on Aristotle. London: Duckworth.

———. (2008) *Alexander Aphrodisiensis De anima libri mantissa: A New Edition of the Greek Text with Introduction and Commentary*. Berlin: Walter de Gruijter.

Todd, R. (1996) *Themistius: On Aristotle on the Soul*. Ancient Commentators on Aristotle. London: Duckworth.

Van Der Eijk, P. (2005) *Philoponus: On Aristotle on the Soul 1.1–2*. Ancient Commentators on Aristotle. London: Duckworth.

———. (2006) *Philoponus: On Aristotle on the Soul 1.3–5*. Ancient Commentators on Aristotle. London: Duckworth.

Verbeke, G. (1966) *Jean Philopon: Commentaire sur le De Anima d'Aristote: Traduction de Guillaume de Moerbeke: Édition critique avec une introduction sur la psychologie de Philopon*. Corpus Latinum Commentariorum in Aristotelem Graecorum 3. Louvain and Paris: Publications Universitaires de Louvain-Éditions Béatrice-Nauwelaerts.

Secondary literature

Barnes, J. (1997) Roman Aristotle. In Barnes, J., and Griffin, M. (eds.) *Philosophia Togata II: Plato and Aristotle at Rome*. Oxford: Oxford University Press, pp. 1–69.

Blumenthal, H. (1996) *Aristotle and Neoplatonism in Late Antiquity: Interpretations of the De anima*. London: Duckworth.

Caston, V. (1999) Aristotle's two intellects: A modest proposal. *Phronesis* 44: 199–227.

Chaniotis, A. (2004) Epigraphic evidence for the philosopher Alexander of Aphrodisias. *Bulletin of the Institute of Classical Studies* 47: 79–81.

Charlton, W. (1987) Aristotle on the place of mind in nature. In Gotthelf, A., and Lennox, J. (eds.) *Philosophical Issues in Aristotle's Biology*. Cambridge and New York: Cambridge University Press, pp. 408–423.

Charrue, J.-M. (1987) *Plotin lecteur de Platon*. Paris: Les Belles Lettres.

De Haas, F. A. J. (1999) Mixture in Philoponus: An encounter with a third kind of potentiality. In Thijssen, J. M. M. H., and Braakhuis, H. A. G. (eds.) *The Commentary Tradition on De generatione et corruptione: Ancient, Medieval and Early Modern*. Turnhout: Brepols, pp. 21–46. Updated reprint in Sorabji, R. (ed.) (2016) *Aristotle Re-Interpreted: New Findings on Seven Hundred Years of the Ancient Commentators*. London: Bloomsbury Academic, pp. 413–435.

———. (2000) Recollection and potentiality in Philoponus. In Kardaun, M., and Spruijt, J. (eds.) *The Winged Chariot: Collected Essays on Plato and Platonism in Honour of L.M. de Rijk*. Brill's Studies in Intellectual History 100. Leiden-Boston-Köln: Brill, pp. 165–184.

———. (forthcoming 2018) Aristotle and Alexander of Aphrodisias on Active Intellectual Cognition. In Mora Márquez, A.M., and Decaix, V. (eds.) *Active Approaches to Intellectual Cognition: From Late Antiquity to the 20th Century*. Dordrecht: Springer.

Diamond, E. (2014) Aristotle's appropriation of Plato's sun analogy in De anima. *Apeiron* 47: 356–389.

Lautner, P. (1992) Philoponus, *in De Anima* III: Quest for an Author. *Classical Quarterly* 42: 510–522.

Sharples, R. (1987) Alexander of Aphrodisias, scholasticism and innovation. *Aufstieg und Niedergang der römischen Welt*, II, 36 (2): 1176–1243. Berlin and New York.

———. (2004) Alexander of Aphrodisias: What is a *Mantissa*? In Adamson, P., Baltussen, H., and Stone, M. (eds.) *Philosophy, Science and Exegesis in Greek, Arabic and Latin Commentaries*. London: Institute of Classical Studies, pp. 51–69.

———. (2005) Implications of the new Alexander of Aphrodisias inscription. *Bulletin of the Institute of Classical Studies* 48: 47–56.

Tempelis, E. (1997) The School of Ammonius on 'logoi' in the human intellect. In Cleary, J. (ed.) *The Perennial Tradition of Neoplatonism*. Leuven: Universitaire Pers Leuven, pp. 310–327.

Wedin, M. (1988) *Mind and Imagination in Aristotle*. New Haven and London: Yale University Press.

INDEX

Academy (Athens) 1, 301
Aëtius 29, 33, 37, 51–53, 216–217
Affected Parts (Galen) 270–271
affection 130, 139n23, 150, 154, 195–196, 216–217, 246, 279–293, 297n40, 302
Affinity Argument 15, 86, 122–125, 127–128
air 31–32, 37–41, 73–75, 78–79
Albert the Great 176
Alexander of Aphrodisias 238, 299–306
Ammonius 229, 307
Anatomical Procedures (Galen) 262
anatomy 71–72
Anaxagoras 4, 19n13, 25, 38–39, 49–53, 120, 207
Anaximenes 1, 5, 18n4, 18n10, 25, 37–38
anger 195–196, 291–293, 297nn47–48
animals 50–51, 156n9, 170, 188–189, 220–221
Annas, Julia 97n2, 227
Anonymus Londiniensis 30, 33
Apology (Plato) 99n15
Archelaus of Athens 120
Aristotle 1–3; in Alexander of Aphrodisias 299, 313n18; atomism in 40; body in 194–210, 295n18; cognition in 155; death in 144; Democritus in 56; Epicurus and 240; in Galen 261, 264, 267–268, 275nn29,36; hylomorphism in 141–155, 173n11; imagination in 182–185; intellect in 39, 160–172, 196–197, 299–300, 305, 312, 312n7; "life-body problem" in 160–161; limits of natural science in 160–172; memory in 182–185; perception in 5, 48–49, 145–149, 156n9, 175–181, 194–210; in Philoponus 299–300, 307–309, 311; Plato in 138n20; in Plotinus 282–283, 296nn24,28; on Pythagoreans 18n4; soul

in 4, 6, 19n12, 31–32, 156n8, 158n19, 168–171, 195, 242, 295n18; Stoics vs. 215; time in 175–190
Arnobius of Sicca 20n29
Art of Medicine (Galen) 273
Aspasius 51
atomism 40, 236–255
atoms 54–58
Augustine 3, 5, 7–8

Barnes, Jonathan 229–230
bipartition of soul 85, 243–246
blood 7, 29–30, 33–36, 72–75, 173n5, 196, 202, 261, 291–293
body: in Aristotle 6, 194–210, 295n18; in atomism 236–243; death and 95–97; deceptions and 92–93; distractions and 90–92; diversions and 88–90; in dualism 6–7; in Epicurus 236–243; in Hippocrates 71–72; intellect and 163; perception and 197–203; in Plato 84–97, 97n4, 293n3, 294n15; in Plotinus 280–283, 287–289; soul and 3–8, 84–88, 142–145, 236–243, 281–283; -soul interaction 128–133; in Stoics 214
brain 76–79
Broadie, Sarah 172n4

Cambridge Platonists 279
Caston, Victor 167, 172n3
Categories (Aristotle) 146, 154, 189–190
Chrysippus 216–217, 228–229
Cicero 37, 224–225, 227, 239
Clarke, Michael 34, 42n6
clinamen 253
cognition 294n15; in Anaxagoras 49–53; in Aristotle 155; in Democritus 53–59; in Hippocrates 66–67, 77–78; in Parmenides 44–49; in Plato 105–106,

317

INDEX

120–137; in *Timaeus* 120–137; *see also* intellect
color 198
cosmic intellects 120–121
cosmic soul, as role model 133–137
counting 177–182, 188–189, 191n20

De Anima (Alexander of Aphrodisias) 299, 301–302, 305–306, 309, 311
De Anima (Aristotle) 56, 141, 149–150, 152–153, 157n10, 166, 176, 179, 185–186, 196–199, 210n3, 238, 242, 299–300
death: in Aristotle 144; body and 95–97; in Diogenes 40–41; in Empedocles 27–30; in Heraclitus 25; in Homer 35–36; metempsychosis and 26–27; in Plato 23, 95–97, 98n15
deceptions 92–93
De fato (Alexander of Aphrodisias) 300–301
De intellectu (Philoponus) 299–300, 306, 308–309, 314n31
De Memoria (Aristotle) 175, 179, 181–184, 186–187, 191n29
Demetrius Laco 245
De mixtione (Alexander of Aphrodisias) 238, 301
Democritus 4, 7, 9, 11, 39–40, 52–59, 237–238, 240
De motu animalium (Aristotle) 150
dependence, of mind on body 195–197, 209–210
De providentia (Alexander of Aphrodisias) 301
De Sensu at Sensibilibus (Aristotle) 196
desire: in Plotinus 289–291
development, mental 249
Diogenes Laertius 49, 59
Diogenes of Apollonia 18n10, 25, 39–41, 120
Diogenes of Babylon 229
Diogenes of Oenoanda 245
distance, of mind from body 195–197, 204–208, 210n3
distractions 90–92
diversions 88–90
Doctrines of Hippocrates and Plato (Galen) 259–263
dreams 69, 80n5
dualism 6–7, 10–11, 18n10, 20n25, 280–281
dual process theories of judgment 115–116, 117n19

Elements of Ethics (Hierocles) 219
Empedocles 4, 10–12, 14, 27–30, 33–34, 36, 46, 53–54, 72
Epictetus 224
Epicurus 9, 236–237, 241–255
epilepsy 74–79

fire 24, 29, 39–40, 131, 134, 145
Freedom From Distress (Galen) 273
Function of the Parts (Galen) 261–262

Galen 1–2, 57, 228–230, 258–274
Gendler, Tamar 117n19
Generation of Animals (Aristotle) 300
Gill, Mary Louise 174n15
Gorgias (Plato) 98n14, 101

harmony theory 6
heat 66–68, 145
Heraclitus 7, 10, 19n17, 24–25, 36–37, 46, 120
Herodotus 26
Herophilus 262
Hierocles 219–220
Hippocrates 7, 65–80
Homer 8, 34–36
Huffman, Carl 32–33
Hume, David 272
hylomorphism 3, 6, 8–9, 141–155, 156n1, 173n11, 195, 282
hylozoism 4

Iliad (Homer) 8
imagination 182–185
immortalism 23–24; conferred 13, 16–17; earned 19n20, 20n29; strong 13, 20n21; types of 13–17; weak 13–14
intellect 38–39, 160–172; in Alexander of Aphrodisias 299–306; in Aristotle 39, 160–172, 196–197, 299–300, 305, 312, 312n7; body and 163; correlatives argument with 164–166, 172; cosmic 120–121; in domain of natural science 162–171; matter and 162–164; in Philoponus 299–300, 306–312; as principle of movement 166–167; time and 182, 185–190; *see also* cognition; reason

Johansen, Thomas 129
judgment: dual process theories of 115–116, 117n19
Justinian 1

INDEX

Kneale, Martha 222
Kneale, William 222

Laws (Plato) 26, 128, 272
Letter to Herodotus (Epicurus) 236–237, 239, 244–245, 254–255
"life-body problem" 160–161
Literalism 199–202, 210n11
Lucretius 3, 7, 9, 11, 19n14, 56, 239, 241–246
Łukasiewicz, Jan 222

Mantissa (Alexander of Aphrodisias) 299, 313n24
Marcus Aurelius 300
Marinus 310
Masi, Francesca 255n1
Mates, Benson 222
memory 182–185, 251–254, 296n30
Meno (Plato) 26, 101
mental development 249
mental states 251–254
Metaphysics (Aristotle) 138n20, 152–153, 177, 188–189, 305, 312
metempsychosis 10–11, 14, 26–28
Mixtures (Galen) 265
monism 6, 9, 243–246
mortalism 8–13
motion: perception of 182–185
movement: intellect as principle of 166–167

Nichomachean Ethics (Aristotle) 188
number 177–178, 191n20; *see also* counting

Odyssey (Homer) 36
Olympiodorus 226
On Difficulties About the Soul (Plotinus) 282
On Disease (Hippocrates) 7, 72–73
On Flesh (Hippocrates) 65–68, 72
On Generation and Corruption (Aristotle) 58
On Nature (Epicurus) 247–248, 253
On Plants (Pseudo-Aristotle) 4, 50
On Regimen (Hippocrates) 7, 67–72
On the Sacred Disease (Hippocrates) 75–79
On Winds (Hippocrates) 73–75
Orphism 8, 19n18, 26

pain 287–289
Parmenides 44–49, 120

Parts and Powers of the Soul, The (Galen) 264
Parts of Animals (Aristotle) 164, 206, 275nn29,36
passions 291–293
perception 5; in Anaxagoras 49–53; in Aristotle 48–49, 145–149, 156n9, 175–181, 194–210; body and 197–203; causes in 197–198; in Democritus 53–59; in Galen 266; in Hippocrates 67, 80n6; memory and 184–185; of motion 182–185; in Parmenides 44–49; in Plato 49, 60n18, 123–124, 130–131; soul and 145–149; in Stoicism 217–218; thought vs. 48–49; of time 175–181
Peripatetics 300–301
Phaedo (Plato) 1, 6–8, 11, 14–16, 18n5, 23, 30–31, 49–50, 64, 69, 85–87, 92–93, 96, 122–126, 128, 136, 138n14, 283, 293n3
Phaedrus (Plato) 104–105, 117nn16,19, 128
phantasia 216–230
Philebus (Plato) 97n4
Philolaus 4–5, 32
Philoponus, John 19n12, 299–300, 306–312
physicalism 160
Physics (Aristotle) 141–142, 152, 154–155, 169, 175–181, 183, 188–190, 191n13
Pindar 69
plants 5, 50–51, 153–154
Plato 1–3, 18n5, 18n10; body in 84–97, 97n4, 293n3, 294n15; cognition in 120–137; death in 23, 26, 30, 95–97, 98n15; dualism in 7–8, 11; in Galen 260–261, 264, 266–268, 272; harmony theory in 6; immortalism in 13–17, 23–24; perception in 49, 123–124, 130–131; in Plotinus 281, 283, 296nn24,28; soul in 6, 11, 14, 18nn5,11, 23, 26–27, 30–31, 35, 41, 84–89, 93–97, 97nn1–2,4–6, 98nn9–10,15, 101–118, 121–139, 260, 282–283, 293n3, 294n16, 311–312; Stoics vs. 215; tripartition of soul in 101–116; *see also specific works*
Plotinus 7–8, 279–293
Posterior Analytics (Aristotle) 156n8, 187
Powers of the Soul Follow Mixtures of the Body, The (Galen) 264–267, 273–274
Praxagoras 262, 264, 275n28
Presocratics 4; *see also specific philosophers*

INDEX

Proportionalism 199–202
Protagoras 60n16
Protagoras (Plato) 101, 106–107, 186
Pseudo-Aristotle 4, 50
Pseudo-Philoponus 185–187
psychological monism 243–246
Pythagoras 4, 10, 14, 26–27
Pythagoreans 7, 18n4, 31–32

reason: and dual process theories of judgment 115–116, 117n19; in Parmenides 45–46; in Plotinus 281–282; in soul 108–110; *see also* cognition; intellect
Recollection Argument 122
Republic (Plato) 23–24, 49, 60n18, 85–86, 88, 98n14, 101–106, 108–112, 117n11, 124, 126, 294n16, 313n19
Riveting Argument 93, 95

sacrifice 10
science: limits of natural, in Aristotle 160–172, 173n8; scope of natural 168–171
Sedley, David 30–31
sensation 51–52
Sextus Empiricus 51–52, 56–58, 218–219, 223–225, 230
sleep 69–70, 155
Socrates *see* Plato
Sophist (Plato) 133–134, 138n16, 139n30
soul 3–8; in Alexander of Aphrodisias 301–302; appetitive part of 111–115; in Aristotle 141–155, 156n8, 158n19, 168–171, 195, 242, 295n18; in atomism 236–243; bipartition of 85, 243–246; body and 3–8, 84–88, 236–243, 281–283; -body interaction 128–133; changes in 284–285; cosmic, as role model 133–137; death and 23–24, 40–41; in Democritus 39–40, 57; as end of living being in unity with body 142–145; in Epicurus 236–243; in Galen 260, 262–268, 274n20; in Heraclitus 24–25; in Hippocrates 66–71, 75; in Homer 8, 35; in hylomorphism 3, 6, 8–9, 141–155; in metempsychosis 10–11; as nature 168–171; in Orphism 8; perception and 145–149; in *Phaedo* 122–125, 136–137; in *Phaedrus* 104–105; in Philoponus 307–308; in Plato 6, 11, 14, 18nn5,11, 23, 26–27, 30–31, 35, 41, 84–89, 93–97, 97nn1–2,4–6, 98nn9–10,15, 101–118, 121–139, 260, 282–283, 293n3, 294n16, 311–312; in Plotinus 279–287, 292–293; as principle vs. subject 149–155; in Pythagoras 27, 31–32; rational part of 108–109, 281–282; in *Republic* 102–104, 108–112; spirited part of 109–111; in Stoicism 9–10, 215–216; as subject of affections 283–287; in *Timaeus* 112–113, 126–137, 137n11; tripartition of 101–116, 173n11; as unitary nature 170–171; unity of 168–171
speech 67, 173n5
Spiritualism 199–201
Stoics 5, 7, 9–10, 214–231, 263–265, 296n30; *see also specific philosophers*
Strato of Lampsacus 14
structuralism 157n14

Thales 4–5
Theaetetus (Plato) 137n11, 222
Themistius 176, 178
Theodoret of Cyrus 30
Theophrastus 29, 47–48, 50–51, 54–56, 301
Therapeutic Method (Galen) 262
Timaeus (Plato) 16–17, 18n10, 20n28, 112–113, 120–121, 125–137, 137n11, 138nn12,14,17–19, 139nn26,30, 268, 294nn3,15
time: in Aristotle 175–190; intellect and 182, 185–190; measurement of 181–182; perception of 175–181
tripartition of soul 101–116, 173n11

vice 296n33

What Is The Living Being? (Plotinus) 279–280

Xenophanes 10, 26, 46, 120
Xenophon 120

For Product Safety Concerns and Information please contact our EU
representative GPSR@taylorandfrancis.com
Taylor & Francis Verlag GmbH, Kaufingerstraße 24, 80331 München, Germany

www.ingramcontent.com/pod-product-compliance
Lightning Source LLC
Chambersburg PA
CBHW071800300426
44116CB00009B/1157